# Critical Security Controls for Effective Cyber Defense

## A Comprehensive Guide to CIS 18 Controls

Dr. Jason Edwards

Apress®

*Critical Security Controls for Effective Cyber Defense: A Comprehensive Guide to CIS 18 Controls*

Dr. Jason Edwards
New Braunfels, TX, USA

ISBN-13 (pbk): 979-8-8688-0505-9          ISBN-13 (electronic): 979-8-8688-0506-6
https://doi.org/10.1007/979-8-8688-0506-6

## Copyright © 2024 by Dr. Jason Edwards

This work is subject to copyright. All rights are reserved by the Publisher, whether the whole or part of the material is concerned, specifically the rights of translation, reprinting, reuse of illustrations, recitation, broadcasting, reproduction on microfilms or in any other physical way, and transmission or information storage and retrieval, electronic adaptation, computer software, or by similar or dissimilar methodology now known or hereafter developed.

Trademarked names, logos, and images may appear in this book. Rather than use a trademark symbol with every occurrence of a trademarked name, logo, or image we use the names, logos, and images only in an editorial fashion and to the benefit of the trademark owner, with no intention of infringement of the trademark.

The use in this publication of trade names, trademarks, service marks, and similar terms, even if they are not identified as such, is not to be taken as an expression of opinion as to whether or not they are subject to proprietary rights.

While the advice and information in this book are believed to be true and accurate at the date of publication, neither the authors nor the editors nor the publisher can accept any legal responsibility for any errors or omissions that may be made. The publisher makes no warranty, express or implied, with respect to the material contained herein.

>    Managing Director, Apress Media LLC: Welmoed Spahr
>    Acquisitions Editor: Susan McDermott
>    Development Editor: Laura Berendson
>    Editorial Project Manager: Jessica Vakili

Cover image by Pixaby

Distributed to the book trade worldwide by Springer Science+Business Media New York, 1 New York Plaza, Suite 4600, New York, NY 10004-1562, USA. Phone 1-800-SPRINGER, fax (201) 348-4505, e-mail orders-ny@springer-sbm.com, or visit www.springeronline.com. Apress Media, LLC is a California LLC and the sole member (owner) is Springer Science + Business Media Finance Inc (SSBM Finance Inc). SSBM Finance Inc is a **Delaware** corporation.

For information on translations, please e-mail booktranslations@springernature.com; for reprint, paperback, or audio rights, please e-mail bookpermissions@springernature.com.

Apress titles may be purchased in bulk for academic, corporate, or promotional use. eBook versions and licenses are also available for most titles. For more information, reference our Print and eBook Bulk Sales web page at http://www.apress.com/bulk-sales.

Any source code or other supplementary material referenced by the author in this book is available to readers on GitHub. For more detailed information, please visit https://www.apress.com/gp/services/source-code.

If disposing of this product, please recycle the paper

# Table of Contents

About the Author .................................................................................. xi

Acknowledgments ............................................................................. xiii

Introduction to the Center for Internet Security (CIS) Controls .......... xv

**Chapter 1: Inventory and Control of Enterprise (Hardware) Assets ..... 1**
    Key Concepts and Terms ............................................................................ 3
    Importance and Relevance ......................................................................... 7
    Risks of Not Implementing the Control .................................................... 11
    What Questions Should You Ask? ............................................................ 13
        Recommended Training .................................................................... 17
    Actionable Recommendations ................................................................. 20
        Simplified Security Controls (SSC) ................................................... 23

**Chapter 2: Inventory and Control of Software Assets ...................... 29**
    Key Concepts and Terms .......................................................................... 32
    Importance and Relevance ....................................................................... 36
    Risks of Not Implementing the Control .................................................... 40
    What Questions Should You Ask? ............................................................ 43
    Recommended Training ........................................................................... 46
    Actionable Recommendations ................................................................. 48
        Simplified Security Controls (SSC) ................................................... 52

TABLE OF CONTENTS

## Chapter 3: Data Protection .................................................................57
- Key Concepts and Terms..............................................................60
- Importance and Relevance ..........................................................65
- Risks of Not Implementing the Control ......................................68
- What Questions Should You Ask?................................................72
- Recommended Training ...............................................................76
- Actionable Recommendations .....................................................79
  - Simplified Security Controls (SSC) ..........................................85

## Chapter 4: Secure Configuration of Enterprise Assets and Software ........................................................................................97
- Key Concepts and Terms............................................................100
- Importance and Relevance ........................................................102
- Risks of Not Implementing the Control ....................................105
- What Questions Should You Ask?..............................................108
- Recommended Training .............................................................110
- Actionable Recommendations ...................................................113
  - Simplified Security Controls (SSC) ........................................116

## Chapter 5: Account Management .....................................................127
- Key Concepts and Terms............................................................130
- Importance and Relevance ........................................................132
- Risks of Not Implementing the Control ....................................136
- What Questions Should You Ask?..............................................140
- Recommended Training .............................................................143
- Actionable Recommendations ...................................................146
  - Simplified Security Controls (SSC) ........................................149

TABLE OF CONTENTS

## Chapter 6: Access Control Management ................................. 155
Key Concepts and Terms ................................................................ 158
Importance and Relevance ............................................................. 160
Risks of Not Implementing the Control ......................................... 164
What Questions Should You Ask? .................................................. 167
Recommended Training .................................................................. 171
Actionable Recommendations ....................................................... 174
    Simplified Security Controls (SSC) ............................................ 176

## Chapter 7: Continuous Vulnerability Management ................. 181
Key Concepts and Terms ................................................................ 184
Importance and Relevance ............................................................. 187
Risks of Not Implementing the Control ......................................... 190
What Questions Should You Ask? .................................................. 193
Recommended Training .................................................................. 196
Actionable Recommendations ....................................................... 200
    Simplified Security Controls (SSC) ............................................ 203

## Chapter 8: Audit Log Management ......................................... 211
Key Concepts and Terms ................................................................ 215
Importance and Relevance ............................................................. 219
Risks of Not Implementing the Control ......................................... 222
What Questions Should You Ask? .................................................. 225
Recommended Training .................................................................. 229
Actionable Recommendations ....................................................... 232
    Simplified Security Controls (SSC) ............................................ 236

TABLE OF CONTENTS

## Chapter 9: Email and Browser Protections ............247
Key Concepts and Terms .................................................250
Importance and Relevance ...............................................253
Risks of Not Implementing the Control ............................256
What Questions Should You Ask? ....................................259
Recommended Training ...................................................263
Actionable Recommendations .........................................266
    Simplified Security Controls (SSC) ...............................270

## Chapter 10: Malware Defenses ..............................277
Key Concepts and Terms .................................................280
Importance and Relevance ...............................................283
Risks of Not Implementing the Control ............................287
What Questions Should You Ask? ....................................291
Recommended Training ...................................................295
Actionable Recommendations .........................................299
    Simplified Security Controls (SSC) ...............................302

## Chapter 11: Data Recovery ....................................309
Key Concepts and Terms .................................................312
Importance and Relevance ...............................................316
Risks of Not Implementing the Control ............................319
What Questions Should You Ask? ....................................322
Recommended Training ...................................................325
Actionable Recommendations .........................................328
    Simplified Security Controls (SSC) ...............................332

TABLE OF CONTENTS

## Chapter 12: Network Infrastructure Management ..........................339
- Key Concepts and Terms ..............................................................342
- Importance and Relevance ..........................................................346
- Risks of Not Implementing the Control ......................................350
- What Questions Should You Ask? ...............................................353
- Recommended Training ...............................................................357
- Actionable Recommendations .....................................................361
  - Simplified Security Controls (SSC) ..........................................364

## Chapter 13: Network Monitoring and Defense ................................371
- Key Concepts and Terms ..............................................................374
- Importance and Relevance ..........................................................378
- Risks of Not Implementing the Control ......................................381
- What Questions Should You Ask? ...............................................384
- Recommended Training ...............................................................387
- Actionable Recommendations .....................................................390
  - Simplified Security Controls (SSC) ..........................................394

## Chapter 14: Security Awareness and Skills Training .......................405
- Key Concepts and Terms ..............................................................409
- Importance and Relevance ..........................................................411
- Risks of Not Implementing the Control ......................................414
- What Questions Should You Ask? ...............................................417
- Recommended Training ...............................................................420
- Actionable Recommendations .....................................................424
  - Simplified Security Controls (SSC) ..........................................427

TABLE OF CONTENTS

## Chapter 15: Service Provider Management .......... 435
Key Concepts and Terms .......... 438
Importance and Relevance .......... 441
Risks of Not Implementing the Control .......... 444
What Questions Should You Ask? .......... 446
Recommended Training .......... 449
Actionable Recommendations .......... 452
   Simplified Security Controls (SSC) .......... 455

## Chapter 16: Application Software Security .......... 463
Key Concepts and Terms .......... 467
Importance and Relevance .......... 470
Risks of Not Implementing the Control .......... 473
What Questions Should You Ask? .......... 476
Recommended Training .......... 478
Actionable Recommendations .......... 482
   Simplified Security Controls (SSC) .......... 485

## Chapter 17: Incident Response Management .......... 497
Key Concepts and Terms .......... 501
Importance and Relevance .......... 504
Risks of Not Implementing the Control .......... 507
What Questions Should You Ask? .......... 511
Recommended Training .......... 514
Actionable Recommendations .......... 517
   Simplified Security Controls (SSC) .......... 520

# TABLE OF CONTENTS

## Chapter 18: Penetration Testing .......................................................527
Key Concepts and Terms..................................................................530
Importance and Relevance ...............................................................534
Risks of Not Implementing the Control ............................................537
What Questions Should You Ask?....................................................539
Recommended Training ...................................................................543
Actionable Recommendations .........................................................546
    Simplified Security Controls (SSC) ..............................................549

## Index.....................................................................................555

# About the Author

**Dr. Jason Edwards** is a seasoned cyber author and professional with over 20 years of experience in the cybersecurity field, having held diverse roles from IT operations and project management to cybersecurity strategy and governance. His strategic approach has enabled him to guide organizations through complex cyber defense challenges, ensuring robust protection against evolving threats. As the author of several books and dozens of articles, Dr. Edwards shares deep knowledge and practical insights with IT professionals, cybersecurity experts, and organizational leaders. Active on LinkedIn, he connects with over 70K professionals through daily and weekly posts and manages a 20K-subscriber mailing list called the Cyber Spear. Passionate about education and community engagement, he offers monthly group sessions, one-on-one consultations, and is a frequent podcast guest discussing cybersecurity trends, strategies, and best practices. For more information, visit his website at jason-edwards.me.

# Acknowledgments

Writing this book has been a journey of immense learning and growth, and I could not have completed it without the unwavering support of many individuals.

First and foremost, I want to thank my family for their endless love and encouragement. To my wife, Selda, your patience, understanding, and belief in me have been my greatest source of strength. To my wonderful children, Michelle, Chris, Celin, and Mayra, thank you for your boundless love and for being my inspiration.

I am deeply grateful to my close friends who have stood by me through thick and thin. Derek B, Rob F, Kurt L, Wendell L, Griffin W, Patrick W, Jason R, Jodi M, and Sam H, your friendship and support have been invaluable.

A heartfelt thanks to my fellow cyber teachers at Hallmark and ThriveDX. Your camaraderie and shared passion for cybersecurity education have enriched my teaching experience immeasurably.

To the students I have taught and am currently teaching, your eagerness to learn and dedication to mastering cybersecurity have been a source of great pride and motivation for me. Thank you for allowing me to be a part of your educational journey.

I would also like to express my gratitude to my coworkers and extended family who, although not individually named, have played a significant role in my professional journey. Your encouragement and assistance have been crucial to my success.

## ACKNOWLEDGMENTS

A special thank you to my LinkedIn followers and all those who have supported my professional efforts by liking, sharing, and engaging with my content. Your enthusiasm and feedback have been a constant source of motivation.

This book is as much yours as it is mine. Thank you for being part of this journey.

With gratitude,

Dr. Jason Edwards

# Introduction to the Center for Internet Security (CIS) Controls

The Center for Internet Security (CIS) Controls, also known as CIS 18, are a set of prioritized cybersecurity best practices designed to help organizations protect themselves against the most common and dangerous cyber threats. Developed by a global community of IT experts, these controls provide a practical and actionable framework for implementing and managing cybersecurity measures. The CIS Controls are widely recognized for their effectiveness in enhancing security posture and are used by organizations of all sizes and across various industries. This introduction provides an overview of the CIS Controls, highlighting their origins, structure, and benefits in mitigating cyber risks and safeguarding critical assets.

## Evolving Cybersecurity Threat Landscape

The cybersecurity landscape is constantly evolving, driven by the rapid pace of technological advancements and the increasing sophistication of cyber adversaries. Organizations adopting new technologies inadvertently expand their attack surface, providing more opportunities for malicious actors to exploit. This dynamic environment requires organizations to stay vigilant and adaptive, continuously updating their security measures to counteract emerging threats. Failure to do so can lead to significant vulnerabilities, putting sensitive data and critical systems at risk.

## INTRODUCTION TO THE CENTER FOR INTERNET SECURITY (CIS) CONTROLS

Emerging threats and attack vectors are becoming more complex and challenging to detect. Cybercriminals leverage advanced machine learning and artificial intelligence techniques to automate attacks and bypass traditional security measures. For instance, ransomware has evolved to include double extortion tactics, where attackers encrypt data and threaten to release it publicly if the ransom is not paid. Additionally, the rise of Internet of Things (IoT) devices has introduced new vulnerabilities, as these often lack robust security features, making them easy targets for exploitation.

Recent high-profile cyber incidents highlight the severe impact of cyber attacks on organizations across various sectors. The SolarWinds attack, for example, demonstrated how sophisticated supply chain attacks can compromise multiple organizations through a single vendor. This incident involved inserting malicious code into a trusted software update, allowing attackers to access numerous government and private sector networks. Another notable case is the Colonial Pipeline ransomware attack, which disrupted fuel supply across the Eastern United States, underscoring the critical importance of securing industrial control systems.

Geopolitical factors significantly influence the cybersecurity landscape, as nation-states increasingly engage in cyber espionage and cyber warfare to achieve strategic objectives. State-sponsored cyber attacks often aim to steal intellectual property, disrupt critical infrastructure, or gain political leverage. For example, tensions between countries can lead to cyber attacks on critical sectors such as energy, finance, and healthcare. These activities pose a threat to national security and create a climate of uncertainty and mistrust, complicating international relations and cooperation on cybersecurity issues.

Advanced Persistent Threats (APTs) represent a significant challenge in cybersecurity due to their sophisticated and stealthy nature. APTs are typically state-sponsored or highly organized groups that engage in prolonged and targeted attacks against specific organizations or sectors.

Their goal is often to gather intelligence, sabotage operations, or exfiltrate sensitive data over an extended period. APTs' ability to remain undetected for long durations makes them particularly dangerous, using advanced techniques such as zero-day exploits and custom malware. Defending against APTs requires a robust, multi-layered security strategy, including advanced threat detection and continuous monitoring.

## Impact on Organizations

The impact of cyber attacks on organizations can be profound and multifaceted, affecting not just the immediate security of systems but also long-term business viability. Organizations of all sizes and sectors are vulnerable to cyber threats, resulting in significant financial losses, reputational harm, operational disruptions, and legal challenges. Understanding these impacts is crucial for organizational leaders to prioritize cybersecurity investments and develop comprehensive risk management strategies.

Cyber attacks can have severe financial consequences for organizations, often resulting in direct costs such as ransom payments, legal fees, and regulatory fines. Additionally, there are indirect costs like loss of business due to system outages, decreased productivity, and the expense of remediation and recovery efforts. For instance, a data breach can lead to substantial expenditures for notification, credit monitoring, and compensation for affected individuals. Moreover, the long-term financial impact can include increased insurance premiums and a potential decline in stock value, especially if the breach affects investor confidence.

Reputational damage is one of the most significant consequences of a cyber attack, as it can erode customer trust and loyalty. When customers perceive that an organization cannot adequately protect their personal information, they may choose to take their business elsewhere. High-profile breaches, such as those experienced by Equifax and Target, demonstrate how a single incident can tarnish a brand's reputation for years. The resulting negative publicity can also attract further scrutiny from regulators and the public, compounding the damage and making recovery efforts more challenging.

Operational disruptions and downtime caused by cyber attacks can impede an organization's ability to function effectively. Ransomware attacks, for example, can lock critical systems and data, halting business operations until the ransom is paid or systems are restored. Even after systems are recovered, there may be lingering effects, such as corrupted data and compromised systems, leading to prolonged periods of reduced operational capacity. The Colonial Pipeline attack is a stark example of how operational disruptions can have widespread consequences, affecting the targeted organization, the broader economy, and public services.

Cyber attacks' legal and regulatory implications are becoming increasingly stringent as governments and regulatory bodies worldwide introduce stricter data protection laws and cybersecurity regulations. Organizations found non-compliant with regulations such as the General Data Protection Regulation (GDPR) or the Health Insurance Portability and Accountability Act (HIPAA) can face hefty fines and sanctions. Additionally, organizations may be subject to lawsuits from customers, partners, and shareholders if it is determined that they failed to take adequate measures to protect sensitive data. Ensuring compliance with these regulations requires a proactive approach to cybersecurity and regular audits to identify and address potential vulnerabilities.

## Human Factor in Cybersecurity

The human factor in cybersecurity is a critical component that often determines the effectiveness of an organization's security measures. While technology and automated defenses play a significant role in protecting against cyber threats, the actions and decisions of individuals within an organization can either fortify or undermine these defenses.

## INTRODUCTION TO THE CENTER FOR INTERNET SECURITY (CIS) CONTROLS

Understanding and addressing the human element is essential for a holistic approach to cybersecurity, as human errors and malicious activities frequently serve as entry points for cyber attacks.

Insider threats and social engineering represent significant risks to organizational cybersecurity. Insider threats can originate from disgruntled employees, contractors, or business partners with legitimate access to systems and data. These individuals might misuse their access for personal gain, to exact revenge, or under coercion from external actors. Social engineering attacks, such as phishing, exploit human psychology to trick individuals into divulging sensitive information or performing actions that compromise security. These tactics can be highly effective, as they often bypass technical defenses by preying on trust and manipulation.

Cybersecurity awareness training equips employees with the knowledge and skills to recognize and respond to threats. Effective training programs educate staff about common attack vectors, such as phishing and social engineering, and provide practical advice on avoiding falling victim to these tactics. Regular training sessions help reinforce best practices and ensure cybersecurity remains a top-of-mind priority. Moreover, fostering a security-conscious culture within the organization encourages employees to remain vigilant and proactive in identifying and reporting suspicious activities.

Human errors are a significant cause of security breaches, often resulting from a lack of awareness or understanding of cybersecurity best practices. Common mistakes include using weak passwords, reusing passwords across multiple accounts, and failing to update software and systems regularly. Additionally, employees might inadvertently click on malicious links or download infected attachments, exposing the organization to malware and other threats. Misconfiguration of systems and inadequate access controls can also create vulnerabilities that attackers can exploit. Addressing these issues requires continuous education, robust policies, and regular audits to identify and mitigate potential weaknesses.

INTRODUCTION TO THE CENTER FOR INTERNET SECURITY (CIS) CONTROLS

# Technological Advancements

Technological advancements continuously reshape the cybersecurity landscape, bringing both opportunities and challenges. Innovations such as the Internet of Things (IoT), artificial intelligence (AI), and blockchain technology offer substantial benefits but also introduce new vulnerabilities and attack vectors. As organizations integrate these technologies into their operations, they must adapt their security strategies to address the evolving threat landscape. Adopting cutting-edge technologies with robust cybersecurity measures is crucial to safeguarding sensitive data and critical systems.

New technologies like IoT, AI, and blockchain present unique cybersecurity challenges requiring specialized approaches. IoT devices, for instance, often lack built-in security features, making them easy targets for attackers. These devices can be used as entry points into more extensive networks or as part of botnets to launch distributed denial-of-service (DDoS) attacks. AI, while valuable for enhancing security measures, can also be weaponized by cybercriminals to automate and scale sophisticated attacks. Blockchain technology, known for its security benefits in certain applications, still faces issues such as the security of smart contracts and the potential for exploitation in decentralized finance (DeFi) platforms. Each of these technologies demands tailored security solutions to mitigate their respective risks.

Digital transformation, characterized by adopting advanced digital technologies to improve business processes and services, has significant security implications. As organizations transition to digital-first operations, they expand their attack surfaces and create new vulnerabilities. Integrating digital technologies often involves using cloud services, mobile devices, and big data analytics, all of which require robust security measures to protect against threats. Additionally, the rapid pace of digital transformation can lead to gaps in security as new technologies are deployed before comprehensive security assessments and implementations are completed. Ensuring that security is a core component of digital transformation initiatives is essential to protecting organizational assets and maintaining trust.

The widespread adoption of cloud computing and the shift to remote work have introduced new security concerns that organizations must address. Cloud environments, while offering scalability and flexibility, also pose risks such as data breaches, misconfigured services, and insecure interfaces. Cloud data protection requires rigorous security practices, including encryption, access controls, and continuous monitoring. Remote work further complicates security efforts, as employees access corporate networks and data from various locations and devices. This increases the risk of unauthorized access, data leaks, and exposure to phishing attacks. Implementing robust endpoint security, virtual private networks (VPNs), and multi-factor authentication (MFA) are critical measures to secure remote work environments.

# Introduction to CIS Controls

The CIS Controls are best practices designed to help organizations improve their cybersecurity posture and defend against the most common and impactful cyber threats. Developed by the Center for Internet Security (CIS), these controls provide a prioritized, actionable framework for implementing and managing security measures. The CIS Controls are widely recognized and adopted across various industries for their effectiveness in reducing risk and enhancing resilience. Understanding their history and development helps contextualize their importance and relevance in today's cybersecurity landscape.

The history and development of the CIS Controls reflect a collaborative effort to address the growing complexity of cyber threats. Initially known as the Consensus Audit Guidelines, these controls were created through the collective expertise of a diverse group of cybersecurity professionals from government, academia, and the private sector. The goal was to establish a practical and prioritized set of actions organizations could implement to protect against the most prevalent and dangerous cyber attacks. Over time, the CIS Controls have evolved to stay ahead of emerging threats and technological advancements, ensuring their continued effectiveness and relevance.

The origins of CIS Controls date back to the early 2000s, a period marked by a significant increase in cyber-attacks and vulnerabilities. Recognizing the need for a standardized approach to cybersecurity, the SANS Institute and other industry leaders developed a set of controls that would be universally applicable and impactful. These early efforts culminated in the publication of the Consensus Audit Guidelines, which later became known as the Critical Security Controls. The foundational principle behind these controls was to focus on a manageable number of high-priority actions that would yield the greatest security benefits.

The CIS Controls have undergone several revisions to adapt to the changing threat landscape and incorporate feedback from the cybersecurity community. Initially comprising 20 controls, the framework was streamlined to 18 controls in its latest iteration to enhance clarity and usability. This evolution reflects the ongoing commitment to refining and updating the controls based on real-world experiences and emerging threats. The transition from CIS 20 to CIS 18 involved re-evaluating and consolidating specific controls and introducing new elements to address contemporary challenges such as cloud security and mobile device management.

The development and ongoing refinement of CIS Controls are made possible through the contributions of a broad coalition of cybersecurity experts and organizations. This collaborative effort includes input from government agencies, private companies, academic institutions, and independent security professionals. Industry leaders' widespread support and endorsement of CIS Controls underscore their value and effectiveness. Many organizations, including Fortune 500 companies and government entities, have adopted CIS Controls as a foundational component of their cybersecurity strategies. This broad adoption validates the controls' relevance and fosters a shared approach to tackling cyber threats across different sectors.

## Core Principles

The CIS Controls are built on several core principles that guide their design and implementation. These principles ensure the controls are effective, manageable, and adaptable to various organizational contexts. By focusing on key areas, balancing different aspects of cybersecurity, and providing flexibility, the CIS Controls offer a comprehensive approach to safeguarding against cyber threats.

One of the core principles of the CIS Controls is prioritization. The controls are organized to allow organizations to focus on the most critical areas first, addressing the most significant risks before moving on to less urgent issues. This prioritized approach helps organizations allocate resources efficiently, ensuring the most impactful security measures are implemented early. The CIS Controls emphasize actions that provide the highest return on investment regarding risk reduction, making them practical for organizations with limited budgets or resources.

The CIS Controls strive to balance prevention, detection, and response. Effective cybersecurity requires not only preventing attacks but also detecting them quickly and responding appropriately. The CIS Controls cover all three aspects: providing guidelines for securing systems and data, monitoring suspicious activities, and planning to respond to incidents. This balanced approach ensures that organizations are prepared to handle the full spectrum of cyber threats, from stopping attacks before they occur to mitigating damage after an incident.

Another core principle of CIS Controls is adaptability. The controls are designed to be flexible and scalable, making them applicable to organizations of all sizes and sectors. Each organization can tailor the CIS

Controls to fit its specific needs and risk profile, whether a small business or a large enterprise. This adaptability ensures the controls remain relevant and effective across diverse environments, from healthcare and finance to manufacturing and education. By providing a customizable framework, the CIS Controls empower organizations to implement security measures that align with their unique circumstances.

## Benefits of Adopting CIS Controls

Adopting CIS Controls offers numerous benefits that can significantly enhance an organization's cybersecurity posture. These benefits include improving security, simplifying compliance, and fostering better organizational collaboration and communication.

Implementing CIS Controls helps organizations improve security by addressing the most critical and common cyber threats. The controls provide a comprehensive set of best practices that, when followed, can significantly reduce the risk of data breaches, system compromises, and other security incidents. Organizations can quickly strengthen their defenses and build a solid foundation for more advanced security measures by focusing on high-priority actions. This proactive approach to cybersecurity helps protect sensitive information and critical assets from malicious actors.

Another significant benefit of adopting the CIS Controls is simplifying compliance efforts. Many regulatory frameworks and standards, such as GDPR, HIPAA, and NIST, align closely with the CIS Controls. By implementing these controls, organizations can simultaneously address multiple compliance requirements, reducing the complexity and cost of meeting regulatory obligations. The CIS Controls provide a clear and structured path for achieving compliance, making it easier for organizations to demonstrate their commitment to cybersecurity and avoid potential fines and penalties.

The CIS Controls also promote enhanced collaboration and communication across different teams within an organization. Effective cybersecurity requires the involvement of various stakeholders, including IT, legal, HR, and executive management. The structured nature of the CIS Controls facilitates clear communication of security priorities and responsibilities, fostering a collaborative approach to managing cyber risks. This cross-functional cooperation ensures that security measures are integrated into the organization's operations, creating a more cohesive and resilient security environment.

# Implementation of Cyber Controls

Implementing cyber controls effectively requires a structured approach that begins with thorough assessment and planning. This process ensures that organizations can identify their specific security needs, allocate resources appropriately, and establish a clear roadmap for enhancing their cybersecurity posture. The initial steps of conducting a cybersecurity risk assessment, identifying critical assets and vulnerabilities, and setting goals and priorities are fundamental to successfully implementing cyber controls.

Assessment and planning form the foundation of any successful cybersecurity strategy. Before implementing specific controls, organizations must understand their current security status, risks, and the resources available for mitigation. This phase involves gathering detailed information about the organization's IT environment, including hardware, software, data, and user practices. By conducting a comprehensive assessment, organizations can develop a clear picture of their security landscape and identify areas that require immediate attention.

## INTRODUCTION TO THE CENTER FOR INTERNET SECURITY (CIS) CONTROLS

A cybersecurity risk assessment is a crucial first step in the implementation process. This assessment involves evaluating the potential threats and vulnerabilities that could impact the organization's information systems and data. The process includes identifying potential threat actors, such as cybercriminals, nation-states, and insiders, and assessing their capabilities and motivations. Additionally, organizations must analyze the likelihood and potential impact of various cyber threats, considering the value of the targeted assets and the effectiveness of existing security measures. The outcome of this assessment provides a prioritized list of risks that need to be addressed.

Identifying critical assets and vulnerabilities is essential for focusing security efforts where they are most needed. Critical assets include data, systems, or processes vital to the organization's success. These might encompass customer information, intellectual property, financial records, and operational systems. Once critical assets are identified, organizations must identify the vulnerabilities that cyber threats could exploit. This involves reviewing current security controls, conducting vulnerability scans, and performing penetration testing. Understanding these vulnerabilities allows organizations to implement targeted controls to protect their most valuable assets.

The next crucial step is setting clear goals and priorities for implementing cyber controls. Based on the risk assessment and vulnerability identification findings, organizations can establish specific, measurable, achievable, relevant, and time-bound (SMART) goals for their cybersecurity initiatives. These goals should align with the organization's overall business objectives and risk tolerance. Prioritization is key, as it ensures that the most critical risks are addressed first. Organizations should focus on implementing high-impact controls that can provide the greatest risk reduction with the available resources. Setting milestones and timelines also helps track progress and ensures accountability throughout the implementation process.

## Integration with Existing Systems

Integrating cyber controls with existing systems is critical to a successful cybersecurity strategy. This process involves aligning new controls with current policies and procedures, leveraging existing security tools and technologies, and ensuring interoperability and scalability. By effectively integrating these controls, organizations can enhance their security posture without causing significant disruption to their operations.

Aligning cyber controls with existing policies and procedures ensures consistency and compliance throughout the organization. This involves reviewing current policies to identify gaps or inconsistencies that need to be addressed. Organizations can streamline implementation and avoid conflicts that could hinder security efforts by harmonizing new controls with established practices. Additionally, updating policies and procedures to reflect the new controls helps reinforce their importance and ensures that all employees are aware of and adhere to the updated security measures.

Leveraging existing security tools and technologies can significantly enhance the efficiency and effectiveness of implementing new controls. Organizations often have a range of security solutions already in place, such as firewalls, intrusion detection systems, and endpoint protection software. Integrating new controls with these existing tools allows for a more seamless transition and maximizes the use of current investments. It is important to evaluate the capabilities of existing tools to determine how they can support the new controls and identify any additional technologies that may be needed to fill gaps.

Ensuring interoperability and scalability is crucial for the long-term success of cybersecurity measures. Interoperability involves ensuring new controls can work seamlessly with existing systems and technologies, reducing the risk of integration issues that could compromise security or operational efficiency. This can be achieved by adhering to industry standards and protocols and facilitating compatibility between solutions.

Scalability, conversely, ensures that the security measures can grow and adapt alongside the organization. As businesses expand and evolve, their security needs will change, and scalable controls can accommodate these changes without requiring a complete overhaul of the security infrastructure.

## Resource Allocation

Effective resource allocation is critical to successfully implementing and managing cybersecurity initiatives. This process involves budgeting for cybersecurity projects, allocating personnel and expertise, and leveraging external resources and partnerships. By strategically distributing resources, organizations can ensure that their cybersecurity efforts are efficient and effective, enhancing their overall security posture.

Budgeting for cybersecurity initiatives requires a detailed understanding of the organization's security needs and priorities. This involves identifying the financial resources necessary to implement and maintain various cybersecurity controls and technologies. Organizations should consider immediate and long-term costs, including hardware and software purchases, ongoing maintenance, and potential costs associated with responding to security incidents. Establishing a clear budget helps ensure sufficient funds are allocated to critical areas, reducing the risk of financial shortfalls that could compromise security efforts.

Allocating the right personnel and expertise is essential for effectively implementing and managing cybersecurity measures. Organizations must have skilled cybersecurity professionals who can design, implement, and monitor security controls. This may involve hiring new staff, training existing employees, or combining both. Additionally, organizations should define roles and responsibilities for cybersecurity tasks to ensure accountability and efficiency. A dedicated cybersecurity team or personnel with specialized expertise can significantly enhance the organization's ability to detect and respond to threats.

Leveraging external resources and partnerships can support an organization's cybersecurity efforts. This can include engaging with cybersecurity consultants, participating in information-sharing networks, and partnering with managed security service providers (MSSPs). External resources can offer specialized expertise, advanced threat intelligence, and additional workforce, which can benefit organizations with limited in-house capabilities. Collaborating with external partners also allows organizations to stay informed about the latest threats and best practices, enhancing their overall security posture.

## Training and Awareness

Developing a comprehensive training and awareness program ensures that all employees understand their role in maintaining cybersecurity. This involves creating training initiatives that educate staff about security policies, common threats, and best practices for preventing breaches. A well-rounded training program should engage stakeholders at all levels, providing continuous education and skill development opportunities.

A comprehensive training program should cover a wide range of topics relevant to cybersecurity. This includes basic concepts such as password management and recognizing phishing attempts, as well as more advanced topics tailored to specific roles within the organization. Training should be interactive and practical, incorporating real-world scenarios and hands-on exercises to reinforce learning. Additionally, the program should be regularly updated to reflect the latest threats and security practices, ensuring employees are always equipped with current knowledge.

Engaging stakeholders at all levels is crucial for creating a security culture within the organization. Senior leadership should demonstrate a solid commitment to cybersecurity, setting the tone for the rest of the organization. Middle managers and team leaders are crucial in reinforcing security practices within their teams, while all employees need to understand their responsibilities. By involving stakeholders at every level, organizations can foster a sense of shared responsibility and encourage proactive security behavior.

Continuous education and skill development are essential for keeping pace with the evolving threat landscape. Cybersecurity training should not be a one-time event but an ongoing process that adapts to new challenges and technologies. Regular training sessions, workshops, and e-learning modules can help maintain high awareness and competence. Additionally, providing opportunities for advanced training and certifications can help cybersecurity professionals stay current with industry developments and enhance their expertise. Continuous education ensures the organization remains resilient against emerging threats and maintains a strong security posture.

# Using the CIS 18 to Determine Necessary Controls

The CIS 18 Controls provide a comprehensive framework organizations can use to enhance their cybersecurity posture. To effectively implement these controls, it is essential to adopt a risk-based approach that tailors the controls to specific organizational risks, prioritizes them based on the current threat landscape, and balances security needs with operational requirements. This strategic approach ensures that the most critical risks are addressed first and that security measures are aligned with the organization's unique context.

A risk-based approach is central to determining the necessary controls using the CIS 18 framework. This methodology involves identifying, assessing, and prioritizing risks based on their potential impact on the organization. By focusing on the most significant threats, organizations can allocate resources more effectively and implement controls that reduce the most critical risk. This approach improves security outcomes and aligns cybersecurity efforts with the organization's overall risk management strategy.

Tailoring controls to specific organizational risks involves customizing the CIS 18 Controls to address the unique vulnerabilities and threat vectors relevant to the organization. This process begins with a thorough risk assessment to identify the assets most critical to the organization, such as sensitive data, key systems, and business processes. Once these critical assets and associated risks are identified, organizations can select and adapt the appropriate CIS Controls to mitigate these risks. This customization ensures that the controls are relevant and effective in the organization's specific context.

Prioritizing controls based on the threat landscape involves evaluating the current and emerging threats that could impact the organization. This requires staying informed about the latest trends in cyber threats, such as new attack vectors, tactics used by threat actors, and industry-specific vulnerabilities. By understanding the threat landscape, organizations can prioritize the implementation of controls that address the most pressing risks. For example, if ransomware attacks are on the rise, an organization might prioritize data backups, patch management, and user training controls to mitigate this threat effectively.

Balancing security needs with operational requirements is crucial for ensuring that implementing controls does not hinder the organization's ability to function effectively. Security measures must be designed and implemented to support, rather than disrupt, business operations. This balance can be achieved by involving key stakeholders from different departments in the planning process to understand their operational needs and constraints. Adopting a phased implementation approach can help integrate controls gradually, allowing time to address any operational challenges. The goal is to enhance security while maintaining productivity and efficiency.

## Metrics and KPIs

Metrics and Key Performance Indicators (KPIs) are essential for measuring the effectiveness and impact of cyber controls. By defining specific KPIs, organizations can track their cybersecurity performance, identify areas for improvement, and communicate results to stakeholders. This structured approach helps ensure cybersecurity efforts align with organizational goals and deliver tangible results.

Defining key performance indicators (KPIs) for controls involves selecting measurable metrics that reflect the effectiveness and efficiency of cybersecurity measures. KPIs should align with the organization's security objectives and risk management strategy. Common KPIs for cyber controls include Incident Detection Time (IDT), which measures the average time taken to detect a security incident, and Incident Response Time (IRT), which tracks the average time to respond to and mitigate a security incident. Other essential KPIs are the number of detected incidents within a specific period, patch management metrics that indicate the percentage of systems with up-to-date patches, user awareness training completion rate, and the false positive rate of security alerts. By defining these KPIs, organizations can establish clear benchmarks for their cybersecurity performance and track progress over time.

Measuring the effectiveness and impact of controls involves collecting and analyzing data related to the defined KPIs. This process starts with data collection from various sources, such as security information and event management (SIEM) systems, incident reports, and audit logs, providing the raw information needed to evaluate control performance. Data analysis follows, assessing how well the controls are performing by identifying trends, patterns, and anomalies that indicate potential issues or areas for improvement. Benchmarking is also crucial, as is comparing the organization's performance against industry standards, best practices, and historical data to highlight areas for improvement. Impact assessment evaluates the broader impact of controls on the organization's security posture, including their effectiveness in reducing risk, preventing incidents, and minimizing the impact of breaches. Organizations can make data-driven decisions to enhance their cybersecurity strategies by systematically measuring control effectiveness and impact.

Reporting and communicating the results of cybersecurity metrics and KPIs to stakeholders is critical for maintaining transparency and accountability. Effective communication ensures that all relevant parties are informed about the organization's security posture and the outcomes of its cybersecurity efforts. Regular reporting involves creating and distributing reports that summarize the performance of cyber controls tailored to the needs of different stakeholders, such as executives, IT teams, and regulatory bodies. These reports might include dashboards, charts, and narratives highlighting key findings and trends. Clear and concise communication is essential, presenting results in a manner that non-technical stakeholders easily understand. Providing actionable insights and recommendations based on the analysis of KPIs helps stakeholders understand the steps needed to address identified issues and improve security measures. Engaging stakeholders in discussions about the results and soliciting their feedback fosters a collaborative approach, building support for cybersecurity initiatives and ensuring alignment with broader business goals.

## About This Book

This book is designed to serve as a comprehensive guide for IT professionals, cybersecurity experts, and organizational leaders aiming to enhance their cybersecurity posture by implementing the CIS 18 Controls. Each chapter is dedicated to one of the controls from the CIS 18, offering a deep dive into its importance, implementation, and management. The structured format of each chapter ensures a thorough understanding and practical application of each control. This approach helps readers systematically improve their organization's cybersecurity defenses.

## INTRODUCTION TO THE CENTER FOR INTERNET SECURITY (CIS) CONTROLS

Each chapter introduces the control, providing context and explaining its relevance in the broader cybersecurity landscape. This section sets the stage for why the control is critical and how it fits into an overall cybersecurity strategy. Understanding the foundational principles of each control is essential for effective implementation. The introduction lays the groundwork for the detailed exploration that follows.

To enhance comprehension, the chapters include a list of key terms associated with the control, each clearly explained. Understanding these terms is essential for grasping the concepts discussed and for effective communication within cybersecurity. This glossary-like section helps readers familiarize themselves with the specific language and terminology used in the industry. Clear definitions ensure that all readers can follow along and understand the material regardless of their prior knowledge.

The book also provides a list of facts demonstrating each control's relevance. These facts are grounded in real-world scenarios and statistical data, underscoring the necessity of implementing the control to protect organizational assets and data. This section highlights the practical importance of control by presenting concrete evidence and examples. Readers can see how the power has been applied successfully in various contexts.

Each chapter details the risks to the business if the control is not implemented. This section outlines the potential consequences, including financial losses, reputational damage, operational disruptions, and legal implications. Understanding these risks helps to emphasize the urgency and importance of the control. This book motivates readers to take proactive measures by clearly identifying the dangers of neglect.

To aid cyber leaders in assessing their organization's security posture, the book includes a list of questions they should ask to gather critical information about the control's implementation and effectiveness. These questions are designed to prompt thorough evaluations and discussions, ensuring that all aspects of the power are considered. By asking the right questions, leaders can uncover weaknesses and areas for

## INTRODUCTION TO THE CENTER FOR INTERNET SECURITY (CIS) CONTROLS

improvement. This section empowers leaders to take a proactive approach to cybersecurity management.

Recommendations on training are provided for each control, focusing on the skills and knowledge that employees and teams need to implement and manage the control effectively. These recommendations help organizations develop targeted training programs that enhance their cybersecurity capabilities. Proper training ensures that staff are well-equipped to handle the demands of the control. This focus on education is crucial for maintaining a solid security posture.

Actionable recommendations for cyber leaders are also included, offering practical steps that can be taken to implement the control. These recommendations provide clear guidance on integrating the control into the organization's security framework. By following these steps, leaders can ensure a structured and effective approach to cybersecurity. Practical advice helps bridge the gap between theory and practice.

Finally, each chapter concludes with a list of Simplified Security Controls (SSC) based on the safeguards in CIS 18 and other relevant frameworks. These controls offer practical examples of how the primary control can be tested, providing actionable insights and methods for validating its effectiveness. This section includes specific testing procedures and scenarios, helping organizations ensure that their controls are implemented and functioning as intended. By providing these examples, the book makes verifying and refining their cybersecurity measures easier for organizations.

By following this structured format, this book provides a detailed and practical guide for enhancing cybersecurity by effectively implementing the CIS 18 Controls. Each section is designed to build on the previous one, creating a comprehensive resource for cybersecurity professionals. This book is an essential tool for any organization looking to strengthen its defenses against the ever-evolving landscape of cyber threats. Its practical, step-by-step approach ensures readers can effectively implement and manage each control, leading to a more secure organizational environment.

# CHAPTER 1

# Inventory and Control of Enterprise (Hardware) Assets

The evolution of hardware asset management within the cybersecurity landscape has become increasingly vital due to technological advancements and evolving regulatory landscapes. Centered initially on reactive measures, the field has progressively shifted toward a proactive approach emphasizing preventing security risks before they emerge. This strategic transformation highlights the necessity of rigorous management practices, as the security of diverse hardware asset classes—including end-user devices (both portable and mobile), network devices, non-computing/Internet of Things (IoT) devices, and servers—is intricately linked to an organization's comprehensive cybersecurity posture.

The role of automation in hardware asset management has expanded significantly, becoming indispensable in addressing the challenges presented by the vast complexity and diversity of assets. Manual processes need to be improved for effectively managing the array of assets such as end-user devices, network hardware, IoT devices, and servers. Automation technologies now play a critical role, enabling organizations to efficiently

CHAPTER 1    INVENTORY AND CONTROL OF ENTERPRISE (HARDWARE) ASSETS

catalog, monitor, and manage these hardware assets on a massive scale. These technologies utilize advanced algorithms and machine learning to accurately identify, classify, and evaluate the security posture of these assets, facilitating rapid and appropriate actions to maintain stringent security standards.

Moreover, integrated security ecosystems have become increasingly crucial in hardware asset management. In today's highly interconnected digital environments, managing hardware assets such as end-user devices, network devices, and servers in isolation is impractical. A holistic approach that acknowledges the interdependencies among these hardware assets and the broader IT and security infrastructure is essential. This approach involves integrating various security tools and technologies, which helps forge a cohesive and robust security framework that enhances the protection of all categories of hardware assets.

Additionally, the progression of hardware asset management has been significantly shaped by the emergence of new regulatory demands. Compliance requirements such as the General Data Protection Regulation (GDPR) in Europe and the California Consumer Privacy Act (CCPA) in the United States have introduced new complexities in managing diverse hardware assets. These regulations demand secure management practices and compliance with stringent privacy and security guidelines, thus making the intersection of hardware asset management and compliance a critical focus area. This necessitates organizations to adopt security-centric and compliance-oriented asset management practices to align with these regulatory standards.

The landscape of hardware asset management is poised for further evolution with the continual advancement of technology. The increasing adoption of artificial intelligence and machine learning is set to revolutionize asset management processes. These cutting-edge technologies promise enhanced levels of automation, predictive analytics, and intelligent decision-making, transforming hardware asset management from a routine tracking function to a strategic capability that significantly influences cybersecurity resilience and innovation.

CHAPTER 1    INVENTORY AND CONTROL OF ENTERPRISE (HARDWARE) ASSETS

Hardware asset management, which encompasses a broad spectrum of hardware types, including end-user devices, network devices, IoT devices, and servers, is a foundational aspect of contemporary cybersecurity strategies. Its role rapidly expands beyond traditional boundaries, establishing it as a cornerstone of strategic cybersecurity initiatives and a crucial element of digital transformation. As organizations navigate this complex and dynamic terrain, embracing innovative, integrated, and proactive asset management practices will be vital for ensuring cybersecurity excellence and maintaining operational integrity. This strategic focus safeguards valuable hardware assets and enhances organizations' overall security posture and compliance readiness, fostering a more secure and resilient digital infrastructure.

# Key Concepts and Terms

Active management encompasses the thorough inventory, tracking, and correction of all enterprise assets, from end-user devices such as portable and mobile gadgets to critical network apparatus, diverse Internet of Things (IoT) devices, and powerful servers. These assets, whether connected to the infrastructure physically, virtually, remotely, or housed within cloud environments, form the foundation of what needs vigilant monitoring and robust protection. The aim is to comprehensively understand the resources that necessitate oversight, ensuring every component is accounted for and safeguarded against cybersecurity threats.

**Enterprise Assets:** "Enterprise assets" encompasses the vast array of hardware, software, and data pivotal to any organization's seamless operation and success. These assets, straddling physical hardware like computers and servers and digital realms such as software applications and data repositories, are the pillars of an organization's technological infrastructure. Their comprehensive management is not just about maintaining operational functionality but is critical to safeguarding against

3

security vulnerabilities and ensuring organizational efficiency. Given their significance, the rigorous oversight of these assets becomes a foundational element of any robust cybersecurity strategy, underpinning the organization's ability to operate securely in an increasingly digitized world.

**Asset Inventory:** Asset inventory is the cornerstone of effective asset management, offering a detailed catalog of an organization's assets. This essential tool records vital details such as the types of assets, their physical or digital locations, ownership details, and operational statuses. By providing a panoramic view of the asset landscape, an asset inventory enables organizations to ensure that every asset, whether a laptop or a piece of critical software, is appropriately accounted for, managed, and secured. Keeping this inventory updated is crucial for its effectiveness, enabling organizations to quickly respond to security threats and manage assets throughout their lifecycle.

**Active Management:** In the dynamic landscape of organizational assets, active management is a critical strategy that involves the meticulous inventorying, tracking, and correction of assets to ensure they align with the organization's security policies and compliance requirements. This proactive approach ensures continuous monitoring and maintenance of assets, enabling the timely identification and mitigation of risks. Active management transcends reactive measures, positioning organizations to anticipate and address potential security vulnerabilities proactively, thereby bolstering the overall cybersecurity posture.

**End-User Devices:** End-user devices, encompassing laptops, desktops, smartphones, and tablets, serve as the primary interfaces employees interact with an organization's digital resources. These devices facilitate access to corporate networks and sensitive information, making them focal points for cybersecurity measures. The necessity to secure these devices cannot be overstated, as they represent common vectors for unauthorized access and data breaches. Ensuring the security of these devices involves a combination of technical safeguards, user education, and policy enforcement to protect against the myriad of threats targeting these accessible assets.

**Portable and Mobile Devices:** The proliferation of portable and mobile devices within the corporate environment, driven by convenience and flexibility, introduces significant management and security challenges. Often encompassed by Bring Your Device (BYOD) policies, these devices blur the lines between personal and professional use, necessitating a careful balance between operational flexibility and security. The inherent mobility of these devices increases their risk of loss or theft, further exacerbating potential data security concerns. Organizations must implement clear, comprehensive guidelines and robust security measures to manage these risks effectively.

**Network Devices:** As the backbone of an organization's network infrastructure, routers, switches, and firewalls are indispensable for ensuring connectivity and facilitating data exchange. Their pivotal role in maintaining the network's integrity and performance makes them prime cyberattack targets. Consequently, proper configuration, management, and security are paramount for these network devices. Implementing stringent security protocols and regular monitoring can significantly mitigate potential vulnerabilities, safeguarding the organization's network against unauthorized access and ensuring the continuity of operations.

**Non-Computing/IoT Devices:** The advent of the Internet of Things (IoT) has significantly expanded the scope of enterprise assets to include non-computing devices such as smart sensors, security cameras, and other connected devices. While enhancing operational efficiency and opening new avenues for innovation, these IoT devices significantly broaden an organization's digital footprint and potential attack surface. Specialized security considerations are imperative for these devices, given their diverse functionalities and operating environments. Managing these assets requires tailored security strategies to address their vulnerabilities and ensure they do not become weak links in the organization's cybersecurity defenses.

CHAPTER 1    INVENTORY AND CONTROL OF ENTERPRISE (HARDWARE) ASSETS

**Servers:** Servers, the powerhouse computers that store, process, and disseminate data to other computers on a network, are central to the operational and informational ecosystems of modern organizations. Their role in data storage, processing, and application hosting makes them critical assets that must be rigorously secured to prevent unauthorized access and cyber attacks. Ensuring the security and availability of servers is a multifaceted endeavor involving physical security measures, cybersecurity defenses, and regular maintenance. The importance of server security is underscored by its direct impact on business continuity, data integrity, and the overall trustworthiness of an organization's IT infrastructure.

**Asset Tracking:** Asset tracking is an essential practice within the broader scope of asset management, enabling organizations to monitor the location and status of their assets in real time. By monitoring asset movements and changes, organizations can prevent loss, theft, and unauthorized use. Asset tracking is not merely about logistical oversight; it is a critical security practice that allows swift responses to potential threats and incidents. Effective asset-tracking systems are indispensable in today's fast-paced and ever-changing operational environments, providing a necessary layer of security and operational control.

**Remote Assets:** The increasing trend of remote work has highlighted the importance of managing and securing remote assets outside the traditional office environment, such as laptops and mobile devices. These assets, often connected over public or unsecured networks, introduce unique security challenges that must be addressed through effective policies and measures. Protecting remote assets is critical for safeguarding sensitive information and maintaining the security of the organization's network. Effective management of these assets requires technological solutions, user education, and policy enforcement, underscoring the multifaceted nature of modern cybersecurity strategies.

**BYOD Policies:** Bring Your Device (BYOD) policies represent a strategic response to the growing integration of personal and corporate device use within the workplace. These policies aim to balance the operational flexibility afforded by personal device use with the need to maintain stringent security controls. BYOD policies outline the responsibilities of both users and the organization in managing and securing portable and mobile devices, playing a pivotal role in the broader asset management and cybersecurity framework. Developing and enforcing comprehensive BYOD policies are crucial for mitigating risks associated with device diversity and ensuring that personal devices do not become vectors for security breaches.

# Importance and Relevance

In today's digital landscape, effective hardware asset management is paramount. As organizations navigate the complexities of cybersecurity threats, the foundational practice of identifying, managing, and securing hardware assets such as end-user devices, network devices, IoT devices, and servers emerges as a critical defense mechanism. The following list highlights the key reasons hardware asset management is indispensable to modern cybersecurity efforts. From securing digital infrastructure to ensuring compliance with regulatory standards and facilitating strategic decision-making, each point underscores the crucial role of this control in strengthening an organization's cyber defenses against the ever-evolving threat landscape.

**Pivotal Role in Security:** Hardware asset management is foundational to securing an organization's digital infrastructure. A comprehensive understanding of all hardware assets within an enterprise is essential for effective defense mechanisms. Unidentified devices pose significant security risks and serve as potential entry points for intruders. By ensuring a thorough inventory of hardware assets, organizations can significantly mitigate vulnerabilities and enhance their security posture, maintaining a resilient defense against evolving cyber threats.

CHAPTER 1   INVENTORY AND CONTROL OF ENTERPRISE (HARDWARE) ASSETS

**Foundation for Risk Management:** Effective hardware asset management is at the heart of risk management. Identifying and classifying hardware assets allows organizations to tailor their security measures, focusing on the most critical and vulnerable assets. This strategic prioritization enables a more efficient allocation of cybersecurity resources, ensuring that protective efforts are concentrated where they are most needed, thereby constructing a robust risk management framework that addresses the unique risks inherent to their operational landscape.

**Compliance and Regulatory Requirements:** Adherence to cybersecurity regulations and standards often hinges on maintaining an accurate hardware asset inventory. This inventory becomes a focal point during compliance audits, highlighting the importance of meticulous hardware asset management. Proper management of hardware assets facilitates compliance and shields organizations from potential legal and financial repercussions. In today's regulatory environment, an up-to-date hardware asset inventory is indispensable for meeting these obligations and maintaining regulatory compliance.

**Enhanced Incident Response:** Swiftly identifying compromised hardware assets is instrumental in formulating an effective response to a security breach. A precise hardware asset inventory provides critical information that enables organizations to isolate threats, minimize damage, and accelerate recovery processes. This readiness and detailed knowledge of hardware assets underpin a rapid and coordinated incident response, which is crucial for mitigating the impact of security breaches and restoring normal operations with minimal delay.

**Optimization of Security Investments:** A deep understanding of the nature and scope of hardware assets allows organizations to make strategic investments in security measures. This insight guides decisions on where resources should be allocated to bolster defenses, ensuring investments are directed toward areas of greatest need. Such a targeted approach to cybersecurity spending enhances security efficiency and maximizes the effectiveness of each investment, contributing to a more robust security framework.

**Improved Network Visibility:** A comprehensive inventory of hardware assets boosts network visibility, empowering IT and security teams to detect unauthorized devices quickly, monitor for unusual behavior, and identify potential security threats. This enhanced visibility is fundamental for proactive threat detection and response, enabling organizations to address vulnerabilities before they can be exploited. Monitoring the network landscape in real time is critical in safeguarding against cyber threats.

**Support for Remote and Cloud Environments:** The proliferation of remote work and cloud-based technologies has introduced additional complexity to asset management. Extending visibility and control to encompass remote devices and cloud assets is vital, as these elements are frequently targeted due to perceived vulnerabilities. Effective hardware asset management practices must adapt to include these environments, ensuring that all assets, regardless of location, are secured and monitored. This adaptability is essential for protecting assets in the evolving digital workspace.

**Dynamic Asset Management:** The rapid evolution of the IT landscape, characterized by the continuous introduction of new devices and the decommissioning of outdated ones, demands dynamic asset management. This approach ensures that the organization's hardware asset inventory accurately reflects current and up-to-date assets, supporting a consistently strong security posture. By embracing dynamic asset management, organizations can stay ahead of changes in the technology ecosystem, maintaining security amid ongoing advancements.

**Resource Optimization:** Effective hardware asset management enables organizations to avoid the costs associated with redundant or underutilized hardware assets. By keeping an accurate and current inventory, organizations can ensure optimal utilization of IT resources, aligning asset use with operational needs and objectives. This optimization reduces unnecessary expenditures and enhances the overall efficiency of the organization's IT operations.

**Data Protection and Privacy:** The security and privacy of sensitive data are paramount, necessitating special attention to hardware assets that store such information. Through hardware asset management, organizations can identify which assets contain sensitive data and implement additional security controls to safeguard against breaches. This focused protection is critical for preventing data leakage and ensuring compliance with privacy regulations, reinforcing the organization's commitment to data security and privacy.

**Facilitates Security Automation:** A well-maintained hardware asset inventory lays the groundwork for the effective implementation of security automation. Automated security solutions can leverage detailed hardware asset information to apply consistent security policies across all assets, ensuring comprehensive coverage. This automation enhances the efficiency of security operations, reducing the manual workload and bolstering the organization's defense mechanisms.

**Strategic Decision-Making:** A thorough understanding of the organization's hardware asset landscape supports informed strategic decision-making regarding cybersecurity policies, budgeting, and IT infrastructure planning. Hardware asset management provides senior management with the data necessary to make decisions that align with the organization's goals and objectives. This strategic alignment is crucial for developing and executing cybersecurity strategies that address current and future challenges, ensuring the organization's resilience in the face of an ever-changing cybersecurity landscape.

# Risks of Not Implementing the Control

In the modern digital ecosystem, securing an organization's hardware assets—including end-user devices, network devices, IoT devices, and servers—is crucial for maintaining operational integrity, customer trust, and a competitive edge. However, failing to implement robust controls for hardware asset management exposes an organization to significant risks that can compromise its security posture, disrupt business operations, and incur substantial financial and reputational damage. Cybersecurity threats continuously evolve, exploiting weaknesses in an organization's defenses, with risks associated with inadequate hardware asset management being particularly insidious. Below are the critical risks companies face when they neglect thorough inventory and control of their hardware assets:

**Vulnerability to Unauthorized Access and Attacks:** A comprehensive understanding of all hardware assets within an organization is critical to ensure that devices are adequately protected. Lack of this knowledge opens up vulnerabilities through unprotected or inadequately secured devices, which malicious actors can exploit. This risk is heightened for unnoticed, unpatched, or misconfigured systems that can be easy entry points for cybercriminals. Identifying and securing every hardware asset against such threats is fundamental to bolstering an organization's cybersecurity posture.

**Compromised Data Security:** An incomplete or outdated inventory of hardware assets, especially those that store, process, or transmit sensitive information, significantly increases the risk of data breaches. This can result in the loss of critical intellectual property and customer data, potentially leading to severe compliance violations and financial penalties. Clarity and accuracy in a hardware asset inventory are paramount in applying necessary security measures to protect sensitive data.

**Inefficient Resource Allocation:** Clear visibility into the needs and statuses of all hardware assets is essential for effectively allocating cybersecurity resources. This visibility is necessary for resources to be misallocated to less critical areas, diminishing the overall effectiveness of cybersecurity measures and potentially wasting valuable security investments. A detailed understanding of the hardware asset landscape is required to ensure that protective efforts are directed where needed.

**Increased Operational Downtime:** Hardware assets not properly managed or monitored are more prone to failures and cyber attacks, leading to significant operational downtime. This not only impacts the organization's productivity but also affects its reputation and customer satisfaction. Quick detection and response to issues with hardware assets are crucial in minimizing downtime and associated costs.

**Challenges in Compliance and Audit Preparedness:** Adhering to regulatory standards often requires organizations to maintain comprehensive hardware asset inventories. Failure to implement such controls can lead to non-compliance, exposing the organization to fines, sanctions, and increased regulatory scrutiny. A well-maintained hardware asset inventory is a regulatory requirement and a critical component of an organization's overall compliance and audit strategy.

**Reduced Incident Response Efficacy:** An accurate and comprehensive hardware asset inventory can significantly help an organization respond effectively to security incidents. Without detailed knowledge of affected systems, identifying and remediating vulnerabilities can be prolonged, exacerbating the impact of incidents. A thorough hardware asset inventory enables faster identification of compromised systems and quicker recovery.

**Blind Spots in Security Coverage:** A lack of a complete hardware asset inventory creates blind spots in an organization's security coverage, leaving certain assets unprotected and without appropriate security measures. These blind spots offer attackers easy targets, increasing the organization's vulnerability to cyber threats. Ensuring comprehensive security coverage requires a thorough inventory of all hardware assets.

**Difficulty in Managing Shadow IT:** Shadow IT, consisting of unauthorized devices and applications, poses significant security vulnerabilities. Detecting and managing shadow IT is a formidable challenge without effective hardware asset control mechanisms. The proliferation of shadow IT can introduce a range of security risks, underscoring the importance of rigorous hardware asset management practices.

**Inability to Prioritize Asset Protection:** Understanding the criticality of different hardware assets is essential for effectively prioritizing security efforts. Without this understanding, organizations may fail to protect high-value assets adequately, exposing them to potential threats. Effective asset prioritization requires a detailed inventory and assessment of hardware assets based on their importance and vulnerability.

**Exposure to Legal and Financial Consequences:** Unsecured hardware assets can lead to data breaches that carry substantial legal and financial consequences for organizations. The fallout from such breaches can include legal challenges, economic losses, and damage to the organization's market position and customer trust. Ensuring that all hardware assets are secured and compliant with relevant regulations is crucial in mitigating these risks.

# What Questions Should You Ask?

In the dynamic world of cybersecurity, safeguarding an organization's hardware assets—such as end-user devices, network devices, IoT devices, and servers—requires thoughtful consideration and strategic planning. For cybersecurity leaders, asking the right questions is the first step in laying the groundwork for effective control implementation. These questions are a diagnostic tool to assess current capabilities and gaps, guiding the organization's cybersecurity strategy. They help identify the scope of the challenge, the resources required, and potential hurdles that may be

CHAPTER 1   INVENTORY AND CONTROL OF ENTERPRISE (HARDWARE) ASSETS

encountered. Furthermore, these questions facilitate a comprehensive understanding of the organization's hardware asset landscape, enabling the ability to apply targeted security measures effectively. By addressing these critical inquiries, cybersecurity leaders can ensure a robust foundation for protecting their organization's hardware assets against the myriad cyber threats they face.

**How frequently is our hardware asset inventory updated?** Regular updates are essential to ensure accuracy and relevance, providing the foundation for effective cybersecurity and compliance management. Leaders must assess how often these updates occur to ensure that the inventory reflects the current state of assets, including newly added or decommissioned items. Frequent updates allow real-time visibility, enabling swift decision-making and comprehensive risk management.

**What types of hardware assets are included in our inventory?** Determining the scope of the hardware asset inventory is critical for effective management. Leaders should inquire about the types of hardware assets cataloged to ensure comprehensive coverage, including mobile devices, network equipment, IoT devices, and servers. A broad and inclusive definition of assets ensures no asset type is overlooked, minimizing security blind spots and enhancing the organization's overall security posture.

**Who is responsible for managing the hardware asset inventory?** It is crucial to identify clear ownership and accountability for the hardware asset management process. Leaders must understand who maintains and updates the hardware asset inventory. Establishing clear roles and responsibilities ensures the asset management process is consistently executed and the inventory remains accurate and current.

**How are hardware assets classified and prioritized for security purposes?** The classification and prioritization of hardware assets are key components of an effective asset management strategy. Leaders should seek to understand the criteria used to classify assets and how these classifications inform security priorities. Knowing how hardware assets are categorized based on their criticality and the sensitivity of the data they handle helps allocate security resources more effectively, focusing efforts on protecting high-risk assets.

**What processes are in place to track the lifecycle of hardware assets?** The lifecycle management of hardware assets, from procurement to decommissioning, is integral to maintaining security. Leaders must inquire about the processes to track hardware assets throughout their lifecycle. Understanding how hardware assets are added, monitored, and eventually retired from the inventory is crucial for ensuring they remain secure at every stage.

**How do we identify and handle unauthorized or rogue hardware assets?** The presence of unauthorized or rogue hardware assets within the network poses a significant security risk. Leaders need to ascertain the mechanisms for detecting and managing such assets. Knowing how the organization identifies and responds to unauthorized hardware assets is essential for maintaining network integrity and security.

**What measures are taken to secure hardware assets in remote or cloud environments?** Securing hardware assets outside the traditional network perimeter has become increasingly important with the proliferation of remote work and cloud technologies. Leaders should explore the strategies and tools to protect remote and cloud-based hardware assets. This inquiry addresses how the organization adapts its security measures to account for the unique challenges presented by these environments.

**How is hardware asset information protected, and who has access to it?** The sensitive information hardware asset inventory requires protection to prevent unauthorized access and potential data breaches. Leaders must understand the safeguards to secure hardware asset information and the access controls implemented. Knowing who has access to the hardware asset inventory and how its confidentiality and integrity are maintained is critical.

CHAPTER 1   INVENTORY AND CONTROL OF ENTERPRISE (HARDWARE) ASSETS

**What integration exists between the hardware asset inventory and other security tools?** The value of a hardware asset inventory is greatly enhanced when integrated with other security tools and systems. Leaders should investigate the extent of this integration and how it facilitates automated processes, improves visibility, and accelerates response times during security incidents.

**How are hardware assets decommissioned securely to ensure no data is left vulnerable?** The decommissioning of hardware assets represents a critical point in their lifecycle, with implications for data security. Leaders must probe into the procedures established for securely decommissioning hardware assets, ensuring that all data is appropriately wiped and that assets are disposed of or repurposed without exposing sensitive information.

**What challenges have we faced in managing and securing hardware assets, and how have these been addressed?** Reflecting on past challenges and the solutions implemented provides valuable insights into the effectiveness of current hardware asset management and security practices. Leaders should inquire about the obstacles encountered in hardware asset management and the strategies to overcome them.

**How does our hardware asset management practice align with industry standards and regulations?** Compliance with industry standards and regulations is crucial to hardware asset management. Leaders must verify that the organization's hardware asset management practices meet operational needs and comply with legal and regulatory requirements. Ensuring alignment with these standards is key to avoiding compliance issues and penalties while reinforcing the organization's commitment to maintaining a secure and compliant operational environment.

# Recommended Training

Effective management of enterprise hardware assets requires a well-trained workforce, skilled not only in the technical aspects but also in the broader organizational procedures that support cybersecurity. This section outlines key training recommendations for IT and cybersecurity staff and general employees. Each training program addresses specific aspects of hardware asset management, enhancing understanding and proficiency in protecting these vital resources. The goal is to foster a culture of cybersecurity awareness across all levels of the organization, thereby reducing risks associated with hardware asset mismanagement. These training programs will equip participants with the necessary skills to contribute effectively to the organization's cybersecurity health.

**Asset Management Fundamentals:** This training is intended for all new employees as part of their onboarding process to instill a foundational understanding of the organization's asset management policies. It should cover the identification, handling, and security of hardware assets, detailing the roles and responsibilities associated with these assets. Participants will learn about the lifecycle of hardware assets, from acquisition to disposal, and the importance of accurate inventory records. This knowledge will help prevent unauthorized assets from entering the network and reduce the risk of security breaches, ensuring all employees understand how their actions can impact the organization's security posture.

**Advanced Hardware Security Management:** Designed for IT and cybersecurity professionals, this training focuses on the complexities of securing hardware assets within an enterprise. It should include hands-on sessions on implementing security controls, conducting regular audits, and responding to security incidents involving hardware. Attendees will learn to apply best practices in hardware security to prevent exploitation and ensure operational continuity. This training aims to develop skills that directly contribute to strengthening the organization's defenses against hardware-related vulnerabilities.

CHAPTER 1   INVENTORY AND CONTROL OF ENTERPRISE (HARDWARE) ASSETS

**Cybersecurity Best Practices for Non-IT Staff:** This training is essential for all non-IT staff, highlighting how everyday interactions with hardware assets can influence the organization's security. It should cover basic security practices such as secure login protocols, recognizing phishing attempts, and adequately using mobile and portable devices. By the end of the session, employees will understand their critical role in maintaining cybersecurity and how adhering to set guidelines minimizes risks. This widespread awareness is crucial for creating a secure operational environment and reducing the incidence of user-related security breaches.

**Device Handling and Responsibility:** Targeting employees who use or manage significant hardware resources, this training emphasizes the correct handling, storage, and disposal of devices. Participants will learn about the risks associated with device mismanagement, including data leakage and unauthorized access. The training will also cover encryption, secure password practices, and physical security measures. Proper training in these areas will ensure that sensitive information remains safe at rest and in transit, significantly lowering the risk of internal and external threats.

**Regulatory Compliance and Hardware Asset Management:** IT staff and administrators should attend this training to understand the regulatory requirements that impact hardware asset management. This session will cover compliance standards relevant to the organization's sector, such as HIPAA for healthcare or GDPR for companies operating in the EU. Knowledge gained will aid in aligning hardware asset management practices with legal and regulatory frameworks, thereby avoiding costly penalties and enhancing the organization's reputation for reliability and trustworthiness.

**Incident Response and Hardware Assets:** IT and cybersecurity teams must be trained in incident response specific to hardware-related issues. This session should focus on identifying, reporting, and responding to security incidents involving hardware assets. Trainees will practice developing coordinated response strategies that minimize downtime and mitigate damage. Skilled response teams can significantly reduce the impact of security breaches, ensuring that the organization can recover swiftly and effectively.

**Inventory Auditing Techniques:** This detailed training should be mandatory for all IT staff involved in asset management. It focuses on auditing techniques that ensure the accuracy and integrity of the hardware asset inventory. The session will include methods for conducting physical and electronic audits, using specialized software tools, and reporting discrepancies. Effective auditing helps maintain a clear picture of the organization's asset landscape, crucial for identifying anomalies and preventing security lapses.

**Network Access Control for Hardware Assets:** Designed for network administrators, this training covers implementing network access controls that regulate hardware connections to the enterprise network. Attendees will learn about the technologies and policies that can prevent unauthorized access, such as NAC systems, MAC address filtering, and port security. Effective network access control is a crucial deterrent against potential attackers, ensuring only authorized and compliant hardware is connected to the network.

**Secure Configuration of Mobile Devices:** Mobile device security is critical, given their potential to access and store sensitive organizational data. This training should focus on secure configuration practices, including VPNs, encryption, and secure Wi-Fi settings. It is ideal for all employees who use mobile devices as part of their job. By securing these devices, the organization can significantly reduce the risk of data breaches from lost, stolen, or compromised mobile hardware.

**Cloud Security and Hardware Assets:** IT professionals handling cloud-connected hardware assets should undergo this training to understand the security challenges and best practices associated with cloud environments. The session will cover cloud infrastructure management, data security, and collaboration with cloud service providers. Mastery of these topics is essential for protecting the organization's data and ensuring seamless and secure cloud operations.

**Physical Security Measures:** This training is appropriate for security personnel and IT staff and focuses on physical security measures critical for protecting hardware assets. Topics include secure facility design, access controls, surveillance, and response strategies for physical breaches. Physical security is fundamental in safeguarding sensitive hardware from theft, tampering, and other physical threats.

**Sustainable Hardware Asset Disposal:** Environmental responsibility and security converge in this training, aimed at IT staff responsible for decommissioning and disposing of hardware. Participants will learn environmentally safe disposal practices that protect sensitive data, such as data wiping and hardware destruction techniques. Proper disposal training ensures the organization meets environmental standards and data protection regulations, reducing legal risks and promoting sustainability.

# Actionable Recommendations

Implementing robust asset management controls is essential for fortifying an organization's cybersecurity posture related to hardware assets such as end-user devices, network devices, IoT devices, and servers. As organizations' digital footprint expands, encompassing a wide array of these devices, maintaining visibility and control over every hardware asset becomes increasingly complex yet critically important. Effective asset management lays the foundation for a secure and resilient digital environment and enables organizations to detect, respond to, and mitigate threats more efficiently. The following recommendations are designed to guide cybersecurity leaders through implementing these controls effectively, ensuring that asset management practices enhance security and support operational efficiency and compliance with regulatory standards.

**Automate Asset Discovery:** Utilizing automated asset discovery tools ensures that all network-connected hardware devices are accurately inventoried. Automation plays a pivotal role in achieving comprehensive coverage of hardware assets, significantly reducing the likelihood of oversight. By regularly scanning and inventorying devices, these tools give organizations a real-time view of their hardware landscape, enabling them to identify and address potential vulnerabilities promptly. This strategic move enhances an organization's ability to maintain a secure and up-to-date hardware inventory.

**Integrate Asset Management Solutions:** Integrating asset management solutions with existing security and IT management tools is a strategic approach that significantly enhances organizational visibility and operational efficiency. This integration facilitates seamless information sharing and streamlines response actions across different platforms, allowing for a more coordinated and effective approach to hardware asset management. Organizations can ensure a unified defense strategy that leverages each component's strengths by choosing solutions that work harmoniously with existing tools.

**Establish Asset Classification Schema:** Developing and implementing an asset classification schema for hardware assets is crucial. By categorizing assets based on their criticality and sensitivity, organizations can prioritize their security efforts and allocate resources more effectively. This strategic classification aids in determining which hardware assets require heightened security measures, ensuring that high-value or sensitive assets are adequately protected against potential threats.

**Define Asset Management Policies:** Establishing clear asset management policies and procedures is crucial for governing the lifecycle processes of hardware assets, including acquisition, modification, and retirement. These policies should be communicated thoroughly across the organization and adhered to uniformly to ensure compliance. By setting explicit guidelines for managing hardware assets, organizations can maintain control over their inventories and mitigate risks associated with asset mismanagement.

**Implement Continuous Monitoring:** Continuous monitoring of hardware assets is imperative for the early detection of unauthorized changes, potential vulnerabilities, and signs of compromise. By setting up systems that monitor assets around the clock, organizations can respond promptly to any anomalies detected, preserving the security and integrity of their assets.

**Regularly Update and Validate Inventory:** Ensuring the accuracy and completeness of the hardware asset inventory requires regular reviews and validations. Organizations should periodically update the inventory to reflect new acquisitions, modifications, or asset decommissions. Keeping the inventory current helps maintain the effectiveness of security and management practices in response to the evolving asset landscape.

**Secure and Monitor Remote and Cloud Assets:** Extending asset management practices to include remote and cloud-based hardware assets is essential in today's distributed work environments. Organizations must apply tailored security measures to these environments and monitor them as diligently as on-premises, ensuring that all hardware assets are adequately protected and managed.

**Leverage Asset Management for Compliance:** Utilizing the hardware asset inventory as a tool for compliance management is a strategic approach to ensuring that all hardware assets adhere to relevant regulatory and industry standards. This comprehensive view facilitates audit readiness and helps organizations avoid non-compliance risks such as fines and legal penalties.

**Create an Asset Decommissioning Process:** Developing a secure process for hardware asset decommissioning is vital to prevent data leakage and ensure the safe disposal or repurposing of assets. This process should include thorough data wiping and confirmation of data removal before decommissioning, mitigating the risk of sensitive data falling into the wrong hands and reflecting the organization's commitment to data security and privacy.

CHAPTER 1  INVENTORY AND CONTROL OF ENTERPRISE (HARDWARE) ASSETS

# Simplified Security Controls (SSC)

Security controls are essential for any organization seeking to protect its digital and physical assets from cyber threats. Tailoring these controls to fit the specific needs of your business environment is crucial, as it ensures that the protection mechanisms are relevant and effective against the specific risks your organization faces. There are numerous sources to draw these controls from, including the well-regarded CIS Top 18, which provides a robust framework for crafting defensive strategies. The recommendations presented in this book are based on the CIS controls, among others, offering a comprehensive guide that can be adapted to serve a wide range of security needs. Before implementing these controls, it is vital to thoroughly review their design to ensure they align with your strategic objectives and operational practices. Additionally, after deployment, it is imperative to regularly test the controls to verify their effectiveness and to make necessary adjustments. This ensures that the controls continue functioning as intended, safeguarding your organization against emerging threats and changing conditions.

## CONTROL 1: COMPREHENSIVE HARDWARE ASSET INVENTORY MANAGEMENT

**Control Objective:** Establish and maintain an accurate, detailed, and up-to-date inventory of all hardware assets across physical, virtual, cloud, and remote environments. This inventory should include end-user devices, network devices, non-computing/IoT devices, and servers, ensuring every asset's status, location, and security compliance are known and managed throughout its lifecycle.

CHAPTER 1   INVENTORY AND CONTROL OF ENTERPRISE (HARDWARE) ASSETS

**Implementation Steps:**

**1.1. Inventory Development:** Create a comprehensive inventory system that records detailed information for each asset, including network address (if static), hardware address, machine name, asset owner, and the department responsible.

**1.2. Regular Updates:** Set a bi-annual or more frequent schedule to update the inventory to reflect new assets, status changes, and asset decommissioning.

**1.3. Integration of MDM Tools:** Deploy Mobile Device Management (MDM) tools and other technologies to support the inventory process for mobile and remote assets, ensuring integration with the inventory system for real-time updates.

**Expected Outcome:** The organization will maintain a continuously updated asset inventory, providing visibility into the entire hardware asset landscape. This enables informed decision-making for asset management, security, and compliance purposes. A comprehensive asset inventory also helps identify and mitigate risks associated with unauthorized access and potential data breaches.

## CONTROL 2: UNAUTHORIZED HARDWARE ASSET MANAGEMENT

**Control Objective:** Identify and manage unauthorized hardware assets within the network to maintain network integrity and security by either regularizing, quarantining, or removing them.

**Implementation Steps:**

**1.1. Process Establishment:** Develop a formal, documented process for weekly identification and management of unauthorized hardware assets, detailing actions such as removal, quarantine, or denial of network access.

CHAPTER 1   INVENTORY AND CONTROL OF ENTERPRISE (HARDWARE) ASSETS

**1.2. Utilization of Discovery Tools:** Deploy active and passive discovery tools to continuously monitor the network for unauthorized hardware assets.

**1.3. Response Protocol:** Establish a protocol for immediate response upon detecting an unauthorized hardware asset, including notification procedures and execution of predetermined management actions.

**Expected Outcome:** A systematic approach to managing unauthorized hardware assets reduces security risks, ensuring all assets on the network are authorized and monitored. The process helps maintain a secure, compliant network environment and mitigates potential disruptions caused by unauthorized assets. Monitoring and managing these assets will enhance the organization's overall security posture.

## CONTROL 3: DYNAMIC HARDWARE ASSET DISCOVERY AND INVENTORY UPDATE

**Control Objective:** Ensure the hardware asset inventory remains current and accurate through dynamic discovery tools and DHCP logging, capturing changes in new and existing assets in real time.

**Implementation Steps:**

**1.1. Deployment of Discovery Tools:** Implement and configure active and passive discovery tools to run at least daily, ensuring comprehensive coverage of network asset detection.

**1.2. DHCP Logging Utilization:** Activate DHCP logging on all DHCP servers or IP address management tools to identify new or changed hardware assets.

**1.3. Inventory Synchronization:** Regularly synchronize discovery and logging data with the asset inventory to ensure all records are current and reflect the network state.

CHAPTER 1    INVENTORY AND CONTROL OF ENTERPRISE (HARDWARE) ASSETS

**Expected Outcome:** Continuous updating of the asset inventory with the latest information enhances the organization's ability to manage hardware assets proactively. This responsiveness to changes supports effective cybersecurity measures and aids in maintaining a secure network environment. Regular inventory updates ensure all hardware assets are accounted for and properly managed throughout their lifecycle.

## CONTROL 4: ENHANCED HARDWARE ASSET TRACKING AND MONITORING

**Control Objective:** Enhance the monitoring and tracking of all hardware assets to ensure comprehensive visibility over asset status, location, and compliance.

**Implementation Steps:**

**1.1. Comprehensive Monitoring:** Implement systems that continuously monitor and track all hardware assets.

**1.2. Real-Time Reporting:** Utilize tools that offer real-time reporting capabilities to promptly detect changes or anomalies in hardware asset status.

**1.3. Periodic Audits:** Conduct periodic audits to verify the accuracy of the hardware asset inventory and the effectiveness of the monitoring tools.

**Expected Outcome:** Robust oversight of all hardware assets enables proactive responses to potential security threats and ensures compliance with regulatory standards. Continuous monitoring and real-time reporting help detect and address issues quickly, maintaining operational integrity and minimizing downtime. Periodic audits verify the accuracy of asset data, reinforcing the security measures in place.

CHAPTER 1  INVENTORY AND CONTROL OF ENTERPRISE (HARDWARE) ASSETS

## CONTROL 5: SECURE CONFIGURATION AND MANAGEMENT OF HARDWARE ASSETS

**Control Objective:** Ensure all hardware assets are securely configured and managed throughout their lifecycle to protect against unauthorized access and vulnerabilities.

**Implementation Steps:**

**1.1. Configuration Standards:** Develop and enforce security configuration standards for all hardware assets, adhering to industry best practices.

**1.2. Change Management:** Implement a change management process to oversee all configuration changes and ensure all modifications are logged and audited.

**1.3. Lifecycle Management:** Establish comprehensive lifecycle management for hardware assets, from procurement to decommissioning.

**Expected Outcome:** Secure configurations and rigorous management practices minimize security risks and enhance the organization's overall security posture. Enforcing best practice standards and thorough change management ensures that all hardware assets are maintained securely and efficiently. Lifecycle management processes help safeguard sensitive data throughout the asset's operational period, preventing data breaches and ensuring compliance with privacy regulations.

CHAPTER 1   INVENTORY AND CONTROL OF ENTERPRISE (HARDWARE) ASSETS

### CONTROL 6: PROACTIVE VULNERABILITY MANAGEMENT FOR HARDWARE ASSETS

**Control Objective:** Proactively manage vulnerabilities in hardware assets to mitigate threats before they can be exploited.

**Implementation Steps:**

**1.1. Regular Vulnerability Scans:** Conduct regular vulnerability scans on all hardware assets to identify and address potential security weaknesses.

**1.2. Patch Management:** Implement a systematic patch management process to ensure the timely application of security patches and updates to hardware assets.

**1.3. Risk Assessment:** Perform risk assessments to prioritize vulnerability remediation based on the criticality of the hardware assets and the potential impact of identified vulnerabilities.

**Expected Outcome:** Regular vulnerability scans and timely patch management maintain the security integrity of hardware assets, reducing the risk of cyber attacks. Proactive risk assessments ensure that resources are allocated effectively to address the most critical vulnerabilities. This comprehensive vulnerability management approach enhances the organization's resilience against cyber threats and supports continuous security improvement.

# CHAPTER 2

# Inventory and Control of Software Assets

The digital infrastructure of modern enterprises is a complex ecosystem consisting of various software applications and operating systems. These components form the backbone of organizational IT environments, powering everything from critical business operations to day-to-day administrative tasks. Managing these software assets, encompassing inventory, tracking, and correction, is an operational necessity and a cornerstone of cybersecurity. Ensuring that only authorized software is installed and can execute. In contrast, unauthorized and unmanaged software is identified and prevented from installation or execution, which is crucial for maintaining IT systems' integrity and security.

At the heart of robust cybersecurity practices is the comprehensive understanding and management of all software assets within an organization's network. This understanding forms the basis for defending against many continuously evolving cyber threats seeking to exploit outdated or unauthorized software vulnerabilities. The challenge is not only in identifying these vulnerabilities but also in managing and mitigating associated risks. A well-maintained inventory of software assets allows organizations to swiftly identify and address these vulnerabilities, significantly reducing the attack surface that cyber adversaries can exploit.

## CHAPTER 2    INVENTORY AND CONTROL OF SOFTWARE ASSETS

Inventory management involves documenting every piece of software within the network, from operating systems to applications, and tracking their usage and lifecycle. This meticulous approach is vital for several reasons. First, it enables the identification of redundant, outdated, or unauthorized software that may pose security risks. Second, it facilitates the rapid deployment of patches and updates, ensuring that software vulnerabilities are addressed promptly. Third, it aids in compliance with regulatory requirements that mandate strict oversight over software assets for data protection and privacy.

The importance of actively managing software assets extends beyond just inventory management. It involves establishing mechanisms to correct discrepancies during inventory audits, such as unauthorized installations or deviations from established IT policies. This proactive stance is indispensable in today's cybersecurity landscape, where attackers relentlessly probe for the weakest link to gain entry into corporate networks.

Unauthorized software, often installed without the knowledge of IT departments, represents a significant security risk. It can be a gateway for malware and other malicious activities, compromising information systems' confidentiality, integrity, and availability. By employing strategies to detect and prevent the execution of such software, organizations can considerably bolster their defenses against these insidious threats.

Moreover, managing software assets is integral to operational efficiency and financial management within organizations. It prevents the wastage of resources on unnecessary or duplicate software licenses and ensures that investments in IT are aligned with business needs. This strategic alignment optimizes IT expenditures and enhances security by minimizing the potential for software-induced vulnerabilities.

Implementing technical controls, such as application allowlisting, ensures that only authorized software can execute on the network. Allowlisting is a preventive security measure that permits the execution of explicitly authorized software while blocking everything else by default. This approach significantly mitigates the risk of malicious software execution, providing a robust layer of security that complements traditional antivirus solutions.

This endeavor's success hinges on the collaborative efforts of IT and cybersecurity teams alongside organizational leadership. A cybersecurity awareness and compliance culture across all levels of the organization is essential for effectively managing software assets. Employees must be educated on the importance of using only authorized software and the risks associated with unauthorized installations. This collective responsibility ensures that cybersecurity practices are not confined to the IT department but woven into the organization's operations.

Furthermore, the dynamic nature of the digital landscape necessitates continuous evaluation and adaptation of software asset management practices. As new technologies emerge and organizational needs evolve, so must the strategies employed to manage software assets. This requires a flexible approach that can adjust to new challenges and opportunities. Regular reviews and updates to the software inventory and ongoing monitoring for unauthorized installations ensure that organizations remain vigilant and responsive to changes in the cyber threat environment.

Therefore, active management of software assets is a critical component of a comprehensive cybersecurity strategy. It encompasses various activities, from inventory and tracking to implementing technical controls like allowlisting. By ensuring that only authorized software is installed and can execute, organizations can protect themselves against a broad spectrum of cyber threats. This not only enhances the security of IT systems but also supports the organization's overall operational efficiency and compliance efforts. Through diligent management and oversight of software assets, enterprises can build a resilient defense against the ever-evolving cyber threat landscape, ensuring the security and continuity of their digital operations.

CHAPTER 2  INVENTORY AND CONTROL OF SOFTWARE ASSETS

# Key Concepts and Terms

Understanding the foundational elements and terminologies in cybersecurity is essential for effectively managing and protecting an organization's digital landscape. The intricacies of software asset management, with its myriad components and processes, demand a deep dive into the specific concepts and terms that form the bedrock of this critical cybersecurity discipline. The following glossary is curated to shed light on the key concepts and terms integral to the proactive management of software assets. Each term encapsulates a vital aspect of the cybersecurity ecosystem, from the initial acquisition and deployment of software to its eventual retirement. It provides insights into the complexities of protecting enterprise assets against ever-evolving threats.

**Asset Management:** In cybersecurity, asset management encompasses the detailed oversight of an organization's digital and physical assets. This includes tracking and maintaining an inventory of hardware and software and ensuring these assets' security and operational readiness. Effective asset management requires a comprehensive strategy integrating IT and security policies, procedures, and tools to monitor and protect assets throughout their lifecycle. This approach enables organizations to optimize asset utilization, improve security postures, and reduce costs by preventing unauthorized access and minimizing the impact of security incidents. It forms a critical part of an organization's cybersecurity framework, ensuring that all assets are accounted for, optimized usage, and adequately protected against cyber threats.

**Software Inventory:** A meticulously maintained software inventory is central to effectively managing an organization's software assets. This inventory should include software names, versions, installation dates, and licensing information for every application installed across the organization's devices. By maintaining this inventory, IT and security teams can quickly respond to security alerts, conduct audits, and ensure compliance with licensing agreements and regulatory requirements. An accurate software inventory also facilitates strategic decision-making regarding software procurement, deployment, and retirement, enabling organizations to avoid redundancies, manage costs, and maintain a secure and efficient IT environment.

**Patch Management:** The complexity of patch management extends beyond simply applying updates; it involves identifying applicable patches, assessing their relevance and potential impact on the IT environment, testing them in a controlled manner, and then systematically deploying them across the affected systems. This process must be performed regularly and efficiently to mitigate vulnerabilities before cyber attackers can exploit them. Effective patch management strategies rely on automation tools to streamline the process, ensuring timely updates while minimizing disruptions to operations. Organizations must prioritize patches based on the severity of the vulnerabilities they address and the criticality of the affected systems to ensure that the most significant risks are mitigated first.

**Vulnerability Management:** An effective vulnerability management program encompasses continuously monitoring new vulnerabilities, assessing the potential impact on the organization's assets, and implementing strategies to mitigate those risks. This proactive approach is essential for maintaining a strong security posture in the face of rapidly evolving cyber threats. Collaboration across departments is required to ensure that vulnerabilities are addressed promptly through patching, configuration changes, or other mitigation techniques. Vulnerability management also involves educating stakeholders about the importance of cybersecurity practices and ensuring that security considerations are integrated into the organization's operational processes.

**Allowlisting:** Implementing allowlisting requires a thorough understanding of an organization's operational needs and the software necessary to meet those needs. This includes establishing a baseline of authorized software necessary for business operations and then enforcing policies that prevent the execution of software not on the allowlist.

Allowlisting strategies must be flexible enough to accommodate necessary updates and changes in software requirements while maintaining strict control over what is permitted to run. This balance is critical for securing the IT environment and ensuring security measures do not hinder business operations.

**Unauthorized Software:** The challenge of managing unauthorized software lies in detecting and removing it and preventing its installation in the first place. This requires a combination of technical controls, such as application allowlisting and endpoint protection solutions, and organizational policies that define acceptable use and software installation procedures. Educating employees about the risks associated with unauthorized software and encouraging adherence to IT policies are crucial to preventing unauthorized software installations. Regular audits and monitoring are also essential for detecting and addressing any unauthorized software that does make it onto the network.

**Software Compliance:** Achieving software compliance involves regular audits to verify that all software is appropriately licensed and adheres to the relevant legal and regulatory requirements. This includes ensuring that software installations do not exceed the number of licenses purchased and that software is used per the terms of service agreements. Organizations must also stay informed about changes in software licensing models and regulatory requirements to maintain compliance. Non-compliance can result in legal penalties, financial losses, and damage to an organization's reputation, making it a critical consideration for businesses of all sizes.

**Security Configuration Management (SCM):** Effective SCM practices involve regularly assessing security configurations against industry standards and best practices to identify misconfigurations and deviations from an organization's security policy. This includes automating the configuration management process to ensure consistency and reduce the likelihood of human error. SCM tools can help in applying configurations, monitoring for changes, and rolling back unauthorized or non-compliant changes. Organizations can protect their assets from known vulnerabilities by maintaining secure configurations and reducing risk exposure.

**Risk Assessment:** Conducting a risk assessment requires identifying potential threats to the organization's assets, assessing the likelihood and impact of those threats, and determining the organization's tolerance for risk. This process helps prioritize risks based on severity and guides the allocation of resources to areas where they will significantly impact risk reduction. Risk assessments should be conducted regularly and whenever significant changes occur within the organization or its operating environment to ensure its risk management strategies remain aligned with current threats and business objectives.

**Software Lifecycle:** Managing the software lifecycle effectively involves planning for the end-of-life of software applications, including migrating data and functionalities to newer, supported platforms before the software becomes obsolete. This planning is critical to avoid security vulnerabilities associated with unsupported software and ensure operations continuity. Lifecycle management also includes evaluating new software for compatibility, security, and compliance requirements before it is introduced into the organization's environment, ensuring it meets its needs without introducing unnecessary risks.

**Digital Signatures:** Utilizing digital signatures requires infrastructure for key management and signature verification to ensure the integrity and authenticity of signed digital content. In cybersecurity, digital signatures verify the source and integrity of software updates, documents, and messages, ensuring they have not been altered or tampered with in transit. This technology is fundamental in establishing trust in digital communications and transactions and protecting against phishing, software tampering, and other cyber threats.

**Cryptographic Hash:** Cryptographic hashes are widespread in cybersecurity practices, from verifying the integrity of downloaded files to ensuring password storage security. Hash functions are designed to be one-way, meaning it is infeasible to reverse the process and retrieve the original input from the hash output. This property makes cryptographic hashes an essential tool in various security applications, including digital forensics, secure information exchange, and tampering or data corruption detection.

# Importance and Relevance

Navigating the complex terrain of cybersecurity necessitates a deep understanding of the multifaceted roles that specific practices play in fortifying an organization's digital defenses. Among these, meticulously managing and overseeing software and hardware assets emerges as a cornerstone strategy, underpinning the security framework that shields enterprises from cyber threats. From bolstering compliance and optimizing resources to enhancing incident response and facilitating strategic planning, the importance and relevance of this practice are manifold. As cyber threats evolve with increasing sophistication, the proactive management of digital assets stands as a bulwark against the vulnerabilities that could compromise the sanctity of an organization's digital and physical resources.

**Pivotal Role in Security:** Asset management is foundational in securing an organization's digital infrastructure. A comprehensive understanding and documentation of all assets within an enterprise are essential for deploying effective defense mechanisms. Unidentified devices and software pose significant security risks and are potential entry points for intruders to exploit. By maintaining a thorough asset inventory, organizations can monitor and protect all access points against unauthorized access, significantly mitigating vulnerabilities and enhancing the overall security posture. This meticulous oversight is indispensable for maintaining a resilient digital environment against evolving cyber threats.

**Compliance and Regulatory Requirements:** In the current digital age, compliance with regulatory standards and frameworks has become paramount for organizations across all sectors. Asset management is critical to meeting these compliance requirements, as it provides a clear view of the software and hardware assets in use, ensuring that they adhere to legal and industry standards. Regular audits and reviews of asset inventories enable organizations to demonstrate their commitment to compliance, avoid potential fines, and maintain trust with clients and partners. Effective asset management ensures that organizations can swiftly adapt to new regulations, maintaining compliance and resilience against legal and operational risks.

**Optimization of Resources:** Effective asset management enables organizations to optimize their use of technological resources. By maintaining an accurate inventory of software and hardware assets, organizations can avoid unnecessary expenditures on unused or redundant licenses and ensure that investments are aligned with business needs. This strategic asset management approach reduces waste and improves operational efficiency by ensuring that resources are allocated where they are most needed. Identifying and decommissioning underutilizing assets allows for a leaner, more efficient IT environment, directly contributing to the organization's bottom line.

**Enhanced Incident Response:** A well-maintained asset inventory improves an organization's incident response capabilities. In the event of a security breach, having detailed information on all assets allows response teams to quickly identify the scope of the compromise, isolate affected systems, and apply necessary mitigations. This rapid response capability minimizes the impact of security incidents, reduces downtime, and protects sensitive information from being exploited. Thus, Asset management is critical in the overall cybersecurity strategy, empowering organizations to respond to and recover from incidents quickly and precisely.

CHAPTER 2   INVENTORY AND CONTROL OF SOFTWARE ASSETS

**Risk Management:** Identifying and classifying assets are key to an effective risk management strategy. Asset management allows organizations to assess the value and sensitivity of their digital assets, enabling them to prioritize security efforts and allocate resources effectively. Understanding which assets are critical to operations and which hold sensitive information helps in crafting tailored security measures, reducing the likelihood of breaches and ensuring the continuity of business operations. This strategic approach to risk management is essential for protecting an organization's most valuable assets and ensuring long-term resilience against cyber threats.

**Improved Software Management:** Keeping an up-to-date software inventory is crucial for managing each application's lifecycle, from procurement to decommissioning. Asset management practices ensure that software is regularly updated and patched, reducing the attack surface available to cyber adversaries. This proactive management of software assets helps avoid security vulnerabilities, ensures compatibility with existing systems, and enhances the overall security and functionality of the IT environment. Furthermore, effective software asset management aids in license compliance, avoiding legal and financial penalties associated with software piracy or under-licensing.

**Prevention of Unauthorized Software:** Asset management includes implementing policies and controls to prevent the installation and execution of unauthorized software. Unauthorized software can introduce security vulnerabilities, compromise data integrity, and lead to compliance issues. Organizations can significantly reduce the risk of malware infection and data breaches by controlling the software installation process and maintaining an allowlist of approved applications. This control mechanism is critical to maintaining a secure and compliant IT environment, ensuring that only software vetted and approved is used within the organization.

**Facilitation of Strategic Planning:** Effective asset management provides organizational leaders with the information needed for strategic planning and decision-making. By clearly understanding the existing

IT infrastructure, leaders can make informed decisions about future investments, technology adoption, and infrastructure upgrades. This foresight helps ensure the IT strategy aligns with the overall business objectives, facilitating growth and adaptation to market changes. Asset management thus bridges IT operations and strategic business planning, contributing to the organization's success and competitiveness.

**Strengthening Security Culture:** Asset management practices encourage a culture of security awareness and responsibility among all employees. By involving users in managing assets, such as reporting unauthorized software or ensuring the security of their devices, organizations can foster a sense of collective responsibility for cybersecurity. This cultural shift is crucial for reinforcing security policies and practices, making security a shared concern across the organization. A strong security culture is a key deterrent against internal and external threats, making it a vital component of the cybersecurity framework.

**Support for Remote Work and Cloud Technologies:** As organizations embrace remote work and cloud-based technologies, asset management has become increasingly crucial for securing dispersed digital environments. Effective management of cloud assets and remote devices ensures that security policies and practices extend beyond the physical office space, protecting data and resources regardless of location. This adaptability is essential for modern organizations, enabling them to leverage the benefits of remote work and cloud technologies while maintaining a secure and controlled IT environment.

**Visibility into Shadow IT:** Asset management helps identify and mitigate the risks associated with shadow IT—technology and systems used within an organization without explicit IT department approval. By providing visibility into all assets in use, organizations can uncover unauthorized devices and applications and assess their impact on security and compliance. Addressing shadow IT through comprehensive asset management reduces the risk of data leaks, compliance violations, and security breaches, ensuring all technology use is aligned with organizational policies and security standards.

**Enhanced Vendor Management:** An integral part of asset management is the oversight of third-party vendors and their impact on the organization's security posture. Organizations can assess the security risks associated with these external entities by maintaining an inventory of all third-party software and hardware. Effective vendor management ensures that third-party products and services meet the organization's security requirements, reducing the risk of supply chain attacks and enhancing the overall security of the IT environment. This comprehensive asset and vendor management approach is critical for safeguarding against complex cyber threats in today's interconnected digital landscape.

# Risks of Not Implementing the Control

Cybersecurity is woven with various controls and practices, each designed to shield organizations from the threats that pervade the digital landscape. Neglecting these protective measures, especially the meticulous management of software and hardware assets, exposes an organization to a spectrum of risks, each carrying the potential to compromise data integrity, disrupt operations, and erode stakeholder trust. With comprehensive asset management, the door is open for security breaches, regulatory non-compliance, and operational inefficiencies, among other pitfalls. The following delineation of risks underscores the imperative of adopting a proactive stance in asset management, highlighting the multifarious dangers organizations face when they overlook this critical control. From vulnerabilities to unauthorized access and the potential for significant financial losses, the consequences of inadequate asset management are far-reaching, underscoring the need for vigilance and strategic foresight in cybersecurity practices.

**Increased Risk of Data Breaches:** Data breaches are a looming threat for organizations neglecting asset management. Without a clear inventory of assets and their security statuses, sensitive data stored across various devices and applications is at risk. Malicious entities exploit these oversights, targeting systems with outdated security measures or unpatched vulnerabilities. The consequences of such breaches extend beyond immediate data loss, affecting an organization's reputation and customer trust and potentially resulting in substantial financial penalties. Effective asset management is a critical barrier, safeguarding data by ensuring all assets are monitored, updated, and protected.

**Compliance Failures:** Regulatory compliance demands stringent oversight of all organizational assets, especially those housing sensitive or regulated data. Failure to implement comprehensive asset management can lead to non-compliance with industry standards and regulations, such as GDPR, HIPAA, or SOX, which prescribe specific data protection and privacy requirements. Such oversights invite legal repercussions and hefty fines and damage an organization's standing in its industry. Proactive asset management ensures that all assets are accounted for, secured, and operated per relevant legal and regulatory frameworks.

**Vulnerability to Unauthorized Access and Attacks:** Companies need a comprehensive understanding and management of all organizational assets to expose themselves to heightened risks of unauthorized access and cyber attacks. This vulnerability stems from inadequate protection of devices and systems, which cybercriminals can readily exploit. Unpatched, unnoticed, or misconfigured systems act as open invitations to malicious actors, serving as easy entry points to infiltrate the network. The absence of rigorous asset management and security practices leaves critical gaps in an organization's defense mechanisms, making identifying and securing every asset imperative. Ensuring a robust cybersecurity posture thus necessitates a foundational commitment to thorough asset inventory and management.

**Operational Disruptions:** Without effective asset management, organizations face significant operational risks. Unmanaged or obsolete assets can fail, causing unplanned downtime and disrupting business operations. These disruptions impact productivity, erode customer confidence, and lead to financial losses. A strategic approach to asset management includes regular reviews and updates of all assets, ensuring that operational capabilities are maintained and potential disruptions are anticipated and mitigated.

**Inefficient Resource Utilization:** Organizations may inadvertently waste resources on redundant or unnecessary software and hardware without a clear view of existing assets. This inefficiency inflates IT costs and diverts funds from critical security investments. Effective asset management optimizes resource allocation, ensuring every asset serves a defined business purpose and contributes to the organization's operational efficiency and security posture.

**Difficulty in Incident Response:** In a security incident, the absence of a comprehensive asset inventory complicates the identification of affected systems and the containment of threats. This hindrance delays response times and can exacerbate the impact of incidents. A well-maintained asset management system is crucial for swift incident response, enabling security teams to isolate affected assets and mitigate threats quickly.

**Exposure to Legacy System Vulnerabilities:** Organizations failing to implement asset management risk overlooking legacy systems that may no longer receive security updates. These systems become prime targets for cybercriminals exploiting known vulnerabilities. A proactive asset management approach involves regular assessments to identify and upgrade or decommission outdated systems, thereby reducing the risk of security breaches through these vulnerabilities.

**Uncontrolled Shadow IT Risks:** The lack of asset management oversight encourages the growth of shadow IT, where employees use unauthorized devices and applications. This practice introduces unknown risks and vulnerabilities into the organization's IT environment.

Organizations can detect and control unauthorized technologies by establishing comprehensive asset management and aligning all IT resources with security policies and standards.

**Reputational Damage:** A cyber attack exploiting poor asset management practices can lead to significant reputational damage. Customers and partners lose trust in organizations that fail to protect their data, leading to lost business and strained relationships. Investing in asset management is a technical necessity and a commitment to stakeholder trust and security.

**Financial Losses from Security Breaches:** The economic implications of not implementing asset management are profound. Beyond the immediate costs associated with responding to cyber attacks, organizations face potential regulatory fines, legal fees, and the long-term impacts of lost business and reputational damage. Effective asset management minimizes these financial risks by ensuring a secure and compliant IT environment.

# What Questions Should You Ask?

In the fast-moving field of cybersecurity, effectively setting up security measures to protect company assets is crucial. It's not just about following rules; it's about making strategic decisions. For those in charge of cybersecurity, asking the right questions is the first important step in building a solid security system. These questions go beyond simple checks. They help define the company's security strategy, understand the current security state, decide where to focus resources to improve protection and identify any challenges that could slow progress. By thoroughly exploring these questions, leaders can better understand what their organization needs to keep its data safe. This understanding allows for the creation of detailed, effective security plans. Through this careful planning, cybersecurity leaders can make their organizations much safer against various cyber threats.

CHAPTER 2    INVENTORY AND CONTROL OF SOFTWARE ASSETS

**How comprehensively does our asset inventory capture software assets?** Understanding the breadth and depth of the asset inventory is crucial for effective cybersecurity management. Cybersecurity leaders should evaluate whether the inventory encompasses all software assets. This comprehensive view is essential for identifying potential vulnerabilities and ensuring that no asset remains unprotected or under-monitored. The completeness of the asset inventory directly influences the organization's ability to enforce security policies and respond to incidents, making it a critical area of inquiry.

**What processes are in place for adding new assets to our inventory?** Incorporating new assets into the inventory reveals the organization's adaptability to change and its readiness to secure new technologies. Leaders should probe into the procedures for updating the asset inventory when new devices, software, or services are deployed. Efficient processes ensure that new assets are promptly accounted for and protected, minimizing the window of vulnerability that cyber threats could exploit.

**How are asset criticality and sensitivity determined and updated?** Identifying assets' criticality and sensitivity is fundamental to prioritizing cybersecurity efforts. Questions should focus on the criteria used to classify assets and how these classifications are reviewed and updated in response to changing business needs and threat landscapes. This understanding helps allocate resources effectively, ensuring that the most critical assets receive the highest level of protection.

**What mechanisms are in place to detect unauthorized assets?** The presence of unauthorized assets can significantly increase the organization's risk profile. Inquiry into the detection mechanisms for such assets is vital for maintaining a secure IT environment. Effective detection capabilities enable the timely identification and remediation of unauthorized assets, reducing the potential for security breaches.

**How is the accuracy of the asset inventory verified?** The reliability of the asset inventory is a cornerstone of effective asset management. Leaders should ask about the methods to validate the inventory's accuracy,

CHAPTER 2   INVENTORY AND CONTROL OF SOFTWARE ASSETS

including regular audits and reconciliation processes. Ensuring the accuracy of the asset inventory is imperative for effective risk management and security planning.

**What strategies are employed to manage the lifecycle of assets?** Asset lifecycle management, from acquisition through decommissioning, impacts the organization's security posture. Questions should explore the strategies for managing this lifecycle, including how assets are maintained, updated, and securely decommissioned. Effective lifecycle management prevents vulnerabilities associated with outdated or unsupported assets.

**How do we ensure compliance with relevant regulations and standards through asset management practices?** Compliance with regulatory requirements and industry standards is a critical consideration. Leaders must understand how asset management practices align with these requirements, ensuring that the organization adheres to best practices and legal obligations. This alignment is crucial for minimizing legal and financial risks.

**What training and awareness programs are in place for managing assets securely?** The human element plays a significant role in asset management. Questions regarding employee training and awareness programs highlight the organization's commitment to cultivating a security-conscious culture. Effective education programs can significantly reduce the risks of human error and insider threats.

**How are assets protected against emerging cyber threats?** In a rapidly evolving threat landscape, the methods used to protect assets against new types of attacks are paramount. Leaders should inquire about the organization's readiness to adapt security measures in response to emerging threats. This adaptability is crucial for ensuring the ongoing security of assets.

**What role does asset management play in our incident response plan?** Integrating asset management into incident response planning is essential for a swift and effective response to security incidents. Understanding how asset information is utilized during an incident enables leaders to evaluate the plan's effectiveness and identify areas for improvement.

CHAPTER 2   INVENTORY AND CONTROL OF SOFTWARE ASSETS

# Recommended Training

Effective management of enterprise software assets is critical to an organization's cybersecurity strategy. Targeted training programs are necessary to ensure that all employees are equipped to protect these valuable assets. These training modules aim to heighten awareness and provide essential skills related to software asset management tailored to different roles within the company. By educating IT professionals and general staff, organizations can mitigate risks, enhance compliance, and optimize the use of software resources. Here, we discuss various recommended training programs that focus specifically on aspects of software asset management and are designed for diverse groups within the company.

**Introduction to Software Asset Management for All Employees**

This training is designed for all employees to foster a basic understanding of software asset management (SAM). The course will introduce participants to the importance of software inventory tracking, licensing compliance, and the risks associated with unauthorized software use. Attendees will learn how to identify approved software, report unlicensed applications, and understand the impact of software management on cybersecurity. The outcome of this training is a workforce that is more aware of how proper software management practices can reduce organizational risk.

**Advanced SAM Techniques for IT Staff**

IT staff members will benefit from advanced training that dives deeper into the technical aspects of software asset management. This session should cover topics such as automated tools for inventory management, techniques for efficient license management, and strategies for integrating SAM with other IT processes. The training will also include case studies on security breaches related to poor software management, highlighting the importance of rigorous SAM practices. This will equip IT professionals with the necessary skills to enhance the security and efficiency of software assets.

CHAPTER 2   INVENTORY AND CONTROL OF SOFTWARE ASSETS

**SAM Compliance and Audit Preparation**

This training is crucial for IT staff and administrators in compliance and audit roles. The focus will be on preparing for audits, understanding compliance requirements, and implementing best practices to ensure adherence to both internal policies and external regulations. Participants will learn about common pitfalls in software audits and how to avoid them by maintaining accurate records and implementing proactive compliance strategies. The outcome is a better-prepared team that can handle audits confidently and ensure compliance efficiently.

**SAM for Project Managers**

Project managers often oversee projects that require new software deployments. This training module will educate them on managing software assets throughout the project lifecycle. Topics include planning for software needs, managing licenses within project budgets, and ensuring software is properly decommissioned or reassigned post-project. This training ensures project managers can incorporate effective SAM practices to avoid overspending and non-compliance risks.

**Security Best Practices for Software Deployment**

This training is tailored for technical teams deploying and managing software applications. It focuses on security best practices during software management's installation, update, and maintenance phases. Participants will learn about securing software environments, managing access controls, and implementing security patches promptly. This training aims to minimize vulnerabilities and ensure that software deployments do not become gateways for cyber threats.

**Software Licensing for Procurement Teams**

Procurement teams must understand the complexities of software licensing to negotiate better terms and manage costs effectively. This training will cover different types of licenses, critical terms in licensing agreements, and strategies for license optimization. Participants will learn how to avoid common mistakes in software procurement that can lead to legal issues or overspending. This will enable them to make informed decisions that align with the organization's software needs and budget.

**Custom Software and Compliance Risks**

Understanding the specific compliance and security risks is crucial for organizations that develop or commission custom software. This training will address the lifecycle of custom software from a compliance perspective, including development, deployment, and maintenance. It will cover intellectual property rights, custom software licensing issues, and security considerations. The aim is to equip teams with the knowledge to manage custom software safely and in compliance with legal and regulatory requirements.

**End-User Responsibilities in SAM**

End-users play a crucial role in software asset management by adhering to organizational policies and procedures. This training will educate all employees on their responsibilities, such as using only approved software, adhering to installation procedures, and reporting discrepancies in software usage. The goal is to cultivate a culture of compliance and vigilance, reducing the risk of unauthorized software installations and potential security breaches.

When effectively implemented, these training modules enhance an organization's security posture and foster a culture of continuous improvement and compliance in managing software assets. Each program is designed to address specific aspects of software asset management, ensuring that all employees, regardless of their role, contribute to the security and efficiency of the organization's software resources.

# Actionable Recommendations

The imperative of robust cybersecurity strategies in today's digital landscape cannot be overstated. Within this context, the diligent management of software assets—encompassing operating systems and

CHAPTER 2   INVENTORY AND CONTROL OF SOFTWARE ASSETS

applications—emerges as a critical safeguard against cyber threats. Effective implementation of this control hinges on strategic, nuanced actions designed to ensure comprehensive visibility, stringent compliance, and proactive defense mechanisms across an organization's digital estate. The recommendations delineated below offer a blueprint for cybersecurity leaders and IT professionals, guiding the establishment and refinement of asset management practices. By embedding these practices within their cybersecurity frameworks, organizations can enhance their defensive posture, ensuring a resilient environment that safeguards against unauthorized software installations and mitigates potential vulnerabilities.

**Automate Asset Discovery:** Leverage advanced automated tools for continuously scanning and cataloging all network-connected devices and software. This automation facilitates the exhaustive and up-to-date mapping of the organization's digital terrain, which is crucial for identifying and managing every asset within the network. By automating this process, organizations eliminate human error and ensure that even transient or previously unnoticed assets are accounted for, thereby significantly bolstering the security framework with minimal manual intervention.

**Implement a Centralized Asset Management System:** A centralized asset management system is vital for consolidating data across the organization's diverse array of assets, offering a singular, comprehensive view of all software and hardware components. This system should seamlessly interface with existing IT and security infrastructures to dynamically update asset inventories, reflecting real-time changes such as new deployments or decommissioning outdated assets. Centralization simplifies the oversight and management of assets and enhances collaborative efforts across departments, ensuring a unified approach to security and compliance.

**Define and Enforce Allowlisting Policies:** Develop stringent allowlisting policies to delineate which applications and operating systems are permitted to operate within the network. These policies should be rigorously enforced, with regular reviews and updates to adapt to evolving

49

organizational needs and emerging security threats. Organizations minimize their attack surface by maintaining a tight rein on allowed software, safeguarding against unauthorized installations that could be conduits for malware or other cyber threats.

**Regularly Update and Patch Software:** Establish a structured, consistent regimen for timely updates and patches to all software assets. This regimen is paramount in closing security vulnerabilities and fortifying defenses against adversaries' exploitation. Organizations should prioritize automation in this sphere, ensuring uniform application of patches and mitigating the risk of oversight or delay that could leave systems susceptible to attack.

**Conduct Frequent Security Audits:** Periodic security audits are instrumental in assessing compliance with established security policies and identifying potential vulnerabilities within the software asset pool. These audits should meticulously evaluate the configuration, usage, and security measures applied to each asset, utilizing findings to continually refine and enhance security protocols and asset management practices. Such proactive scrutiny is essential for maintaining a robust, adaptive security posture in the face of evolving threats and regulatory landscapes.

**Integrate Asset Management with Incident Response:** The seamless integration of asset management systems with the organization's broader incident response framework is crucial for rapidly identifying and containing security breaches. Detailed, readily accessible information about impacted assets can dramatically accelerate the response process, mitigating potential damage and facilitating a more effective recovery. This integration underscores the strategic value of asset management in preventative measures and as a critical component of reactive security strategies.

**Utilize Security Configuration Management (SCM):** Implementing SCM practices enables organizations to standardize and enforce secure configurations across all assets, significantly reducing the risk of misconfiguration and unauthorized modifications. Regular reviews and adjustments of these configurations in alignment with best practices and organizational policy changes are critical for ensuring that assets remain secure throughout their lifecycle. SCM acts as a dynamic safeguard, adapting asset defenses to continuous changes in the threat environment and organizational infrastructure.

**Enhance Visibility with Network Segmentation:** Network segmentation plays a pivotal role in enhancing the manageability and security of assets by dividing the more extensive network into smaller, more controllable segments. This strategic division allows for the tailored application of security policies based on the criticality and function of assets within each segment, improving monitoring capabilities and reducing the potential impact of breaches. Segmentation bolsters security and facilitates more efficient asset management by categorizing assets into manageable cohorts.

**Train and Educate Staff:** Comprehensive training programs are essential for cultivating a culture of security awareness among all organizational members. These programs should cover the importance of adhering to asset management policies, recognizing and reporting unauthorized software, and understanding each individual's critical role in the organization's cybersecurity ecosystem. Education and awareness are vital deterrents against inadvertent breaches, reinforcing the human element as a cornerstone of a comprehensive cybersecurity strategy.

**Monitor for Unauthorized Software:** Continuous monitoring for unauthorized software is imperative for early detection and remediation. Implementing sophisticated monitoring tools that promptly alert IT and security teams to unapproved installations allows for swift action, minimizing potential exposure to security risks. This vigilant oversight is critical to an effective asset management strategy, ensuring that only authorized, secure software operates within the network.

**Document and Maintain an Asset Register:** A meticulously maintained asset register is an indispensable tool for effective asset management. It provides a detailed record of all assets, including their configurations, ownership, and associated risk levels. This documentation facilitates day-to-day management and security assessments and supports compliance efforts and strategic planning. Regular updates to the asset register ensure that it remains an accurate, valuable resource for decision-making and risk-management processes.

**Leverage Cloud Asset Management Solutions:** For organizations utilizing cloud services, cloud-specific asset management solutions offer specialized tools for extending visibility and control over cloud-hosted assets. These solutions address cloud environments' unique challenges, providing dynamic discovery, management, and security capabilities tailored to the cloud. Adopting cloud-focused asset management tools ensures that organizations maintain a consistent security posture across both on-premises and cloud environments, effectively managing and securing assets regardless of location.

# Simplified Security Controls (SSC)

Security controls are essential for any organization seeking to protect its digital and physical assets from cyber threats. Tailoring these controls to fit the specific needs of your business environment is crucial, as it ensures that the protection mechanisms are relevant and effective against the specific risks your organization faces. There are numerous sources to draw these controls from, including the well-regarded CIS Top 18, which provides a robust framework for crafting defensive strategies. The recommendations presented in this book are based on the CIS controls, among others, offering a comprehensive guide that can be adapted to serve a wide range of security needs. Before implementing these controls, it is vital to thoroughly review their design to ensure they align with your strategic objectives and operational practices. Additionally, after deployment, it is imperative to regularly test the controls to verify their effectiveness and to make necessary adjustments. This ensures the controls continue functioning as intended, safeguarding your organization against emerging threats and changing conditions.

CHAPTER 2   INVENTORY AND CONTROL OF SOFTWARE ASSETS

## CONTROL 1: COMPREHENSIVE SOFTWARE INVENTORY MANAGEMENT

**Control Objective:** To maintain an up-to-date and detailed inventory of all software assets within the organization to ensure visibility and control over software usage and compliance.

**Implementation Steps:**

**1.1. Inventory Initialization:** Develop a centralized inventory system to document all software on enterprise assets, including titles, versions, publishers, and usage details.

**1.2. Regular Updates:** Schedule bi-annual inventory updates, incorporating changes such as new installations, upgrades, and software decommissioning.

**1.3. Integration of Discovery Tools:** Implement automated tools that continuously monitor and update the software inventory.

**Expected Outcome:** An accurate and comprehensive software inventory that enhances visibility across the organization's software assets, aiding in compliance and security monitoring.

## CONTROL 2: VALIDATION OF SOFTWARE AUTHORIZATION

**Control Objective:** Ensure that all software used within the organization is authorized, supported, and compliant with internal policies to reduce the risks associated with outdated or unauthorized applications.

**Implementation Steps:**

**1.1. Authorization Checks:** Regularly verify that only currently supported and authorized software is in use, and establish protocols for rapid response if unauthorized software is detected.

**1.2. Documentation of Exceptions:** Document exceptions clearly for necessary but unsupported software, detailing mitigating controls and accepted residual risks.

**1.3. Continuous Monitoring:** Implement monthly reviews to assess and validate the authorization status of all software used across the enterprise.

**Expected Outcome:** A controlled environment with only authorized and supported software, minimizing potential security vulnerabilities.

## CONTROL 3: UNAUTHORIZED SOFTWARE REMEDIATION

**Control Objective:** To detect and remediate instances of unauthorized software usage to maintain system integrity and compliance.

**Implementation Steps:**

**1.1. Regular Scans for Compliance:** Conduct monthly scans to identify and document unauthorized software installations.

**1.2. Removal Processes:** Establish a standardized process for removing unauthorized software or the documentation and approval of necessary exceptions.

**1.3. Employee Awareness Training:** Educate employees about the risks associated with unauthorized software and the importance of adhering to company policies.

**Expected Outcome:** Reduced incidence of unauthorized software, enhancing security and compliance with internal and external regulations.

CHAPTER 2   INVENTORY AND CONTROL OF SOFTWARE ASSETS

## CONTROL 4: AUTOMATED MANAGEMENT OF SOFTWARE INVENTORIES

**Control Objective:** Leverage technology to automate the tracking and management of software inventories, improving accuracy and efficiency.

**Implementation Steps:**

**1.1. Selection of Tools:** Identify and deploy robust software inventory tools that integrate seamlessly with existing IT infrastructure.

**1.2. Automation of Inventory Updates:** Set up these tools to automatically detect and record software installation and usage changes.

**1.3. Regular System Audits:** Use the data from automated tools to conduct regular audits, ensuring completeness and accuracy.

**Expected Outcome:** A highly efficient and accurate system for managing software inventories, reducing the administrative burden and increasing compliance.

## CONTROL 5: IMPLEMENTATION OF SOFTWARE ALLOWLISTING

**Control Objective:** To ensure that only pre-approved software can execute on corporate systems, significantly reducing the risk of malware and other security threats.

**Implementation Steps:**

**1.1. Develop Allowlist Policies:** Define and document policies regarding which software and software versions are authorized to run on enterprise systems.

**1.2. Technical Enforcement:** Implement technical controls that enforce these allowlist policies, blocking all non-approved software by default.

CHAPTER 2    INVENTORY AND CONTROL OF SOFTWARE ASSETS

**1.3. Bi-annual Review of Allowlist:** Regularly review and update the allowlist to accommodate necessary changes and updates to software assets.

**Expected Outcome:** Enhanced security posture through strict control over software execution, ensuring that only secure and authorized applications run on enterprise assets.

## CONTROL 6: SECURE MANAGEMENT OF SOFTWARE LIBRARIES

**Control Objective:** Control and monitor the use of software libraries within the enterprise to prevent security vulnerabilities associated with unauthorized or malicious libraries.

**Implementation Steps:**

**1.1. Library Verification:** Implement controls to verify and authorize libraries before they are allowed to load into system processes.

**1.2. Block Unauthorized Libraries:** Automatically prevent unauthorized or unrecognized libraries from loading.

**1.3. Regular Review and Updates:** Periodically review the list of authorized libraries and update control mechanisms to reflect changes in the software environment.

**Expected Outcome:** A secure software environment where only authorized libraries can execute protects the systems from potential vulnerabilities and attacks.

# CHAPTER 3

# Data Protection

Data protection stands as a critical pillar in the edifice of cybersecurity. In the digital age, where data is both a valuable asset and a potential liability, effectively managing and securing this data is paramount. This extends beyond mere compliance or safeguarding against external threats; it encompasses a holistic approach to how data is identified, classified, handled, retained, and disposed of. The importance of data protection is magnified in a landscape where data breaches not only result in financial loss but also erode trust and can cause irreparable damage to an organization's reputation.

The foundation of robust data protection lies in developing comprehensive processes and technical controls. These mechanisms serve as the frontline defense and the last line of resilience against attempts to compromise data integrity and confidentiality. They ensure that only authorized personnel can access sensitive information and monitor and record their actions. This framework deters potential internal and external threats and ensures that the organization can swiftly respond and recover should a breach occur.

Implementing effective data protection strategies requires a nuanced understanding of the data lifecycle. From the moment data is created or received, it embarks on a journey through various stages of use, sharing, storage, and, eventually, destruction. Each stage presents unique challenges and vulnerabilities. For instance, data can be intercepted or altered during the transmission phase if not properly secured. Similarly, improperly disposed data can lead to unintentional exposure long after it is presumed safe. Thus, a comprehensive approach to data protection must address these vulnerabilities head-on, ensuring data integrity and confidentiality throughout its lifecycle.

The role of classification in data protection cannot be overstated. By distinguishing between different types of data based on their sensitivity and value to the organization, entities can allocate resources and tailor protection mechanisms more effectively. This hierarchical approach ensures that the most sensitive data, which could cause the most significant harm if compromised, receives the highest level of security. Classification also aids in compliance, as regulatory frameworks often mandate differing levels of protection for various data types.

Technical controls form the backbone of data protection, encompassing a range of tools and technologies designed to secure data across its lifecycle. These include encryption, access controls, data loss prevention (DLP) technologies, and more. Encryption, for example, ensures that even if data is intercepted or accessed without authorization, it remains unintelligible and useless to the attacker. Access controls prevent unauthorized access, ensuring that only individuals who need to interact with the data for legitimate purposes can do so.

Another critical aspect of data protection is securely handling data. This includes the physical and digital security measures and policies and procedures that govern how data is accessed, shared, and transferred. Employee training plays a crucial role in this context, as human error remains one of the most significant vulnerabilities in data protection. By fostering a culture of security awareness, organizations can mitigate the risk of accidental disclosures or mishandling of sensitive information.

Data retention and disposal practices are equally important components of the data protection framework. Retention policies ensure that data is kept only as long as necessary, reducing the volume of data that could be compromised. Conversely, secure disposal practices ensure that once data is no longer needed, it is destroyed to prevent recovery or unauthorized access. This could involve physical destruction, digital wiping, or other methods, depending on the nature of the data and the medium on which it is stored.

Software management on the network is intrinsically linked to data protection. Unauthorized or unmanaged software can introduce vulnerabilities through which attackers can access sensitive data. Thus, maintaining an inventory of authorized software and ensuring that only these approved applications can execute is a crucial defensive measure. This also involves promptly addressing vulnerabilities in existing software through updates and patches, further reducing the attack surface.

The challenge of unauthorized software highlights the importance of active management and monitoring within data protection. Tools and technologies that provide visibility into network activity and automatically detect unauthorized software installations or attempts to execute such software are critical. These capabilities enable organizations to quickly respond to potential threats, minimizing the window of opportunity for attackers to exploit vulnerabilities.

Collaboration between IT and cybersecurity teams is vital in implementing data protection strategies. While IT teams deeply understand the organization's technology infrastructure, cybersecurity teams bring expertise in threat identification and mitigation. This collaboration ensures that data protection measures are technically feasible and aligned with the organization's broader security objectives.

Compliance with legal and regulatory requirements adds another layer of complexity to data protection. Laws and regulations often dictate specific protection measures, data handling practices, and breach notification procedures. Navigating this regulatory landscape requires a detailed understanding of applicable laws and a proactive approach to compliance. This protects against legal and financial repercussions and builds trust with customers and partners by demonstrating a commitment to data security.

Finally, cyber threats' evolving nature necessitates a dynamic data protection approach. What is considered a robust defense today may need to be improved tomorrow. Continuous assessment, improvement, and adaptation of data protection strategies are crucial. This includes staying abreast of emerging threats, technological advancements, and changes in regulatory requirements. By doing so, organizations can ensure that their data protection efforts remain effective and resilient in the face of an ever-changing threat landscape.

In summary, data protection is a multifaceted challenge that requires a comprehensive and nuanced approach. Each aspect is vital in safeguarding sensitive information, from technical controls and processes to human factors and compliance. As organizations navigate the complexities of the digital era, the principles of effective data protection outlined in this section will serve as a foundational guide in developing robust cybersecurity strategies.

# Key Concepts and Terms

At its heart, data protection is about ensuring data confidentiality, integrity, and availability. It encompasses various practices, technologies, and policies to secure data from unauthorized access, disclosure, alteration, and destruction. From the inception of data in an organization's systems to its eventual disposal, every phase of the data lifecycle presents unique challenges and requires specific strategies to mitigate risks effectively. The terms defined in this section represent the foundational building blocks of comprehensive data protection strategies, providing readers with the knowledge to develop, implement, and manage them within their organizations.

**Asset Management:** In cybersecurity, asset management is identifying, cataloging, and overseeing an organization's assets to ensure they are utilized effectively and protected adequately. This encompasses physical devices such as computers and servers and software applications and data, particularly pertinent to data protection efforts. The process facilitates a clear understanding of an organization's assets, where they are located, and how they are connected. It also plays a critical role in risk management by identifying the assets that hold the most value or contain sensitive information, requiring heightened security measures. Effective asset management is foundational to developing comprehensive data protection strategies, ensuring that all potential points of vulnerability are known and safeguarded against.

**Data Lifecycle Management (DLM):** Data Lifecycle Management represents a holistic approach to handling the information within an organization from its inception to disposal. DLM strategies encompass the creation, storage, use, sharing, archiving, and destruction of data, with a strong focus on implementing security controls at each stage to protect data integrity and confidentiality. This concept is essential in data protection, as it recognizes that data's value and sensitivity can change over time, necessitating different security measures as it moves through its lifecycle. Implementing effective DLM helps organizations maintain compliance with various data protection regulations and minimize the risk of data breaches by ensuring appropriate safeguards are in place throughout the data's existence. Moreover, DLM aids in optimizing data storage, reducing costs, and improving organizational efficiency by eliminating redundant or obsolete data.

**Data Classification:** Data classification involves systematically sorting data into categories based on its level of sensitivity, regulatory compliance requirements, and business significance. This foundational process in data protection strategy allows organizations to apply the principle of least privilege, ensuring that only the necessary individuals have access to sensitive data and that such data is protected according to its classification level. Furthermore, data classification simplifies the task of regulatory compliance by identifying which datasets fall under specific legal protections. It also enhances the efficiency of data management and

CHAPTER 3    DATA PROTECTION

security operations by prioritizing the allocation of resources to the most critical data. Effective data classification is a dynamic process that requires regular review and updating to reflect changes in business processes, regulatory requirements, and the evolving cyber threat landscape.

**Encryption:** Encryption is a critical security control that involves transforming readable data into an unreadable format, using algorithms to ensure that only authorized parties can decipher and access the original information. This method is indispensable for protecting the confidentiality and integrity of data, especially in transit over the Internet or stored on portable media, where it is vulnerable to interception or theft. Encryption technologies enable secure communication and safeguard sensitive information, rendering it useless to unauthorized individuals even if they bypass other security measures. In data protection, encryption strategies must be robust, employing strong encryption standards and managing encryption keys securely to prevent unauthorized access. The application of encryption extends beyond protecting data from external threats; it is also crucial for ensuring privacy and compliance with global data protection regulations, such as the GDPR and HIPAA.

**Access Control:** Access control systems are vital for enforcing security policies restricting access to organizational resources, including data. These systems work by identifying, authenticating, and authorizing individuals to access specific resources based on predefined policies. Effective access control mechanisms are tailored to an organization's particular needs, ensuring that employees and other stakeholders have access only to the data and resources necessary for their roles, thus minimizing the potential for unauthorized access or data breaches. These controls range from traditional password-based systems to more sophisticated biometric authentication methods encompassing physical and digital assets. Implementing robust access control is a cornerstone of data protection, ensuring that sensitive information remains confidential and accessible only to those with legitimate needs.

**Data Loss Prevention (DLP):** Data Loss Prevention technologies and strategies are designed to monitor, detect, and prevent unauthorized access or distribution of sensitive data. DLP solutions provide real-time visibility and control over data movement across an organization, helping to safeguard against both internal and external threats. By applying policies based on data classification, DLP systems can block sensitive information from being transmitted outside the corporate network, copied to unsecured devices, or uploaded to cloud services without authorization. The effectiveness of DLP in data protection lies in its ability to protect data at rest, in use, and in motion, addressing a wide array of potential data leak scenarios. Organizations deploy DLP to meet compliance requirements, protect intellectual property, and prevent financial loss from data breaches.

**Data Retention Policy:** A data retention policy outlines how long data should be retained for operational or compliance reasons and the procedures for its secure deletion once it is no longer needed. These policies are critical for data protection as they help organizations manage the risks associated with data storage, including unauthorized access to or theft of stored data. A well-crafted data retention policy balances the need to retain data for business operations, legal compliance, and historical reference with the risks and costs associated with long-term data storage. It also specifies secure deletion practices, ensuring that data is rendered unrecoverable once it has served its purpose. Adhering to a data retention policy not only aids in compliance with data protection regulations but also minimizes the potential attack surface for cyber threats.

**Data Disposal:** Proper data disposal involves the secure destruction or deletion of data to prevent unauthorized access or recovery after its intended use is complete. Effective data disposal practices are integral to data protection strategies, ensuring that sensitive information is irretrievably destroyed when no longer required. This can involve physically destroying hardware, using secure erasure software to wipe data from storage devices, or employing data shredding services. The goal is to mitigate the risk of data breaches and protect privacy by ensuring unauthorized parties cannot reconstruct or retrieve data. Secure data disposal is a best practice for safeguarding sensitive information and is often a legal requirement under data protection laws.

**Data Inventory and Mapping:** Conducting a data inventory and mapping exercise is essential for understanding the data flow within an organization. This process involves identifying all data assets, classifying them according to sensitivity, and documenting how data moves through the organization's systems and processes. Data inventory and mapping provide critical insights for implementing effective data protection measures by highlighting where sensitive data resides, how it is used, and who has access to it. This visibility is crucial for risk management, enabling organizations to apply targeted security controls where they are most needed. Furthermore, data inventory and mapping facilitate compliance with data protection regulations, often requiring detailed knowledge of data flows and storage locations.

**Security Configuration Management (SCM):** Security Configuration Management maintains systems securely by managing their configurations. SCM involves establishing baseline security configurations, monitoring systems for deviations from these baselines, and correcting any identified issues. This practice is vital for data protection, as improperly configured systems can provide easy entry points for attackers seeking to access sensitive data. SCM tools enable organizations to automate the detection and remediation of misconfigurations, thereby enhancing their security posture. By ensuring that systems are always configured according to industry best practices and compliance standards, organizations can significantly reduce their vulnerability to cyber attacks.

CHAPTER 3   DATA PROTECTION

# Importance and Relevance

Data is the lifeblood of organizations, driving operations, innovation, and strategic decision-making. As the volume of data organizations generate and store skyrockets, so does its attractiveness to cybercriminals. Protecting this data is not merely a regulatory compliance issue but a critical component of organizational resilience and reputation management. This section delves into data protection's multifaceted importance and relevance within modern cybersecurity practices. Each point outlined below underscores the imperative for robust data protection measures, providing compelling reasons for organizations to prioritize this control in their cybersecurity frameworks.

**Mitigation of Data Breaches:** Data breaches can have devastating consequences, from financial losses to long-term reputational damage. Effective data protection controls are critical to preventing unauthorized access to sensitive information. By identifying, classifying, securely handling, retaining, and disposing of data, organizations can significantly reduce the likelihood and impact of data breaches. These measures ensure that even if attackers penetrate perimeter defenses, the critical data remains inaccessible or unusable, minimizing potential damage. This strategic approach to data protection is essential for maintaining the confidentiality, integrity, and availability of sensitive information.

**Pivotal Role in Security:** Asset management is the foundation for securing an organization's digital and physical infrastructure. Understanding all assets within an enterprise is crucial for deploying effective defense mechanisms against cyber threats. Devices and software that are unidentified or unmanaged can introduce significant security risks, acting as potential entry points for attackers. A comprehensive asset inventory allows organizations to monitor and secure every access point, significantly reducing vulnerabilities and strengthening the overall security posture. This proactive approach is indispensable for safeguarding against the continually evolving landscape of cyber threats.

**Regulatory Compliance:** Adhering to data protection standards is about enhancing security and legal and regulatory compliance. Numerous laws and regulations across the globe mandate strict management, protection, and handling of data, especially personally identifiable information (PII). Organizations failing to comply with these regulations face hefty fines, legal repercussions, and damage to their reputation. Implementing rigorous data protection controls helps ensure compliance with these regulatory requirements, reducing legal risks and fostering trust among clients and partners. Moreover, it positions the organization as a responsible custodian of data, a critical attribute in today's data-centric world.

**Enhanced Customer Trust:** In an age where data breaches frequently make headlines, customer trust has become a valuable commodity. Organizations that commit to data protection through comprehensive controls are better positioned to build and maintain this trust. Customers are more likely to engage with businesses that can assure the security and confidentiality of their personal and financial information. By prioritizing data protection, organizations protect their assets and enhance their reputation and customer relationships, increasing loyalty and competitive advantage.

**Protection Against Insider Threats:** Not all threats to data security originate from outside the organization. Whether malicious or unintentional, insider threats pose a significant risk to data integrity and confidentiality. Data protection controls that include access management, data classification, and encryption are vital for mitigating the risks posed by insider actions. These controls ensure that employees have access only to the data necessary for their roles, reducing the potential for accidental or intentional data breaches. Addressing insider threats is a critical component of a holistic data protection strategy.

**Enabling Secure Data Sharing:** In the interconnected business environment, the ability to share data securely with partners, vendors, and customers is necessary. Data protection controls facilitate secure data sharing by ensuring that sensitive information is encrypted, classified, and only accessible to authorized parties. This protects the data and enables organizations to collaborate more effectively without compromising security. Secure data sharing is essential for innovation and operational efficiency, making data protection controls a key enabler of business growth.

**Cost Savings:** The financial repercussions of a data breach can be staggering, encompassing regulatory fines, legal fees, and costs associated with breach mitigation efforts. Investing in data protection controls can significantly reduce these costs by preventing breaches in the first place. Additionally, efficient data management practices, such as proper data classification and disposal, can save storage and management costs. By reducing the risk of financial losses and optimizing data storage, data protection controls offer a cost-effective strategy for managing cybersecurity risks.

**Reputation Management:** An organization's reputation is one of its most valuable assets. Data breaches can cause irreparable damage to a brand, eroding customer trust and leading to lost business. Effective data protection measures help safeguard an organization's reputation by preventing the exposure of sensitive information. A robust data protection framework can facilitate a more effective response in a breach, mitigating potential damage and demonstrating the organization's commitment to security.

**Supporting Remote Work:** The rise of remote work has expanded the data security perimeter, introducing new vulnerabilities. Data protection controls are essential for securing data across distributed networks and devices, ensuring employees can access and use data securely, regardless of location. These controls include secure data storage solutions, encryption of data in transit, and robust authentication mechanisms. As remote work becomes a permanent feature of the business landscape, data protection controls enable productivity and security.

**Cloud Security:** With the increasing adoption of cloud-based technologies, data protection controls are vital for securing data stored and processed in the cloud. These controls ensure that data in the cloud is encrypted, access is tightly controlled, and data residency and sovereignty requirements are met. Implementing data protection measures in cloud environments protects against unauthorized access and data breaches, enabling organizations to leverage the benefits of cloud computing while minimizing security risks.

**Competition and Market Position:** In competitive markets, an organization's approach to data protection can be a differentiating factor. Companies known for stringent data security measures may have a competitive edge, attracting customers who prioritize privacy and security. This competitive advantage can translate into market growth, higher customer retention rates, and an enhanced brand image.

**Future-proofing the Organization:** Finally, investing in data protection controls is an investment in the future resilience of the organization. As cyber threats evolve and data becomes increasingly central to business operations, protecting this data becomes more critical. Organizations with robust data protection measures are better positioned to adapt to future challenges, whether from technological advancements, regulatory changes, or emerging cyber threats. Future-proofing through data protection is not just about preventing breaches today; it's about ensuring the organization can thrive in the cybersecurity landscapes of tomorrow.

# Risks of Not Implementing the Control

Data is invaluable to any organization, driving decision-making, operations, and strategic planning. However, cybercriminals, insider threats, and accidental breaches constantly threaten this invaluable asset. The failure to implement robust data protection controls exposes an organization to significant risks, compromising its operational integrity, financial stability, and reputational standing. Data protection controls, encompassing the identification, classification, secure handling, retention, and disposal of data, are critical in mitigating these risks. Without these controls, organizations are vulnerable to myriad threats, each capable of inflicting severe damage. The following elucidates the multifaceted risks associated with neglecting data protection controls, highlighting the imperatives for organizations to prioritize their implementation.

**Vulnerability to Unauthorized Access and Attacks:** Organizations are susceptible to unauthorized access and cyber attacks without comprehensive data protection strategies. The absence of stringent controls such as data encryption, access management, and intrusion detection systems creates open avenues for cybercriminals to exploit. Sensitive data stored without adequate protection can be easily accessed and exfiltrated, leading to significant financial and reputational damage. This vulnerability becomes particularly acute in the case of systems that are unpatched, misconfigured, or otherwise neglected, serving as prime targets for malicious actors. Therefore, establishing robust data protection measures is essential for securing organizational data against cyber threats.

**Increased Risk of Data Breaches:** The failure to implement data protection controls significantly elevates the risk of data breaches. Cybercriminals and insider threats actively seek to exploit weaknesses in data security practices. Without proper controls, sensitive information, including customer data, intellectual property, and financial records, is exposed to potential compromise. Data breaches can result in the loss of critical information, financial penalties, legal repercussions, and damage to the organization's reputation. Implementing data protection controls is crucial for minimizing the likelihood of such breaches and their associated impacts.

**Legal and Regulatory Non-compliance:** Data protection is not just a best practice but a legal requirement in the modern regulatory environment. Numerous laws and regulations mandate the protection of personal and sensitive data. Organizations failing to implement adequate data protection measures risk non-compliance with these regulatory requirements, leading to hefty fines, sanctions, and legal challenges. The implications of non-compliance extend beyond financial penalties, affecting organizational reputation and stakeholder trust. Data protection controls are thus essential for ensuring compliance with applicable laws and regulations, safeguarding the organization from legal and financial repercussions.

**Financial Losses from Cyber Incidents:** The direct and indirect costs of cyber incidents stemming from inadequate data protection can be staggering. These costs include incident response efforts, system restoration, legal fees, regulatory fines, and compensation to affected parties. Additionally, organizations may face increased insurance premiums and investment losses. The financial impact of these incidents can strain organizational resources, diverting funds from critical operations and strategic initiatives. Adequate data protection controls can significantly mitigate the risk of such incidents and their associated financial burdens.

**Damage to Reputation and Customer Trust:** An organization's reputation is one of its most valuable assets. Data breaches and other incidents resulting from inadequate data protection can severely damage this asset, eroding customer trust and loyalty. The recovery from such reputational damage can be lengthy and costly, requiring significant efforts to rebuild trust and confidence among customers, partners, and stakeholders. Organizations prioritizing data protection are committed to safeguarding their stakeholders' interests, which is crucial for maintaining and enhancing their reputational standing.

**Operational Disruptions:** Cybersecurity incidents caused by inadequate data protection can lead to significant operational disruptions. Attacks like ransomware can paralyze critical systems, halt operations, and require extensive recovery efforts. The downtime associated with these incidents can lead to lost productivity, unmet customer needs, and missed business opportunities. Implementing data protection controls helps prevent such disruptions, ensuring the continuity of operations even in the face of cyber threats.

**Intellectual Property Theft:** For many organizations, intellectual property (IP) is a cornerstone of their competitive advantage. Without adequate data protection measures, IP is vulnerable to theft and espionage. Competitors or cybercriminals can exploit weak data security practices to steal patents, designs, and trade secrets, significantly undermining the organization's market position and prospects. Robust data protection controls are essential for safeguarding intellectual property against unauthorized access and theft.

**Exposure to Insider Threats:** Insider threats, both malicious and unintentional, pose a significant risk to organizations lacking strong data protection measures. Employees, contractors, or partners with access to sensitive information can inadvertently or deliberately leak or compromise data. Implementing data protection controls, including access controls and user activity monitoring, is vital for mitigating the risks posed by insider threats. These measures ensure that sensitive data is accessible only on a need-to-know basis and that suspicious activities are promptly detected and addressed.

**Increased Vulnerability to Phishing and Social Engineering Attacks:** Organizations with inadequate data protection are more susceptible to phishing and social engineering attacks. These attacks exploit human vulnerabilities to gain unauthorized access to sensitive data. Effective data protection measures, including employee training and awareness programs, are critical for equipping staff with the knowledge and skills to recognize and respond to these threats. By fostering a culture of security awareness, organizations can enhance their resilience against social engineering tactics.

**Loss of Competitive Advantage:** Protecting sensitive data is a crucial differentiator in the competitive business landscape. Organizations that fail to implement effective data protection measures risk losing their competitive edge. Sensitive business strategies, customer data, and innovation insights can fall into the hands of competitors, eroding

CHAPTER 3   DATA PROTECTION

market share and growth potential. Data protection controls are a security measure and a strategic imperative for maintaining and enhancing competitive positioning.

**Compliance Risks with International Data Protection Laws:** The global nature of business operations means that organizations must often comply with international data protection laws and regulations. Failure to implement appropriate data protection controls can result in non-compliance with these laws, leading to legal challenges and financial penalties. Organizations operating across borders must ensure that their data protection practices align with the requirements of all applicable jurisdictions, safeguarding against the risks of international legal entanglements.

**Challenges in Data Recovery and Continuity:** Organizations face significant challenges in recovering from data loss incidents without robust data protection measures. The loss of critical data can disrupt business continuity and lead to long-term damage, whether due to cyber attacks, system failures, or human error. Data protection controls, including regular backups and disaster recovery plans, are crucial for ensuring that data can be quickly and effectively restored, minimizing the impact on operations, and ensuring business continuity.

# What Questions Should You Ask?

Deploying effective data protection controls is not merely a technical challenge but a strategic imperative that requires careful planning, insight, and foresight. For leaders safeguarding their organization's data assets, formulating and asking the right questions is crucial in establishing a solid foundation for these controls. These questions are instrumental in diagnosing the current state of data protection, understanding the unique risks faced by the organization, and identifying the measures necessary to mitigate these risks. By diving into these inquiries, cybersecurity leaders can better understand their organization's data ecosystem, enabling them to tailor their data protection strategies to be robust and resilient. Moreover, these questions facilitate a proactive approach to cybersecurity, ensuring that leaders are not merely reacting to threats as they occur but anticipating and neutralizing them through strategic planning and implementation.

**What types of data does our organization handle and store?** Initiating a precise inventory of the data types managed by the organization is critical. This inquiry lays the groundwork for all subsequent data protection efforts, necessitating a detailed analysis of data flows, storage practices, and usage patterns across the organization. Leaders must delve into the specifics of each data category, considering not just the apparent repositories of sensitive information but also less conspicuous data pools that might be overlooked. This comprehensive audit will help identify which data is most vulnerable or would have the most severe consequences if compromised, thereby guiding the prioritization of protection efforts.

**How is data classified, and who is responsible for its classification?** Delving into data classification processes reveals how information is segmented according to sensitivity and accessibility requirements. This question goes beyond the mere existence of a classification scheme to probe the effectiveness and clarity of classification criteria, the regularity of classification reviews, and the accountability mechanisms in place for ensuring data is accurately categorized. It also opens up discussions on the training and awareness initiatives necessary for all stakeholders to understand and respect these classifications.

**What measures are in place to ensure the secure handling of data?** Investigating the safe handling of data encompasses a broad spectrum of practices, from initial data creation or acquisition to its deletion or destruction. Leaders must examine technical safeguards like encryption and secure access protocols and the policies and practices surrounding data sharing, both internally and externally. This includes scrutinizing data security in transit and at rest, as well as the controls over who can access data, under what circumstances, and how unauthorized access attempts are detected and managed.

**How are data retention and disposal managed?** Questions on data retention and disposal practices delve into information lifecycle management, seeking to understand how data is stored and archived or deleted over time. This involves evaluating the criteria used to determine retention periods, the processes for securely deleting data at the end of its lifecycle, and how these practices are audited for compliance and effectiveness. It's also important to consider the environmental impact of data disposal methods, ensuring they are secure and responsible.

**What technical controls are in place to protect data?** This inquiry requires a deep dive into the technical infrastructure safeguarding data, from firewalls and intrusion detection systems to encryption protocols and anomaly detection mechanisms. Leaders should seek to understand how these controls integrate into a cohesive defense strategy, how they're monitored and updated in response to emerging threats, and how their effectiveness is measured. This also includes an evaluation of the resilience of these controls against sophisticated cyber threats and their adaptability to future technological advancements.

**How do we manage access to sensitive data?** Access management is a linchpin of data protection, requiring meticulous scrutiny of how permissions are granted, reviewed, and revoked. This question explores the granularity of access controls, the mechanisms for authenticating identity, and the oversight processes for ensuring access rights remain aligned with job requirements and data sensitivity. It also covers the training and awareness efforts that underpin a secure access management culture, ensuring all stakeholders understand their responsibilities and the risks associated with data access.

**What training and awareness programs are in place for data protection?** Exploring the scope and effectiveness of training and awareness programs is crucial for building a data protection culture within the organization. Leaders should investigate these programs' frequency, coverage, and methods, assessing how well they prepare employees to recognize and respond to data security threats. This includes evaluating the programs' adaptability to changing threat landscapes and their success in fostering a proactive security mindset among all organizational members.

**How do we detect and respond to data breaches?** Understanding an organization's capacity to detect and respond to data breaches involves examining the tools, processes, and teams for identifying security incidents and mitigating their impacts. This question probes the readiness of the organization to act swiftly and effectively in the face of a data breach, including the clarity of response protocols, the training of response teams, and the mechanisms for communicating with stakeholders, including regulatory bodies, in the aftermath of a breach.

**What is our policy for working with third-party vendors who handle our data?** Third-party vendors often represent a significant vector for data breaches, making it imperative for leaders to understand the safeguards and agreements with these partners. This encompasses the due diligence processes for selecting vendors, the security requirements imposed on them, and the ongoing monitoring and assessment of their compliance with these requirements. Leaders should also consider contingency plans when responding to a breach originating from a third-party vendor.

**How do we ensure compliance with relevant data protection regulations?** Navigating the complex landscape of data protection regulations requires a multifaceted approach. Leaders must inquire about the processes for staying abreast of regulatory changes, the strategies for ensuring ongoing compliance, and how compliance efforts are documented and demonstrated. This also involves understanding the interplay between regulatory requirements and how the organization prioritizes actions to meet these diverse obligations.

**What is our strategy for securing data in the cloud?** As organizations increasingly rely on cloud services, securing cloud-stored data becomes critical. This question explores the security measures specific to cloud environments, including encryption practices, access controls, and collaboration with cloud service providers to ensure data security. It also covers evaluating cloud services for compliance with organizational security policies and regulatory requirements.

**How do we evaluate and improve our data protection practices?** Continuous improvement is essential for keeping pace with evolving cyber threats and technological advancements. Leaders should ask about the mechanisms for monitoring the effectiveness of data protection practices, including regular security audits, risk assessments, and feedback channels for identifying and implementing improvements. This also includes a willingness to invest in new technologies and practices to enhance the organization's data protection capabilities.

# Recommended Training

Data protection is an essential component of organizational security and compliance. Training for IT/cybersecurity staff and general employees is crucial to reinforce best practices and mitigate risks associated with data handling. Effective training programs educate participants on the importance of protecting sensitive information, understanding potential cyber threats, and adhering to organizational policies. These programs should be tailored to the specific roles of the attendees, ensuring that each individual understands their responsibilities and the actions they must take to safeguard data. Well-designed training reduces the risk of data breaches and promotes a culture of security awareness throughout the organization.

**Recommended Training for General Security Awareness:** General Security Awareness training is fundamental for all employees. This training should cover the basics of cybersecurity, including common threats like phishing, malware, and social engineering. Participants will learn how to recognize suspicious activities and the proper steps to report them. The outcome of this training is a workforce that acts as a first line of defense, equipped to identify and avoid potential security threats. Regularly updated to reflect the latest threat landscape, this training significantly reduces the risk of successful cyber attacks by promoting vigilant and informed behaviors among all staff members.

**Data Handling and Compliance Training:** Data Handling and Compliance training is essential for employees who regularly interact with sensitive data. This training should focus on the proper procedures for accessing, processing, and storing data and compliance with relevant data protection regulations such as GDPR or HIPAA. Attendees will learn about the legal implications of mishandling data and the organizational policies that govern data security. The training aims to minimize legal risks and ensure that all personnel know the importance of compliance, reducing the likelihood of data breaches and regulatory penalties.

**Advanced Security Training for IT Staff:** Advanced Security Training is crucial for IT and cybersecurity teams. This program should cover network security, encryption, and threat analysis. Participants will gain hands-on experience with tools and techniques for securing organizational data against advanced threats. The training will enhance their ability to detect, respond to, and mitigate cyber incidents, thus strengthening the organization's security posture. This specialized training ensures the IT staff is prepared to handle complex challenges in the rapidly evolving cybersecurity landscape.

**Incident Response and Management Training:** Incident Response and Management training is vital for IT staff managing security breaches. This training includes simulations of data breach scenarios to teach staff the steps necessary for an effective response. It aims to minimize the impact of breaches by ensuring that employees can act swiftly and effectively to contain and remediate issues. This training is critical for maintaining business continuity and protecting organizational reputation during a security incident.

CHAPTER 3   DATA PROTECTION

**Data Privacy Training for Admin Staff:** Admin staff often handle personal data and thus require Data Privacy training. This training should emphasize the importance of confidentiality and the legal aspects of data handling, tailored to the specifics of the industry and applicable privacy laws. The outcome is a more compliant workforce that understands how to handle personal information properly, reducing the risk of data leakage and enhancing trust with clients and customers.

**Phishing Defense Training:** Phishing Defense training should be mandatory for all employees to recognize and respond to phishing attempts and social engineering scams. This training will include practical exercises like identifying malicious emails and links. The goal is to reduce the incidence of successful phishing attacks, a common entry point for security breaches. This training is particularly effective in mitigating one of the most significant risks to organizational security.

**Secure Data Disposal Training:** Secure Data Disposal training is necessary for employees involved in decommissioning hardware or handling outdated data. Participants will learn the correct procedures for securely erasing data using approved tools and techniques. This training ensures that sensitive information is permanently removed and unrecoverable, protecting against data breaches from discarded devices and media.

**Mobile Device Security Training:** As mobile devices become integral to business operations, Mobile Device Security training becomes crucial. This training should cover the secure use of smartphones, tablets, and laptops, emphasizing the risks associated with these devices. The training will teach employees how to secure their devices against unauthorized access and data loss, significantly reducing the risk of security breaches through mobile platforms.

**Cloud Security Training:** Cloud Security Training is essential for IT staff working with cloud-based technologies. This training should address the specific security challenges associated with the cloud, such as data access and control, vendor management, and encryption. It aims to enhance the security of cloud environments, ensuring that data stored in the cloud is protected against unauthorized access and other cyber threats.

**Business Continuity Planning Training:** Business Continuity Planning (BCP) Training is crucial for key personnel in ensuring the organization's resilience in the face of data breaches or other cyber incidents. This training covers the development and execution of business continuity plans, focusing on maintaining operations during and after a security incident. It prepares staff to manage disruptions effectively, ensuring critical business functions continue with minimal impact.

**Security Software Usage Training:** Training in Security Software Usage is vital for employees who use security tools as part of their daily responsibilities. This training should cover the correct operation of these tools, including anti-virus programs, firewalls, and intrusion detection systems. Proper training ensures these tools are used effectively, maximizing their potential to protect organizational data.

**Third-Party Security Management Training:** Third-Party Security Management training is crucial for staff managing vendor relationships involving data access. This training should cover the assessment and management of third-party risks, contractual obligations, and the monitoring of vendor compliance with security requirements. This training reduces the risk associated with third-party vendors, a common source of data breaches.

# Actionable Recommendations

Protecting an organization's data assets against many cyber threats is not just essential—it's imperative. Implementing robust data protection controls requires a strategic approach, combining the latest technological solutions with best practices in cybersecurity management. This section offers a set of actionable recommendations that organizations can follow to enhance their data protection efforts. These guidelines are designed to help cybersecurity leaders develop, implement, and maintain effective data protection controls that safeguard sensitive information from unauthorized access, disclosure, alteration, and destruction. By adhering to these recommendations, organizations can strengthen their cybersecurity posture, ensure compliance with regulatory requirements, and build trust with customers and stakeholders.

**Automate Asset Discovery:** Utilizing automated asset discovery tools facilitates a comprehensive and continuous inventory of all network-connected devices and software. This is crucial for ensuring that every asset, whether newly deployed or previously unnoticed, is accounted for and appropriately secured. Automation aids in overcoming the limitations of manual inventory processes, which can be time-consuming and prone to human error, thereby enhancing the accuracy and efficiency of asset management. An up-to-date asset inventory is indispensable for identifying vulnerabilities and implementing targeted security measures. It also provides a foundational understanding for developing a coherent data protection strategy covering the entire organization's digital environment.

**Implement Data Classification Schemes:** Establishing a systematic data classification scheme enables organizations to categorize their data based on sensitivity and the criticality of its protection. This step is essential for determining the security controls required for different data types, ensuring that the most sensitive or valuable information receives the highest level of protection. A well-defined classification scheme facilitates the efficient allocation of resources and helps comply with regulatory data handling and privacy requirements. Engaging stakeholders from various departments in the classification process ensures a comprehensive understanding of data flows and uses across the organization, fostering a unified approach to data protection. Regular training and awareness efforts are crucial for maintaining the effectiveness of the classification scheme, as they ensure that all employees understand their roles in protecting classified data.

CHAPTER 3  DATA PROTECTION

**Adopt a Least Privilege Access Model:** Implementing a least privilege access model is pivotal in minimizing the risk of unauthorized data access and potential breaches. This approach entails granting users only the access necessary for their specific job functions, significantly reducing the attack surface for potential cyber threats. Regular access rights and privileges reviews should complement rigorous access controls to ensure they remain aligned with current job requirements and organizational structures. Adopting this model also requires robust mechanisms for monitoring and auditing access to sensitive data, allowing for the prompt detection and remediation of inappropriate access patterns or security policy violations. Training employees on access control and the principles of least privilege is essential for reinforcing adherence to this model and enhancing the organization's overall data security posture.

**Encrypt Sensitive Data:** Encryption is a critical safeguard for protecting the confidentiality and integrity of data, both at rest and in transit. Organizations should employ strong encryption standards and manage encryption keys securely to prevent unauthorized access to sensitive information. Implementing encryption across various platforms and data storage environments ensures consistent protection, irrespective of where the data resides or how it is transmitted. Regularly reviewing and updating encryption practices in light of new technological developments and emerging threats is essential for maintaining the effectiveness of this control. Additionally, educating staff on the importance of encryption and properly handling encrypted data reinforces the organization's commitment to data protection.

**Establish Comprehensive Data Handling Policies:** Developing and enforcing detailed data handling policies provides clear guidelines for the creation, storage, sharing, and disposal of data within the organization. These policies should address the entire data lifecycle, incorporating best practices for data protection and specifying the roles and responsibilities of all employees in maintaining data security. Effective communication and training on these policies ensure that staff understand the procedures for securely handling data and the implications of policy violations. Regular audits of data handling practices help identify areas for improvement and ensure compliance with internal policies and external regulatory requirements. Engaging with organizational stakeholders in developing and periodically reviewing these policies ensures they remain relevant and effective in addressing current data protection challenges.

**Deploy Data Loss Prevention (DLP) Solutions:** Data Loss Prevention (DLP) technologies are crucial in monitoring and controlling the movement and storage of sensitive data within an organization's network. Organizations can prevent data leaks and breaches by configuring DLP solutions to detect and block unauthorized attempts to access, share, or transfer sensitive information. DLP policies should be tailored to the organization's specific data protection needs and regulatory obligations, providing a flexible yet robust mechanism for safeguarding critical information. Training employees on the importance of DLP measures and their role in preventing data loss is vital to fostering a security-aware culture. Ongoing evaluation and adjustment of DLP policies and technologies ensure they remain effective despite evolving data usage patterns and emerging security threats.

**Regularly Update and Patch Systems:** Keeping software and systems up-to-date with the latest patches and updates is essential for protecting against known vulnerabilities that cybercriminals could exploit. A structured patch management process, prioritizing critical updates based on the severity of vulnerabilities and the potential impact on the organization's data, ensures timely protection against threats. Where possible, automating the patch management process can enhance efficiency and reduce the likelihood of human error leading to missed updates. Educating employees about regular updates, particularly for remote or BYOD (Bring Your Device) environments, reinforces the organization's commitment to data security. Regular vulnerability assessments and penetration testing can further identify unpatched systems and areas requiring attention, ensuring a comprehensive approach to system maintenance and data protection.

**Conduct Regular Security Audits and Assessments:** Periodic security audits and risk assessments are vital for identifying vulnerabilities and gaps in an organization's data protection strategy. These evaluations provide insights into the effectiveness of existing controls and highlight areas where enhancements are necessary. Involving external experts in these audits can offer an objective perspective and uncover issues internal teams might overlook. The findings from these assessments should inform the development of action plans to address identified risks, with priorities assigned based on the potential impact on data security. Continuous monitoring and reassessment ensure that the organization's data protection measures evolve in line with changing threat landscapes and technological advancements.

**Develop and Practice an Incident Response Plan:** An effective incident response plan outlines the procedures to follow for a data breach or security incident, ensuring a coordinated and efficient response. This plan should designate specific roles and responsibilities, including communication strategies for internal and external stakeholders. Regular training and simulation exercises prepare the response team to act swiftly and effectively, minimizing the impact of incidents on the organization's operations and reputation. Continuous improvement of the incident response plan, based on lessons learned from drills and actual incidents, ensures that the organization remains prepared to address future threats. Collaboration with law enforcement and industry partners can also enhance the organization's response capabilities and access to threat intelligence.

**Secure Data Across Its Lifecycle:** Implementing controls to secure data throughout its lifecycle, from creation to disposal, is essential for comprehensive data protection. This includes establishing secure storage solutions, implementing effective access controls, and ensuring secure data transfer. Data retention policies should be developed to determine how long data is kept and the procedures for its secure deletion or destruction at the end of its lifecycle. Regular training on data lifecycle management practices ensures employees understand their responsibilities in maintaining data security throughout its lifecycle. Regular reviews of these practices help to ensure they remain effective and compliant with current regulatory requirements and organizational needs.

**Monitor and Manage Third-Party Risks:** Managing the security risks associated with third-party vendors who access or handle the organization's data is critical for comprehensive data protection. Conducting thorough security assessments of vendors before engagement and regular reviews after that ensures that third parties adhere to the organization's data security standards. Contractual agreements should specify data protection requirements and responsibilities, providing a legal framework for enforcement. Implementing mechanisms for continuous monitoring of third-party compliance with security requirements helps identify and mitigate risks promptly. Establishing clear communication channels and incident response protocols with vendors ensures coordinated efforts to safeguard sensitive data.

**Foster a Culture of Security Awareness:** Cultivating a culture of security awareness within the organization is fundamental to the success of data protection efforts. Ongoing education and training programs should inform employees about the latest cyber threats, data protection best practices, and their role in safeguarding sensitive information. Engaging leadership in promoting data security reinforces its significance across the organization. Recognizing and rewarding compliance with data protection policies can motivate employees to adhere to security practices. Continuous feedback mechanisms allow for the refinement of training programs and addressing emerging security challenges, ensuring that the organization's workforce remains a strong line of defense against data breaches.

CHAPTER 3   DATA PROTECTION

# Simplified Security Controls (SSC)

Security controls are essential for any organization seeking to protect its digital and physical assets from cyber threats. Tailoring these controls to fit the specific needs of your business environment is crucial, as it ensures that the protection mechanisms are relevant and effective against the specific risks your organization faces. There are numerous sources to draw these controls from, including the well-regarded CIS Top 18, which provides a robust framework for crafting defensive strategies. The recommendations presented in this book are based on the CIS controls, among others, offering a comprehensive guide that can be adapted to serve a wide range of security needs. Before implementing these controls, it is vital to thoroughly review their design to ensure they align with your strategic objectives and operational practices. Additionally, after deployment, it is imperative to regularly test the controls to verify their effectiveness and to make necessary adjustments. This ensures that the controls continue to function as intended, safeguarding your organization against emerging threats and changing conditions.

## CONTROL 1: ESTABLISH AND MAINTAIN A DATA MANAGEMENT PROCESS

**Control Objective:** To create a comprehensive data management process that encompasses the identification, handling, retention, and disposal of data based on its sensitivity and value.

**Implementation Steps:**

**1.1. Define Data Sensitivity and Ownership:** Identify and classify data based on sensitivity. Assign ownership to specific roles within the organization to ensure accountability for the handling and security of each data category.

**1.2. Develop Handling and Retention Protocols:** Establish protocols for how different data types should be handled and retained. Include physical and digital data format guidelines addressing storage, access, and transfer procedures.

CHAPTER 3   DATA PROTECTION

**1.3. Formalize Disposal Procedures:** Create formal procedures for the secure disposal of data that are no longer required based on its classification and legal retention requirements.

**1.4. Annual Review and Update:** Regularly review and update the data management process at least annually or following significant organizational changes that could impact data security.

**Expected Outcome:** A well-defined data management process will ensure that all data within the organization is handled, stored, retained, and disposed of in a secure and compliant manner, reducing the risk of data breaches and ensuring compliance with data protection regulations.

## CONTROL 2: ESTABLISH AND MAINTAIN A DATA INVENTORY

**Control Objective:** To maintain an accurate inventory of all data, especially sensitive data, to manage and protect it effectively.

**Implementation Steps:**

**1.1. Inventory Creation:** Develop a comprehensive inventory that includes all data, emphasizing sensitive data and detailing its format, location, and responsible party.

**1.2. Integration with Data Management:** Ensure the data inventory is integrated with the organization's data management process to maintain consistency in handling and protection standards.

**1.3. Regular Updates:** Update the data inventory annually or more frequently if required, focusing on changes to sensitive data assets.

**1.4. Priority on Sensitive Data:** Prioritize the inventory review and update sensitive data to apply heightened security measures consistently.

**Expected Outcome:** A well-maintained data inventory allows for effective management and protection of organizational data, particularly sensitive data, by providing clear visibility into data assets and locations.

CHAPTER 3   DATA PROTECTION

## CONTROL 3: CONFIGURE DATA ACCESS CONTROL LISTS

**Control Objective:** To restrict data access based on the principle of least privilege, ensuring that individuals have access only to the data necessary for their job functions.

**Implementation Steps:**

**1.1. Define Access Levels:** Establish different levels of data access that correspond to the organization's structure and employee roles.

**1.2. Implement Access Controls:** Apply these access control lists to all systems, including file servers, databases, and applications, both locally and remotely.

**1.3. Regular Review and Adjustment:** Periodically review access controls to ensure they remain appropriate as roles and responsibilities evolve within the organization.

**1.4. Automation of Access Control Updates:** Where possible, automate the updates to access control lists to enhance efficiency and reduce the risk of human error.

**Expected Outcome:** Effective implementation of data access control lists will minimize the risk of unauthorized data access and potential data breaches, reinforcing the organization's data security posture.

CHAPTER 3   DATA PROTECTION

## CONTROL 4: ENFORCE DATA RETENTION

**Control Objective:** To ensure that data is retained only as long as necessary for legal, regulatory, and business requirements and securely disposed of afterward.

**Implementation Steps:**

**1.1. Define Retention Periods:** Establish minimum and maximum retention periods based on the nature of the data and its relevance to business operations and compliance requirements.

**1.2. Implement Retention Policies:** Apply these retention policies across all data storage systems and formats.

**1.3. Monitor Compliance:** Regularly monitor compliance with data retention policies to ensure that data is neither retained too long nor disposed of prematurely.

**1.4. Update Retention Policies:** Review and update retention policies annually or in response to legal or business conditions changes.

**Expected Outcome:** Strict enforcement of data retention policies will reduce the volume of data that needs to be protected and decrease the risk associated with data breaches while ensuring compliance with legal and regulatory requirements.

CHAPTER 3  DATA PROTECTION

## CONTROL 5: SECURELY DISPOSE OF DATA

**Control Objective:** To ensure that all data is disposed of securely and in accordance with its sensitivity and the organization's data management policies.

**Implementation Steps:**

**1.1. Define Disposal Methods:** Establish secure data disposal methods appropriate for the sensitivity level of the data, such as physical destruction or digital wiping.

**1.2. Integrate Disposal into Data Management:** Ensure that disposal methods are integrated into the overall data management process to maintain compliance and security consistency.

**1.3. Employee Training:** Train relevant personnel on proper disposal techniques to prevent data leaks or breaches.

**1.4. Regular Audits:** Conduct regular audits to ensure that data disposal practices are followed correctly and consistently throughout the organization.

**Expected Outcome:** Properly implementing secure data disposal practices will ensure that sensitive data is irrecoverably erased when no longer needed, minimizing the risk of unauthorized access and maintaining compliance with data protection regulations.

CHAPTER 3   DATA PROTECTION

## CONTROL 6: ENCRYPT DATA ON END-USER DEVICES

**Control Objective:** To protect the confidentiality and integrity of data stored on end-user devices by implementing strong encryption methods.

**Implementation Steps:**

**1.1. Select Encryption Tools:** Choose appropriate encryption technologies, such as Windows BitLocker, Apple FileVault, or Linux dm-crypt, based on the operating systems in use.

**1.2. Implement Encryption:** Deploy encryption across all end-user devices that contain sensitive data.

**1.3. Train Users:** Educate users on the importance of encryption and how to ensure it is always enabled.

**1.4. Monitor and Verify:** Regularly verify that encryption is active on all devices and monitor compliance to prevent data exposure.

**Expected Outcome:** Encrypting data on end-user devices will significantly reduce the risk of data breaches, especially in device loss or theft cases, by ensuring that data remains inaccessible without proper authorization.

## CONTROL 7: ESTABLISH AND MAINTAIN A DATA CLASSIFICATION SCHEME

**Control Objective:** To categorize data based on its sensitivity and value to the organization, ensuring appropriate security measures are applied.

**Implementation Steps:**

**1.1. Develop Classification Labels:** Create a set of data classification labels, such as "Sensitive," "Confidential," and "Public."

**1.2. Apply Classification:** Classify all data according to these labels and integrate classification into the lifecycle management processes.

CHAPTER 3   DATA PROTECTION

**1.3. Employee Training:** Train all employees on the classification scheme to ensure correct data handling based on its classification.

**1.4. Regular Reviews:** Annually review and update the classification scheme to reflect changes in business processes or the threat landscape.

**Expected Outcome:** A well-defined data classification scheme will facilitate the proper handling and protection of data throughout the organization, enhancing security and compliance.

## CONTROL 8: DOCUMENT DATA FLOWS

**Control Objective:** To map and document how data flows through the organization, including transfers to and from service providers, to identify and mitigate potential security vulnerabilities.

**Implementation Steps:**

**1.1. Map Data Flows:** Identify and document data movement within and outside the organization, particularly for sensitive data.

**1.2. Integration with Data Management:** Ensure data flow documentation is integrated with the data management process to enhance data protection measures.

**1.3. Regular Updates:** Update documentation annually or whenever significant changes occur in data processing or business operations.

**1.4. Training and Awareness:** Ensure employees understand their roles within these data flows and the importance of securing data in transit.

**Expected Outcome:** Comprehensive documentation of data flows will help the organization manage data more securely, recognize potential security vulnerabilities, and implement appropriate safeguards.

CHAPTER 3    DATA PROTECTION

## CONTROL 9: ENCRYPT DATA ON REMOVABLE MEDIA

**Control Objective:** To ensure the security of data stored on removable media by implementing strong encryption measures.

**Implementation Steps:**

**1.1. Select Encryption Technologies:** Implement robust encryption standards such as AES for encrypting data on removable media.

**1.2. Policy Implementation:** Develop and enforce policies that mandate the encryption of sensitive data on all removable media.

**1.3. Employee Training:** Train employees on the importance of using encrypted removable media and the procedures for encrypting data before transfer.

**1.4. Compliance Monitoring:** Regularly monitor the use of removable media to ensure compliance with encryption policies.

**Expected Outcome:** Encryption of data on removable media will prevent unauthorized access to sensitive information in the event of loss or theft, thereby enhancing data security.

## CONTROL 10: ENCRYPT SENSITIVE DATA IN TRANSIT

**Control Objective:** To protect sensitive data from interception and unauthorized access during transmission.

**Implementation Steps:**

**1.1. Implement Secure Protocols:** Use secure communication protocols such as TLS and OpenSSH for all data transmissions.

**1.2. Enforce Policy Compliance:** Ensure that policies requiring the encryption of data in transit are strictly enforced across the organization.

CHAPTER 3    DATA PROTECTION

**1.3. Regular Security Assessments:** Conduct regular security assessments to verify the integrity of the encryption protocols and techniques used.

**1.4. Training and Awareness:** Educate employees on encrypting data in transit and the technologies used to secure data.

**Expected Outcome:** Implementing robust encryption for data in transit will significantly reduce the risk of data interception and unauthorized access, maintaining the confidentiality and integrity of sensitive data.

## CONTROL 11: ENCRYPT SENSITIVE DATA AT REST

**Control Objective:** To ensure that sensitive data is encrypted at rest to prevent unauthorized access, especially in storage environments.

**Implementation Steps:**

**1.1. Select Encryption Methods:** Use advanced encryption methods such as storage-layer encryption and, where applicable, client-side encryption to protect data at rest.

**1.2. Integrate Encryption into Data Storage:** Apply encryption consistently across all storage solutions, including servers, databases, and cloud storage.

**1.3. Regular Encryption Key Management:** Implement robust encryption key management practices to ensure the security of encryption keys.

**1.4. Continuous Monitoring:** Continuously monitor data storage environments to ensure encryption measures are always in place and functioning correctly.

**Expected Outcome:** Encryption of sensitive data at rest will safeguard against unauthorized access and breaches, strengthening the organization's overall security posture.

## CONTROL 12: SEGMENT DATA PROCESSING AND STORAGE BASED ON SENSITIVITY

**Control Objective:** To segment processing and storage systems based on the sensitivity of the data they handle, ensuring that systems are appropriately secured.

**Implementation Steps:**

**1.1. Define Segmentation Policies:** Develop clear policies for data segmentation based on sensitivity levels.

**1.2. Implement Segmentation Controls:** Apply physical and logical controls to separate high-sensitivity data processing and storage from lower-sensitivity operations.

**1.3. Regular Policy Review:** Periodically review segmentation policies and controls to ensure they continue to protect sensitive data effectively.

**1.4. Training and Compliance:** Train employees on the importance of segmentation and regularly audit systems for compliance with segmentation policies.

**Expected Outcome:** Effective data processing and storage segmentation will reduce the risk of sensitive data exposure and provide additional security, especially against insider threats and system breaches.

CHAPTER 3    DATA PROTECTION

## CONTROL 13: DEPLOY A DATA LOSS PREVENTION SOLUTION

**Control Objective:** To implement a comprehensive Data Loss Prevention (DLP) strategy that detects potential data breaches or data ex-filtration transmissions and prevents them by monitoring, detecting, and blocking sensitive data handling in violation of security policies.

**Implementation Steps:**

**1.1. Implement DLP Tools:** Deploy enterprise-wide DLP solutions to monitor and protect data in use, in motion, and at rest.

**1.2. Integrate DLP with Existing Security Tools:** Ensure DLP solutions are integrated with other security systems for enhanced data protection.

**1.3. Continuous Monitoring and Response:** Set up continuous monitoring with real-time alerts to detect and respond to policy violations or suspicious data activity.

**1.4. Regular Updates and Tuning:** Regularly update DLP rules and policies based on evolving data protection needs and threat landscape changes.

**Expected Outcome:** A robust DLP system will help prevent data leaks and unauthorized data transmissions, protecting sensitive information from internal and external threats.

CHAPTER 3    DATA PROTECTION

## CONTROL 3.14: LOG SENSITIVE DATA ACCESS

**Control Objective:** To maintain comprehensive logs of all access to sensitive data, including modifications and disposal, to ensure traceability and accountability.

**Implementation Steps:**

**1.1. Establish Logging Standards:** Define what constitutes sensitive data and ensure all access to such data is logged.

**1.2. Secure and Centralize Logs:** Ensure logs are securely stored and centrally managed to prevent unauthorized access and manipulation.

**1.3. Regular Log Review:** Implement routine log reviews and audits to detect unauthorized access or anomalous activities.

**1.4. Integration with Incident Response:** Ensure log analysis is integrated with the organization's incident response plan to facilitate quick detection and remediation of security breaches.

**Expected Outcome:** Effective logging of sensitive data access will enhance the organization's ability to detect, investigate, and respond to potential security incidents, thereby reducing the risk of data breaches and ensuring compliance with regulatory requirements.

# CHAPTER 4

# Secure Configuration of Enterprise Assets and Software

The challenge of maintaining secure configurations does not end at the initial setup; it extends throughout the lifecycle of the assets and software. It involves ongoing updates, patches, and monitoring any changes that could introduce vulnerabilities. Effective configuration management ensures compliance, incident response, and supporting audits. This process helps maintain that configurations do not drift into less secure states over time. Consequently, organizations must establish rigorous processes to track and verify the security of their configurations.

The role of service providers is increasingly important in modern digital infrastructures, particularly for smaller enterprises. These providers often set up flexible configurations to accommodate various customer needs. Unfortunately, these settings tend not to prioritize security, leaving significant gaps unless the enterprise takes action. Enterprises must take responsibility for configuring these services securely, necessitating a vigilant and proactive approach to configuration management. This includes modifying and customizing default settings to meet specific security standards and requirements.

Developing a strong security posture begins with applying a secure baseline configuration. Enterprises are advised to start with publicly available security benchmarks, guidelines, and checklists to establish these baselines. These should be adjusted to align with specific enterprise security policies, regulatory requirements, and business needs. Such alignment is critical to creating an effective defense mechanism against potential cyber threats. Moreover, documenting any deviations from standard configurations helps in future reviews or audits.

The implementation of secure configurations involves several detailed steps. These range from determining the risk classification of the data handled by the assets to applying necessary security patches and conducting regular security assessments. For example, a security configuration script that aligns with the risk level of data on an asset can significantly mitigate potential breaches. Each step is critical in building a secure foundation that protects sensitive information and maintains system integrity.

Configuration management tools are pivotal in maintaining the security of enterprise assets. These tools assess compliance with established security baselines and detect deviations that could expose the organization to risks. Whether these tools operate agent-based or agentless, they provide visibility and control to manage configurations effectively. They are essential for ensuring that all assets remain within the organization's security parameters and that any discrepancies are quickly addressed.

Training and awareness among staff are indispensable in the secure configuration process. All personnel should understand the importance of security settings and be equipped to implement and maintain these settings. Embedding security into the organizational culture ensures that it is not viewed merely as a technical requirement but as a fundamental operational practice. This holistic approach helps mitigate human errors and enhance the organization's security posture.

As technology evolves, so do cyber adversaries' tactics. This dynamic landscape requires organizations to establish secure configurations and continuously monitor and adapt these configurations to new threats. Changes in technology, updates to existing systems, and variations in user behavior can all necessitate adjustments to security configurations. Staying ahead of these changes is crucial for maintaining the effectiveness of security measures.

Documentation and policy development play crucial roles in a robust security configuration strategy. Clear documentation of all configurations and deviations helps maintain clarity and accountability within the organization. It also aids in audits and compliance reviews, providing a clear trail of decisions and actions to secure systems. Well-documented policies and procedures are the backbone of effective cybersecurity governance and are indispensable for long-term security management.

The complexity of today's enterprise environments often means that different assets require tailored security configurations. These configurations should reflect the specific security needs and data classifications relevant to those assets. For instance, a high-risk data server will have different security requirements than a low-risk employee workstation. Tailoring configurations enhances security and optimizes system performance and usability, making it a critical practice for modern enterprises.

Adhering to these principles and continuously adapting to the changing threat landscape can help organizations establish a secure configuration framework that significantly reduces their cyberattack vulnerability. This foundational element of cybersecurity is vital in building a resilient digital infrastructure capable of withstanding the evolving threats of the digital age. Secure configuration remains a cornerstone of effective cyber defense strategies through diligent management and a commitment to continuous improvement.

CHAPTER 4   SECURE CONFIGURATION OF ENTERPRISE ASSETS AND SOFTWARE

# Key Concepts and Terms

In cybersecurity, precise knowledge of key concepts and terms is essential for the effective management and secure configuration of enterprise assets. This section offers a detailed glossary of critical cybersecurity terms fundamental to robust security practices. These definitions cover everything from asset management to incident response and provide the foundational knowledge to implement and manage security measures effectively. Understanding these terms enables IT professionals, cybersecurity experts, and organizational leaders to strengthen their security frameworks and protect their digital environments.

**Baseline Security Configuration:** Baseline security configuration sets the minimum security controls necessary for a secure operating environment. It is derived from industry standards and tailored to specific organizational needs, establishing a benchmark for consistent security posture. These baseline configurations help measure system-setting deviations and maintain uniform security standards across all enterprise assets. This approach is fundamental in managing and mitigating potential security risks effectively.

**Configuration Drift:** Configuration drift refers to unintended system setting changes that deviate from baseline security configurations. Such drifts can occur due to ongoing system updates and changes, exposing organizations to potential security risks. Regular audits and continuous monitoring are necessary to detect and correct drift, ensuring compliance with established security policies. Managing configuration drift is vital for maintaining the security integrity of enterprise assets.

**Patch Management:** Patch management is a critical security function that involves acquiring, testing, and applying updates to software and systems. This process corrects vulnerabilities and software bugs, protecting enterprise assets from exploitation by cyber threats. Effective patch management ensures systems' operational integrity and security by promptly addressing known vulnerabilities. It is a cornerstone of proactive cybersecurity practices.

# CHAPTER 4   SECURE CONFIGURATION OF ENTERPRISE ASSETS AND SOFTWARE

**Vulnerability Management:** Vulnerability management is a proactive approach to identifying, classifying, remediating, and mitigating vulnerabilities within an organization's assets. This continuous process is essential for maintaining system security by addressing potential weaknesses before exploiting them. It involves regular scans and assessments to keep security measures up-to-date. Effective vulnerability management is critical for safeguarding an organization's digital infrastructure.

**Change Management:** Change management in cybersecurity is the structured approach to handling changes to the IT infrastructure. This includes managing the addition, modification, or removal of any hardware, software, or system configuration. Such management minimizes risks associated with changes and ensures that they do not compromise system security or disrupt business operations. Effective change management is essential for maintaining system security in a dynamic IT environment.

**Security Compliance:** Security compliance involves adhering to relevant laws, regulations, and standards to protect sensitive information and avoid penalties. It requires thorough documentation, regular audits, and alignment of IT policies with compliance requirements. Compliance is crucial for protecting sensitive data and maintaining the trust of stakeholders. Organizations must continuously monitor and adjust their compliance strategies to align with legal and regulatory changes.

**Security Policy:** A security policy is a formal statement that outlines an organization's approach to protecting its physical and IT assets. It sets clear guidelines for staff and management regarding their responsibilities and expected security practices. These policies help ensure consistent implementation of security measures across an organization. A well-defined security policy is foundational to effective cybersecurity governance.

**Access Control:** Access control is a fundamental security measure that ensures only authorized users can access specific resources. It protects sensitive information from unauthorized access and potential breaches.

Effective access control systems are based on comprehensive policies and are enforced through robust technological solutions. Maintaining stringent access controls is crucial for the security of sensitive data.

**Security Audits:** Security audits are systematic evaluations that measure the effectiveness of an organization's security measures. They identify risks, assess policy compliance, and help maintain security standards. Regular security audits are essential for ensuring ongoing adherence to security best practices. They are a key component of proactive security management.

**Risk Assessment:** Risk assessment is a critical cybersecurity process involving identifying and evaluating risks associated with an organization's assets. It helps make informed decisions about the security measures to protect those assets. This process is integral to risk management strategies, guiding security investments and policy decisions. Effective risk assessment is essential for minimizing potential security threats.

**Incident Response:** Incident response is the organized approach to managing the aftermath of security breaches or cyber attacks. It aims to limit damage, reduce recovery time and costs, and prevent future incidents. An effective incident response plan includes preparation, detection, analysis, containment, eradication, and recovery activities. This proactive approach is crucial for minimizing the impact of security incidents on an organization.

# Importance and Relevance

The secure configuration of enterprise assets and software is a technical necessity and a strategic imperative affecting various aspects of organizational cybersecurity. From compliance with regulatory frameworks to enhancing incident response capabilities, the importance of this practice cannot be overstated. In this section, we will explore the

## CHAPTER 4   SECURE CONFIGURATION OF ENTERPRISE ASSETS AND SOFTWARE

multifaceted benefits and the critical role secure configuration plays in maintaining robust cyber defenses. Each aspect discussed will underscore why adhering to security best practices is essential for minimizing risks, reducing costs, and building trust across all stakeholder interactions in today's digital landscape.

**Compliance with Regulations:** Secure configuration of enterprise assets and software ensures compliance with various regulatory frameworks that mandate strict cybersecurity measures. Organizations across different sectors must often adhere to standards such as GDPR, HIPAA, or PCI DSS, which include directives on secure configurations. Failing to comply can result in severe financial penalties and damage to reputation. Thus, maintaining secure configurations protects information and aligns with legal and regulatory obligations.

**Minimization of Attack Surfaces:** A well-configured system minimizes the number of attack vectors accessible to cybercriminals. Disabling unnecessary services, closing unused ports, and removing default accounts or passwords significantly reduce opportunities for malicious access. Each reduction in the attack surface decreases the organization's overall risk profile, making it a less attractive target for attackers. This proactive approach is vital in a landscape where threat actors continuously seek new vulnerabilities to exploit.

**Enhanced Incident Response:** Secure configurations significantly aid incident response and forensic activities. When systems are configured according to best practices, detecting anomalies and responding to incidents is easier. Secure baselines provide a clear reference that helps quickly identify unauthorized changes or suspicious activities, enabling faster containment and mitigation of threats, thereby reducing potential damage and recovery time.

**Cost Reduction in Security Management:** Secure configuration is a cost-effective measure in the long term. By investing in proper configuration management from the outset, organizations can avoid the higher costs of responding to security breaches and incidents. Preventative measures such as secure configurations are generally less resource-intensive than the remediation of security failures, which often include legal fees, fines, and the costs of restoring operations and reputation.

**Support for Remote and Cloud Environments:** As organizations increasingly adopt remote work and cloud-based technologies, secure configurations become even more critical. These environments often expand the security perimeter and introduce new asset control and vulnerability management challenges. Secure configurations tailored for remote access devices and cloud platforms ensure that security is not compromised despite the expanded attack surface.

**Foundation for Advanced Security Technologies:** Secure configuration is a baseline for implementing more sophisticated security measures, such as intrusion detection systems, advanced threat protection, and security information and event management (SIEM) systems. These technologies rely on the assumption that the underlying assets are securely configured. With this foundation, the effectiveness of these advanced solutions can be significantly improved.

**Improved System Performance and Stability:** Secure configurations enhance security and contribute to IT systems' overall performance and stability. Systems can run more efficiently and reliably by eliminating unnecessary software and turning off redundant services. This optimization of system resources often leads to better performance and reduced downtime, which is crucial for maintaining business continuity.

**Enhanced User Confidence and Trust:** Customers and partners place higher trust in organizations that demonstrate a commitment to cybersecurity. The secure configuration of enterprise assets and software signals stakeholders that the organization is protecting its digital resources seriously. This trust is fundamental in building and maintaining strong business relationships in the digital age.

**Support for Compliance Audits:** Secure configurations simplify the process of compliance audits. Auditors often look for adherence to industry best practices and regulatory requirements during their assessments. By maintaining configured systems securely, organizations can provide auditors with clear evidence of compliance, thus facilitating smoother audit processes and demonstrating due diligence.

**Scalability of Security Practices:** Secure configuration practices are scalable and can grow with the organization. As enterprises expand, the complexity of their IT environments also increases. A solid foundation in secure configuration practices ensures that new assets and technologies can be integrated securely into the organization's infrastructure, maintaining security consistency as the business scales.

**Proactive Threat Mitigation:** Secure configuration is inherently proactive rather than reactive. By establishing and maintaining secure settings, organizations can prevent many threats from materializing rather than dealing with the consequences of security breaches. This proactive stance is essential in an era where new vulnerabilities and attack methodologies constantly emerge, requiring organizations to stay ahead of potential threats.

# Risks of Not Implementing the Control

The failure to implement secure configurations for enterprise assets and software exposes organizations to a broad spectrum of cybersecurity risks. These vulnerabilities can compromise data integrity, disrupt business operations, and result in substantial financial losses. In an era where digital threats are increasingly sophisticated and pervasive, securing enterprise assets through well-defined configurations is not merely an option but a necessity. This section outlines the risks of neglecting this crucial cybersecurity measure, demonstrating the potential consequences on organizational security, compliance, and operational stability.

**Increased Vulnerability to Cyber Attacks:** Enterprise assets are significantly more susceptible to attacks without secure configuration. Default settings often prioritize convenience over security, leaving systems open to exploitation. Hackers can easily target these vulnerabilities, potentially gaining unauthorized access to sensitive information. This risk is compounded as the organization grows and its digital footprint expands, making consistent security configurations more crucial.

**Compliance Violations and Legal Repercussions:** Organizations are bound by various regulatory requirements that dictate stringent data protection and security measures. Failing to secure asset configurations can lead to non-compliance with regulations such as GDPR, HIPAA, or PCI DSS, resulting in hefty fines and legal actions. This not only affects the organization's financial standing but also damages its reputation in the industry.

**Data Breaches and Loss of Confidential Information:** Insecure configurations can lead to data breaches, where sensitive or confidential information is accessed without authorization. The impact of such violations extends beyond immediate financial losses to long-term reputational damage and loss of customer trust. Organizations may also face legal consequences if customer data is compromised due to inadequate security practices.

**Operational Disruptions:** Unsecured configurations can be exploited to cause operational disruptions. For instance, an attacker could disable critical systems or corrupt key data, leading to downtime and significant business interruptions. These disruptions can cascade effects on service delivery, customer satisfaction, and business revenues, often requiring extensive resources.

**Increased IT Costs:** The absence of secure configurations often results in higher IT costs. Organizations must spend more on incident response and remediation when vulnerabilities are exploited. Proactive investment in secure configurations can significantly reduce these costs by preventing security breaches and their associated expenses from occurring in the first place.

**Diminished Customer Trust:** Customers expect their data to be protected. If an organization fails to secure its configurations and a breach occurs, customer trust will be severely eroded. This loss of trust can result in a decline in business as customers move to competitors perceived as more secure, impacting the organization's market position and profitability.

**Exploitation of IoT Devices:** In today's interconnected environment, insecure configurations of non-computing IoT devices present a significant risk. These devices often lack robust built-in security, making them easy targets for attackers who can use them as entry points into wider organizational networks, thereby multiplying the potential for damage.

**Loss of Intellectual Property:** Companies that fail to implement secure configurations risk intellectual property theft. Cybercriminals can exploit vulnerabilities to steal patents, designs, business strategies, and other proprietary information, giving competitors an undue advantage and potentially causing irreparable harm to the victim organization's market standing and prospects.

**Resource Misallocation:** Without a secure configuration strategy, organizations might allocate resources inefficiently, reacting to threats ad hoc rather than addressing them systematically. This often leads to duplicated efforts and wasted resources, which could be better spent on strategic initiatives that advance business objectives.

**Weakened Incident Response:** An organization's ability to respond effectively to security incidents is compromised when assets are not securely configured. The lack of a robust configuration complicates identifying how breaches occurred and the best steps for remediation, thereby extending recovery times and increasing the breach's impact.

**Scalability Challenges:** As an organization grows, so does the complexity of its asset management. Insecure configurations can severely hamper the scalability of security practices, making it difficult to ensure consistent security as new technologies and devices are integrated into the existing infrastructure.

**Increased Insider Threat Risk:** Insecure configurations increase the risk of insider threats, as employees or contractors might exploit weak configurations for malicious purposes or inadvertently cause security incidents. Strong configuration controls help mitigate this risk by restricting unnecessary access to systems and data, thus reducing opportunities for insider breaches.

# What Questions Should You Ask?

Implementing secure configurations for enterprise assets and software is a strategic endeavor that requires thorough planning and precise execution. Cybersecurity leaders play a pivotal role in shaping the direction and effectiveness of this initiative. To successfully implement this vital security control, leaders must ask targeted questions that clarify the organization's current security posture, identify vulnerabilities, and align security efforts with broader business objectives. These questions are the foundation for a robust cybersecurity strategy, ensuring that all asset and software security aspects are comprehensively addressed. This approach enhances protection and integrates security into the organization's operations and culture.

**What are our most critical assets and software?** Identifying which assets and software are crucial to the organization's operations is essential for prioritizing security efforts. This question helps determine where to focus initial configuration efforts and resource allocation. Understanding the criticality of assets ensures that the most sensitive and valuable resources receive the highest level of protection, aligning security measures with business priorities.

**How are our assets currently configured?** Before any new policies are implemented, it's crucial to understand the existing configuration state of all assets. This question leads to a comprehensive audit of current configurations against best practices and security standards. Knowing the baseline configuration helps identify deviations that may pose security risks.

CHAPTER 4   SECURE CONFIGURATION OF ENTERPRISE ASSETS AND SOFTWARE

**What configuration standards are we following?** This question ensures that the organization aligns its configuration practices with industry standards, such as those from NIST, CIS, or specific regulatory compliance requirements. It highlights the importance of maintaining consistent, standardized security practices that are recognized and respected industry-wide.

**Who can configure our assets and software, and how is this access controlled?** Controlling who can configure assets is critical for maintaining security integrity. This question addresses the need for strict access controls and permissions monitoring to prevent unauthorized changes that could expose the organization to risk. It also involves establishing protocols for granting, reviewing, and revoking access as necessary.

**What is our process for updating and patching software, and how often is it reviewed?** Regular updates and patches are vital for securing software against known vulnerabilities. This question prompts the establishment of a systematic, timely patch management process. It also ensures that the process is reviewed and updated regularly to adapt to new threats and changes in the software environment.

**How do we monitor configuration changes and ensure they comply with our security policies?** Continuous monitoring of configuration changes is necessary to ensure compliance with security policies. This question leads to implementing auditing and logging tools to track real-time changes and alert security teams to unauthorized modifications.

**What measures are in place to prevent configuration drift?** Configuration drift can occur when settings are changed inadvertently or without approval, leading to potential security gaps. This question is essential for establishing mechanisms such as configuration management tools and regular audits to ensure configurations remain secure over time.

**How do we handle the security configurations of remote and mobile devices?** Securing mobile and remote devices has become increasingly important with the rise of remote work. This question addresses the need for specific policies and technologies to manage the unique risks associated with these devices, ensuring they are securely configured to prevent data leakage and unauthorized access.

**What is our strategy for securing cloud environments?** As more organizations move to cloud-based services, securing these environments must be addressed explicitly. This question ensures that cloud configurations are included in the security strategy, tailored to the specific services and platforms used, and compliant with cloud security best practices.

**How do we ensure compliance with industry regulations through our configuration practices?** This question emphasizes aligning configuration practices with legal and regulatory requirements. It prompts establishing a compliance framework that integrates secure configurations to adhere to necessary standards.

**What training do we provide to our team on secure configuration practices?** Educating the team about secure configuration practices is crucial for maintaining security across the organization. This question ensures that all relevant personnel are trained on the importance of secure configurations, how to implement them, and how to recognize potential security violations.

**How do we evaluate the effectiveness of our configuration controls?** Regular evaluation is necessary to determine their effectiveness and identify areas for improvement. This question leads to implementing testing and assessment protocols, such as penetration testing and security audits, to validate the strength of the configurations in place.

# Recommended Training

In the realm of cybersecurity, the secure configuration of enterprise assets and software demands not only technical solutions but also a well-informed workforce. Effective training programs ensure that IT professionals and general staff understand their roles in maintaining security. This section outlines a series of recommended training sessions tailored to different organizational roles, aiming to enhance security by equipping employees with the knowledge and skills necessary to support secure operations. By providing this training, organizations can reduce risks associated with human error and increase the effectiveness of their security protocols. Each training module is designed to address specific needs, ensuring relevance and usefulness.

**Foundations of Cybersecurity for Non-IT Staff:** This training is intended for all employees outside the IT department. It should cover basic cybersecurity principles, common threats such as phishing and malware, and the importance of secure password practices. The outcome will be a heightened awareness of cybersecurity across the organization, reducing the risk of data breaches initiated through human error. This foundational knowledge empowers all employees to act as a first line of defense against cyber threats.

**Secure Configuration Management for IT Admins:** Specifically designed for IT administrators, this training should delve into advanced concepts of secure configuration for both hardware and software. Participants will learn about the best practices for setting up and maintaining secure configurations, understanding compliance requirements, and managing access controls. The goal is to enable IT staff to effectively secure critical assets, thus minimizing the risk of unauthorized access and data breaches.

**Incident Response Training:** Essential for IT staff and selected non-IT personnel, this training focuses on acting swiftly and effectively when a security breach occurs. It includes identifying signs of a breach, the steps to take immediately following detection, and how to communicate during an incident. Training in incident response reduces the potential damage from breaches and speeds up recovery times, directly impacting the organization's resilience to attacks.

**Data Privacy Regulations Compliance:** Aimed at IT professionals and any staff involved in data management, this training covers relevant data protection regulations such as GDPR, HIPAA, or PCI DSS. Participants learn about the legal requirements for protecting data and non-compliance penalties. This training helps ensure that employees know regulatory obligations, reducing the risk of costly legal issues and enhancing data privacy practices.

**Secure Use of Cloud Services:** With the increasing reliance on cloud-based technologies, training on secure cloud practices is crucial for IT teams. This session should cover the configuration of cloud services, risk management in a cloud environment, and best practices for securely using cloud storage and applications. Such training ensures that cloud technologies are leveraged safely, protecting organizational data from exposure or loss.

**Mobile Device Security:** This training is appropriate for all employees and focuses on securing mobile devices, which are often overlooked entry points for security threats. Topics include setting strong passwords, recognizing unsafe applications, and securing data transmission. The outcome is a reduced risk of data leakage through mobile platforms, which is increasingly important as remote work becomes more prevalent.

**Phishing Defense Techniques:** Targeting all company staff, this training educates on recognizing and responding to phishing attempts. By simulating phishing scenarios, employees learn to identify suspicious links and messages, reducing the likelihood of successful phishing attacks within the organization.

**Advanced Encryption Techniques:** Intended for IT staff, particularly those in roles involving sensitive data, this training explores encryption methods and their application in protecting data. Participants learn how to implement encryption effectively, ensuring data integrity and confidentiality. The training reduces the risk of data breaches by enhancing data security in transit and at rest.

**Secure Software Development:** This training emphasizes secure coding practices for IT staff involved in software development. It covers common security vulnerabilities in code, such as injection attacks and cross-site scripting, and how to avoid them. This reduces the risk of security flaws in applications, which can serve as entry points for attackers.

**User Access Control:** Crucial for IT administrators, this training teaches effective management of user access controls and the principle of least privilege. It includes creating, modifying, and revoking access permissions to ensure that users have only the access necessary for their roles. This training helps prevent insider threats and accidental data exposure.

**Security Audit Procedures:** This training, aimed at IT staff responsible for compliance and security oversight, covers how to conduct internal security audits and reviews. It ensures that staff can proactively identify and rectify security issues, maintaining high-security compliance and readiness.

**Business Continuity and Disaster Recovery:** This training is designed for key personnel across various departments. It focuses on developing and implementing business continuity and disaster recovery plans that include provisions for maintaining IT security in the face of disruptions. This training ensures organizational resilience, allowing the business to continue operations securely even under adverse conditions.

# Actionable Recommendations

Implementing secure configurations of enterprise assets and software is critical in safeguarding an organization against cyber threats. This section provides actionable recommendations to guide IT professionals and organizational leaders in effectively applying security measures. These recommendations are designed to optimize the security configurations of all digital and physical assets, ensuring they are robust, compliant, and capable of resisting the most prevalent cyber threats. By following these structured guidelines, organizations can enhance their security posture, minimize vulnerabilities, and better manage their cyber risk in an ever-evolving digital landscape. Each recommendation focuses on practical steps and strategic considerations to help achieve a comprehensive and sustainable security framework.

**Develop a Baseline Configuration Standard:** Establishing a baseline configuration for all enterprise assets and software is essential. This standard should reflect the minimum security settings for protecting your organization's data and systems. Defining and documenting these baselines ensures consistency in deploying and maintaining secure configurations. The baseline should be reviewed and updated regularly to adapt to new threats, technologies, and business requirements.

**Automate Configuration Management:** Utilize automated tools to manage and enforce security configurations across your entire asset base. Automation reduces the risk of human error and ensures configurations are applied consistently and efficiently. Tools that detect deviations from established baselines and automatically remediate these discrepancies are particularly valuable. Automation streamlines security processes and provides a scalable solution for managing configurations as the organization grows.

**Implement Strict Access Controls:** Restrict configuration access to authorized personnel only. Implement role-based access controls (RBAC) to ensure that individuals can only make changes within their area of responsibility. This minimizes the risk of unauthorized changes that could compromise system integrity. Access to configuration settings should also be logged and monitored for auditing and forensic purposes.

**Conduct Regular Security Audits:** Regularly audit your configurations against the established baselines to identify unauthorized changes or non-compliance with internal standards and external regulations. These audits should include automated tools and manual reviews to ensure a comprehensive assessment. Audit findings should be documented and followed by prompt action to remediate any identified issues.

**Engage in Continuous Monitoring:** Monitor configurations to quickly detect and respond to unauthorized changes and potential security incidents. Monitoring should leverage real-time alerting systems to provide immediate notifications of suspicious activities. This ongoing vigilance helps maintain the integrity of your security posture and reduces the window of opportunity for attackers.

**Integrate Secure Configuration into Change Management Processes:** Secure configurations should be integral to your organization's change management protocol. Any changes to hardware, software, or settings must go through a formal process that includes security review and approval. This integration ensures that security considerations are embedded in the lifecycle of your assets from procurement to decommissioning.

**Train Staff on Secure Configuration Practices:** Provide comprehensive training to IT staff responsible for configuring and maintaining enterprise assets. This training should cover best practices, company policies, and the tools used for managing configurations. Equipping your team with the necessary knowledge and skills is crucial for maintaining the security integrity of your IT environment.

**Leverage Security Configuration Frameworks:** Adopt and customize security configuration frameworks provided by organizations such as the Center for Internet Security (CIS) or the National Institute of Standards and Technology (NIST). These frameworks offer industry-validated best practices that can be tailored to meet specific organizational needs and regulatory requirements.

**Secure Remote Access:** Ensure that remote access solutions are securely configured to prevent unauthorized access. Use multi-factor authentication (MFA), encrypted connections, and secure virtual private networks (VPNs). Policies should also be in place to control and monitor remote access activities.

**Document Configuration Policies and Procedures:** Maintain detailed documentation of all configuration policies and procedures. This documentation should be easily accessible and regularly updated to reflect the latest security practices and organizational changes. Documentation is essential not only for internal use but also for compliance and auditing purposes.

**Patch and Update Regularly:** Implement a robust patch management process to ensure all software is up-to-date with the latest security patches. This reduces the attack surface by closing vulnerabilities that cyber threats could exploit. A structured approach to patching is critical to maintaining the security of your systems.

**Review and Refine Configuration Policies:** Regularly review and refine your configuration policies to align with evolving security landscapes and business objectives. This includes reassessing risk tolerance, technological advancements, and compliance requirements. Continuously improving your configuration management practices is key to avoiding potential security challenges.

# Simplified Security Controls (SSC)

Security controls are essential for any organization seeking to protect its digital and physical assets from cyber threats. Tailoring these controls to fit the specific needs of your business environment is crucial, as it ensures that the protection mechanisms are relevant and effective against the specific risks your organization faces. There are numerous sources to draw these controls from, including the well-regarded CIS Top 18, which provides a robust framework for crafting defensive strategies. The recommendations presented in this book are based on the CIS controls, among others, offering a comprehensive guide that can be adapted to serve a wide range of security needs. Before implementing these controls, it is vital to thoroughly review their design to ensure they align with your strategic objectives and operational practices. Additionally, after deployment, it is imperative to regularly test the controls to verify their effectiveness and to make necessary adjustments. This ensures the controls continue functioning as intended, safeguarding your organization against emerging threats and changing conditions.

## CONTROL 1: ESTABLISHING AND MAINTAINING A SECURE CONFIGURATION PROCESS FOR ENTERPRISE ASSETS

**Control Objective:** Ensure the integrity and security of all enterprise assets, including end-user devices, IoT devices, and servers, through consistent, secure configuration practices.

**Implementation Steps:**

**1.1. Define Security Configuration Standards:** Develop standardized, secure configuration guidelines for all types of enterprise assets based on industry best practices and organizational requirements.

**1.2. Continuous Documentation:** Maintain up-to-date documentation of configuration standards and practices, reviewing and updating these documents annually or whenever significant changes occur in the enterprise environment.

**1.3. Compliance Audits:** Regularly audit the configurations of all enterprise assets to ensure compliance with documented standards and proactively address deviations.

**Expected Outcome:** A robust and consistently applied secure configuration process that enhances the security of enterprise assets and reduces the risk of unauthorized access or data breaches.

CHAPTER 4   SECURE CONFIGURATION OF ENTERPRISE ASSETS AND SOFTWARE

## CONTROL 2: SECURE CONFIGURATION OF NETWORK DEVICES

**Control Objective:** To protect network integrity and prevent unauthorized access by maintaining a secure configuration of all network devices.

**Implementation Steps:**

**2.1. Establish Configuration Baselines:** Define and document baseline configurations for all network devices, including routers, switches, and firewalls.

**2.2. Implement Configuration Management Tools:** Utilize automated configuration management tools to apply, monitor, and maintain secure configurations across network devices.

**2.3. Regular Review and Adjustment:** Conduct annual reviews and more frequent adjustments of network device configurations to adapt to new threats and changes in the network architecture.

**Expected Outcome:** Enhanced security of network devices through stringent configuration practices, minimizing the risk of network-based attacks and ensuring reliable network performance.

## CONTROL 3: AUTOMATIC SESSION LOCKING

**Control Objective:** Minimize the risk of unauthorized access to enterprise assets by implementing automatic session locking after defined periods of inactivity.

**Implementation Steps:**

**3.1. Define Lockout Timers:** Establish specific inactivity durations, after which automatic session locking will be triggered for different devices.

**3.2. Configure Devices:** Apply these settings across all applicable enterprise assets, including general-purpose operating systems and mobile devices.

CHAPTER 4   SECURE CONFIGURATION OF ENTERPRISE ASSETS AND SOFTWARE

**3.3. User Awareness and Training:** Educate users on the importance of logging off or securing devices when not in use and the functionality of automatic locking.

**Expected Outcome:** Reduced instances of unauthorized access due to unattended devices enhance enterprise security.

## CONTROL 4: FIREWALL MANAGEMENT ON SERVERS AND END-USER DEVICES

**Control Objective:** To safeguard enterprise assets from unauthorized access and potential threats by implementing robust firewall solutions on servers and end-user devices.

**Implementation Steps:**

**4.1. Selection and Installation of Firewalls:** Choose and install appropriate firewall solutions tailored to the specific needs of servers and end-user devices.

**4.2. Configuration of Firewall Rules:** Establish and maintain a strict set of firewall rules that default to deny all traffic except for explicitly allowed services and ports.

**4.3. Regular Updates and Rule Reviews:** Ensure firewalls are regularly updated and rules are reviewed to adapt to evolving security needs and threat landscapes.

**Expected Outcome:** Strong perimeter and internal defenses against unauthorized access and network threats, provided by effectively managed firewalls.

CHAPTER 4  SECURE CONFIGURATION OF ENTERPRISE ASSETS AND SOFTWARE

## CONTROL 5: ADDITIONAL CONTROLS FOR MANAGING ENTERPRISE ASSETS AND SOFTWARE

**Control Objective:** Enhance the security and management of enterprise assets through additional specific measures.

**Implementation Steps:**

**5.1. Manage Default Accounts:** Identify and disable or secure default accounts on all enterprise assets to prevent unauthorized use.

**5.2. Uninstall Unnecessary Services:** Review and remove unneeded services or applications from enterprise assets to reduce potential attack surfaces.

**5.3. Enforce Device Lockout and Remote Wipe:** Implement strict policies for device lockout after multiple failed authentication attempts and enable remote wipe capabilities for lost or stolen devices.

**5.4. Separate Workspaces on Mobile Devices:** Management profiles safeguard corporate information by separating enterprise and personal data on mobile devices.

**Expected Outcome:** Strengthened security of enterprise assets through comprehensive management practices, reducing the risk of data leakage, unauthorized access, and malware infections.

CHAPTER 4    SECURE CONFIGURATION OF ENTERPRISE ASSETS AND SOFTWARE

## CONTROL 6: SECURE CONFIGURATION MANAGEMENT OF ENTERPRISE ASSETS AND SOFTWARE

**Control Objective:** Ensure robust management of configurations and access protocols to maintain security integrity across all enterprise software and hardware.

**Implementation Steps:**

**6.1. Implement Version-Controlled Infrastructure:** Adopt infrastructure-as-code practices to maintain and deploy configuration changes in a controlled and versioned manner.

**6.2. Secure Access Protocols:** Ensure all access to administrative interfaces is conducted via secure network protocols such as SSH and HTTPS, avoiding insecure protocols like Telnet and HTTP.

**6.3. Regular Security Training:** Conduct ongoing security training for IT staff responsible for managing enterprise assets, emphasizing the importance of secure practices and the dangers of insecure protocols.

**6.4. Audit and Response Procedures:** Set up regular audits of asset and software configurations and establish protocols for immediate response and rectification of any identified issues.

**Expected Outcome:** Enhanced security and control over enterprise assets, reduced risk of unauthorized access, and potential security breaches due to outdated or insecure management practices.

CHAPTER 4   SECURE CONFIGURATION OF ENTERPRISE ASSETS AND SOFTWARE

## CONTROL 7: MANAGEMENT OF DEFAULT ACCOUNTS

**Control Objective:** Mitigate risks associated with default accounts on enterprise assets and software to prevent unauthorized access.

**Implementation Steps:**

**7.1. Inventory of Default Accounts:** Compile a comprehensive list of all default accounts provided with enterprise assets and software.

**7.2. Disable or Modify Default Credentials:** Actively disable or change default usernames and passwords to custom, strong credentials as part of the initial setup process.

**7.3. Regular Review of Account Usage:** Regularly review the use of all accounts, ensuring that default accounts are not re-enabled or misused.

**7.4. Enforce Account Management Policies:** Implement and enforce strict policies regarding creating, modifying, and deleting user accounts.

**Expected Outcome:** Significant reduction in the security risks posed by default accounts, ensuring that all user credentials are appropriately managed and safeguarded.

## CONTROL 8: UNINSTALLATION OR DISABLING OF UNNECESSARY SERVICES

**Control Objective:** Eliminate potential vulnerabilities by removing or turning off services that are not necessary for business operations.

**Implementation Steps:**

**8.1. Identify Redundant Services:** Conduct comprehensive assessments to identify any unnecessary services running on enterprise assets.

**8.2. Develop a Removal or Disablement Plan:** Create detailed plans and procedures for safely removing or disabling these services without impacting essential functions.

CHAPTER 4   SECURE CONFIGURATION OF ENTERPRISE ASSETS AND SOFTWARE

**8.3. Monitor for Unauthorized Services:** Implement monitoring tools to detect and alert IT staff of any unauthorized services that may be activated on systems.

**8.4. Ongoing Compliance and Auditing:** Regularly audit systems to ensure compliance with the service management policy and adapt to new business needs.

**Expected Outcome:** A cleaner, more secure operating environment with minimized exposure to vulnerabilities associated with unnecessary services.

## CONTROL 9: CONFIGURATION OF TRUSTED DNS SERVERS

**Control Objective:** Enhance network security by configuring enterprise assets to utilize trusted DNS servers that prevent DNS-based attacks and filtering.

**Implementation Steps:**

**9.1. Select Reputable DNS Providers:** Choose DNS providers known for robust security features and reliable service.

**9.2. Configure DNS Settings:** Apply settings across the enterprise to direct DNS traffic through these trusted providers.

**9.3. Implement DNS Security Extensions (DNSSEC):** Deploy DNSSEC to protect against DNS spoofing and ensure the authenticity of response data.

**9.4. Regular DNS Performance and Security Reviews:** Periodically review DNS configurations and performance to ensure optimal security and functionality.

**Expected Outcome:** Improved network security and reduced risk of DNS attacks, contributing to safer Internet navigation and data integrity.

CHAPTER 4   SECURE CONFIGURATION OF ENTERPRISE ASSETS AND SOFTWARE

## CONTROL 10: ENFORCEMENT OF AUTOMATIC DEVICE LOCKOUT

**Control Objective:** Protect enterprise data by automatically locking devices after multiple failed authentication attempts to prevent unauthorized access.

**Implementation Steps:**

**10.1. Set Failed Authentication Thresholds:** Establish clear policies on the maximum number of failed authentication attempts before a device is locked.

**10.2. Configure Lockout Mechanisms:** Implement these settings across all susceptible devices, particularly portable and mobile devices.

**10.3. User Education on Device Security:** Train users on the importance of device security and the implications of failed access attempts.

**10.4. Monitoring and Response System:** Set up monitoring systems to track failed login attempts and alert security personnel to potential breach attempts.

**Expected Outcome:** Increased device security, minimizing the risk of unauthorized access through brute force attacks or accidental credential exposure.

## CONTROL 11: REMOTE WIPE CAPABILITY

**Control Objective:** Ensure the ability to remotely wipe data from enterprise-owned devices if lost, stolen, or no longer under the control of an authorized user.

**Implementation Steps:**

**11.1. Enable Remote Wipe Features:** Activate and configure remote wipe capabilities on all enterprise mobile devices and laptops.

**11.2. Develop Remote Wipe Activation Protocols:** Establish clear protocols defining when and how remote wipes should be executed, including necessary approvals.

**11.3. Test Remote Wipe Functionality:** Regularly test the effectiveness of the remote wipe features to ensure they function as intended under various scenarios.

**11.4. User Awareness and Training:** Inform and train users on the circumstances and processes involved in remote data wiping to prepare them for potential data loss scenarios.

**Expected Outcome:** Enhanced security posture to prevent sensitive data exposure in the event of device loss or theft, maintaining data confidentiality and compliance.

## CONTROL 12: SEPARATION OF ENTERPRISE WORKSPACES ON MOBILE DEVICES

**Control Objective:** Secure and separate enterprise data from personal data on mobile devices to protect organizational information.

**Implementation Steps:**

**12.1. Implement Mobile Device Management (MDM) Solutions:** Deploy MDM solutions that support the creation of separate workspaces for enterprise applications and data.

**12.2. Configure Workspace Settings:** Define security settings for the enterprise workspace that restrict data sharing between enterprise and personal spaces.

**12.3. Regular Security Audits of Mobile Devices:** Conduct periodic security audits to maintain the separation and prevent data leakage between spaces.

**12.4. Training and Compliance:** Train employees to use segregated workspaces correctly and monitor compliance to ensure adherence to security policies.

**Expected Outcome:** Effective separation of personal and business data on mobile devices reduces the risk of unauthorized access to sensitive enterprise information and ensures compliance with data protection regulations.

# CHAPTER 5

# Account Management

Effective account management is fundamental to securing any enterprise's cyber environment. In today's digital landscape, user credentials are not just simple access tokens but critical assets that require stringent oversight and robust management practices. The ease with which internal and external threat actors can exploit valid user credentials underscores the need for meticulous account management strategies. Unlike traditional hacking, which often involves breaching complex security systems, obtaining legitimate user credentials can provide unfettered access to sensitive data and systems, making account management a linchpin in cybersecurity defense.

Unauthorized access through compromised credentials can occur in various ways, highlighting the importance of comprehensive account oversight. Weak passwords, outdated accounts, and dormant test accounts create vulnerabilities that can be easily exploited. Additionally, the reuse of passwords across different platforms and services can lead to significant security breaches if one account is compromised. Social engineering tactics, such as phishing and malware to capture credentials, further complicate the threat landscape, necessitating a multifaceted approach to account management.

## CHAPTER 5   ACCOUNT MANAGEMENT

With their elevated privileges, administrative accounts are desirable targets for attackers. These accounts can alter system settings, add new users, and access critical data, making their compromise potentially catastrophic. Therefore, managing these high-privilege accounts requires extra vigilance, including stringent password policies, regular audits, and multifactor authentication (MFA). Service accounts, often shared among multiple users and sometimes overlooked, pose significant risks if not properly managed. Identifying and securing these accounts is essential to maintaining a robust security posture.

An effective account management strategy starts with a detailed inventory of all user accounts and credentials. Just as enterprise assets and software are tracked, credentials must be meticulously inventoried, too. This ensures that every account is accounted for and that no unauthorized or orphaned accounts linger in the system. Regular audits are crucial in this process, as they help to identify and rectify discrepancies, ensuring that all accounts are tied to active and authorized users.

Password policies play a vital role in securing user credentials. Organizations must develop and enforce strong password policies that mandate complex passwords and discourage reuse across different platforms. The CIS Password Policy Guide offers comprehensive recommendations for creating and managing passwords effectively. Alongside password policies, organizations should promote password managers, which help users manage their credentials securely, reducing the risk of passwords being stored in unsecured locations like spreadsheets or text files.

Single Sign-On (SSO) solutions provide a streamlined and secure method for managing multiple user accounts. By allowing users to access multiple applications with a single set of credentials, SSO reduces the number of passwords that need to be managed and remembered, thereby decreasing the likelihood of password reuse. Additionally, SSO can enhance security by centralizing authentication processes and providing better oversight of user access. Coupled with MFA, SSO can significantly bolster an organization's defense against credential-based attacks.

If not properly managed, inactive user accounts present a significant security risk. Automatically logging out users after inactivity and deactivating dormant accounts can mitigate this risk. Organizations should implement policies that ensure inactive accounts are regularly reviewed and deactivated if they are no longer needed. This reduces the attack surface and ensures that only active, authorized users can access enterprise systems and data.

Training and awareness programs are critical components of an effective account management strategy. Users must be educated on the importance of securing their credentials, recognizing phishing attempts, and following best practices for password management. Regular training sessions and security awareness campaigns can foster a culture of security within the organization, ensuring that users are vigilant and proactive in protecting their accounts.

Finally, logging and monitoring account activities are essential for detecting and responding to potential security incidents. By maintaining detailed logs of account activities, organizations can identify suspicious behavior, such as unauthorized access attempts or changes to critical settings. This proactive monitoring enables swift responses to potential threats, minimizing the impact of any security breaches. While account logging and monitoring are covered more under CIS Control 8, their integration into a comprehensive Identity and Access Management (IAM) program must be balanced.

In summary, robust account management is the cornerstone of any effective cybersecurity strategy. Organizations can protect their critical assets from unauthorized access by implementing stringent policies for password management, auditing, and monitoring. Administrative and service accounts require special attention due to their elevated privileges and potential impact if compromised. Regular training and using tools like SSO and MFA further enhance the security of user credentials. As cyber threats evolve, maintaining a vigilant and proactive approach to account management remains crucial in safeguarding enterprise systems and data.

CHAPTER 5   ACCOUNT MANAGEMENT

# Key Concepts and Terms

Understanding key concepts and terms related to account management is essential for effectively securing user credentials and ensuring robust cybersecurity practices. This section delves into fundamental terms crucial for comprehending the intricacies of account management within an enterprise setting.

**User Credentials:** User credentials combine a username and password that allows access to enterprise systems and data. These credentials are critical assets that must be protected through strong password policies and regular monitoring. Compromised credentials can lead to unauthorized access and significant security breaches. Effective management of user credentials involves implementing multifactor authentication (MFA) and educating users on creating strong, unique passwords.

**Administrative Accounts:** Administrative accounts have elevated privileges that allow users to make significant system changes, including adding or removing users, installing software, and altering security settings. These accounts are high-value targets for attackers because they can provide broad access to enterprise assets. Securing administrative accounts involves strict access controls, regular audits, and ensuring that administrative activities are performed using separate accounts from those used for day-to-day tasks.

**Service Accounts:** Service accounts are specialized accounts used by applications or scripts to perform automated tasks. These accounts often run with elevated privileges and are shared among multiple users or systems, making them attractive targets for attackers. Proper management of service accounts includes regular audits, ensuring they are not tied to individual users, and implementing strict controls to limit their access to only necessary resources.

**Password Policies:** Password policies are rules and guidelines that dictate how passwords should be created, managed, and maintained within an organization. These policies typically require passwords to be complex, unique, and changed regularly. Effective password policies help mitigate the risk of password-related breaches by ensuring that users create strong passwords and do not reuse them across different systems.

**Password Managers:** Password managers help users securely store and manage their passwords. These tools generate complex passwords and store them in an encrypted format, reducing the risk of password reuse and the likelihood of passwords being stored insecurely. Encouraging password managers can significantly enhance the overall security of user credentials within an organization.

**Single Sign-On (SSO):** Single Sign-On (SSO) is an authentication process that allows users to access multiple applications with a single set of credentials. SSO simplifies user access management and reduces the number of passwords users need to remember, decreasing the risk of password fatigue and reuse. Implementing SSO can streamline the login process and enhance security by centralizing authentication.

**Multifactor Authentication (MFA):** Multifactor Authentication (MFA) is a security mechanism requiring users to provide two or more verification factors to access a system. This can include something they know (password), something they have (security token), or something they are (biometric verification). MFA adds an extra layer of security, making it more difficult for attackers to gain unauthorized access, even if they have obtained user credentials.

**Dormant Accounts:** Dormant accounts are user accounts that have not been used for a prolonged period. If not managed properly, these accounts can pose significant security risks, as they may be forgotten and left with unchanged default passwords. Regularly auditing and disabling dormant accounts is crucial to minimizing the attack surface and ensuring that only active, authorized users can access enterprise systems.

**Account Auditing:** Account auditing involves regularly reviewing user accounts to ensure they are still required and are being used appropriately. This process helps identify and remove unauthorized or unnecessary accounts, reducing the risk of account-based attacks. Effective account auditing includes verifying that all accounts are associated with active users and ensuring that privileged accounts are used correctly.

**Account Logging:** Account logging is recording user activities within a system. These logs can provide valuable insights into user behavior and help detect suspicious activities that may indicate a security breach. Maintaining comprehensive account activity logs is essential for promptly identifying and responding to potential security incidents.

**Social Engineering:** Social engineering is a tactic used by attackers to manipulate individuals into divulging confidential information, such as user credentials. Common social engineering techniques include phishing emails, pretexting, and baiting. Educating users about the dangers of social engineering and how to recognize and respond to these tactics is crucial for protecting user credentials and maintaining overall security.

**Credential Stuffing:** Credential stuffing is an attack method where attackers use lists of compromised usernames and passwords to gain unauthorized access to multiple accounts. This technique exploits users who reuse passwords across different services. Implementing strong password policies, using MFA, and monitoring unusual login activities are effective measures to defend against credential-stuffing attacks.

## Importance and Relevance

Account management is crucial for maintaining a secure IT environment in the modern digital landscape. Properly managing user accounts, including those with administrative privileges and service accounts, helps prevent unauthorized access and mitigates cyber threats. Mismanagement of accounts can lead to significant vulnerabilities, making it imperative for organizations to prioritize effective account management practices. The following points highlight the importance and relevance of account management in today's cybersecurity landscape.

**Prevents Unauthorized Access:** Effective account management prevents unauthorized access to enterprise systems and data. Proper procedures for creating, managing, and deactivating user accounts ensure that only authorized individuals can access sensitive information. Organizations can significantly reduce the risk of unauthorized access by enforcing strong authentication methods and regularly auditing accounts. This is particularly important for administrative and service accounts, which can have extensive access and control over IT resources. Ensuring these accounts are managed correctly helps maintain the integrity and security of the organization.

**Reduces Risk of Insider Threats:** Insider threats, intentional or accidental, pose a significant risk to organizations. Proper account management can mitigate these threats by implementing strict controls over account creation and access levels and monitoring user activities. By ensuring that employees only have access to the information and systems necessary for their roles, organizations can minimize the potential for misuse. Regular audits and monitoring can detect unusual behavior, allowing for timely intervention. This proactive approach helps protect against data breaches and other malicious activities from within the organization.

**Enhances Compliance:** Many regulatory frameworks and industry standards, such as GDPR, HIPAA, and PCI-DSS, require robust account management practices. Compliance with these regulations is essential to avoid legal penalties and maintain the trust of customers and partners. Proper account management helps organizations meet these requirements by ensuring that access to sensitive data is controlled and monitored. Regular audits and documentation of account management activities demonstrate compliance efforts. This protects the organization from regulatory fines and enhances its reputation for data security.

**Improves Incident Response:** Effective account management supports rapid and efficient incident response. In the event of a security breach, having a clear and accurate inventory of user accounts allows security teams to identify and isolate compromised accounts quickly. This minimizes potential damage and helps contain the breach. Detailed logging and monitoring of account activities provide valuable information for investigating incidents. This data is crucial for understanding the scope of the breach and implementing corrective measures. Therefore, a well-managed account system is essential for timely and effective incident response.

**Supports Least Privilege Principle:** The principle of least privilege dictates that users should only have the minimum level of access necessary to perform their job functions. Effective account management enforces this principle by carefully controlling and regularly reviewing user permissions. This reduces the risk of granting excessive access rights, which attackers can exploit. Implementing the least privilege helps limit the potential impact of compromised accounts. Organizations can better protect their sensitive data and critical systems by minimizing unnecessary access.

**Enhances Accountability:** Proper account management enhances accountability within an organization. By ensuring that each user account is tied to a specific individual, organizations can track and attribute actions to the appropriate user. This is especially important for auditing and forensic analysis. Clear accountability helps deter malicious activities, as users are aware that their actions are being monitored. In the event of an incident, having detailed records of user activities aids in identifying the responsible parties and understanding the sequence of events.

**Facilitates Employee Lifecycle Management:** Effectively managing user accounts is crucial throughout the entire employee lifecycle, from onboarding to offboarding. When new employees join, they need prompt access to the systems and data necessary for their roles. Effective account management ensures that this access is granted quickly and securely. Similarly, when employees leave the organization, their accounts must be deactivated to prevent unauthorized access. Proper management of the employee lifecycle helps maintain security and operational efficiency.

**Reduces the Risk of Credential Theft:** Account management practices such as enforcing strong passwords, implementing multifactor authentication (MFA), and regularly updating credentials are essential for protecting against credential theft. Attackers often exploit weak or reused passwords to gain unauthorized access. Organizations can strengthen their defenses by promoting complex passwords and providing tools like password managers. MFA adds a layer of security, making it more difficult for attackers to compromise accounts. Regularly updating credentials ensures that any stolen passwords become useless over time.

**Supports Single Sign-On (SSO):** Implementing Single Sign-On (SSO) solutions can streamline account management and enhance security. SSO allows users to access multiple applications with a single set of credentials, reducing the number of passwords they need to remember. This decreases the likelihood of password reuse and simplifies the user experience. SSO also centralizes authentication, making enforcing security policies and monitoring access easier. Organizations can improve security and user convenience by integrating SSO with account management practices.

**Improves Security Awareness:** Effective account management includes educating users about the importance of securing their credentials and recognizing potential threats. Regular training and awareness programs help users understand best practices for password management and how to identify phishing attempts. This proactive approach reduces the risk of compromised user accounts through social engineering attacks. By fostering a culture of security awareness, organizations can empower their employees to contribute to the overall cybersecurity effort. Educated users are a critical line of defense against cyber threats.

**Facilitates Access Management:** Managing access to various systems and applications is a complex task that requires clear policies and procedures. Effective account management simplifies this process by providing a structured approach to granting, reviewing, and revoking access. This ensures that users have the appropriate level of access based on their roles and responsibilities. Automated tools can assist in managing access requests and approvals, reducing administrative overhead. Proper access management helps maintain security while enabling users to perform their duties efficiently.

**Enhances Monitoring and Auditing:** Continuous monitoring and auditing of user accounts are essential to effective account management. Organizations can detect unusual behavior and potential security incidents by keeping detailed logs of account activities. Regular audits help ensure that access permissions are appropriate and that any anomalies are investigated. This ongoing oversight is crucial for maintaining security and compliance. Effective monitoring and auditing practices provide the visibility needed to promptly identify and address security issues.

# Risks of Not Implementing the Control

Failure to implement effective account management can expose a company to many cybersecurity risks. Mismanagement of user, administrative, and service accounts can lead to unauthorized access, data breaches, and other security issues. The absence of robust account management practices can ensure the integrity, confidentiality, and availability of an organization's assets and data is maintained. This section outlines the key risks of neglecting proper account management, emphasizing the critical need for stringent procedures and tools to safeguard user credentials and access permissions.

**Unauthorized Access:** When account management is neglected, unauthorized users can gain access to sensitive information. Without proper oversight, accounts may have excessive privileges or former employees' accounts may remain active. This lack of control can lead to unauthorized individuals accessing confidential data, compromising the entire organization's security. Preventing unauthorized access requires diligent account monitoring and regular audits to ensure that only authorized users can access critical systems and data.

**Data Breaches:** Poor account management practices can result in significant data breaches. Weak passwords, shared accounts, and unmanaged service accounts create vulnerabilities that attackers can exploit to steal sensitive information. Data breaches can lead to financial losses, legal penalties, and damage to an organization's reputation. To mitigate this risk, organizations must enforce strong password policies, monitor account activities, and secure all user credentials. Effective account management is essential to protecting against data breaches.

**Insider Threats:** Insider threats pose a significant risk to organizations when account management is inadequate. Employees or contractors with malicious intent can misuse their access privileges to steal data or disrupt operations. Even well-intentioned insiders can cause harm through negligence or error if their access is improperly controlled. Implementing strict account management practices helps minimize the risk of insider threats by ensuring that users have only the access they need and that their activities are monitored. Regular audits and access reviews are crucial in detecting and preventing insider threats.

**Regulatory Non-Compliance:** Many regulations and industry standards mandate robust account management practices to protect sensitive data. Failure to comply with these requirements can result in fines, legal action, and reputational damage. Organizations that do not manage accounts effectively may struggle to demonstrate compliance during audits. Adhering to best account management practices helps ensure compliance with GDPR, HIPAA, and PCI-DSS regulations. Compliance avoids legal repercussions and builds trust with customers and stakeholders.

**Operational Disruptions:** Inadequate account management can lead to operational disruptions, impacting productivity and business continuity. Uncontrolled account access may result in unauthorized changes to critical systems, causing system outages or data loss. Efficient account management ensures system access is properly controlled and any changes are authorized and tracked. This reduces the likelihood of disruptions and helps maintain smooth business operations. Ensuring continuity of operations is a key benefit of effective account management.

**Reputational Damage:** Data breaches and security incidents resulting from poor account management can damage an organization's reputation. Customers, partners, and stakeholders expect companies to protect their information and maintain robust security practices. A breach can erode trust and lead to business and market share loss. Maintaining stringent account management practices demonstrates a commitment to security and helps preserve an organization's reputation. Trust and reputation are critical assets that must be protected through diligent security measures.

**Increased Attack Surface:** Unmanaged or poorly managed accounts increase an organization's attack surface, providing more opportunities for attackers to exploit. Dormant accounts, shared credentials, and weak password policies create vulnerabilities that can be easily targeted. Reducing the attack surface requires regular account audits, strong authentication measures, and the removal of unnecessary accounts. Organizations can better protect their systems and data by minimizing the number of potential entry points. Effective account management is essential in reducing the overall attack surface.

**Financial Losses:** Security incidents and breaches resulting from poor account management can lead to significant financial losses. These losses may stem from fines, legal fees, remediation costs, and loss of business. The cost of recovering from a data breach, including restoring data and systems, can also be substantial. Implementing robust account management practices helps prevent security incidents and reduces the financial impact of breaches. Protecting financial resources is a key consideration for all organizations.

**Ineffective Incident Response:** Without proper account management, detecting and responding to security incidents becomes challenging. Lack of visibility into account activities and unauthorized access makes identifying and containing breaches difficult. Effective account management includes detailed logging and monitoring of user activities, enabling swift detection of suspicious behavior. Prompt incident response minimizes damage and helps organizations recover more quickly from attacks. Enhancing incident response capabilities is a crucial benefit of robust account management.

**Loss of Intellectual Property:** Intellectual property (IP) is a valuable asset that must be protected from unauthorized access and theft. Poor account management can lead to the exposure of proprietary information, giving competitors an unfair advantage. Securing accounts with access to IP is essential to preserving an organization's competitive edge. Implementing strict access controls and monitoring user activities helps protect intellectual property from internal and external threats. Safeguarding IP is a vital component of overall business security.

**Employee Productivity:** Inadequate account management can affect employee productivity, causing access to necessary systems and data delays. Poorly managed accounts may result in users having insufficient or excessive access, hindering their ability to perform their job functions effectively. Streamlined account management ensures that employees have access to perform their tasks without unnecessary delays. Efficient access management supports overall productivity and operational efficiency. A key aspect of account management is facilitating smooth and secure employee access.

**Weak Security Posture:** Failing to implement effective account management weakens an organization's security posture. A strong security framework relies on properly managed accounts to control access and protect sensitive information. Neglecting account management can lead to multiple vulnerabilities and increase the risk of security incidents. Strengthening account management practices is essential to building a resilient cybersecurity defense. A robust security posture protects against threats and ensures the safety of critical assets.

CHAPTER 5    ACCOUNT MANAGEMENT

# What Questions Should You Ask?

Cybersecurity leaders must ask critical questions to implement account management practices that guide their strategy and operations. These questions help identify potential gaps, assess current practices, and ensure appropriate controls are in place to protect enterprise assets and data. By addressing these questions, organizations can develop a comprehensive approach to managing user accounts, including administrator and service accounts, that aligns with their security goals. Each question is a foundation for evaluating and enhancing account management practices, ensuring robust protection against unauthorized access and cyber threats.

**What accounts currently exist within our system?** Understanding the full inventory of user, administrative, and service accounts. This includes identifying active and dormant accounts, ensuring no unnecessary or unauthorized accounts are in the system. Regularly auditing and updating this inventory helps maintain control and visibility over who has access to what resources. Knowing the current state of accounts allows for better management and mitigation of potential security risks associated with unused or misconfigured accounts.

**How are new accounts created and authorized?** The process for creating and authorizing new accounts must be clearly defined and strictly followed. This ensures that only authorized personnel can create accounts and that each new account is appropriately vetted and necessary. Establishing robust procedures for account creation helps prevent unauthorized access and ensures that new accounts adhere to security policies. It is essential to have a formal approval process to maintain accountability and control over account creation.

**What password policies are in place?** Strong password policies are fundamental to securing user accounts. These policies should mandate the use of complex passwords, regular password changes, and the prohibition of password reuse. Enforcing stringent password requirements helps protect against brute force attacks and credential theft. Regularly reviewing and updating password policies ensures they remain effective against evolving threats.

**How is multifactor authentication (MFA) implemented?** MFA adds a layer of security by requiring users to provide two or more verification forms. Understanding how MFA is implemented, which accounts are covered, and how users are enrolled is essential. MFA should be mandatory for high-privilege accounts and sensitive systems to reduce the risk of unauthorized access significantly. Evaluating the effectiveness and coverage of MFA helps strengthen overall account security.

**What mechanisms are in place to monitor account activities?** Monitoring account activities is critical for detecting and responding to suspicious behavior. This includes tracking login attempts, changes to account permissions, and unusual access patterns. Implementing comprehensive logging and monitoring tools allows security teams to identify potential security incidents in real-time. Regular analysis of account activity logs helps in early detection and mitigation of threats.

**How are inactive or dormant accounts managed?** Dormant accounts pose significant security risks if not properly managed. It is important to have policies for regularly reviewing and deactivating accounts no longer in use. Implementing automatic deactivation mechanisms for inactive accounts for a certain period helps reduce the attack surface. Regular audits should ensure that all active accounts are necessary and authorized.

**What is the process for handling account terminations?** When employees leave the organization, their accounts must be promptly deactivated to prevent unauthorized access. Having a clear process for account termination ensures that all access rights are revoked in a timely manner. This includes coordination with HR and IT departments to ensure that account deactivation aligns with the employee's departure. Proper handling of account terminations helps protect against potential security breaches from former employees.

CHAPTER 5    ACCOUNT MANAGEMENT

**How are privileged accounts managed and monitored?** Privileged accounts have elevated access that can cause significant damage if compromised. Therefore, strict controls and monitoring are essential for these accounts. This includes limiting the number of privileged accounts, implementing MFA, and regularly auditing their use. Ensuring privileged accounts are used only for necessary tasks helps mitigate the risk of misuse or compromise.

**What training and awareness programs are in place for users?** It is crucial to educate users about the importance of account security and best practices. Training programs should cover topics such as recognizing phishing attempts, creating strong passwords, and the importance of MFA. Regularly updating and reinforcing training helps ensure that users remain vigilant and informed about current security threats. Awareness programs contribute to a security-conscious culture within the organization.

**How are service accounts managed and secured?** Due to their high level of access, service accounts, often used by applications and scripts, require careful management. Understanding how these accounts are created, managed, and monitored is important. Service accounts should follow the same stringent security policies as user accounts, including strong passwords and regular audits. Proper management of service accounts helps prevent unauthorized access and potential misuse.

**What is the process for conducting regular account audits?** Regular audits are essential for maintaining the integrity and security of user accounts. These audits should review account permissions, ensure compliance with security policies, and identify any anomalies. Establishing a schedule for regular audits helps keep account management practices up-to-date and effective. Audits provide an opportunity to detect and address potential security issues before they can be exploited.

**How are access requests and changes documented and tracked?** Documenting and monitoring access requests and changes ensures accountability and transparency. This includes maintaining detailed records of who requested access, what was granted, and when changes were made. Having a clear trail of documentation helps in audits and investigations. Proper tracking and documentation of access changes support effective account management and security.

# Recommended Training

Implementing effective training programs for IT/cyber staff and employees is crucial to maintaining robust account management practices. These training programs should educate staff on the importance of account security, the risks associated with poor account management, and the best practices to follow. Tailored training sessions can ensure that all employees, regardless of their role, understand their responsibilities in protecting enterprise assets and data. Organizations can significantly reduce the risk of unauthorized access and other cybersecurity threats by equipping employees with the knowledge and skills to manage accounts securely.

**Security Awareness Training:** All employees should attend security awareness training to understand basic cybersecurity principles and the importance of account security. This training should cover topics such as recognizing phishing attempts, creating strong passwords, and the significance of multifactor authentication (MFA). The outcome of this training is to make employees more vigilant and capable of identifying potential security threats. By increasing awareness, the organization can reduce the risk of social engineering attacks and credential theft.

**Password Management Training:** IT/cyber staff and admins should participate in password management training to learn about creating and enforcing strong password policies. This training should include guidelines for setting complex passwords, the use of password managers, and policies for regular password updates. The goal is to ensure that all accounts are protected with strong, unique passwords, reducing the risk of brute force attacks and unauthorized access. Effective password management is a critical component of overall account security.

**Multifactor Authentication (MFA) Training:** Admins and IT/cyber staff should receive specialized training on implementing and managing MFA solutions. This training should cover the technical aspects of setting up MFA and best practices for enrolling users and handling MFA-related issues. The outcome is to enhance user account security by adding layer verification. MFA significantly reduces the risk of account compromise, even if passwords are stolen.

**Privileged Access Management Training:** IT/cyber staff and admins should be trained on managing privileged accounts with elevated access. This training should include best practices for controlling access to critical systems, monitoring privileged account activities, and using privileged access management (PAM) tools. Properly managing privileged accounts helps prevent unauthorized access to sensitive information and critical systems. Reducing the misuse of privileged accounts is essential for maintaining a secure IT environment.

**Account Lifecycle Management Training:** Admins and IT/cyber staff should be trained on creating, modifying, and deactivating user accounts. This training should emphasize the importance of timely account deactivation for departing employees and the regular review of active accounts. The outcome is a streamlined account lifecycle management process that minimizes the risk of unauthorized access through dormant or unused accounts. Efficient account management is crucial for maintaining security and compliance.

**Incident Response Training:** All employees, especially IT/cyber staff, should participate in incident response training to understand their roles in the event of a security breach. This training should cover the steps to take when a security incident is detected, how to report suspicious activities, and the procedures for containing and mitigating breaches. A well-prepared incident response team can quickly address security incidents, minimizing damage and reducing recovery time. Effective incident response is vital for protecting enterprise assets and data.

**Service Account Management Training:** IT/cyber staff should receive training on managing service accounts used by applications and scripts. This training should include best practices for securing service accounts, monitoring their usage, and regularly auditing their access rights. Proper service account management helps prevent unauthorized access and potential misuse. Ensuring that service accounts are secure is essential for maintaining the integrity of automated processes.

**Access Control Training:** All employees should be trained on the principles of access control, including the importance of the principle of least privilege. This training should teach employees how to request access appropriately and the procedures for granting and revoking access. Understanding access control helps employees recognize the importance of limiting access to only what is necessary for their job functions. Implementing access control measures reduces the risk of unauthorized access to sensitive information.

**Security Policy Training:** All employees should know the organization's security policies and procedures. This training should cover the rationale behind security policies, the specific policies in place, and the consequences of non-compliance. The outcome is ensuring all employees know and adhere to the organization's security policies. Clear understanding and compliance with security policies are critical for maintaining a secure environment.

**Audit and Compliance Training:** IT/cyber staff should participate in training focused on audit and compliance requirements related to account management. This training should include best practices for conducting regular audits, documenting account activities, and ensuring compliance with relevant regulations. The goal is to maintain accurate records and demonstrate compliance during security audits. Regular audits and compliance checks help identify and rectify security gaps.

**User Education Programs:** Regular user education programs should be conducted for all employees to keep them updated on the latest security threats and best practices. These programs should include interactive sessions, real-life case studies, and practical exercises. The outcome is a well-informed workforce that can proactively identify and respond to security threats. Continuous education is key to adapting to the evolving cybersecurity landscape.

**Social Engineering Awareness Training:** All employees should undergo training to recognize and respond to social engineering attacks. This training should cover various social engineering tactics, such as phishing, pretexting, and baiting, and provide strategies for avoiding these traps. Educating employees about social engineering helps prevent attackers from exploiting human vulnerabilities to gain unauthorized access. Awareness and vigilance are essential defenses against social engineering attacks.

# Actionable Recommendations

Implementing effective account management practices is crucial for ensuring enterprise assets and data security and integrity. Proper user, administrator, and service account management can significantly reduce the risk of unauthorized access and cyber threats. The following recommendations provide actionable steps organizations can take to enhance their account management processes. By adopting these best practices, organizations can ensure that their accounts are managed securely, efficiently, and in compliance with relevant regulations.

**Conduct Regular Account Audits:** Regularly auditing user accounts helps identify and remove inactive or unnecessary accounts. This process ensures that only authorized and active users have access to enterprise resources. Audits should include reviewing account permission usage patterns and ensuring compliance with security policies. Conducting regular audits helps maintain a clean and secure user account database. It also helps detect and address potential security issues before they can be exploited.

**Implement Strong Password Policies:** Enforce strong password policies that require complex, unique passwords for all user accounts. Password policies should mandate regular password changes and prohibit the reuse of old passwords. Educating users on the importance of creating strong passwords and using password managers can further enhance security. Strong password policies help protect against brute-force attacks and unauthorized access. Ensuring that passwords are robust and frequently updated is a fundamental security measure.

**Enable Multifactor Authentication (MFA):** Implementing MFA adds an extra layer of security by requiring users to provide additional verification beyond just a password. MFA should be mandatory for accessing critical systems and high-privilege accounts. Factors such as biometrics, security tokens, or SMS codes can significantly reduce the risk of account compromise. MFA helps protect against credential theft and phishing attacks. Enforcing MFA across the organization strengthens overall account security.

**Enforce the Principle of Least Privilege:** Limit user access to the minimum necessary to perform their job functions. Regularly review and adjust access permissions to ensure they are appropriate and up-to-date. This principle helps minimize the risk of unauthorized access and potential misuse of privileges. Implementing the least privilege reduces the attack surface and limits the potential damage from compromised accounts. Ensuring users only have necessary access enhances security.

**Automate Account Management Processes:** Utilize automated tools for managing user accounts, including provisioning, de-provisioning, and access reviews. Automation reduces the risk of human error and ensures consistency in account management practices. Automated systems can also provide real-time monitoring and alerts for suspicious account activities. Leveraging automation enhances efficiency and accuracy in managing user accounts. It also helps ensure that account management policies are consistently enforced.

CHAPTER 5  ACCOUNT MANAGEMENT

**Conduct Security Awareness Training:** Regularly train employees on security best practices, including recognizing phishing attempts, creating strong passwords, and the importance of MFA. Training should be tailored to organizational roles to address specific risks and responsibilities. Educated users are more likely to follow security policies and report suspicious activities. Continuous security awareness training helps maintain a vigilant and security-conscious workforce. A well-informed staff is a critical component of effective account management.

**Implement Robust Logging and Monitoring:** Enable detailed logging and monitoring of all account activities to detect and respond to suspicious behavior. Logs should include information on login attempts, account permissions changes, and sensitive data access. Regularly reviewing these logs helps identify potential security incidents early. Effective logging and monitoring provide valuable insights for incident response and forensic analysis. Maintaining comprehensive logs is essential for tracking and investigating account-related issues.

**Use Privileged Access Management (PAM) Solutions:** Deploy PAM solutions to manage and monitor privileged accounts with elevated access. PAM tools can enforce strict access controls, monitor usage, and provide detailed audit trails for privileged activities. Regularly reviewing and auditing privileged account usage helps prevent misuse and detect anomalies. Implementing PAM solutions enhances the security of high-risk accounts. Properly managing privileged accounts is crucial for protecting critical systems and data.

**Regularly Review and Update Security Policies:** Security policies should be regularly reviewed and updated to address emerging threats and changes in the IT environment. Policies should cover all aspects of account management, including password requirements, MFA, and access control. Ensuring that policies are clear, comprehensive, and communicated to all employees is essential. Regular policy reviews help maintain alignment with best practices and regulatory requirements. Keeping policies up-to-date ensures they remain effective in mitigating risks.

CHAPTER 5   ACCOUNT MANAGEMENT

**Ensure Proper Offboarding Procedures:** Implement and enforce procedures for promptly deactivating accounts of employees who leave the organization. This includes revoking access to all systems and recovering company-owned devices and credentials. Timely account deactivation helps prevent unauthorized access by former employees. Effective offboarding procedures are critical for maintaining security and protecting sensitive information. Properly managing employee exits reduces the risk of data breaches and other security incidents.

**Regularly Test and Evaluate Security Measures:** Conduct regular tests and evaluations of security measures, including penetration and vulnerability assessments. These tests help identify weaknesses in account management practices and provide insights for improvement. Regular evaluations ensure that security controls are adequate and up-to-date. Testing and assessments are essential for maintaining a strong security posture. Proactively identifying and addressing vulnerabilities strengthens overall account security.

**Promote a Security-First Culture:** Foster a security culture within the organization where all employees understand their role in protecting sensitive information. Encourage employees to follow security best practices and report any suspicious activities. Leadership should demonstrate a commitment to security and provide the necessary resources and support. Promoting a security-first culture helps ensure that account management practices are consistently followed. A strong security culture is fundamental to effective account management.

## Simplified Security Controls (SSC)

Security controls are essential for any organization seeking to protect its digital and physical assets from cyber threats. Tailoring these controls to fit the specific needs of your business environment is crucial, as it ensures that the protection mechanisms are relevant and effective against the specific risks your organization faces. There are numerous sources to draw these

CHAPTER 5  ACCOUNT MANAGEMENT

controls from, including the well-regarded CIS Top 18, which provides a robust framework for crafting defensive strategies. The recommendations presented in this book are based on the CIS controls, among others, offering a comprehensive guide that can be adapted to serve a wide range of security needs. Before implementing these controls, it is vital to thoroughly review their design to ensure they align with your strategic objectives and operational practices. Additionally, after deployment, it is imperative to regularly test the controls to verify their effectiveness and to make necessary adjustments. This ensures that the controls continue to function as intended, safeguarding your organization against emerging threats and changing conditions.

## CONTROL 1: ESTABLISH AND MAINTAIN AN INVENTORY OF ACCOUNTS

**Control Objective:** To maintain a comprehensive and up-to-date inventory of all user and administrator accounts within the enterprise, ensuring that each account is authorized and monitored regularly.

**Implementation Steps:**

**1.1. Inventory Creation:** Establish an initial inventory of all existing user and administrator accounts. Ensure the inventory includes critical details such as the person's name, username, start and stop dates, and department.

**1.2. Regular Validation:** Schedule recurring inventory validation, at least quarterly, to confirm that all active accounts are authorized. Use automated tools where possible to streamline this process.

**1.3. Update Procedures:** Implement procedures for regularly updating the inventory to reflect new hires, terminations, and role changes. Ensure that these updates are prompt and accurate.

**Expected Outcome:** A well-maintained inventory of accounts ensures that only authorized individuals have access to enterprise resources. This practice helps prevent unauthorized access and facilitates the timely detection and deactivation of inactive or unnecessary accounts.

CHAPTER 5    ACCOUNT MANAGEMENT

## CONTROL 2: USE UNIQUE PASSWORDS

**Control Objective:** To enhance security by ensuring all enterprise accounts use unique passwords, reducing the risk of unauthorized access due to password reuse.

**Implementation Steps:**

**2.1. Policy Development:** Develop and implement a password policy that mandates using unique passwords for all enterprise accounts. Specify the minimum password length requirements—8 characters for accounts with MFA and 14 characters for accounts without MFA.

**2.2. User Education:** Educate users on the importance of using unique passwords and provide training on creating strong, secure passwords. Promote the use of password managers to help users manage their passwords effectively.

**2.3. Enforcement Mechanisms:** Deploy technical controls to enforce the password policy, including checks for uniqueness and complexity. Regularly audit password compliance to ensure adherence to the policy.

**Expected Outcome:** Implementing a unique password policy strengthens the security of enterprise accounts by reducing the likelihood of password-related breaches. Users are less likely to fall victim to credential stuffing and other password-based attacks.

CHAPTER 5    ACCOUNT MANAGEMENT

## CONTROL 3: DISABLE DORMANT ACCOUNTS

**Control Objective:** To minimize security risks by identifying and disabling dormant accounts after inactivity, ensuring only active and necessary accounts remain enabled.

**Implementation Steps:**

**3.1. Inactivity Monitoring:** Implement monitoring tools to track account activity and identify dormant accounts that have not been used for 45 days.

**3.2. Automated Deactivation:** Configure automated processes to disable dormant accounts after the specified period of inactivity. Ensure that these processes are documented and auditable.

**3.3. Regular Reviews:** Conduct periodic reviews to ensure that dormant accounts are correctly identified and disabled. Reactivate accounts only when justified and approved through appropriate channels.

**Expected Outcome:** Disabling dormant accounts reduces the risk of unauthorized access through unused accounts. This practice helps maintain a secure and streamlined account management system.

## CONTROL 4: RESTRICT ADMINISTRATOR PRIVILEGES TO DEDICATED ADMINISTRATOR ACCOUNTS

**Control Objective:** To enhance security by restricting administrator privileges to dedicated accounts, ensuring that general computing activities are conducted from non-privileged accounts.

**Implementation Steps:**

**4.1. Account Segregation:** Establish dedicated administrator accounts for users with elevated privileges. Ensure these accounts are used solely for administrative tasks.

CHAPTER 5    ACCOUNT MANAGEMENT

**4.2. Policy Enforcement:** Develop and enforce policies that prohibit using administrator accounts for general computing activities such as Internet browsing, email, and productivity tasks.

**4.3. Regular Audits:** Conduct regular audits to ensure compliance with the policy, verifying that administrative tasks are performed only from dedicated administrator accounts.

**Expected Outcome:** Restricting administrator privileges to dedicated accounts minimizes the risk of privilege misuse and enhances overall security. This segregation of duties helps protect critical systems from potential exploitation.

## CONTROL 5: ESTABLISH AND MAINTAIN AN INVENTORY OF SERVICE ACCOUNTS

**Control Objective:** To maintain a comprehensive inventory of service accounts, ensuring that each account is authorized and its use is regularly reviewed.

**Implementation Steps:**

**5.1. Initial Inventory:** Create an inventory of all service accounts, including department ownership, review dates, and the purpose of each account.

**5.2. Regular Validation:** Perform quarterly reviews of the service account inventory to validate that all active accounts are authorized and necessary.

**5.3. Update Procedures:** Implement procedures to keep the inventory current, reflecting changes such as creating or deactivating service accounts. Ensure all changes are documented and reviewed.

**Expected Outcome:** A well-maintained inventory of service accounts ensures that these accounts are appropriately managed and monitored. Regular reviews help prevent unauthorized use and mitigate security risks associated with service accounts.

## CONTROL 6: CENTRALIZE ACCOUNT MANAGEMENT

**Control Objective:** To streamline and secure account management by centralizing it through a directory or identity service, ensuring consistent application of policies and easier oversight.

**Implementation Steps:**

**6.1. Directory Service Implementation:** Deploy a centralized directory or identity service to manage all user, administrator, and service accounts.

**6.2. Integration and Synchronization:** Integrate all enterprise systems with the centralized directory to ensure consistent and synchronized account management across the organization.

**6.3. Policy Application:** Use the centralized directory to enforce account management policies, including password policies, MFA, and access controls. Regularly audit the directory service for compliance and effectiveness.

**Expected Outcome:** Centralizing account management improves security by ensuring consistent application of policies and easier oversight of all accounts. This approach enhances efficiency and reduces the risk of mismanagement.

# CHAPTER 6

# Access Control Management

Access control management is a foundational element in cybersecurity, serving as the gatekeeper to an organization's critical assets and data. The primary goal is to ensure that individuals within an organization have access only to the information and systems necessary for their roles and nothing more. This principle of least privilege minimizes the potential for unauthorized access and reduces the risk of insider threats. Effective access control management protects sensitive data and enhances overall organizational security by establishing a structured framework for granting, managing, and revoking access rights.

Role-based access control (RBAC) is a key strategy employed in access control management. It involves defining access rights based on roles within the organization, aligning access permissions with the responsibilities and duties associated with each role. This approach simplifies assigning access rights and ensures consistency across the organization. By clearly delineating roles and related access levels, RBAC helps prevent the accidental granting of excessive privileges, which can lead to security vulnerabilities.

Implementing multi-factor authentication (MFA) is another critical aspect of access control management. MFA requires users to provide two or more verification factors to access a system, significantly enhancing security by making it more difficult for unauthorized users to breach accounts. MFA is essential for privileged or administrative accounts, as these accounts have elevated access rights that can cause substantial damage if compromised. Modern MFA solutions often leverage smartphone applications, which generate time-sensitive codes, adding an extra layer of security beyond traditional passwords.

Privileged Access Management (PAM) tools are crucial in safeguarding administrative accounts. PAM solutions enforce strict controls over high-privilege accounts, often requiring one-time passwords and limiting access to specific tasks or time frames. This reduces the risk of misuse or exploitation of administrative privileges. Additionally, PAM tools often include monitoring and auditing capabilities, allowing security teams to track the use of privileged accounts and detect any suspicious activity promptly.

Provisioning and de-provisioning access is a critical component of access control management. When new employees join an organization, their access rights must be carefully assigned based on their role. Equally important is the prompt revocation of access when an employee leaves or changes roles within the organization. Automated systems can streamline this process, ensuring access rights are consistently and accurately managed, reducing the risk of lingering access that could be exploited.

Centralizing access control through a directory service or single sign-on (SSO) provider can greatly enhance security and manageability. A centralized system provides a unified framework for managing user credentials and access rights, simplifying the administration of access controls across the organization. This centralization also enables more efficient auditing and monitoring of access activities, helping to detect and respond to potential security incidents more quickly.

Maintaining an inventory of authentication and authorization systems is essential for effective access control management. Organizations must keep track of all systems that manage access to their assets, whether hosted onsite or by a third-party provider. Regularly reviewing and updating this inventory ensures that the organization comprehensively understands its access control landscape and can identify and address any gaps or vulnerabilities.

Periodic access control reviews are crucial for validating that all access privileges are appropriate and authorized. These reviews should be conducted annually if not more frequently, to ensure that access rights remain aligned with current roles and responsibilities. Organizations can identify and rectify discrepancies by systematically auditing access permissions, reinforcing their security posture.

The concept of least privilege should be a guiding principle in access control management. Organizations can limit the potential damage from compromised accounts by ensuring that users have only the minimum level of access necessary to perform their duties. This approach requires a thorough understanding of each role's requirements and a diligent effort to tailor access permissions accordingly.

Another important aspect of access control management is addressing the unique challenges of managing service accounts. Service accounts, often used for automated processes and applications, can pose significant security risks if not properly managed. Organizations must inventory these accounts, ensure credentials are securely stored and managed, and monitor their use to detect anomalous activity.

Effective access control management also involves educating employees about the importance of access controls and their role in maintaining organizational security. Training programs should emphasize the need to safeguard credentials, recognize phishing attempts, and understand the potential consequences of access control breaches. By fostering a culture of security awareness, organizations can enhance their defense against cyber threats.

In conclusion, access control management is critical to any robust cybersecurity strategy. By implementing structured and consistent processes for granting, managing, and revoking access rights, leveraging advanced tools like MFA and PAM, and fostering a culture of security awareness, organizations can significantly enhance their protection against unauthorized access and cyber threats. Regular audits and reviews ensure that access controls remain effective and aligned with organizational needs, providing a resilient defense in the ever-evolving landscape of cybersecurity.

# Key Concepts and Terms

Understanding access control management requires familiarity with several key concepts and terms that form the backbone of this critical cybersecurity practice. These concepts are foundational to designing and implementing effective access control mechanisms that protect an organization's assets and data. A clear grasp of these terms enables IT professionals to create robust access control policies, ensuring users have appropriate access while minimizing security risks. The following sections provide detailed explanations of twelve essential terms related to access control management. Mastery of these concepts is crucial for maintaining a secure and efficient cybersecurity posture.

**Role-Based Access Control (RBAC):** This approach assigns access rights based on the roles within an organization. A set of responsibilities defines each role, and access permissions are tailored to these duties. RBAC simplifies user permissions management by categorizing access based on job functions, reducing the complexity and potential for errors that arise from manually assigning permissions to individuals.

**Least Privilege:** The principle of least privilege ensures that users have only the minimum level of access necessary to perform their job functions. This reduces the risk of accidental or intentional misuse of privileges. By limiting access rights, organizations can minimize the potential damage from compromised accounts or insider threats, enhancing overall security.

**Multi-Factor Authentication (MFA):** MFA adds an extra layer of security by requiring users to provide multiple verification forms before accessing a system. These factors typically include something the user knows (a password), something the user has (a smartphone or hardware token), and something the user is (biometric verification). Implementing MFA is crucial for protecting sensitive and administrative accounts.

**Privileged Access Management (PAM):** PAM solutions are designed to control and monitor access to high-privilege accounts. These tools enforce stringent access controls, often requiring one-time passwords and limiting access to specific tasks or periods. PAM systems also provide auditing and reporting capabilities, enabling organizations to track the use of privileged accounts and detect suspicious activities.

**Access Provisioning:** This process involves granting access rights to users based on their roles and responsibilities within the organization. Effective access provisioning ensures new employees receive the necessary permissions to perform their duties without unnecessary delays. Automated provisioning systems can streamline this process, reducing administrative overhead and ensuring consistency.

**Access De-provisioning:** De-provisioning revokes access rights when an employee leaves or changes roles. Prompt and thorough de-provisioning is critical to prevent former employees from retaining access to sensitive information. Automated de-provisioning systems help ensure access rights are revoked consistently and quickly, reducing the risk of unauthorized access.

**Single Sign-On (SSO):** SSO allows users to access multiple applications and systems with a single login credentials. This simplifies the user experience and reduces the number of passwords users need to remember. Centralizing authentication through an SSO provider enhances security by providing a unified access control mechanism and making enforcing consistent security policies across all systems easier.

**Authentication:** Authentication is verifying the identity of a user attempting to access a system. It typically involves validating a username and password but includes other factors such as biometric data or tokens. Robust authentication mechanisms ensure only authorized users can access sensitive information and systems.

**Authorization:** Once a user's identity is authenticated, authorization determines what resources and actions the user is permitted to access. This step involves checking the user's permissions against the requested resource or action. Effective authorization mechanisms ensure that users can only perform actions that are within their role's scope of responsibilities.

**Audit Trails:** Audit trails are records of user activities within a system, including login attempts, accessed resources, and performed actions. Maintaining comprehensive audit trails is crucial for monitoring user behavior, detecting potential security incidents, and supporting forensic investigations. Audit trails provide visibility into how access controls are being used and help ensure accountability.

**Separation of Duties (SoD):** SoD is a security principle that divides tasks and privileges among multiple individuals to reduce the risk of fraud or error. Organizations can prevent conflicts of interest and reduce the likelihood of malicious activities by ensuring that no single individual controls all aspects of a critical process. SoD is particularly important in financial and administrative processes.

**Service Accounts:** These are special accounts used by applications or automated processes rather than by human users. Service accounts often require elevated privileges to perform their functions, making them a potential security risk if improperly managed. Organizations must ensure that service account credentials are securely stored and regularly monitored to prevent misuse.

# Importance and Relevance

Access control management is a cornerstone of modern cybersecurity practices. Ensuring that users, administrators, and service accounts have appropriate access to enterprise assets is critical in protecting sensitive data and maintaining the integrity of systems. With the increasing complexity of enterprise environments and the ever-evolving threat landscape, robust access control measures are essential. Effective access control mitigates risks associated with unauthorized access and helps organizations comply with regulatory requirements and industry standards. This section explores the key reasons why access control management is crucial for cybersecurity today.

**Principle of Least Privilege:** The principle of least privilege ensures that users only have the access necessary to perform their roles. This minimizes the potential damage that compromised accounts can cause. By restricting access, organizations can limit the exposure of sensitive data and critical systems. Implementing the least privilege reduces the attack surface, making it more difficult for attackers to gain unauthorized access. This approach also helps monitor and manage user activities more effectively.

**Multi-Factor Authentication:** Multi-factor authentication (MFA) is a vital component of access control management, providing an additional layer of security. MFA requires users to present multiple verification forms before gaining access, making it significantly harder for attackers to compromise accounts. The use of MFA is especially important for accounts with elevated privileges or those that access sensitive information. This added security measure helps protect against phishing attacks, credential theft, and other common cyber threats. Organizations that enforce MFA are better positioned to safeguard their assets.

**Role-Based Access Control:** Role-based access control (RBAC) simplifies user permissions management by assigning access rights based on roles within the organization. This approach ensures that access is granted in a consistent and controlled manner. RBAC helps prevent unauthorized access by clearly defining what each role can and cannot do. It also facilitates easier audits and compliance checks, as roles and permissions are systematically documented. Implementing RBAC can improve overall security posture and operational efficiency.

**Centralized Access Control:** Centralizing access control through a directory service or single sign-on (SSO) provider streamlines the management of user identities and permissions. This centralization makes it easier to enforce security policies uniformly across the enterprise. It also enhances visibility into user activities, detecting and responding to suspicious behavior. Centralized access control can reduce administrative overhead and improve the user experience by simplifying login processes. Organizations can better protect their assets with a unified approach to access management.

**Regular Review and Updating of Permissions:** Regular review and updating of access permissions are crucial for maintaining security over time. As employees change roles or leave the organization, their access must be adjusted to prevent lingering access. Periodic reviews help identify and remediate excessive or outdated permissions, reducing the risk of insider threats. This practice ensures that access controls remain aligned with the organization's current state and its security requirements. Continuous monitoring and updating of access permissions are essential for effective cybersecurity.

**Privileged Access Management Tools:** Privileged Access Management (PAM) tools provide additional security for accounts with elevated privileges. These tools help manage and monitor the use of privileged accounts, ensuring that only authorized actions are performed. PAM solutions often include features like session recording, password vaulting, and automated workflows for granting and revoking access. By controlling and auditing privileged access, organizations can better protect critical systems and data from abuse. Implementing PAM is a key strategy in defending against advanced cyber threats.

**Temporary Access Permissions:** Using temporary or time-bound access permissions helps minimize the risk of granting elevated privileges. This approach ensures that users only have the access they need for a specific period, reducing the potential for misuse. Temporary access can be particularly useful for contractors, temporary employees, or projects requiring elevated permissions. By limiting the duration of access, organizations can better control and monitor user activities. This practice adds an extra layer of security to the access management process.

**Comprehensive De-Provisioning Processes:** Comprehensive de-provisioning processes are essential for removing access when users leave the organization or change roles. This ensures that former employees or contractors can no longer access enterprise assets, reducing the risk of unauthorized access. Effective de-provisioning involves disabling accounts and revoking permissions promptly. It is important to maintain audit trails for accountability and compliance purposes. Ensuring access is revoked correctly is critical in maintaining a secure environment.

**Monitoring and Auditing User Activities:** Monitoring and auditing user activities are key components of access control management. By tracking how and when users access systems, organizations can detect and respond to suspicious behavior. Auditing helps ensure compliance with security policies and regulatory requirements. It also provides valuable insights into potential vulnerabilities and areas for improvement. Regular monitoring and auditing are essential for maintaining the integrity and security of enterprise assets.

**Access Control Policies:** Access control policies help establish clear guidelines for granting, managing, and revoking access permissions. These policies ensure consistency in how access is managed across the organization. Well-defined policies help prevent ad hoc or arbitrary permission granting, which can lead to security gaps. They also provide a framework for training employees on security best practices. Implementing robust access control policies is fundamental to an effective cybersecurity strategy.

**Protecting Sensitive Data:** Protecting sensitive data from unauthorized access is a primary objective of access control management. Ensuring only authorized users can access sensitive information helps prevent data breaches and leaks. Access control measures like encryption, tokenization, and fine-grained permissions play a crucial role in data protection.

Organizations must safeguard sensitive data to maintain trust and comply with data protection regulations. Effective access control is essential for protecting the confidentiality and integrity of sensitive information.

**Addressing Cloud and Remote Work Environments:** The increasing use of cloud services and remote work environments necessitates robust access control measures. As more enterprise assets move to the cloud and employees access systems remotely, the risk of unauthorized access increases. Implementing access control solutions that support cloud environments and remote access is critical. These solutions must provide secure authentication, authorization, and monitoring capabilities. Ensuring secure access in a distributed environment is a crucial challenge for modern cybersecurity.

# Risks of Not Implementing the Control

Failing to implement robust access control management can expose an organization to numerous cybersecurity risks. These risks can compromise sensitive data, disrupt operations, and damage the organization's reputation. Without proper access controls, unauthorized users may gain access to critical systems and data, leading to potential data breaches and other security incidents. Additionally, improper management of user privileges can result in insider threats and compliance issues. Understanding these risks is crucial for organizations to prioritize and implement effective access control measures.

**Risk of Unauthorized Access:** Unauthorized access is significant when access controls are not properly implemented. Without appropriate access restrictions, malicious actors can infiltrate systems and gain access to sensitive data. This can lead to data breaches, where confidential information is exposed or stolen. Unauthorized access can also result in system disruptions, as attackers may alter or destroy critical data. Protecting against unauthorized access is essential to maintaining the integrity and confidentiality of organizational data.

**Risk of Data Breaches:** Data breaches are a major consequence of inadequate access control. When user access is not managed correctly, it becomes easier for attackers to exploit vulnerabilities and access sensitive information. Data breaches can result in customer data, financial information, and intellectual property loss. These incidents often lead to severe financial penalties, legal repercussions, and a loss of trust from customers and partners. Implementing stringent access controls is critical to preventing data breaches and protecting valuable data assets.

**Risk of Insider Threats:** Insider threats pose a significant risk to organizations that do not enforce proper access control measures. Employees or contractors with excessive access privileges can intentionally or unintentionally cause harm to the organization. This can include data theft, fraud, or sabotage of critical systems. Insider threats are often more challenging to detect and mitigate, making implementing access controls that restrict privileges based on role and need essential. Regular monitoring and auditing of user activities can help identify and respond to insider threats.

**Risk of Compliance Violations:** Organizations that fail to implement adequate access control measures risk non-compliance with industry regulations and standards. Many regulatory frameworks, such as GDPR, HIPAA, and PCI DSS, mandate specific access control requirements to protect sensitive data. Non-compliance can result in hefty fines, legal actions, and reputational damage. Ensuring compliance through effective access control is essential for avoiding these consequences and maintaining a strong security posture.

**Risk of Privilege Escalation:** Privilege escalation occurs when users gain higher access levels than intended, often exploiting system vulnerabilities. Without proper access control, attackers can escalate their privileges and gain control over critical systems and data. This can lead to significant security breaches and the potential for widespread damage within the organization. Implementing strict access controls and regularly reviewing user privileges can prevent privilege escalation attacks.

**Risk of Malware Infections:** Inadequate access controls can increase the risk of malware infections within an organization. Users with excessive privileges may inadvertently download or execute malicious software, leading to system compromises. Malware infections can cause data loss, system downtime, and financial losses. Restricting user access to only necessary functions and implementing strong authentication measures can help mitigate the risk of malware infections.

**Risk of Operational Disruptions:** Operational disruptions are common when access control measures are not adequately enforced. Unauthorized access or privilege misuse can result in system outages, data corruption, and loss of productivity. These disruptions can have a cascading effect on business operations, leading to financial losses and customer dissatisfaction. Effective access control helps ensure that only authorized users can make critical changes, reducing the likelihood of operational disruptions.

**Risk of Data Integrity Compromise:** Data integrity is at risk when access controls are not adequately managed. Unauthorized users or insiders with excessive privileges can alter or delete critical data, compromising its accuracy and reliability. This can have severe consequences for decision-making processes and business operations. Implementing strict access controls and regularly auditing user activities are essential for maintaining data integrity.

**Risk of Financial Losses:** Financial losses are a significant risk associated with inadequate access control management. Data breaches, operational disruptions, and compliance violations can all result in substantial financial penalties and costs. Additionally, the loss of sensitive information can have long-term financial impacts, such as loss of business and competitive advantage. Investing in robust access control measures is crucial to mitigating these financial risks.

**Risk of Reputational Damage:** Reputational damage is a critical consequence of failing to implement effective access control. Data breaches and security incidents can erode customer trust and tarnish the organization's reputation. Adverse publicity and loss of confidence can have lasting effects on the business, including loss of customers and market share. Protecting against reputational damage requires strong access control measures to prevent security incidents and demonstrate a commitment to cybersecurity.

**Risk of Unmonitored Access:** Unmonitored access poses a significant threat to organizations that do not implement proper access controls. Without monitoring, it becomes difficult to detect unauthorized activities and potential security breaches. Unmonitored access can lead to prolonged threat exposure and increased damage before detection. Implementing access controls with comprehensive monitoring and auditing capabilities is essential for early detection and response to security incidents.

**Risk of Resource Misuse:** Resource misuse is a risk when access controls are not enforced, allowing users to exploit system resources for unauthorized purposes. This can include using company assets for personal gain or engaging in activities that violate organizational policies. Resource misuse can result in financial losses, legal issues, and reduced system performance. Implementing strict access controls and monitoring user activities can help prevent resource misuse and protect organizational assets.

# What Questions Should You Ask?

Implementing effective access control management is critical for safeguarding enterprise assets and ensuring compliance with security standards. Cybersecurity leaders must ask the right questions to identify gaps and develop robust processes for managing access credentials and privileges. These questions should cover various aspects of access control, including user authentication, privilege management, and monitoring. By addressing these questions, organizations can create a comprehensive strategy for access control that protects sensitive data and supports overall cybersecurity objectives. Here are key questions to guide cybersecurity leaders in effectively implementing access control management.

**What are the current processes for granting and revoking access?** Understanding the existing methods for granting and revoking access is fundamental. This question helps identify whether the current procedures are manual, automated, or a mix of both. It also reveals any gaps or inefficiencies in the system, such as delays in revoking access for terminated employees. Ensuring access is granted and revoked promptly is crucial to maintaining security and preventing unauthorized access. Cybersecurity leaders must evaluate these processes to determine if improvements or automation can enhance security and efficiency.

**How is role-based access control (RBAC) implemented?** RBAC is a key method for managing user permissions. This question helps assess how well RBAC is implemented and whether roles are clearly defined and regularly updated. Proper implementation of RBAC ensures that users have the necessary access to their roles without excessive permissions. Evaluating RBAC can identify areas where roles need refinement or users may have unnecessary access. Effective RBAC reduces the risk of insider threats and ensures compliance with the principle of least privilege.

**Are multi-factor authentication (MFA) mechanisms in place?** Multi-factor authentication adds an extra layer of security by requiring multiple verification forms. This question is crucial for understanding how MFA is implemented across the organization. Assessing the use of MFA for both standard and privileged accounts helps identify vulnerabilities where additional security measures may be needed. MFA significantly reduces the risk of unauthorized access due to compromised credentials. Ensuring comprehensive MFA implementation is vital for protecting sensitive systems and data.

**How are privileged accounts managed and monitored?** Privileged accounts have elevated access that can pose significant risks if mismanaged. This question focuses on the management and monitoring of these high-risk accounts. Effective privileged access management (PAM) includes controls such as session recording, password vaulting, and periodic audits. Understanding how privileged accounts are handled helps identify weaknesses that malicious insiders or external attackers could exploit. Proper management and monitoring of privileged accounts are essential for preventing misuse and ensuring accountability.

**What tools and technologies are used for access control?** The tools and technologies used for access control play a crucial role in the effectiveness of security measures. This question aims to identify the software and systems in place, such as directory services, single sign-on (SSO) solutions, and PAM tools. Evaluating the current technology stack helps determine if gaps or outdated systems need upgrading. Modern tools can offer advanced features like automated provisioning, real-time monitoring, and enhanced security protocols. Investing in the right technologies is key to maintaining robust access control.

**How frequently are access rights reviewed and updated?** Regular access rights reviews are necessary to ensure they remain appropriate over time. This question addresses the frequency and thoroughness of these reviews. Periodic audits help identify users with excessive privileges, outdated roles, or accounts that should be deactivated. Keeping access rights up-to-date is critical for minimizing security risks and maintaining compliance with regulatory requirements. Establishing a schedule for regular reviews can help ensure that access rights consistently align with current needs.

**What procedures are in place for emergency access?** Emergency access procedures allow authorized users to gain necessary access during critical situations. This question examines whether such procedures are well-defined and secure. Emergency access should be granted in a controlled manner, with proper logging and oversight to prevent misuse. Understanding these procedures helps ensure the organization can respond effectively to emergencies without compromising security. Well-designed emergency access protocols are essential for maintaining operations during unexpected events.

CHAPTER 6   ACCESS CONTROL MANAGEMENT

**How is access control integrated with other security measures?** Integration of access control with other security measures enhances overall protection. This question explores how access control links identity management, network security, and data protection strategies. Effective integration ensures access control works seamlessly with other security components to provide comprehensive coverage. Assessing this integration helps identify gaps where access control may need to fully align with broader security policies. Coordinated security measures provide a stronger defense against complex threats.

**How is user access to external applications managed?** User access to external applications, such as cloud services, requires careful management to ensure security. This question focuses on the processes for granting and monitoring access to third-party applications. Ensuring that external access is secure involves implementing measures like MFA and SSO for cloud services. Understanding how external access is managed helps identify data-sharing and remote work risks. Proper controls for external applications are essential for protecting sensitive information outside the corporate network.

**Are there policies for monitoring and logging access activities?** Monitoring and logging access activities are crucial for detecting and responding to security incidents. This question examines whether clear policies and tools are in place for tracking user actions—comprehensive logging records access attempts, changes, and other critical events, aiding in forensic analysis. Regular monitoring helps detect suspicious activities in real time, enabling prompt response to potential threats. Implementing robust logging and monitoring policies is key to maintaining security and accountability.

**How are temporary access permissions handled?** Temporary access permissions are often needed for contractors, temporary staff, or specific projects. This question assesses the processes for granting and revoking temporary access. Ensuring that temporary permissions are controlled and time-bound reduces the risk of lingering access after the need has passed.

Clear policies for temporary access help prevent unauthorized access and ensure that permissions are promptly revoked when no longer required. Managing temporary access effectively is vital for maintaining a secure environment.

**What training is provided to users about access control policies?**
User awareness and training are critical for effectively implementing access control policies. This question examines the training programs that educate users about security practices and their responsibilities. Well-informed users are more likely to follow best practices and report suspicious activities. Regular training helps reinforce the importance of access control and ensures that users understand the policies. Ongoing education is essential for fostering a security-conscious culture within the organization.

# Recommended Training

Ensuring all employees understand the importance of access control within an organization is paramount to maintaining security integrity. Training should be comprehensive and tailored to different roles within the company, from IT staff to everyday users, to help them recognize their part in protecting the company's assets. Effective training equips employees with the necessary knowledge to handle daily access control tasks and heightens their awareness of potential security threats. This proactive approach to education helps mitigate risks associated with improper access management and reinforces the company's overall security posture.

**Comprehensive Security Awareness Training**
Regardless of their role, every employee should participate in a comprehensive security awareness program. This training should cover the basics of corporate security policies, the importance of safeguarding

sensitive information, and the specific protocols for accessing company resources. The outcome should be that employees understand their role in maintaining security and recognize potential threats. By raising awareness, this training significantly reduces the risk of security breaches resulting from human error.

### Role-Based Access Control Training for IT and Cybersecurity Teams

IT and cybersecurity teams require specialized training in role-based access control systems. This training should delve into the technical aspects of setting up and managing access permissions according to organizational roles. Participants will learn how to implement least privilege principles effectively and ensure access rights comply with current security policies. The outcome is a more secure environment where access is strictly managed and aligned with the business's specific needs, thus reducing the likelihood of unauthorized access.

### MFA Implementation Workshops

Multi-factor authentication (MFA) is crucial for protecting sensitive systems and data. MFA implementation workshops should be mandatory for IT administrators and security professionals. These sessions should include hands-on activities for setting up MFA and integrating it with existing systems and applications. The training will ensure that these critical staff members are proficient in deploying MFA, enhancing the security layers, and protecting sensitive assets.

### Privileged Access Management (PAM) Training

Specifically designed for system administrators and security personnel, PAM training focuses on the tools and practices needed to manage and monitor privileged accounts. Attendees will learn about the risks associated with privileged accounts and the best security practices, including using jump boxes and session monitoring. This training is crucial for preventing unauthorized access and potential insider threats.

### Customized Training for Non-IT Staff on Specific Access Protocols

Non-IT staff often interact with systems that require specific access protocols. Customized training for these employees should focus on the systems they use and the correct procedures for securely accessing them. This training should include practical guidelines on who to contact for access issues, how to handle access credentials safely, and the importance of reporting suspicious activities. Well-informed employees are less likely to compromise security protocols inadvertently.

### Incident Response Training for Access Control Breaches

This training is vital for IT staff and selected employees who might be involved in managing a security breach. It should simulate access control breach scenarios and guide attendees through detecting, responding to, and recovering from these incidents. The training aims to prepare participants for real-world breaches, ensuring they can act swiftly and effectively to minimize damages and restore security.

### Annual Refresher Courses on Access Control Changes

Annual refresher courses should be mandatory for all employees to keep them updated on access control policies and technology changes. These courses reinforce previous training and introduce new practices that may have been adopted since the last session. Keeping employees informed about updates ensures continuous compliance with best practices and maintains a high level of security awareness throughout the organization.

### Security Training for Remote Workers

Given the rise in remote work, specific training tailored to remote employees is essential. This training should address the unique risks of accessing corporate networks outside the office. Topics might include the secure use of VPNs, the importance of secure home networks, and best practices for using company devices in unsecured environments. This training helps mitigate the risks associated with remote access points and ensures remote workers are not vulnerable to attacks.

CHAPTER 6   ACCESS CONTROL MANAGEMENT

# Actionable Recommendations

Effective access control management is vital for safeguarding an organization's digital assets. This involves a strategic approach where best practices and proven methods guide access credentials' creation, assignment, management, and revocation. These recommendations aim to provide organizations with a framework for enhancing their security posture through robust access control strategies. By adopting these guidelines, organizations can better protect against unauthorized access and ensure that privileges are accurately aligned with users' roles and responsibilities. Such an approach secures data and streamlines operations, making managing and auditing access rights easier.

**Develop Comprehensive Access Policies:** Organizations should develop comprehensive access control policies defining access granted, reviewed, and revoked access. These policies must include criteria for assigning user roles and the types of access permitted for each role. Establishing strong policies helps set the foundation for secure access management and ensures that every action is governed by clearly stated rules, reducing the scope for errors and inconsistencies. Furthermore, these policies should be regularly updated to reflect new security challenges and changes in business operations. Effective communication of these policies ensures that all stakeholders know their responsibilities and the procedures they must follow.

**Implement Role-Based Access Control (RBAC):** Role-based access control should ensure that employees only have access to the resources necessary for their job functions. This minimizes the risk of accidental or malicious data breaches by limiting access to sensitive information on a need-to-know basis. Regular audits should be conducted to ensure that the roles are aligned with current organizational needs and that the RBAC system is functioning as intended. Implementing RBAC effectively reduces administrative overhead and enhances compliance with regulatory requirements. Moreover, it simplifies user permissions management, making it easier to adjust them as needed.

**Enforce Multi-Factor Authentication (MFA):** Multi-factor authentication must be enforced for all users, particularly for accessing critical systems and data. MFA adds a layer of security by requiring users to provide two or more verification factors to gain access, significantly reducing the likelihood of unauthorized access due to compromised credentials. This practice should be standardized across the organization to maintain consistency in security protocols. Additionally, training sessions should be held to ensure that all employees understand how to use MFA tools effectively. Enforcing MFA can greatly diminish the impact of phishing attacks and credential theft.

**Regular Access Reviews:** Periodic access rights reviews should be conducted to ensure they remain appropriate over time. These reviews help identify discrepancies, such as access rights that no longer align with an individual's current role or overly permissive access that has not been revoked. Scheduled reviews contribute to maintaining a secure and compliant access environment. They also provide an opportunity to reassess the effectiveness of the current access control measures and make necessary adjustments. Regular Audits are essential for catching potential security lapses before threat actors exploit them.

**Use Automated Tools for Access Assignment and Revocation:** Organizations should use automated tools for assigning and revoking access to minimize human error and increase efficiency. Automation ensures that access rights are granted based on predefined roles and are revoked or adjusted immediately upon role change or termination of employment. This reduces the risk of lingering access rights becoming potential security vulnerabilities. Automated tools also provide a clear audit trail, which is crucial for compliance and security audits. By streamlining the access management process, organizations can ensure timely access rights updates, enhancing overall security.

**Provide Training on Access Control Procedures:** Training is crucial for ensuring that all employees understand their roles and responsibilities related to access control. Regular training sessions should be conducted to inform staff about access control policies, the importance of security practices such as MFA, and the consequences of non-compliance. Training should be tailored to different organizational roles to address security needs and concerns. This educational approach ensures that all employees can handle their access rights responsibly. Moreover, well-informed employees are more likely to comply with security protocols, reducing the risk of accidental breaches.

# Simplified Security Controls (SSC)

Security controls are essential for any organization seeking to protect its digital and physical assets from cyber threats. Tailoring these controls to fit the specific needs of your business environment is crucial, as it ensures that the protection mechanisms are relevant and effective against the specific risks your organization faces. There are numerous sources to draw these controls from, including the well-regarded CIS Top 18, which provides a robust framework for crafting defensive strategies. The recommendations presented in this book are based on the CIS controls, among others, offering a comprehensive guide that can be adapted to serve a wide range of security needs. Before implementing these controls, it is vital to thoroughly review their design to ensure they align with your strategic objectives and operational practices. Additionally, after deployment, it is imperative to regularly test the controls to verify their effectiveness and to make necessary adjustments. This ensures that the controls continue to function as intended, safeguarding your organization against emerging threats and changing conditions.

CHAPTER 6   ACCESS CONTROL MANAGEMENT

## CONTROL 1: ESTABLISH AN ACCESS GRANTING PROCESS

**Control Objective:** To create a standardized, possibly automated, process for granting access to enterprise assets in response to new hires, rights grants, or role changes within the organization.

**Implementation Steps:**

**1.1. Define Access Levels:** Clearly define different organizational access levels based on roles and responsibilities. This ensures that access is appropriately aligned with job functions.

**1.2. Automate Provisioning:** Implement an automated system for provisioning access. This system should integrate with human resources and IT operations to streamline the process from onboarding to role changes.

**1.3. Review and Approval:** Establish a protocol for review and approval of access requests. This step involves the direct supervisor and IT security to validate the necessity of access before it is granted.

**Expected Outcome:** Establishing a systematic access-granting process ensures that employees have appropriate access rights when joining or changing roles. This minimizes security risks associated with overprivileged accounts and enhances operational efficiency.

## CONTROL 2: ESTABLISH AN ACCESS REVOKING PROCESS

**Control Objective:** To implement a reliable and possibly automated process for revoking access rights, particularly focusing on accounts terminated or changed due to role adjustments.

**Implementation Steps:**

**2.1. Immediate Deactivation:** Ensure immediate deactivation of access rights upon employee termination or role change to prevent unauthorized access.

177

CHAPTER 6   ACCESS CONTROL MANAGEMENT

**2.2. Automate De-provisioning:** Automate de-provisioning using automated tools to revoke access, reducing dependency on manual processes and decreasing the likelihood of errors or delays.

**2.3. Audit and Compliance:** Regularly audit access rights and compliance to ensure that de-provisioning policies are strictly followed and documented for audit trails.

**Expected Outcome:** The process ensures access rights are promptly and effectively revoked when no longer needed, maintaining security integrity and compliance with internal and external regulations.

## CONTROL 3: ENFORCE MULTI-FACTOR AUTHENTICATION (MFA) FOR CRITICAL APPLICATIONS AND ACCESS POINTS

**Control Objective:** To enhance the security of externally exposed applications and remote network access by enforcing multi-factor authentication.

**Implementation Steps:**

**3.1. Identify Critical Systems:** Identify and categorize all externally exposed remote access systems requiring enhanced security measures.

**3.2. Implement MFA:** Deploy MFA technology across these identified systems. Choose robust authentication methods beyond basic SMS-based verification.

**3.3. Continuous Monitoring and Review:** Regularly monitor the effectiveness of MFA implementations and update the security measures as needed based on emerging threats and technological advances.

**Expected Outcome:** With MFA enforced, the organization significantly reduces the risk of unauthorized access caused by compromised credentials, strengthening the overall security posture.

CHAPTER 6   ACCESS CONTROL MANAGEMENT

## CONTROL 4: MAINTAIN A COMPREHENSIVE INVENTORY OF AUTHENTICATION SYSTEMS

**Control Objective:** To establish and maintain a detailed inventory of all authentication and authorization systems, whether onsite or hosted remotely, and review it periodically.

**Implementation Steps:**

**4.1. Document Authentication Systems:** Document all authentication systems and mechanisms, including those used for internal and cloud-based applications.

**4.2. Regular Updates:** Update the inventory annually or more frequently as changes occur, ensuring all new systems and modifications are recorded.

**4.3. Review and Assessment:** Conduct periodic assessments to ensure the inventory's accuracy and completeness and that all systems comply with current security policies.

**Expected Outcome:** Maintaining an up-to-date inventory allows the organization to manage better and secure its authentication systems, ensuring that all components are known and adequately controlled.

## CONTROL 5: CENTRALIZE AND STREAMLINE ACCESS CONTROL

**Control Objective:** To centralize access control management through directory services or SSO providers to enhance security and simplify the administration of user credentials and access rights.

**Implementation Steps:**

**5.1. Implement Centralized Management Systems:** Adopt a centralized access control system, such as SSO or directory services, to streamline access rights management across various platforms and applications.

## CHAPTER 6  ACCESS CONTROL MANAGEMENT

**5.2. Integrate Existing Systems:** Ensure integration of all existing systems with the centralized access control solution to maintain consistency and control.

**5.3. Ongoing Management and Improvement:** Regularly review and refine the access control processes to adapt to new business needs and emerging security challenges.

**Expected Outcome:** Centralizing access control not only simplifies the management of user access and reduces the complexity of the IT infrastructure but also enhances security across the organization by providing a unified view of user activities and permissions.

## CONTROL 6: DEFINE AND MAINTAIN ROLE-BASED ACCESS CONTROL (RBAC)

**Control Objective:** To define, implement, and maintain a role-based access control system that ensures users are granted access strictly based on their organizational roles and responsibilities.

**Implementation Steps:**

**6.1. Define Roles and Access Requirements:** Clearly define roles within the organization and specify the access rights necessary for each role to perform its functions.

**6.2. Implement RBAC System:** Deploy an RBAC system that enforces access controls based on the predefined roles and their access rights.

**6.3. Regular Reviews and Adjustments:** Regularly review roles and their access rights to ensure they remain appropriate as roles evolve and organizational needs change.

**Expected Outcome:** Implementing and maintaining RBAC ensures that all personnel have access only to the resources necessary for their roles, minimizing the risk of unauthorized access and enhancing overall operational security.

# CHAPTER 7

# Continuous Vulnerability Management

Continuous vulnerability management is a cornerstone for maintaining a secure organizational infrastructure in the ever-evolving cybersecurity landscape. The constant influx of new threats necessitates an ongoing, proactive approach to identifying and mitigating vulnerabilities within enterprise assets. As cyber attackers become more sophisticated, they continuously seek out weaknesses in systems to exploit, underscoring the need for defenders to stay one step ahead. Swiftly identifying and addressing vulnerabilities is critical for minimizing the window of opportunity that attackers can exploit.

Cybersecurity professionals must develop comprehensive plans encompassing continuous vulnerability assessment and tracking. This involves monitoring public and private industry sources for the latest threat and vulnerability information. It is essential to be informed about the latest security updates, patches, advisories, and threat bulletins. Regularly reviewing the enterprise environment helps identify potential vulnerabilities before attackers can exploit them. This proactive stance is a crucial element in any organization's defense strategy.

## CHAPTER 7  CONTINUOUS VULNERABILITY MANAGEMENT

The challenge for defenders is not only in detecting vulnerabilities but also in managing them efficiently. This process requires dedicated time, attention, and resources. Attackers often have access to the same information as defenders and can exploit vulnerabilities more quickly than patches can be applied. The time gap between discovering a vulnerability and its remediation can be critical. Therefore, it is imperative to prioritize vulnerabilities based on their potential impact and the likelihood of exploitation. This prioritization ensures that the most dangerous vulnerabilities are addressed first, reducing the risk to the enterprise.

Vendors must develop and deploy patches and updates when new vulnerabilities are reported. Defenders must then assess the risk of these vulnerabilities to their specific environment, perform regression testing, and install the patches. This process is not infallible, as attackers may exploit vulnerabilities not yet known to the security community, known as "zero-day" exploits. Once a vulnerability is publicly disclosed, the race patches it before it can be widely exploited. Defenders must remain vigilant, knowing that some vulnerabilities may have been known within a closed community before public disclosure.

Effective vulnerability management also involves understanding that not all vulnerabilities can be immediately remediated. In some cases, organizations must rely on other controls to mitigate the risk posed by these vulnerabilities. This layered approach to security ensures that even if one control fails, others are in place to provide protection. Enterprises must continuously assess their infrastructure, address discovered flaws, and remain aware of potential vulnerabilities.

Scaling remediation efforts across an entire enterprise presents additional challenges. Organizations must prioritize actions amidst conflicting priorities, ensuring remediation efforts do not negatively impact business operations. This balance requires careful planning and coordination, often involving cross-functional teams to address vulnerabilities without disrupting critical business processes. The ability to scale and prioritize effectively is key to maintaining robust cybersecurity defenses.

# CHAPTER 7  CONTINUOUS VULNERABILITY MANAGEMENT

The use of advanced tools and procedures is essential in vulnerability management. Numerous vulnerability scanning tools are available to evaluate the security configuration of enterprise assets. Some enterprises utilize commercial services with remotely managed scanning appliances to achieve this. Standardizing the definitions of discovered vulnerabilities using industry-recognized schemes and languages, such as Common Vulnerabilities and Exposures (CVE) and Common Vulnerability Scoring System (CVSS), helps streamline this process. These tools and standards are integral components of the Security Content Automation Protocol (SCAP), providing a structured approach to vulnerability management.

The frequency of scanning activities should be tailored to the diversity and complexity of an enterprise's assets. Different vendors have varying patch cycles, necessitating more frequent scans to promptly identify and address all vulnerabilities. Authenticated scans, which use user credentials to perform comprehensive assessments, offer deeper insights into the security posture of enterprise assets. These detailed scans can uncover vulnerabilities that unauthenticated scans might miss, providing a more accurate picture of the organization's security status.

In addition to scanning for vulnerabilities, various tools can evaluate enterprise asset security settings and configurations. These tools detect unauthorized changes and inadvertent security weaknesses introduced by administrators. Linking vulnerability scanners with problem-ticketing systems is an effective strategy for tracking and reporting progress on fixing vulnerabilities. This integration helps highlight critical vulnerabilities to senior management, ensuring they receive the attention needed for timely resolution.

Enterprises should track how long it takes to remediate vulnerabilities once they are identified or patches are issued. This data supports compliance requirements and can be reviewed in IT security steering committee meetings. These meetings, which bring together leaders from IT and business units, prioritize remediation efforts based on business impact. Regularly reviewing remediation timelines and effectiveness helps organizations refine their vulnerability management processes, making them more resilient against evolving cyber threats.

Effective vulnerability management is not a one-time effort but an ongoing continuous improvement process. Security personnel must compare the results of current scans with previous ones to identify trends and changes in the vulnerability landscape. This trend analysis helps understand how vulnerabilities are evolving and whether the organization's security posture is improving. Regular assessments and quality assurance processes ensure configuration updates and patches are implemented correctly across all relevant enterprise assets.

# Key Concepts and Terms

Understanding the critical concepts and terminology associated with continuous vulnerability management is essential for implementing effective cybersecurity strategies. This section introduces and explains key terms fundamental to grasping the principles and practices of maintaining a robust security posture in the face of evolving threats.

**Vulnerability:** A vulnerability is a weakness or flaw in software, hardware, or organizational processes that cyber attackers can exploit to gain unauthorized access, disrupt operations, or cause damage. Identifying vulnerabilities is the first step in the vulnerability management process. These weaknesses can arise from coding errors, misconfigurations, or design flaws and need to be regularly assessed and addressed to prevent exploitation.

**Zero-Day Exploit:** A zero-day exploit is an attack that targets a vulnerability unknown to the security community or the software vendor. Because the vulnerability is not publicly known or patched, it provides attackers with a significant advantage. Zero-day exploits are perilous as they can cause extensive damage before detection and remediation.

CHAPTER 7   CONTINUOUS VULNERABILITY MANAGEMENT

Organizations must adopt proactive monitoring and advanced threat detection techniques to mitigate the risks associated with zero-day exploits.

**Patch Management:** Patch management involves acquiring, testing, and applying updates to software and systems to fix vulnerabilities and improve security. This process is critical in vulnerability management as timely patching reduces the window of opportunity for attackers. Effective patch management requires coordination across different teams, prioritization based on risk, and thorough testing to ensure patches do not disrupt business operations.

**Authenticated Scans:** Authenticated scans are vulnerability assessments conducted using valid credentials to log into systems and perform a comprehensive evaluation. These scans provide deeper insights into an organization's security posture by examining configurations, installed software, and potential vulnerabilities that unauthenticated scans might miss. Authenticated scans are essential for identifying and addressing security issues that require administrative access to detect.

**Common Vulnerabilities and Exposures (CVE):** The Common Vulnerabilities and Exposures (CVE) system is a standardized list of publicly known cybersecurity vulnerabilities. Each vulnerability is assigned a unique identifier, which helps share data across different security products and services. CVE is essential for improving communication and coordination within the security community, enabling organizations to prioritize and address vulnerabilities effectively.

**Common Vulnerability Scoring System (CVSS):** The Common Vulnerability Scoring System (CVSS) provides a standardized method for rating the severity of security vulnerabilities. CVSS scores range from 0 to 10, with higher scores indicating more severe vulnerabilities. The scoring system considers factors such as exploitability, impact, and the complexity of attacks. CVSS helps organizations prioritize their vulnerability management efforts based on the potential impact of each vulnerability.

**Security Content Automation Protocol (SCAP):** The Security Content Automation Protocol (SCAP) is a suite of standards for automating vulnerability management, policy compliance, and security measurement. SCAP includes various components, such as CVE, CVSS, and others, to standardize identifying and remedying security issues. Utilizing SCAP-compliant tools enables organizations to streamline their vulnerability management processes and improve their overall security posture.

**Indicators of Compromise (IOCs):** Indicators of Compromise (IOCs) are pieces of forensic data that indicate a potential breach or malicious activity within a network or system. IOCs can include file hashes, IP addresses, domain names, or unusual network traffic patterns. Monitoring for IOCs helps in the early detection of security incidents and enables a swift response to mitigate damage. Incorporating IOC data into vulnerability management processes enhances threat detection and response capabilities.

**Remediation:** Remediation refers to correcting or mitigating identified vulnerabilities to reduce risk. This can involve applying patches, changing configurations, or implementing additional security controls. Effective remediation requires a clear understanding of the vulnerability, its potential impact, and the steps necessary to address it. Timely remediation is crucial for minimizing the risk of exploitation and maintaining a secure environment.

**Regression Testing:** Regression testing is the process of re-testing software or systems after changes, such as applying patches or updates, to ensure that existing functionalities remain unaffected. This testing is vital in patch management to confirm that new patches do not introduce new issues or vulnerabilities. Implementing robust regression testing helps maintain system stability and security after changes.

**Problem-Ticketing Systems:** Problem-ticketing systems are tools used to track and manage the lifecycle of identified vulnerabilities, from discovery to resolution. These systems facilitate communication and coordination among different teams, ensuring that vulnerabilities are addressed promptly. Integrating problem-ticketing systems with vulnerability scanners helps prioritize remediation efforts and provides visibility into the status of security issues.

**Threat Intelligence:** Threat intelligence involves collecting, analyzing, and disseminating information about potential or current threats to an organization's cybersecurity. This intelligence includes data on emerging threats, attack patterns, and vulnerabilities. Leveraging threat intelligence helps organizations anticipate and defend against cyber attacks more effectively. Incorporating threat intelligence into vulnerability management processes enhances the ability to prioritize and address the most relevant threats.

## Importance and Relevance

In today's dynamic cybersecurity landscape, the importance and relevance of continuous vulnerability management cannot be overstated. This control is crucial for organizations striving to protect their assets against evolving cyber threats. A robust vulnerability management process helps organizations identify and address vulnerabilities and strengthen their overall security posture. The following points highlight why continuous vulnerability management is vital in cybersecurity.

**Proactive Threat Mitigation:** Continuous vulnerability management enables organizations to identify and mitigate threats before they can be exploited proactively. By regularly scanning for vulnerabilities and addressing them promptly, enterprises can significantly reduce the risk of successful cyber attacks. This proactive approach ensures that potential security weaknesses are identified and fixed early, preventing attackers from exploiting them to gain unauthorized access or cause damage.

**Reduced Attack Surface:** Regularly assessing and addressing vulnerabilities helps reduce an organization's attack surface, which refers to the sum of all potential points where an attacker could exploit a system.

By minimizing the number of vulnerabilities, organizations can make it more difficult for attackers to find and exploit weaknesses, enhancing their overall security posture.

**Compliance with Regulations:** Many regulatory frameworks and industry standards require organizations to implement continuous vulnerability management in their cybersecurity practices. Compliance with these regulations is essential to avoid legal penalties and maintain trust with stakeholders. Regular vulnerability assessments and timely remediation demonstrate an organization's commitment to maintaining a secure environment and complying with relevant laws and standards.

**Enhanced Risk Management:** Effective vulnerability management is critical to an organization's risk management strategy. Organizations can allocate resources more effectively by identifying and prioritizing vulnerabilities based on their potential impact and likelihood of exploitation. This targeted approach helps mitigate the most significant risks and ensures that security efforts focus on the areas that matter most.

**Improved Incident Response:** Continuous vulnerability management contributes to improved incident response capabilities. By regularly monitoring for vulnerabilities and applying necessary patches, organizations can reduce the likelihood of incidents occurring in the first place. Additionally, a well-maintained vulnerability management process provides valuable data that can be used to enhance incident response strategies, ensuring a swift and effective reaction to any security breaches.

**Protection Against Zero-Day Exploits:** Zero-day exploits pose a significant threat as they target vulnerabilities that are not yet known to the security community. Continuous vulnerability management helps organizations stay ahead of these threats by maintaining an up-to-date understanding of their security posture and implementing advanced threat detection techniques. This vigilance allows for quicker identification and mitigation of unknown vulnerabilities, reducing the risk of zero-day attacks.

**Business Continuity:** Maintaining business continuity is a top organizational priority, and effective vulnerability management is crucial. By addressing vulnerabilities promptly, organizations can prevent disruptions caused by cyber attacks. Ensuring that systems and data remain secure and available supports the business's ongoing operations and minimizes the impact of potential security incidents.

**Cost Efficiency:** Proactively managing vulnerabilities can result in significant cost savings for organizations. The cost of addressing vulnerabilities before they are exploited is typically much lower than the cost of dealing with the aftermath of a cyber attack. Investing in continuous vulnerability management helps prevent costly breaches, data loss, and damage to an organization's reputation.

**Data Protection:** Protecting sensitive data is a fundamental aspect of cybersecurity. Continuous vulnerability management helps safeguard personal, financial, and proprietary information by ensuring secure systems and applications. Preventing unauthorized access to data through timely identification and remediation of vulnerabilities is essential for maintaining trust and compliance with data protection regulations.

**Adaptability to Emerging Threats:** The cybersecurity landscape constantly evolves, with new threats and vulnerabilities emerging regularly. Continuous vulnerability management enables organizations to adapt to these changes by staying informed about the latest security developments. This adaptability is crucial for maintaining a resilient security posture in the face of ever-changing cyber threats.

**Support for Digital Transformation:** As organizations increasingly adopt digital technologies and move to cloud-based environments, the complexity of their IT infrastructure grows. Continuous vulnerability management supports digital transformation by ensuring that new systems and applications are secure. This proactive approach helps organizations leverage the benefits of digital technologies while minimizing security risks.

**Strengthened Organizational Reputation:** A strong security posture enhances an organization's reputation with customers, partners, and stakeholders. Demonstrating a commitment to continuous vulnerability management shows that an organization takes cybersecurity seriously and is dedicated to protecting its assets and data. This trust is vital for maintaining and growing business relationships in an increasingly security-conscious market.

# Risks of Not Implementing the Control

Failing to implement continuous vulnerability management exposes organizations to many risks that can have severe consequences. If left unaddressed, vulnerabilities within enterprise assets can be exploited by cyber attackers, leading to breaches, financial losses, and reputational damage. The dynamic nature of cyber threats means that organizations must continuously monitor and address vulnerabilities to protect their infrastructure. Companies increase their susceptibility to attacks without a proactive approach and undermine their overall security posture. The following points highlight the significant risks associated with neglecting continuous vulnerability management.

**Increased Susceptibility to Cyber Attacks:** Organizations without continuous vulnerability management are more susceptible to cyber attacks. Attackers can exploit unpatched vulnerabilities to gain unauthorized access, steal data, or disrupt operations. Cybercriminals often scan for these weaknesses, and the lack of a proactive management system makes it easier for them to find and exploit security gaps. This susceptibility increases the likelihood of successful attacks and subsequent breaches.

**Data Breaches:** Neglecting vulnerability management significantly raises the risk of data breaches. Sensitive information, including personal data, financial records, and intellectual property, becomes vulnerable to unauthorized access. Data breaches can result in substantial financial losses, legal penalties, and loss of customer trust. Protecting data is a fundamental aspect of cybersecurity, and continuous monitoring is essential to prevent unauthorized access through known vulnerabilities.

**Regulatory Non-Compliance:** Many industries are governed by regulations mandating specific cybersecurity practices, including continuous vulnerability management. Failure to comply with these regulations can result in severe penalties, legal actions, and loss of business opportunities. Regulatory non-compliance affects an organization's financial standing and damages its reputation and trustworthiness in the market.

**Financial Losses:** Organizations face significant financial risks by not managing vulnerabilities. The costs associated with data breaches, ransomware attacks, and other cyber incidents can be exorbitant. These costs include remediation expenses, legal fees, regulatory fines, and compensation for affected parties. Additionally, the loss of business due to reputational damage can have a long-term impact on revenue.

**Operational Disruptions:** Cyber attacks exploiting unaddressed vulnerabilities can lead to significant operational disruptions. These disruptions can halt business processes, affect service delivery, and result in downtime that impacts productivity and profitability. Continuous vulnerability management is essential to ensure business operations remain uninterrupted and resilient against potential threats.

**Reputational Damage:** An organization's reputation can suffer greatly from a security incident resulting from unmanaged vulnerabilities. Customers, partners, and stakeholders expect robust security measures to protect their data and interactions. A breach can erode trust and confidence, leading to business loss and difficulty acquiring new customers. Rebuilding a damaged reputation is a lengthy and challenging process.

**Loss of Competitive Advantage:** Companies that fail to implement continuous vulnerability management may fall behind their competitors, who prioritize security. The loss of competitive advantage can be particularly damaging in industries where trust and security are paramount. Ensuring robust vulnerability management helps maintain a strong market position.

**Legal Liabilities:** Organizations may face legal liabilities if vulnerabilities lead to security breaches and data loss. Affected parties can file lawsuits, resulting in costly legal battles for the company's image. Effective vulnerability management reduces the risk of such legal challenges by proactively addressing potential security issues.

**Intellectual Property Theft:** Unaddressed vulnerabilities can provide an entry point for attackers to steal intellectual property. This includes proprietary technologies, trade secrets, and other valuable information that gives an organization a competitive edge. Intellectual property theft can have long-term negative impacts on innovation and market position.

**Increased Remediation Costs:** The longer a vulnerability remains unaddressed, the more costly it becomes to remediate. Attackers can exploit these vulnerabilities, causing more damage and requiring extensive resources to fix. Proactive vulnerability management minimizes these costs by addressing issues before they can be exploited, reducing the overall financial burden on the organization.

**Compromised Customer Trust:** Customers expect organizations to protect their data with the highest level of security. A breach resulting from neglected vulnerabilities can severely compromise customer trust. Once trust is lost, customers may take their business elsewhere, leading to a decline in customer base and revenue. Maintaining continuous vulnerability management is crucial for retaining customer trust.

# What Questions Should You Ask?

Effective implementation of continuous vulnerability management requires cybersecurity leaders to ask the right questions. These questions help identify the current security posture, understand the scope of vulnerabilities, and determine the necessary steps to enhance the organization's defenses. By addressing these critical areas, leaders can develop a robust vulnerability management strategy that aligns with their organization's goals and risk tolerance. The following questions serve as a foundational guide to shape the work required for successful implementation.

**What are our critical assets?** Identifying critical assets is the first step in vulnerability management. This involves determining which systems, applications, and data are essential for the organization's operations and mission. Critical assets often include financial data, intellectual property, customer information, and core business applications. Knowing what needs the most protection helps prioritize vulnerability scanning and remediation efforts. This focus ensures that resources are allocated efficiently and that the most important assets are safeguarded against potential threats.

**What is our current vulnerability landscape?** Understanding the current vulnerability landscape involves conducting comprehensive assessments to identify existing weaknesses. Regular vulnerability scans and analyses are essential to determine the extent and severity of vulnerabilities within the organization. This knowledge allows cybersecurity leaders to develop targeted strategies to address these issues. By having a clear picture of the vulnerability landscape, leaders can prioritize remediation efforts and allocate resources effectively to mitigate risks.

**How frequently are we conducting vulnerability scans?** The frequency of vulnerability scans should be aligned with the organization's risk profile and the nature of its assets. Regular scans help promptly identify new vulnerabilities and ensure that existing ones are tracked and addressed. Determining the right frequency involves considering factors such as the criticality of assets, the changing threat landscape, and compliance requirements. Consistent scanning practices enable organizations to avoid potential threats and maintain a robust security posture.

**Are we using authenticated scans?** Authenticated scans use valid credentials to access systems and perform a more thorough assessment. By examining configurations and installed software, they provide deeper insights into the security posture of enterprise assets. Authenticated scans can uncover vulnerabilities that unauthenticated scans might miss, offering a more comprehensive view of the organization's security status. Utilizing authenticated scans ensures that the vulnerability management process is thorough and accurate.

**How are we prioritizing vulnerabilities for remediation?** Prioritizing vulnerabilities based on their potential impact and likelihood of exploitation is crucial for effective management. This involves using frameworks like the Common Vulnerability Scoring System (CVSS) to assess severity and impact. Prioritization helps allocate resources to address the most critical vulnerabilities first, reducing the risk of exploitation. A structured approach to prioritization ensures that remediation efforts are focused on areas that pose the greatest threat to the organization.

**Do we have a patch management process in place?** A robust patch management process is essential for addressing vulnerabilities identified through scans. This process includes acquiring, testing, and applying patches to systems and applications. Effective patch management ensures that vulnerabilities are mitigated promptly, reducing the risk of exploitation. A systematic approach to patch management helps maintain the security and integrity of the organization's IT infrastructure.

CHAPTER 7   CONTINUOUS VULNERABILITY MANAGEMENT

**What tools and technologies are we using for vulnerability management?** The choice of tools and technologies significantly impacts the effectiveness of the vulnerability management program. This includes vulnerability scanners, configuration management tools, and threat intelligence platforms. Selecting the right tools involves evaluating their capabilities, compatibility with existing systems, and ease of use. Leveraging advanced tools and technologies enhances the efficiency and accuracy of the vulnerability management process.

**Are we integrating vulnerability management with incident response?** Integrating vulnerability management with incident response ensures a cohesive approach to addressing security issues. This integration allows for seamless team communication and coordination, improving the organization's ability to respond to threats. By linking these processes, organizations can quickly remediate vulnerabilities exploited during incidents. A unified approach enhances overall security and resilience.

**How are we educating and training our staff on vulnerability management?** Educating and training staff on vulnerability management is crucial for the program's success. This includes regular training sessions, workshops, and awareness programs to ensure employees understand their roles and responsibilities. An informed workforce can identify and report vulnerabilities more effectively, contributing to the organization's security efforts. Continuous education helps keep staff updated on the latest threats and best practices in vulnerability management.

**What metrics are we using to measure the effectiveness of our vulnerability management program?** Establishing metrics to measure the effectiveness of the vulnerability management program is essential for continuous improvement. Key metrics include the number of vulnerabilities identified, time to remediation, and the success rate of patches applied. These metrics provide insights into the program's performance and areas that need improvement. Reviewing and analyzing these metrics help refine strategies and enhance the program's effectiveness.

CHAPTER 7   CONTINUOUS VULNERABILITY MANAGEMENT

**How are we ensuring compliance with relevant regulations and standards?** Compliance with regulations and standards is a critical aspect of vulnerability management. This involves understanding the specific requirements of frameworks such as GDPR, HIPAA, and PCI-DSS and ensuring that the vulnerability management practices align with these standards. Regular audits and assessments help maintain compliance and identify areas for improvement. Ensuring compliance reduces legal risks and enhances the organization's reputation and trustworthiness.

**How are we incorporating threat intelligence into our vulnerability management process?** Incorporating threat intelligence into the vulnerability management process helps understand the evolving threat landscape. Threat intelligence provides insights into emerging threats, attack patterns, and vulnerabilities attackers exploit. This information can be used to prioritize vulnerabilities and tailor remediation efforts based on the most current threat data. Leveraging threat intelligence enhances the organization's ability to anticipate and mitigate potential threats effectively.

# Recommended Training

Implementing continuous vulnerability management requires a comprehensive training program tailored to different roles within the organization. Practical training ensures that IT and cybersecurity staff, administrators, and all other employees understand their responsibilities in identifying, reporting, and mitigating vulnerabilities. This program should address technical aspects and general cybersecurity awareness to create a well-informed workforce capable of contributing to the organization's security posture. The following training recommendations provide a structured approach to educating staff and reducing risks associated with vulnerabilities.

**Vulnerability Assessment and Management Training:** IT and cybersecurity staff should undergo specialized vulnerability assessment and management training. This training should cover using vulnerability scanning tools, interpreting scan results, prioritizing vulnerabilities, and remediation techniques. The outcome is a skilled team capable of conducting thorough vulnerability assessments and efficiently addressing identified issues. By enhancing their technical skills, the organization can ensure timely detection and mitigation of vulnerabilities, reducing the risk of exploitation.

**Patch Management Best Practices:** Administrators and IT staff responsible for maintaining systems should attend patch management best practices training. This training includes understanding the patch management lifecycle, testing patches before deployment, and strategies for scheduling patches without disrupting business operations. The goal is to ensure that patches are applied promptly and correctly, minimizing the window of opportunity for attackers. Effective patch management reduces the risk of exploited vulnerabilities and maintains systems' integrity.

**Security Configuration Management:** Training on security configuration management is essential for IT and cybersecurity staff. This training should focus on configuring systems securely, monitoring for unauthorized changes, and maintaining compliance with security policies. Attendees will learn how to apply secure configurations to various systems and regularly audit these configurations. Proper configuration management helps prevent the introduction of security weaknesses, thus enhancing the organization's overall security posture.

**Incident Response Training:** Both IT and cybersecurity teams, as well as key administrators, should participate in incident response training. This program should cover the development of incident response plans, identifying and responding to security incidents, and post-incident analysis. The outcome is a prepared team that can swiftly and effectively handle security breaches, minimizing damage and recovery time. Strong incident response capabilities are crucial for mitigating the impact of exploited vulnerabilities.

**Security Awareness Training for All Employees:** All employees should receive regular security awareness training regardless of their role. This training should cover basic cybersecurity principles, recognizing phishing attempts, and safe Internet practices. The goal is to create a security-conscious culture where employees can identify and report suspicious activities. A well-informed workforce reduces the likelihood of successful social engineering attacks and other exploits that target human vulnerabilities.

**Role-Based Access Control Training:** Administrators and IT staff should be trained in implementing role-based access control (RBAC) principles. This training includes understanding the importance of least privilege, creating and managing user roles, and auditing access controls. Proper implementation of RBAC ensures that employees have access only to the information and systems necessary for their job functions, reducing the risk of unauthorized access.

**Phishing Simulation and Awareness Training:** Employees should participate in phishing simulation and awareness training to recognize and respond to phishing attempts. This training involves simulated phishing attacks to test and reinforce employees' ability to identify fraudulent emails. The outcome is a vigilant workforce capable of avoiding phishing scams, a common vector for exploiting vulnerabilities. Regular simulations and training help to keep phishing awareness high and improve overall security.

**Secure Coding Practices:** Developers should attend training on secure coding practices to prevent introducing vulnerabilities during software development. This training covers common vulnerabilities, secure coding standards, and code review processes. The goal is to ensure that applications are built with security, reducing the likelihood of vulnerabilities in the final product. Secure coding practices are essential for maintaining the integrity and security of software applications.

**Data Protection and Privacy Training:** Employees handling sensitive data should receive data protection and privacy principles training. This training includes understanding data classification, data handling procedures, and compliance with privacy regulations. The outcome is an informed staff that can adequately manage and protect sensitive information, ensuring compliance and reducing the risk of data breaches. Effective data protection practices are crucial for safeguarding organizational and customer data.

**Network Security Essentials:** Network administrators and IT staff should attend training on network security essentials. This training covers firewall configuration, intrusion detection systems, and network segmentation. The goal is to equip staff with the knowledge to secure the organization's network infrastructure against potential threats. Proper network security practices are vital for preventing unauthorized access and protecting the organization's data and systems.

**Mobile Device Security Training:** Employees using mobile devices for work should undergo mobile device security training. This training includes best practices for securing mobile devices, such as using strong passwords, enabling encryption, and recognizing security threats. The outcome is a workforce understanding the importance of securing their mobile devices, reducing the risk of data breaches from lost or compromised devices. Mobile device security is essential as more employees use mobile technology remotely.

**Continuous Learning and Certification Programs:** IT and cybersecurity staff should be encouraged to participate in continuous learning and certification programs. This includes pursuing certifications such as CISSP, CEH, and CompTIA Security+ to stay updated with the latest cybersecurity trends and best practices. The goal is to maintain high expertise within the organization, ensuring staff can effectively manage and respond to evolving threats. Continuous learning helps keep the organization's security strategies current and effective.

# Actionable Recommendations

Effective implementation of continuous vulnerability management requires a strategic approach tailored to an organization's unique needs and infrastructure. By following structured and actionable recommendations, organizations can establish a robust framework for identifying, assessing, and mitigating vulnerabilities. The following recommendations provide a comprehensive guide to optimizing vulnerability management processes, ensuring enterprises are well-prepared to address current and emerging cyber threats. Each recommendation focuses on critical aspects contributing to the organization's security posture and resilience.

**Develop a Comprehensive Vulnerability Management Policy:** Establishing a comprehensive vulnerability management policy is essential. This policy should outline the procedures for vulnerability scanning, assessment, prioritization, and remediation. It must define roles and responsibilities, ensuring accountability across the organization. A well-documented policy provides a clear framework for all stakeholders, aligning efforts and facilitating consistent application of best practices. Regularly reviewing and updating this policy ensures it remains effective and relevant.

**Implement Regular and Automated Vulnerability Scanning:** Automated vulnerability scanning tools should be deployed to scan all networked assets regularly. These tools enable continuous monitoring and provide real-time insights into the security posture. Scheduling scans to run at frequent intervals ensures that new vulnerabilities are promptly identified. Automated scans reduce the likelihood of human error and increase the efficiency of the vulnerability management process. Ensuring that scans cover all assets, including endpoints, servers, and network devices, is crucial for comprehensive security.

**Utilize Authenticated Scans for In-Depth Analysis:** Authenticated scans should be employed to gain deeper insights into system vulnerabilities. These scans use valid credentials to access systems and thoroughly assess configurations and installed software. Authenticated scans can uncover vulnerabilities that unauthenticated scans might miss, offering a more comprehensive view of the security landscape. By conducting authenticated scans, organizations can ensure higher accuracy and detail in their vulnerability assessments. This approach enhances the effectiveness of the overall vulnerability management strategy.

**Prioritize Vulnerabilities Based on Risk:** Establish a risk-based approach to prioritize vulnerabilities. Use frameworks like the Common Vulnerability Scoring System (CVSS) to assess each vulnerability's severity and potential impact. Factors such as exploitability, impact on business operations, and exposure should be considered when prioritizing remediation efforts. Organizations can efficiently allocate resources and reduce the risk of significant security incidents by focusing on the most critical vulnerabilities. This method ensures that efforts are directed where they are most needed.

**Integrate Vulnerability Management with Patch Management Processes:** Vulnerability management should be closely integrated with patch management processes. Ensure that identified vulnerabilities are promptly addressed through the application of appropriate patches. Develop a systematic approach for testing and deploying patches to avoid disruptions. Coordinating these efforts improves the timeliness and effectiveness of remediation activities. Maintaining a seamless connection between vulnerability identification and patch application is vital for maintaining a secure environment.

**Establish Clear Communication Channels:** Effective communication channels should be established to facilitate the timely sharing of vulnerability information. This includes internal communications among IT and security teams and external communications with vendors and third-party service providers. Clear and efficient communication ensures all relevant parties know vulnerabilities and remediation efforts. Regular updates and status reports help keep stakeholders informed and aligned. Effective communication reduces delays and enhances coordination.

**Leverage Threat Intelligence for Informed Decision-Making:** Incorporate threat intelligence to enhance vulnerability management efforts. Threat intelligence provides valuable insights into emerging threats, attack patterns, and vulnerabilities that are being actively exploited. By leveraging this information, organizations can prioritize vulnerabilities based on the current threat landscape. Integrating threat intelligence into the decision-making process improves the accuracy and relevance of vulnerability management activities. This proactive approach helps anticipate and mitigate potential threats more effectively.

**Conduct Regular Training and Awareness Programs:** Regular training and awareness programs should be conducted for all employees. These programs should cover the basics of cybersecurity, including recognizing phishing attempts and safe online practices. Specialized IT and security staff training should focus on vulnerability assessment and management techniques. Keeping the workforce informed and vigilant is crucial for maintaining a solid security posture. Continuous education ensures that employees can support the organization's security efforts.

**Establish Metrics and Key Performance Indicators (KPIs):** Develop metrics and KPIs to measure the effectiveness of the vulnerability management program. Key metrics might include the number of vulnerabilities identified, the time to remediation, and the success rate of patch applications. Regularly reviewing these metrics helps assess the program's performance and identify areas for improvement. Establishing clear KPIs provides a basis for continuous improvement and accountability. Tracking progress and outcomes ensures that the program remains aligned with organizational goals.

**Implement a Vulnerability Disclosure Program:** Consider establishing a vulnerability disclosure program to encourage responsible reporting of vulnerabilities by external parties. This program should

CHAPTER 7  CONTINUOUS VULNERABILITY MANAGEMENT

provide clear guidelines for reporting vulnerabilities and outline the organization's commitment to addressing reported issues. A well-managed disclosure program can enhance security by leveraging the broader community's insights. Encouraging external reporting helps identify vulnerabilities that internal teams might overlook. This collaborative approach strengthens overall security.

**Regularly Review and Update Security Configurations:** Regular reviews and updates of security configurations are essential to maintain a secure environment. Configuration management tools should be used to ensure that systems are configured according to security best practices. Regular audits and assessments help identify and rectify any deviations or misconfigurations. Keeping configurations up-to-date reduces the risk of vulnerabilities caused by improper settings. Ongoing vigilance in configuration management is key to maintaining robust security defenses.

**Foster a Culture of Continuous Improvement:** Promote a culture of continuous improvement within the organization's cybersecurity practices. Encourage feedback and suggestions from employees on how to enhance vulnerability management processes. Regularly review and refine strategies based on lessons learned and evolving threats. Fostering a continuous improvement mindset ensures that the organization remains adaptable and resilient. This proactive approach helps in staying ahead of potential security challenges.

# Simplified Security Controls (SSC)

Security controls are essential for any organization seeking to protect its digital and physical assets from cyber threats. Tailoring these controls to fit the specific needs of your business environment is crucial, as it ensures that the protection mechanisms are relevant and effective against the specific risks your organization faces. There are numerous sources to draw these controls from, including the well-regarded CIS Top 18, which provides a robust framework for crafting defensive strategies.

# CHAPTER 7   CONTINUOUS VULNERABILITY MANAGEMENT

The recommendations presented in this book are based on the CIS controls, among others, offering a comprehensive guide that can be adapted to serve a wide range of security needs. Before implementing these controls, it is vital to thoroughly review their design to ensure they align with your strategic objectives and operational practices. Additionally, after deployment, it is imperative to regularly test the controls to verify their effectiveness and to make necessary adjustments. This ensures the controls continue functioning as intended, safeguarding your organization against emerging threats and changing conditions.

## CONTROL 1: ESTABLISH AND MAINTAIN A VULNERABILITY MANAGEMENT PROCESS

**Control Objective:** To develop and sustain a comprehensive vulnerability management process for all enterprise assets, ensuring continuous protection against vulnerabilities.

**Implementation Steps:**

1. **Document Vulnerability Management Procedures:** Develop detailed documentation outlining the vulnerability identification, assessment, and remediation processes.

2. **Annual Review and Updates:** Schedule annual reviews of the vulnerability management process documentation to ensure it remains current and effective.

3. **Adjust for Significant Changes:** Update the vulnerability management process documentation whenever significant changes in the enterprise environment could impact vulnerability management.

4. **Assign Roles and Responsibilities:** Clearly define and assign roles and responsibilities for vulnerability management within the organization to ensure accountability.

5. **Implement Training Programs:** Conduct regular staff training in vulnerability management to inform them about the latest tools and techniques.

**Expected Outcome:** A well-documented and regularly updated vulnerability management process ensures that all enterprise assets are consistently monitored and protected against vulnerabilities, reducing the risk of exploitation and enhancing overall security.

## CONTROL 2: ESTABLISH AND MAINTAIN A REMEDIATION PROCESS

**Control Objective:** To develop and maintain a risk-based remediation strategy, ensuring timely and effective mitigation of identified vulnerabilities.

**Implementation Steps:**

1. **Document the Remediation Process:** Create a detailed remediation process document that outlines the steps for addressing identified vulnerabilities based on risk assessment.

2. **Monthly Reviews:** Conduct monthly reviews of the remediation process to ensure it aligns with the latest threat intelligence and organizational changes.

3. **Risk-Based Prioritization:** Implement a risk-based approach to prioritize vulnerabilities for remediation, focusing on those with the highest potential impact.

4. **Automate Tracking and Reporting:** Use automated tools to track and report the status of remediation efforts, ensuring transparency and accountability.

CHAPTER 7    CONTINUOUS VULNERABILITY MANAGEMENT

5. **Communicate with Stakeholders:** Establish clear communication channels to inform all relevant stakeholders about remediation activities and progress.

**Expected Outcome:** A structured and dynamic remediation process ensures that vulnerabilities are addressed promptly and effectively, reducing the risk of exploitation and enhancing the organization's resilience against cyber threats.

## CONTROL 3: PERFORM AUTOMATED OPERATING SYSTEM PATCH MANAGEMENT

**Control Objective:** To ensure that operating system updates are applied promptly through automated patch management, minimizing vulnerabilities.

**Implementation Steps:**

1. **Deploy Automated Patch Management Tools:** Implement tools that automate the patch management process for operating systems across all enterprise assets.

2. **Schedule Monthly Updates:** Schedule automated updates to run on a monthly basis or more frequently if required to ensure timely patch application.

3. **Test Patches Before Deployment:** Establish a testing process to verify patches in a controlled environment before deploying them to production systems.

4. **Monitor Patch Deployment:** Use monitoring tools to track the deployment of patches and ensure that all systems are updated as scheduled.

5. **Document Patch Management Procedures:** Maintain detailed documentation of the patch management process, including schedules, testing procedures, and deployment protocols.

CHAPTER 7    CONTINUOUS VULNERABILITY MANAGEMENT

**Expected Outcome:** Automated and regularly scheduled operating system patch management reduces the risk of exploited vulnerabilities, ensuring that systems remain secure and up-to-date.

## CONTROL 4: PERFORM AUTOMATED APPLICATION PATCH MANAGEMENT

**Control Objective:** To ensure that application updates are applied promptly through automated patch management, minimizing vulnerabilities.

**Implementation Steps:**

1. **Implement Automated Patch Management Tools:** Use tools that automate the patch management process for applications across all enterprise assets.

2. **Schedule Regular Updates:** Schedule automated updates to run on a monthly basis or more frequently if needed to ensure the timely application of patches.

3. **Test Application Patches:** Develop a testing protocol to validate application patches in a controlled environment before deployment.

4. **Track and Monitor Updates:** Use monitoring systems to track the deployment of application patches and ensure compliance with update schedules.

5. **Document Procedures:** Maintain comprehensive documentation of the application patch management process, including schedules, testing, and deployment procedures.

**Expected Outcome:** Automated and regular application patch management ensures that vulnerabilities in software applications are addressed promptly, reducing the risk of exploitation.

## CONTROL 5: PERFORM AUTOMATED VULNERABILITY SCANS OF INTERNAL ENTERPRISE ASSETS

**Control Objective:** To conduct regular automated vulnerability scans of internal enterprise assets, identifying and mitigating security weaknesses.

**Implementation Steps:**

1. **Deploy SCAP-Compliant Tools:** Use SCAP-compliant vulnerability scanning tools to ensure thorough, standardized assessments.

2. **Schedule Quarterly Scans:** Schedule automated scans to run at least quarterly or more frequently if required by the organization's risk profile.

3. **Conduct Authenticated Scans:** Perform authenticated scans using valid credentials to gain deeper insights into system configurations and vulnerabilities.

4. **Conduct Unauthenticated Scans:** Perform unauthenticated scans to identify vulnerabilities from an external perspective.

5. **Analyze and Remediate Findings:** Analyze scan results to identify vulnerabilities and prioritize remediation efforts based on risk.

**Expected Outcome:** Regular automated vulnerability scans of internal assets help identify and mitigate security weaknesses, enhancing the organization's overall security posture.

CHAPTER 7    CONTINUOUS VULNERABILITY MANAGEMENT

## CONTROL 6: PERFORM AUTOMATED VULNERABILITY SCANS OF EXTERNALLY-EXPOSED ENTERPRISE ASSETS

**Control Objective:** To conduct regular automated vulnerability scans of externally exposed enterprise assets, identifying and mitigating security risks.

**Implementation Steps:**

1. **Use SCAP-Compliant Scanning Tools:** Deploy SCAP-compliant tools for consistent and comprehensive vulnerability assessments of external assets.

2. **Schedule Monthly Scans:** Schedule automated scans to run monthly or more frequently if needed to ensure timely detection of vulnerabilities.

3. **Focus on Externally-Exposed Assets:** Target scans on externally exposed assets, such as web servers, cloud services, and network gateways.

4. **Perform Comprehensive Analysis:** Analyze scan results to identify vulnerabilities and assess their potential impact on the organization.

5. **Prioritize Remediation Efforts:** Prioritize remediation based on the severity and exploitability of identified vulnerabilities.

**Expected Outcome:** Regular automated vulnerability scans of externally exposed assets help identify and address security risks, protecting the organization from external threats.

CHAPTER 7   CONTINUOUS VULNERABILITY MANAGEMENT

## CONTROL 7: REMEDIATE DETECTED VULNERABILITIES

**Control Objective:** To ensure timely and effective remediation of detected vulnerabilities, reducing the risk of exploitation.

**Implementation Steps:**

1. **Establish Remediation Processes:** Develop and document remediation processes that outline steps for addressing identified vulnerabilities.

2. **Use Automated Tools:** Implement automated tools to facilitate the remediation process, tracking the status and progress of vulnerability fixes.

3. **Schedule Monthly Reviews:** Conduct monthly reviews to ensure that remediation efforts are on track and aligned with risk-based priorities.

4. **Assign Responsibilities:** Clearly define and assign responsibilities for remediation activities to ensure accountability and timely action.

5. **Report Progress to Stakeholders:** Regularly update stakeholders on the status of remediation efforts, providing transparency and oversight.

**Expected Outcome:** A structured and efficient remediation process ensures that detected vulnerabilities are addressed promptly, reducing the risk of exploitation and enhancing the organization's security posture.

# CHAPTER 8

# Audit Log Management

Effective audit log management is a cornerstone of robust cybersecurity strategies. Audit logs serve as the digital footprints of all activities within an information system, providing a trail of evidence that is invaluable in both detecting and responding to cyber threats. These logs are essential for understanding the sequence of events leading up to and following a security incident, offering insights crucial for forensic analysis. Organizations can significantly enhance their ability to identify and mitigate potential security breaches by systematically collecting, reviewing, and retaining audit logs.

The importance of audit log management must be balanced in the context of modern cybersecurity. In many cases, audit logs are the only sources of evidence that reveal the presence and activities of an intruder within a network. Attackers often exploit that organizations do not actively analyze their logs, using this oversight to remain undetected for extended periods. This can lead to prolonged unauthorized access, data exfiltration, and other malicious activities that can severely affect the organization. Therefore, establishing a comprehensive audit log management process is critical for maintaining the integrity and security of information systems.

Audit logs can be broadly categorized into system logs and audit logs. System logs typically capture system-level events, such as process start and end times, system crashes, and other operational activities. These logs are

## CHAPTER 8   AUDIT LOG MANAGEMENT

easier to enable and require minimal configuration. In contrast, audit logs focus on user-level events, such as login attempts, file access, and other user interactions. Setting up audit logs requires more detailed planning and configuration to capture all relevant events accurately. Both logs are essential for providing a complete picture of the system and user activities.

The role of audit logs extends beyond real-time threat detection. They are also vital for incident response and post-incident analysis. When a security incident occurs, having detailed and comprehensive log records allows security teams to reconstruct the sequence of events, identify the methods used by attackers, and assess the extent of the damage. This information is crucial for containing the incident, preventing further damage, and developing strategies to prevent future occurrences. Additionally, audit logs can be instrumental in legal and compliance contexts, providing evidence that may be required for investigations and regulatory reporting.

Retention of audit logs is another critical aspect of audit log management. Logs should be retained for a sufficient period to ensure they are available for analysis in case of a delayed discovery of a security incident. The retention period may vary depending on regulatory requirements, the nature of the organization, and the potential risks involved. Proper retention practices ensure that logs are available when needed without overburdening storage resources. Regular reviews of retention policies help maintain a balance between availability and resource management.

Centralized Logging is a best practice that enhances the efficiency and effectiveness of audit log management. Organizations can simplify the log analysis and correlation process by aggregating logs from various sources into a centralized system. Centralized Logging enables security teams to quickly identify patterns and anomalies that may indicate malicious activities. It also facilitates the implementation of automated alerting mechanisms that can notify security personnel of potential threats in real time. This approach improves threat detection accuracy and streamlines audit logs' overall management.

Time synchronization across all logging sources is essential for ensuring the accuracy and reliability of audit logs. Discrepancies in timestamps can create confusion and hinder the analysis of security incidents. By standardizing time synchronization, organizations can ensure that all logs are recorded with consistent timestamps, making correlating events across different systems easier. This consistency is crucial for reconstructing timelines and understanding the sequence of events during an incident. Implementing multiple synchronized time sources helps maintain this accuracy even in the event of a failure of the primary time source.

Detailed audit logging is significant for systems handling sensitive data. These logs should capture comprehensive information about each event, including the event source, date, username, timestamp, source and destination addresses, and other relevant details. Such granularity is essential for conducting thorough forensic investigations and understanding the full impact of a security incident. Detailed logs enable security teams to trace attackers' actions, identify compromised accounts, and determine which data may have been accessed or exfiltrated. This level of detail is indispensable for effective incident response and remediation.

In addition to traditional system and user activities, specific events should be logged to enhance security monitoring. For example, DNS query logs can provide insights into potential domain-based threats, while URL request logs can reveal attempts to access malicious websites. Command-line audit logs are useful for detecting unauthorized use of administrative commands and scripts. By collecting and analyzing these specialized logs, organizations can better understand the threat landscape and improve their ability to detect and respond to sophisticated attacks.

CHAPTER 8   AUDIT LOG MANAGEMENT

Regular reviews of audit logs are essential for maintaining an effective security posture. Periodic log reviews help identify anomalies and abnormal events that may indicate a security threat. These reviews should be conducted on a scheduled basis, such as weekly or more frequently, depending on the organization's risk profile. Automated tools can assist in identifying patterns and anomalies, but human analysis is also critical for interpreting the context and significance of the findings. Proactive log reviews enable organizations to detect potential threats early and take appropriate actions to mitigate them.

Ensuring adequate storage for audit logs is a fundamental requirement of audit log management. Logs should be stored in a manner that prevents tampering and unauthorized access. The storage solution should be scalable to accommodate the growing volume of log data over time. Implementing redundancy and backup measures helps protect log data from loss due to hardware failures or other incidents. Secure storage practices ensure that logs are preserved in their integrity, making them available for analysis when needed.

Access control logs are an important component of audit log management. These logs record attempts to access resources without appropriate privileges, providing insights into potential unauthorized access attempts. By monitoring access control logs, organizations can identify and investigate suspicious activities, such as repeated failed login attempts or access attempts to restricted areas. This information can help detect insider threats and external attacks, enabling security teams to respond promptly to prevent potential breaches.

Collecting logs from service providers is another crucial aspect of comprehensive audit log management. Many organizations rely on third-party services for various functions, such as cloud computing, authentication, and data storage. Ensuring that logs from these service providers are collected and integrated into the organization's logging system enhances visibility into all activities affecting the organization's security. These logs should include key authentication and authorization events, data creation and disposal activities, and user management actions. Integrating service provider logs helps provide a complete picture of the security landscape, facilitating more effective threat detection and response.

Effective audit log management is essential for maintaining a robust cybersecurity posture. Organizations can significantly enhance their ability to detect, respond to, and recover from cyber threats by systematically collecting, analyzing, and retaining audit logs. Implementing best practices such as centralized Logging, time synchronization, and detailed Logging for sensitive systems ensures that audit logs provide valuable insights into security events. Regular log reviews and secure storage practices further strengthen the organization's ability to protect its information assets and maintain compliance with regulatory requirements.

# Key Concepts and Terms

Understanding key concepts and terms related to audit log management is crucial for effectively implementing and maintaining robust cybersecurity measures. This section delves into essential terminology that underpins audit log management, providing clarity and context for IT professionals, cybersecurity experts, and organizational leaders. By grasping these concepts, readers can better appreciate the intricacies of audit log management and its pivotal role in detecting, analyzing, and mitigating cyber threats.

**Audit Logs:** Audit logs are detailed records of system and user activities within an information system. These logs capture many events, such as login attempts, file accesses, and system changes. They provide a comprehensive trail of actions, which is invaluable for forensic investigations and incident response. Audit logs help security teams understand what occurred during a security incident, who was involved, and how the attack was executed. Proper management of audit logs is essential for maintaining the integrity and security of an organization's information systems.

**System Logs:** System logs record system-level events, such as process start and end times, system crashes, and other operational activities. These logs are native to operating systems and require minimal configuration to activate. They are crucial for monitoring systems' health and performance, identifying issues, and ensuring smooth operations. By analyzing system logs, administrators can detect hardware failures, software errors, and other technical problems that could impact system performance. System logs complement audit logs by providing a broader view of system activity.

**Log Analysis:** Log analysis examines audit and system logs to identify patterns, anomalies, and potential security threats. This involves using specialized tools and techniques to sift through large volumes of log data, extracting meaningful insights. Effective log analysis can detect unusual behaviors, such as repeated failed login attempts or unauthorized access to sensitive files. Regular log analysis is critical for early threat detection and helps organizations respond swiftly to potential security incidents. It also aids in compliance with regulatory requirements by ensuring logs are actively monitored and reviewed.

**Forensic Investigation:** Forensic investigation in cybersecurity involves analyzing digital evidence, including audit logs, to understand the details of a security incident. This process helps determine the extent of an attack, the methods used by the attackers, and the impact on the organization. Forensic investigators rely heavily on detailed and accurate audit logs to reconstruct events and identify the incident's root cause. The findings from forensic investigations are essential for improving security measures and preventing future breaches.

**Centralized Logging:** Centralized Logging refers to aggregating log data from various sources into a single, centralized system. This approach simplifies the management and analysis of logs, making correlating events and identifying security threats easier. Centralized Logging enhances the visibility of activities across the entire network, allowing for more efficient monitoring and quicker response times. It also supports compliance efforts by providing a unified log repository that can be audited and reviewed systematically.

**Time Synchronization:** Time synchronization ensures that all log entries across different systems have consistent timestamps. This is crucial for accurately correlating events and understanding the sequence of actions during a security incident. Discrepancies in timestamps can create confusion and hinder the investigation process. Implementing synchronized time sources, such as Network Time Protocol (NTP) servers, across all logging systems helps maintain the integrity and reliability of log data.

**Retention Policies:** Retention policies define the duration for which audit logs should be stored. These policies are influenced by regulatory requirements, organizational needs, and the nature of the data being logged. Adequate retention periods ensure that logs are available for analysis in case of delayed discovery of security incidents. Retention policies must balance the need for long-term storage with the constraints of storage resources, ensuring logs are preserved without overwhelming system capacities.

**Anomaly Detection:** Anomaly detection involves identifying deviations from normal behavior within log data. This can indicate potential security threats like unusual login patterns or unexpected data transfers. Anomaly detection tools use machine learning and statistical analysis to recognize patterns and flag anomalies. Security teams can prioritize their efforts to investigate and mitigate genuine threats by focusing on outliers, enhancing the organization's overall security posture.

**Access Control Logs:** Access control logs record attempts to access system resources, including successful and failed attempts. These logs are vital for monitoring user activities and detecting unauthorized access to sensitive information. Organizations can identify potential insider threats and external attacks by reviewing access control logs. Detailed access logs provide a clear picture of who accessed what resources, when, and from where, facilitating thorough investigations and strengthening access management policies.

**DNS Query Logs:** DNS query logs capture requests made to the Domain Name System (DNS), which translates domain names into IP addresses. Monitoring these logs can reveal attempts to access malicious domains or command-and-control servers used by attackers. DNS query logs are an important source of information for identifying and blocking malicious activities at the network level. Analyzing these logs helps prevent threats from reaching critical systems and enhances overall network security.

**Command-Line Audit Logs:** Command-line audit logs track commands executed in command-line interfaces such as PowerShell, BASH, or remote administrative terminals. These logs are useful for detecting unauthorized use of administrative privileges and monitoring administrative activities. Command-line audit logs provide detailed insights into the actions performed by users with elevated privileges, helping to identify potential misuse or compromise of administrative accounts. This level of auditing is crucial for maintaining the security of critical systems and ensuring accountability.

**Service Provider Logs:** Service provider logs capture activities related to third-party services used by an organization, such as cloud computing, authentication, and data storage services. These logs include events like authentication and authorization actions, data creation and deletion, and user management events. Collecting and analyzing service provider logs enhances visibility into the security posture of third-party services, ensuring they align with the organization's security policies. Integrating these logs into the centralized system provides a comprehensive view of all activities affecting the organization's security.

# Importance and Relevance

Understanding the importance and relevance of audit log management in today's cybersecurity landscape is crucial for organizations aiming to protect their information systems effectively. This section outlines the key reasons audit log management is indispensable for maintaining robust security practices. By appreciating these factors, IT professionals, cybersecurity experts, and organizational leaders can prioritize and implement comprehensive logging strategies that enhance their overall security posture.

**Early Detection of Malicious Activity:** Audit logs are fundamental for the early detection of malicious activity. They record various events, such as failed login attempts, unauthorized access, and abnormal user behavior, which can indicate the presence of an intruder. Early detection is critical to preventing further damage, allowing security teams to respond swiftly to potential threats. Organizations can continuously monitor and analyze audit logs to identify and mitigate risks before they escalate into significant security incidents.

**Forensic Investigations and Incident Response:** Effective audit log management is vital for forensic investigations and incident response. When a security breach occurs, audit logs provide a detailed account of the events leading up to and following the incident. This information is essential for understanding the attack vectors used by cybercriminals and the extent of the damage. Comprehensive log records enable security teams to reconstruct the sequence of events, identify compromised systems, and implement remediation measures to prevent future attacks.

**Compliance with Regulatory Requirements:** Many industries are subject to strict regulatory requirements that mandate the collection and retention of audit logs. Regulations such as the General Data Protection Regulation (GDPR), the Health Insurance Portability and Accountability Act (HIPAA), and the Sarbanes-Oxley Act (SOX) require organizations to maintain detailed logs for compliance purposes. Adhering to these regulations helps organizations avoid legal penalties and demonstrates their commitment to protecting sensitive information. Proper audit log management ensures that organizations can meet these regulatory obligations effectively.

**Understanding User Behavior:** Audit logs provide valuable insights into an information system's user behavior. By analyzing these logs, organizations can identify patterns and trends that may indicate potential security risks. For example, frequent access to sensitive files by a single user or unusual login times can signal insider threats. Understanding user behavior through audit logs allows organizations to implement targeted security measures and reduce the likelihood of data breaches caused by internal actors.

**Proactive Threat Hunting:** Proactive threat hunting involves actively searching for signs of malicious activity within an organization's network. Audit logs are a critical resource for threat hunters, as they contain detailed records of system and user activities. By leveraging audit logs, threat hunters can identify indicators of compromise (IOCs) and potential attack vectors that traditional security tools may not detect. Proactive threat hunting helps organizations avoid cybercriminals and enhances their overall security posture.

**Enhancing Incident Response Plans:** Well-maintained audit logs are essential for enhancing incident response plans. They provide a wealth of information that can be used to refine and improve response strategies. Organizations can identify weaknesses in their incident response processes by analyzing past incidents and the corresponding audit logs and making necessary adjustments. This continuous improvement cycle ensures that incident response plans remain effective and can address emerging threats.

**Data Integrity Audit logs:** Audit logs ensure data integrity within an information system. They record all actions taken on data, including creation, modification, and deletion events. This transparency helps organizations verify that data has not been tampered with and maintains its accuracy and reliability. Data integrity is particularly important for industries that rely on accurate data for decision-making, such as healthcare and finance.

**Supporting Accountability and Transparency:** Maintaining detailed audit logs supports accountability and transparency within an organization. Logs provide a traceable record of all activities, making it possible to determine who performed specific actions and when. This accountability is essential for internal audits, investigations, and regulatory compliance. Transparent logging practices foster a culture of responsibility and trust, as employees know their actions are being recorded and reviewed.

**Improving Security Policies and Controls:** Audit logs offer valuable feedback on the effectiveness of an organization's security policies and controls. By analyzing log data, security teams can assess whether existing measures adequately protect the system or if adjustments are needed. For example, if logs reveal frequent failed login attempts, it may indicate the need for more robust authentication mechanisms. Continuous evaluation and improvement of security policies based on log analysis help organizations stay resilient against evolving threats.

**Facilitating Root Cause Analysis:** When a security incident occurs, it is essential to identify the root cause to prevent recurrence. Audit logs provide the detailed information necessary for a thorough root cause analysis. By examining log entries, security teams can trace the origin of the incident, understand how it propagated, and determine what vulnerabilities were exploited. This knowledge is crucial for implementing effective countermeasures and strengthening the organization's security framework.

**Supporting Legal and Investigative Processes:** In the event of a cybercrime, audit logs can serve as crucial evidence in legal and investigative processes. They provide a detailed and chronological account of events, which can be used to support claims and demonstrate the occurrence of malicious activities. Legal authorities and investigators rely on audit logs to build cases against cybercriminals and understand the full impact of their actions. Proper log management ensures this critical evidence is preserved and accessible when needed.

**Mitigating Insider Threats:** Insider threats pose a significant risk to organizations as they involve individuals with legitimate access to sensitive information. Audit logs are an essential tool for detecting and mitigating insider threats. Organizations can identify suspicious behavior that may indicate malicious intent by monitoring and analyzing user activities. Effective audit log management helps organizations protect against insider threats by providing the visibility needed to detect and respond to potentially harmful actions by employees or contractors.

# Risks of Not Implementing the Control

Failing to implement effective audit log management poses significant risks to any organization. Without comprehensive Logging, companies are left vulnerable to undetected cyber threats, prolonged security breaches, and substantial financial and reputational damage. The absence of detailed logs hampers the ability to conduct forensic investigations, complicates compliance with regulatory requirements, and diminishes the overall security posture. Organizations that overlook audit logs' importance may need help responding adequately to security incidents, leading to severe consequences. This section explores the various risks associated with neglecting audit log management.

**Undetected Security Breaches:** Security breaches can go undetected for extended periods without proper audit log management. Malicious actors exploit systems without leaving obvious traces; logs are often the only evidence of their presence. If an organization fails to monitor and analyze logs, attackers can operate unnoticed, gaining access to sensitive data and systems. The longer a breach remains undetected, the greater the potential damage, including data theft, financial loss, and operational disruption.

**Inadequate Incident Response:** The absence of detailed audit logs severely hampers incident response efforts. When a security incident occurs, logs provide the essential information needed to understand the nature and scope of the attack. Without this data, security teams struggle to determine the cause, contain the threat, and remediate the damage. Inadequate incident response can lead to prolonged recovery times, increased costs, and ongoing vulnerabilities that attackers can exploit again.

**Non-Compliance with Regulations:** Many industries are subject to stringent regulatory requirements that mandate collecting, retaining, and reviewing audit logs. Failure to comply with these regulations can result in substantial fines, legal penalties, and damage to an organization's Reputation. Regulatory bodies require audit logs to verify that security measures are functioning correctly. Non-compliance exposes the organization to legal risks and undermines customer and stakeholder trust.

**Difficulty in Forensic Investigations:** Forensic investigations rely heavily on audit logs to reconstruct the events leading up to and following a security incident. Without comprehensive logs, investigators lack the necessary data to identify the attack vector, understand the methods used, and determine the extent of the breach. This lack of information can prevent organizations from learning from incidents and improving their security posture, leaving them vulnerable to repeat attacks.

**Increased Risk of Insider Threats:** Insider threats, whether from malicious employees or inadvertent actions, pose a significant risk to organizations. Audit logs provide a detailed record of user activities, helping to identify unusual behavior that may indicate an insider threat. These logs are necessary for detecting and mitigating insider threats to be much easier. Organizations may be unaware of unauthorized access to sensitive information, leading to data breaches and other security incidents.

**Lack of Accountability:** Audit logs establish accountability by providing a record of actions taken by users and administrators. This accountability is crucial for ensuring that individuals follow security policies and procedures. Holding users accountable for their actions without logs is challenging, leading to potential policy violations and security risks. A lack of accountability can result in a culture of complacency, where employees need to take security seriously.

**Inability to Detect Anomalies:** Detecting anomalies and unusual behavior patterns is essential for identifying potential security threats. Audit logs are a primary data source for anomaly detection tools and processes. Without these logs, organizations lose a critical mechanism for spotting signs of compromise. This inability to detect anomalies early can result in undetected threats and increased cyberattack exposure.

**Impaired Security Policy Evaluation:** Audit logs provide valuable insights into the effectiveness of security policies and controls. Organizations can identify weaknesses and gaps in their security posture by analyzing log data. Evaluating whether existing policies are adequate or need improvement is not easy without this feedback. This lack of evaluation can result in outdated or ineffective security measures that fail to protect against evolving threats.

**Prolonged System Downtime:** Security incidents often lead to system downtime as organizations work to contain and remediate the threat. With detailed logs, understanding the full impact of an incident and restoring systems to regular operation becomes more manageable. Prolonged downtime can disrupt business operations, leading to lost revenue, decreased productivity, and dissatisfied customers. Effective audit log management helps minimize downtime by enabling faster and more efficient incident response.

**Damage to Reputation:** A failure to implement proper audit log management can result in high-profile security breaches that damage an organization's Reputation. Customers, partners, and stakeholders expect organizations to protect their data and maintain robust security measures.

Publicized breaches, especially those that could have been prevented with better log management, can erode trust and confidence. The long-term impact on Reputation can be difficult to repair and may result in lost business opportunities.

**Financial Losses:** Security breaches and incidents can lead to significant financial losses, including direct costs such as fines, legal fees, and remediation expenses, as well as indirect costs like lost revenue and damage to brand value. Without effective audit log management, organizations are at a higher risk of experiencing breaches that result in financial harm. Investing in proper log management can help mitigate these risks and protect the organization's bottom line.

**Operational Disruption:** Cybersecurity incidents can cause severe operational disruptions, impacting the ability to deliver products and services. Without audit logs, diagnosing and addressing the cause of these disruptions becomes more complex and time-consuming. Operational disruptions can affect customer satisfaction, competitive positioning, and overall business performance. Proper audit log management helps organizations quickly identify and resolve issues, maintaining continuity and minimizing the impact on operations.

# What Questions Should You Ask?

Effective audit log management requires careful planning and consideration. Cybersecurity leaders must ask the right questions to ensure their organization's logging processes are comprehensive, efficient, and aligned with best practices. These questions help identify potential gaps in the logging strategy, clarify requirements, and guide robust audit log management implementation. By addressing these critical questions, organizations can enhance their ability to detect, respond to, and recover from cyber threats.

**What are our logging requirements?** Understanding the organization's specific logging requirements is fundamental. This includes identifying the types of events that need to be logged, the systems and applications that should generate logs, and the level of detail required. Clearly defined logging requirements help capture all relevant activities, providing a comprehensive view of the system and user behavior. Organizations may miss critical security monitoring and incident response events without this clarity.

**How will logs be collected and stored?** Determining the methods for log collection and storage is crucial for maintaining the integrity and availability of log data. This involves deciding whether to use centralized or decentralized logging systems, selecting appropriate tools and technologies, and defining storage capacities and retention periods. Effective log collection and storage solutions ensure that logs are accessible for analysis and protected against tampering or loss. Proper storage also supports compliance with regulatory requirements for data retention.

**What tools and technologies will we use for log analysis?** Selecting the right tools and technologies for log analysis is essential for efficient and effective monitoring. This includes identifying software that can automate log parsing, correlation, anomaly detection, and tools for manual log review and forensic investigation. Advanced log analysis tools help security teams quickly identify suspicious activities and potential threats, enhancing their ability to respond promptly. The right tools also enable the organization to scale its logging efforts as the volume of log data grows.

**How will we ensure the accuracy and reliability of logs?** Ensuring the accuracy and reliability of logs is critical for meaningful analysis and incident response. This involves synchronizing time across all logging sources, validating log integrity, and ensuring logs are generated consistently. Accurate and reliable logs provide a trustworthy record of events, which is essential for forensic investigations and compliance audits. With this assurance, organizations may be able to create an accurate timeline of events during a security incident.

**Who will have access to log data?** Defining who has access to log data is important for maintaining security and confidentiality. This involves establishing role-based access controls, ensuring only authorized personnel can view or modify logs, and regularly auditing access to log data. Controlled access helps prevent unauthorized tampering with log data and protects sensitive information contained within logs. It also ensures that security teams can rely on the integrity of log data for their analyses and investigations.

**How often will logs be reviewed?** Determining the frequency of log reviews is essential for timely threat detection and response. This involves setting a schedule for regular log reviews, which may vary based on the criticality of the systems being monitored and the organization's risk profile. Regular reviews help identify anomalies and potential security incidents early, allowing prompt action. Consistent log review practices also support compliance with industry standards and regulatory requirements.

**What are our retention policies for log data?** Establishing retention policies for log data is crucial for balancing storage costs with the need for historical data. This involves defining how long logs should be kept, considering regulatory requirements, and the organization's operational needs. Effective retention policies ensure that logs are available for analysis during investigations and audits without overwhelming storage resources. Proper retention practices also help organizations manage data lifecycle and disposal processes securely.

**How will we protect log data from tampering and unauthorized access?** Protecting log data from tampering and unauthorized access is vital for maintaining its integrity and confidentiality. This involves implementing encryption, secure storage solutions, and access controls to safeguard logs. Ensuring log data security helps maintain trust in the information used for security monitoring and incident response. It also supports compliance with regulations that mandate the protection of sensitive data.

CHAPTER 8  AUDIT LOG MANAGEMENT

**How will we handle log data from third-party service providers?** Managing log data from third-party service providers is important for comprehensive security monitoring. This involves defining how logs from cloud services, external applications, and other third-party systems will be collected, integrated, and analyzed. Ensuring that third-party logs are included in the organization's logging strategy provides a complete view of the security landscape. It also helps identify potential threats originating from or involving third-party services.

**What procedures are in place for incident response based on log data?** Defining procedures for incident response based on log data is essential for effective threat management. This involves establishing protocols for analyzing logs during an incident, determining the roles and responsibilities of team members, and outlining the steps for containment, eradication, and recovery. Clear incident response procedures ensure the organization can quickly and effectively respond to security incidents, minimizing damage and disruption. These procedures also support continuous improvement by incorporating lessons learned from previous incidents.

**How will we ensure continuous improvement of our logging practices?** Ensuring continuous improvement of logging practices involves regularly reviewing and updating policies, procedures, and technologies. This includes conducting periodic audits, staying informed about industry best practices, and integrating feedback from security incidents and log analyses. Continuous improvement helps organizations adapt to evolving threats and maintain effective logging strategies. It also ensures that the organization's logging efforts align with its security goals and compliance requirements.

**What training will be provided to staff on log management?** Providing training to staff on log management is crucial for the effective implementation and maintenance of logging practices. This involves educating team members on the importance of audit logs, how to generate and review logs, and the tools and techniques used for log analysis.

Well-trained staff are better equipped to identify and respond to security incidents, ensuring that logging practices are followed consistently and accurately. Regular training also helps keep the team updated on new technologies and best practices in log management.

# Recommended Training

Effective audit log management hinges on robust policies and tools and comprehensive training programs for all employees, from IT and cybersecurity staff to general administrative and operational personnel. Training ensures that everyone understands the importance of Logging, knows how to handle log data, and recognizes their role in maintaining security. This section outlines recommended training initiatives that organizations can implement to enhance their overall cybersecurity posture and ensure the effective use of audit logs.

**Log Management Basics for IT and Cybersecurity Staff:** IT and cybersecurity staff should undergo training that covers the fundamentals of log management. This includes understanding the types of logs, how logs are generated and collected, and the tools used for log analysis. The training should also emphasize the importance of log integrity and retention policies. Organizations can ensure that logs are managed effectively and accurately by equipping staff with this knowledge. This training helps reduce the risk of missed or misinterpreted log data, enhancing overall security monitoring.

**Advanced Log Analysis Techniques for Security Analysts:** Security analysts should receive advanced training in log analysis techniques. This training should cover the use of specialized tools and methodologies for detecting anomalies, correlating events, and identifying potential threats. Analysts should also learn to interpret complex log data and conduct forensic investigations. By enhancing their analytical skills, security analysts can more effectively identify and respond to security incidents. This advanced training helps reduce the time to detect and mitigate threats, minimizing potential damage.

**Incident Response Training for IT Staff:** IT staff should be trained in incident response procedures, specifically focusing on using log data during an incident. This training should include identifying indicators of compromise (IOCs) in logs, steps for containing and eradicating threats, and methods for documenting and reporting incidents. Effective incident response training ensures that IT staff can quickly and accurately respond to security breaches. This preparedness reduces the impact of incidents and helps maintain system integrity.

**Log Management Policies and Procedures for Administrators:** Administrators responsible for implementing and overseeing log management should receive training on organizational policies and procedures. This training should include guidelines for log configuration, collection, storage, retention, and access control measures. Understanding these policies ensures administrators can enforce consistent and compliant log management practices. Proper training in policies and procedures helps prevent gaps in Logging that attackers could exploit.

**Awareness Training for General Employees:** All employees should receive general awareness training on the importance of audit logs and their role in maintaining security. This training should cover basic concepts such as what logs are, why they are essential, and how employee actions can impact log data. By raising awareness, organizations can foster a security-conscious culture where employees understand the significance of their actions. This awareness helps reduce inadvertent actions that could compromise log data.

**Role-Based Training for Specific Departments:** Departments with unique security needs, such as finance or human resources, should receive role-based training tailored to their specific requirements. This training should cover the types of logs relevant to their operations, how to recognize suspicious activities and best practices for safeguarding sensitive

CHAPTER 8   AUDIT LOG MANAGEMENT

data. Role-based training ensures that employees in critical departments are equipped to handle security challenges pertinent to their functions. This targeted approach helps mitigate risks specific to different areas of the organization.

**Regular Refresher Courses and Updates:** To keep pace with evolving threats and technologies, all staff should participate in regular refresher courses and updates on log management and cybersecurity best practices. These sessions should review key concepts, introduce new tools and techniques, and address recent security incidents and lessons learned. Continuous education helps maintain a high level of vigilance and adaptability among employees. Regular updates ensure that the organization's security practices remain effective and current.

**Phishing and Social Engineering Awareness:** Training on phishing and social engineering should be provided to all employees to help them recognize and respond to these common threats. This training should include real-world examples of phishing attempts, techniques for verifying the legitimacy of communications, and steps to take if a phishing attempt is suspected. Organizations can reduce the likelihood of successful social engineering attacks by educating employees about these tactics. Awareness training helps protect against threats that could lead to compromised log data and other security breaches.

**Training on Compliance and Regulatory Requirements:** Employees responsible for ensuring compliance should receive training on relevant regulatory requirements related to log management. This training should cover the specific logs required by regulations such as GDPR, HIPAA, and SOX, as well as retention and reporting obligations. Understanding these requirements ensures that the organization remains compliant with legal standards. Compliance training helps prevent regulatory violations and the associated penalties.

**Secure Configuration and Maintenance Training:** IT staff and administrators should receive training on the secure configuration and maintenance of systems and applications that generate logs. This training should cover best practices for setting up logging features, maintaining log security, and ensuring logs are not inadvertently disabled. Proper configuration and maintenance are critical for the reliability and integrity of log data. This training helps reduce the risk of configuration errors that could lead to gaps in Logging.

**Integration of Third-Party Logs:** Training on integrating third-party service provider logs into the organization's framework is essential. This training should include methods for collecting, normalizing, and analyzing logs from external services such as cloud providers and SaaS applications. Ensuring seamless integration of third-party logs enhances the overall visibility of the organization's security posture. This integration training helps identify and mitigate threats from or involving third-party services.

**Incident Simulation Exercises:** Conducting incident simulation exercises, such as tabletop scenarios and live drills, helps staff practice using log data in real-time incident response situations. These exercises should simulate various security incidents, allowing participants to apply their training in a controlled environment. Simulations help identify strengths and weaknesses in the organization's incident response capabilities. Regular exercises ensure that staff are well-prepared to handle actual security incidents effectively.

## Actionable Recommendations

Implementing effective audit log management requires a strategic approach encompassing best practices, tools, and processes. These recommendations provide actionable steps for organizations to enhance their logging capabilities, ensuring comprehensive monitoring, timely detection of anomalies, and efficient incident response. By following these recommendations, IT professionals and cybersecurity teams can strengthen their organization's security posture and improve their ability to respond to and recover from cyber threats.

**Establish Clear Logging Policies:** Organizations should develop clear policies that define the scope, objectives, and requirements for log management. These policies outline what events need to be logged, how logs should be collected and stored, and the retention periods for different types of logs. By establishing clear policies, organizations can ensure consistency and compliance across all systems and applications. Well-defined logging policies help prevent gaps in coverage and ensure that critical events are captured and available for analysis.

**Implement Centralized Logging Solutions:** Centralized logging solutions aggregate data from various sources into a single platform, simplifying management and analysis. Organizations should deploy centralized logging tools to collect logs from servers, applications, network devices, and cloud services. Centralized Logging enhances visibility into system activities and allows for more efficient correlation and detection of anomalies. This approach also facilitates easier compliance with regulatory requirements by providing a unified repository for log data.

**Utilize Automated Log Analysis Tools:** Automated log analysis tools can help organizations efficiently process and analyze large volumes of log data. These tools use machine learning and pattern recognition to detect anomalies, correlate events, and identify potential security threats. Implementing automated analysis tools reduces the manual effort required for log review and increases the speed and accuracy of threat detection. Automated tools help security teams prioritize alerts and focus on critical incidents.

**Ensure Time Synchronization Across Systems:** Time synchronization is crucial for maintaining the accuracy and reliability of log data. Organizations should configure all systems and devices to use synchronized time sources, such as Network Time Protocol (NTP) servers. Consistent timestamps across logs ensure that events can be accurately correlated and timelines reconstructed during incident investigations. Time synchronization helps avoid confusion and ensures the integrity of log data.

CHAPTER 8   AUDIT LOG MANAGEMENT

**Regularly Review and Update Logging Configurations:** Regular reviews and updates of logging configurations ensure that logging practices remain effective and aligned with evolving security requirements. Organizations should periodically audit their logging settings to verify that all necessary events are captured and that log data is stored securely. Updates should be made in response to changes in the threat landscape, regulatory requirements, and organizational needs. Continuous improvement of logging configurations helps maintain comprehensive coverage and effective monitoring.

**Conduct Routine Log Reviews:** Routine log reviews are essential for identifying anomalies and potential security incidents. Organizations should establish a schedule for regular log reviews, with frequency based on the criticality of the systems and the organization's risk profile. These reviews can be performed manually or with automated tools, but human oversight is crucial for interpreting context and significance. Regular log reviews help detect threats early and enable prompt responses to mitigate risks.

**Implement Access Controls for Log Data:** Access controls are vital for protecting the integrity and confidentiality of log data. Organizations should enforce role-based access controls (RBAC) to ensure only authorized personnel can view or modify logs. Regular audits of access permissions should be conducted to verify that access rights are appropriate and up-to-date. Secure access controls help prevent unauthorized tampering with log data and protect sensitive information contained within logs.

**Ensure Adequate Log Storage and Retention:** Adequate storage and retention practices are critical for preserving log data for analysis and compliance purposes. Organizations should ensure that their log storage solutions can handle the volume of log data generated and that retention policies comply with regulatory requirements. Implementing scalable storage solutions and defining clear retention periods help manage storage costs and ensure logs are available when needed. Proper storage and retention practices support effective incident response and forensic investigations.

**Integrate Logs from Third-Party Services:** Integrating logs from third-party services, such as cloud providers and SaaS applications, provides a comprehensive view of the security landscape. Organizations should work with their service providers to collect relevant log data and integrate it into their centralized logging solution. This integration enhances visibility into activities across all network parts and helps identify potential threats involving third-party services. Effective integration of third-party logs supports a holistic approach to security monitoring.

**Develop Incident Response Procedures Based on Log Data:** Incident response procedures should be developed focusing on utilizing log data effectively. These procedures should outline the steps for analyzing logs during an incident, identifying indicators of compromise, and coordinating response efforts. Organizations can ensure they have the necessary information to mitigate threats by incorporating log data into incident response plans. Clear procedures help streamline incident response and minimize the impact of security incidents.

**Provide Training on Log Management Best Practices:** Training is essential for ensuring that staff understand and adhere to log management best practices. Organizations should provide regular training sessions for IT, cybersecurity, and administrative staff on log collection, analysis, and incident response topics. Training should also cover the importance of log integrity and confidentiality. Well-trained staff are better equipped to manage logs effectively and respond to security incidents.

**Conduct Regular Audits and Assessments:** Regular audits and assessments of log management practices help identify areas for improvement and ensure compliance with policies and regulations. Organizations should conduct internal audits to review logging configurations, access controls, and retention practices. External assessments by third-party experts can provide additional insights and recommendations. Regular audits help maintain effective log management and demonstrate a commitment to cybersecurity best practices.

## Simplified Security Controls (SSC)

Security controls are essential for any organization seeking to protect its digital and physical assets from cyber threats. Tailoring these controls to fit the specific needs of your business environment is crucial, as it ensures that the protection mechanisms are relevant and effective against the specific risks your organization faces. There are numerous sources to draw these controls from, including the well-regarded CIS Top 18, which provides a robust framework for crafting defensive strategies. The recommendations presented in this book are based on the CIS controls, among others, offering a comprehensive guide that can be adapted to serve a wide range of security needs. Before implementing these controls, it is vital to thoroughly review their design to ensure they align with your strategic objectives and operational practices. Additionally, after deployment, it is imperative to regularly test the controls to verify their effectiveness and to make necessary adjustments. This ensures the controls continue functioning as intended, safeguarding your organization against emerging threats and changing conditions.

CHAPTER 8   AUDIT LOG MANAGEMENT

## CONTROL 1: ESTABLISH AND MAINTAIN AN AUDIT LOG MANAGEMENT PROCESS

**Control Objective:** To define and maintain a comprehensive audit log management process that addresses collecting, reviewing, and retaining audit logs for enterprise assets.

**Implementation Steps:**

**1.1. Define Logging Requirements:** Establish clear requirements for what events must be logged, including user activities, system events, and network traffic. Specify the level of detail required for each type of log.

**1.2. Develop Logging Policies:** Create policies that outline log collection, review, and retention procedures. Ensure these policies comply with relevant regulatory requirements and industry best practices.

**1.3. Implement Logging Solutions:** Deploy the tools and technologies to collect and manage audit logs according to the defined policies. Ensure these solutions are integrated across all enterprise assets.

**1.4. Review and Update Annually:** Conduct an annual review of the audit log management process and update documentation to reflect changes in the enterprise environment or regulatory requirements.

**Expected Outcome:** A well-defined audit log management process that ensures consistent and comprehensive Logging across all enterprise assets. This process facilitates effective monitoring, incident response, and compliance with regulatory requirements.

CHAPTER 8    AUDIT LOG MANAGEMENT

## CONTROL 2: COLLECT AUDIT LOGS

**Control Objective:** To ensure that audit logs are collected across all enterprise assets in accordance with the organization's logging policies.

**Implementation Steps:**

**2.1. Enable Logging on All Assets:** Ensure that Logging is enabled on all enterprise systems, applications, and network devices. Verify that all relevant events are being captured.

**2.2. Standardize Log Formats:** Use standardized formats for log entries to facilitate more accessible analysis and correlation across different systems.

**2.3. Verify Log Collection:** Regularly check that logs are collected correctly and are complete. Address any gaps or issues in log collection promptly.

**2.4. Maintain Log Integrity:** Implement measures to protect the integrity of log data, such as encryption and access controls.

**Expected Outcome:** Comprehensive and accurate collection of audit logs across all enterprise assets, providing a reliable foundation for security monitoring and incident response.

## CONTROL 3: ENSURE ADEQUATE AUDIT LOG STORAGE

**Control Objective:** To maintain adequate storage for audit logs to ensure they are available for analysis and compliance.

**Implementation Steps:**

**3.1. Assess Storage Requirements: Consider the volume of log data generated to determine the storage capacity needed to retain logs for the required retention period.**

## CHAPTER 8   AUDIT LOG MANAGEMENT

**3.2. Implement Scalable Storage Solutions:** Deploy scalable storage solutions that can accommodate the growing volume of log data. Ensure these solutions support quick retrieval and analysis of logs.

**3.3. Regularly Monitor Storage Utilization:** Monitor storage utilization to ensure adequate available space and proactively expand storage as needed.

**3.4. Establish Archiving Procedures:** Implement procedures for archiving older log data to maintain storage efficiency while ensuring access to historical logs.

**Expected Outcome:** Sufficient and scalable storage for audit logs, ensuring logs are retained for the required period and can be accessed for analysis and compliance.

## CONTROL 4: STANDARDIZE TIME SYNCHRONIZATION

**Control Objective:** To standardize time synchronization across all enterprise assets to ensure accurate and consistent timestamps in log data.

**Implementation Steps:**

**4.1. Configure Time Sources:** Set up at least two synchronized time sources across all systems and devices, such as Network Time Protocol (NTP) servers.

**4.2. Implement Time Sync Policies:** Develop policies that require regular synchronization of system clocks with the designated time sources.

**4.3. Regularly Audit Time Settings:** Periodically audit the time settings on all systems to ensure they remain synchronized. Address any discrepancies promptly.

**4.4. Educate Staff on Time Sync Importance:** Provide training for IT staff on the importance of time synchronization and how to configure and maintain time settings.

**Expected Outcome:** Consistent and accurate timestamps in log data enable reliable correlation and event analysis across different systems.

CHAPTER 8   AUDIT LOG MANAGEMENT

## CONTROL 5: COLLECT DETAILED AUDIT LOGS

**Control Objective:** Configure detailed audit logging for enterprise assets containing sensitive data to facilitate forensic investigations.

**Implementation Steps:**

**5.1. Identify Sensitive Assets:** Determine which enterprise assets contain sensitive data and require detailed audit logging.

**5.2. Configure Detailed Logging:** Set up detailed Logging on these assets, including event source, date, username, timestamp, source addresses, and destination addresses.

**5.3. Verify Log Detail:** Regularly verify that the generated logs include the necessary details to support forensic analysis.

**5.4. Protect Sensitive Logs:** Implement additional security measures to protect the logs from sensitive assets, such as encryption and restricted access.

**Expected Outcome:** Detailed audit logs from sensitive assets, providing comprehensive data for forensic investigations and enhancing the ability to respond to security incidents.

## CONTROL 6: COLLECT DNS QUERY AUDIT LOGS

**Control Objective:** To collect DNS query audit logs on enterprise assets to monitor and analyze DNS traffic for security threats.

**Implementation Steps:**

**6.1. Enable DNS Logging:** Configure enterprise DNS servers and relevant systems to log DNS queries.

CHAPTER 8  AUDIT LOG MANAGEMENT

**6.2. Integrate DNS Logs:** Ensure DNS query logs are integrated into the centralized logging system for correlation with other log data.

**6.3. Analyze DNS Traffic:** Regularly analyze DNS query logs to identify unusual patterns or potential indicators of compromise.

**6.4. Respond to DNS Threats:** Develop procedures for responding to threats identified through DNS query log analysis, such as blocking malicious domains.

**Expected Outcome:** Enhanced monitoring and analysis of DNS traffic, improving the ability to detect and respond to DNS-based security threats.

## CONTROL 7: COLLECT URL REQUEST AUDIT LOGS

**Control Objective:** Collect URL request audit logs on enterprise assets to monitor and analyze web traffic for security threats.

**Implementation Steps:**

**7.1. Enable URL Logging:** Configure web proxies, firewalls, and relevant systems to log URL requests.

**7.2. Integrate URL Logs:** Ensure URL request logs are integrated into the centralized logging system for comprehensive analysis.

**7.3. Analyze Web Traffic:** Regularly analyze URL request logs to identify access to malicious or unauthorized websites.

**7.4. Block Malicious URLs:** Implement procedures for blocking access to identified malicious URLs to prevent potential threats.

**Expected Outcome:** Improved visibility into web traffic, enabling the detection and prevention of security threats associated with malicious or unauthorized web activity.

## CONTROL 8: COLLECT COMMAND-LINE AUDIT LOGS

**Control Objective:** To collect command-line audit logs to monitor administrative activities and detect potential misuse of administrative privileges.

**Implementation Steps:**

**8.1. Enable Command-Line Logging:** Configure systems to log command-line activities, including commands executed in PowerShell, BASH, and remote administrative terminals.

**8.2. Integrate Command-Line Logs:** Ensure command-line logs are integrated into the centralized system for comprehensive monitoring.

**8.3. Monitor Administrative Actions:** Regularly review command-line logs to detect unusual or unauthorized administrative activities.

**8.4. Investigate Suspicious Commands:** Develop procedures for investigating suspicious command-line activities and taking appropriate action.

**Expected Outcome:** Enhanced monitoring of administrative activities, improving the ability to detect and respond to potential misuse of administrative privileges.

## CONTROL 9: CENTRALIZE AUDIT LOGS

**Control Objective:** To centralize the collection and retention of audit logs across enterprise assets for efficient management and analysis.

**Implementation Steps:**

**9.1. Deploy Centralized Logging Solution:** Implement a centralized logging solution to aggregate log data from all enterprise assets.

CHAPTER 8   AUDIT LOG MANAGEMENT

**9.2. Integrate All Logs:** Ensure logs from servers, applications, network devices, and third-party services are integrated into the centralized system.

**9.3. Standardize Log Formats: Standardized log formats** facilitate more straightforward correlation and analysis within the centralized system.

**9.4. Monitor Centralized Logs:** Regularly monitor and analyze logs within the centralized system to detect potential security incidents.

**Expected Outcome:** Centralized collection and retention of audit logs, enabling efficient management, comprehensive analysis, and improved detection of security threats.

## CONTROL 10: RETAIN AUDIT LOGS

**Control Objective:** To retain audit logs for at least 90 days to ensure availability for analysis and compliance purposes.

**Implementation Steps:**

**10.1. Define Retention Periods:** Establish retention periods for different types of logs, ensuring compliance with regulatory requirements.

**10.2. Implement Retention Policies:** Configure log storage solutions to retain logs for the defined periods, with automatic archiving and deletion processes.

**10.3. Monitor Retention Compliance:** Regularly verify that log retention practices comply with the established policies and adjust as needed.

**10.4. Secure Archived Logs:** Ensure that archived logs are stored securely and remain accessible for the required retention period.

**Expected Outcome:** Adequate retention of audit logs, ensuring they are available for analysis, investigations, and compliance audits.

CHAPTER 8   AUDIT LOG MANAGEMENT

## CONTROL 11: CONDUCT AUDIT LOG REVIEWS

**Control Objective:** Conduct regular audit log reviews to detect anomalies or abnormal events that could indicate a potential threat.

**Implementation Steps:**

**11.1. Establish a Review Schedule:** Define a schedule for regular log reviews, with frequency based on the criticality of the systems and risk profile.

**11.2. Use Automated Tools:** Implement automated tools to assist with log reviews, highlighting anomalies and potential security incidents.

**11.3. Perform Manual Reviews:** Conduct manual reviews of logs to interpret context and significance, focusing on high-risk systems and events.

**11.4. Document and Respond:** Document findings from log reviews and develop procedures for responding to identified threats or anomalies.

**Expected Outcome:** Regular and thorough reviews of audit logs, enhancing the ability to detect and respond to security incidents promptly.

## CONTROL 12: COLLECT SERVICE PROVIDER LOGS

**Control Objective:** To collect and integrate logs from service providers to ensure comprehensive monitoring of all activities affecting the organization's security.

**Implementation Steps:**

**12.1. Identify Service Providers:** Identify all third-party service providers and the types of logs they generate.

**12.2. Integrate Provider Logs:** Ensure logs from service providers are collected and integrated into the centralized logging system.

CHAPTER 8   AUDIT LOG MANAGEMENT

**12.3. Monitor and Analyze:** Regularly monitor and analyze service provider logs to detect unusual activities and potential threats.

**12.4. Coordinate with Providers:** Develop procedures for coordinating with service providers in case of detected security incidents involving their services.

**Expected Outcome:** Comprehensive monitoring of all activities affecting the organization's security, including those involving third-party service providers, enhancing the ability to detect and respond to threats.

# CHAPTER 9

# Email and Browser Protections

The digital landscape is rife with threats that target email and web browsers, making them critical entry points for cyber attackers. These vectors are particularly vulnerable due to their direct interaction with users, offering numerous opportunities for manipulation and exploitation. Cybercriminals can craft content to deceive users into revealing sensitive information or unwittingly allowing access to their systems. This heightened risk underscores the necessity of robust protection and detection mechanisms to safeguard organizational assets.

Email and web browsers are essential tools for modern communication and information exchange, but their ubiquitous nature makes them prime targets for malicious activities. Attackers frequently exploit these avenues to deploy phishing schemes, malware, and other forms of social engineering. The consequences of such breaches can be severe, ranging from data theft to significant operational disruptions. Therefore, improving security measures in these areas is not just advisable but imperative for any organization.

The nature of email as an interactive medium makes it especially susceptible to exploitation. Attackers can use phishing emails to deceive users into clicking on malicious links or downloading harmful attachments. Business Email Compromise (BEC) schemes are also prevalent, where attackers impersonate trusted contacts to manipulate employees into transferring funds or sharing confidential information. The interactive element of email necessitates not only technical defenses but also rigorous training and awareness programs for users.

On the other hand, web browsers are gateways to the vast expanse of the Internet, including both legitimate and malicious websites. Attackers can exploit vulnerabilities in web browsers or their plugins to gain unauthorized access to systems. These exploits can be executed through malicious websites that exploit known browser vulnerabilities. Hence, maintaining updated browsers and plugins and employing robust content filtering mechanisms is crucial for minimizing risks.

Browser-based attacks often utilize social engineering tactics to lure users into compromising their security. Pop-ups and misleading advertisements can trick users into downloading malware or revealing personal information. Implementing strict browser settings to block pop-ups and prevent the automatic execution of potentially harmful content can significantly reduce these risks. Additionally, subscribing to DNS filtering services can help block access to known malicious domains at the network level, providing an added layer of defense.

The evolution of email and web access technologies further complicates the security landscape. With the shift toward web-based and mobile email clients, traditional security controls embedded in full-featured email clients often need to be included. This transition requires organizations to adopt new security measures tailored to these platforms, ensuring that encryption, authentication, and phishing reporting mechanisms are effectively implemented.

Technical defenses are only sufficient with proper user education and awareness. Employees must be trained to recognize phishing attempts and understand the importance of reporting suspicious activities. Conducting regular phishing simulations and providing feedback can help users improve their ability to identify and respond to threats. This combination of technical and educational measures is essential for a comprehensive defense strategy.

Regular audits and updates to email and web security protocols are necessary to keep pace with the evolving threat landscape. Cybercriminals continually develop new techniques to bypass existing defenses, making it vital for organizations to stay informed about the latest threats and vulnerabilities. Implementing a proactive approach to security, including frequent assessments and updates, can help mitigate the risk of breaches.

Organizations should also foster a culture of cybersecurity awareness, where all employees understand their role in protecting the enterprise. This involves technical staff and all users who interact with email and web browsers. Encouraging a security-first mindset can lead to more vigilant and cautious behavior, reducing the likelihood of successful attacks.

Collaboration between IT security teams and business units is crucial for effective email and web browser protection. Understanding different departments' specific needs and workflows can help tailor security measures that do not impede productivity. For example, restricting certain file types in emails may require coordination to ensure that necessary documents can be exchanged without exposing the organization to unnecessary risks.

Investing in advanced security tools and technologies can also enhance email and web protection. Solutions such as advanced threat protection (ATP) for email, which uses machine learning and behavioral analysis to detect and block sophisticated attacks, can provide additional layers of security. Similarly, web filtering and isolation technologies can prevent users from accessing malicious websites or downloading harmful content.

Continuous monitoring and incident response capabilities are essential to a robust email and web security strategy. Implementing systems that can detect anomalies and respond to potential threats in real time can help mitigate the impact of attacks. A well-defined incident response plan ensures organizations can quickly address and recover from security breaches, minimizing damage and downtime.

## CHAPTER 9  EMAIL AND BROWSER PROTECTIONS

Securing email and web browsers is a multifaceted challenge requiring technical measures, user education, and continuous vigilance. By understanding the tactics used by cybercriminals and implementing comprehensive protection strategies, organizations can significantly reduce their vulnerability to these common attack vectors. As the digital landscape continues to evolve, so must the defenses that protect it, ensuring that enterprises can operate securely and efficiently in an increasingly connected world.

# Key Concepts and Terms

Understanding the specific terms and concepts of email and web browser protections is crucial in cybersecurity. This section will delve into key terminology professionals must grasp to effectively defend against threats targeting these vectors. Each term is fundamental to comprehending the strategies and mechanisms to secure email and web browser interactions, providing a solid foundation for implementing robust cybersecurity measures.

**Phishing:** Phishing is a deceptive practice where attackers send fraudulent emails purporting to be from reputable sources to trick recipients into revealing sensitive information, such as login credentials or financial details. These emails often mimic the look and feel of legitimate communications, exploiting the trust users place in known entities. Victims unknowingly compromise their security by clicking on malicious links or downloading harmful attachments. Phishing remains a prevalent threat due to its effectiveness in manipulating human behavior, making user education and awareness critical components of defense strategies.

**Business Email Compromise (BEC):** Business Email Compromise (BEC) is a sophisticated scam targeting businesses that regularly conduct wire transfers and deal with foreign suppliers. Attackers infiltrate or spoof email accounts of executives or high-level employees to trick unsuspecting employees into transferring money or sensitive information. These attacks leverage social engineering tactics and detailed knowledge of business operations, making them difficult to detect. The financial and reputational damage from BEC incidents can be substantial, necessitating stringent email security measures and verification protocols.

**Malware:** Malware, short for malicious software, encompasses various harmful programs designed to damage or disrupt systems, steal data, or gain unauthorized access. Common types include viruses, worms, trojans, ransomware, and spyware. Malware can be delivered via email attachments, malicious links, or compromised websites. Effective defenses against malware involve a combination of antivirus software, regular system updates, and user education to recognize and avoid potential threats.

**DNS Filtering:** DNS filtering is a security measure that blocks access to malicious or harmful websites at the domain name system (DNS) level. By intercepting DNS requests and preventing connections to known malicious domains, DNS filtering helps protect users from phishing sites, malware distribution, and other web-based threats. This proactive approach enhances network security by stopping threats before they can reach users' browsers, adding a critical layer of defense.

**Content Filtering:** Content filtering involves using software or hardware solutions to control the types of content accessed over the Internet. This includes blocking access to inappropriate or harmful websites, preventing the download of malicious files, and filtering out phishing attempts. Content filters are essential for protecting users from accidental or intentional exposure to dangerous content, reducing the risk of security breaches.

**Pop-up Blockers:** Pop-up blockers are browser features or extensions designed to prevent unwanted pop-up windows from appearing while users browse the Internet. Pop-ups can be annoying and disruptive, but they also pose significant security risks, as they can contain malicious code or deceptive messages to trick users into compromising their security. Enabling pop-up blockers helps mitigate these risks by automatically preventing such content from displaying.

**Encryption:** Encryption converts data into a coded format to prevent unauthorized access. In the context of email security, encryption ensures that messages and attachments are only readable by the intended recipients. This protects sensitive information from being intercepted and exploited by attackers. Encryption protocols are fundamental for securing email communications and maintaining data privacy.

**DMARC (Domain-based Message Authentication, Reporting, and Conformance):** DMARC is an email authentication protocol that protects domain owners from unauthorized use, such as email spoofing. It allows domain owners to publish policies specifying which mechanisms (SPF and DKIM) are employed and how receivers should handle unauthenticated emails. By enabling DMARC, organizations can reduce the incidence of phishing and spam, improving overall email security. Proper implementation requires effective collaboration between email administrators and domain owners to configure and monitor DMARC policies.

**Web Browser Plugins:** Web browser plugins are small software modules that add specific features or functionalities to web browsers. While they enhance user experience, they can also introduce security vulnerabilities if not properly managed. Attackers can exploit malicious plugins or outdated versions to access the browser or underlying system. Regularly reviewing and updating plugins and restricting the installation of untrusted plugins are essential for maintaining browser security.

**Social Engineering:** Social engineering is a manipulation technique that exploits human psychology to gain unauthorized access to information or systems. Attackers use tactics, such as phishing emails, pretexting, or baiting, to deceive individuals into divulging confidential information or performing actions that compromise security. Understanding and recognizing social engineering tactics is vital for users to avoid falling victim to these schemes. Training and awareness programs are crucial for educating employees about the signs and dangers of social engineering.

**Browser Vulnerabilities:** Browser vulnerabilities are security flaws within web browsers that attackers can exploit to compromise user systems. These vulnerabilities can arise from bugs in the browser code, insecure default settings, or unpatched security holes. Exploiting these vulnerabilities, attackers can execute malicious code, steal data, or take control of the affected systems. Regularly updating browsers and applying security patches are key practices for mitigating the risks associated with browser vulnerabilities.

**Spam Filtering:** Spam filtering is a technique for identifying and blocking unsolicited and potentially harmful email messages. By analyzing email content and metadata, spam filters can detect and quarantine suspicious emails before they reach users' inboxes. This reduces the likelihood of users interacting with phishing attempts, malware, or other malicious content. Effective spam filtering involves continuously updating filter rules to adapt to evolving spam tactics and improve detection accuracy.

# Importance and Relevance

In the current cybersecurity landscape, the importance and relevance of email and web browser protections cannot be overstated. These protections are essential for mitigating risks associated with two of the most commonly exploited entry points for cyber attackers. Email and web browsers serve as primary communication tools and gateways to the Internet, respectively, making them frequent targets for malicious activities. The following points underscore the critical nature of implementing robust security measures for these vectors, emphasizing why organizations must prioritize this aspect of their cybersecurity strategies.

**High Frequency of Use:** Nearly every member of an organization uses email and web browsers daily, increasing the likelihood of encountering threats. Given their ubiquitous nature, attackers often exploit these tools to reach many potential victims quickly. This widespread usage necessitates comprehensive security measures to protect against the constant barrage of phishing attempts, malware, and other malicious activities.

**Sophistication of Attacks:** Cyber threats targeting email and web browsers have become increasingly sophisticated. Attackers employ advanced techniques such as spear phishing, which involves highly personalized and convincing emails and drive-by downloads, where malicious software is downloaded without the user's knowledge. These sophisticated tactics can easily bypass basic security measures, requiring advanced defenses and continual updates to protective technologies.

**Human Vulnerability:** Email and web browsers are prime targets for social engineering attacks, which exploit human psychology rather than technical vulnerabilities. Phishing emails often use emotions like fear or curiosity to trick users into divulging sensitive information. This human element makes training and awareness programs as crucial as technical defenses in preventing successful attacks.

**Evolving Threat Landscape:** The threat landscape constantly changes, with new vulnerabilities and attack methods emerging regularly. The attack surface expands as organizations adopt new technologies and platforms, such as cloud-based email and remote working solutions. This dynamic environment necessitates ongoing vigilance and adaptation of security measures to protect email and web browser interactions effectively.

**Economic Impact:** Cyber attacks via email and web browsers can have significant financial repercussions. Costs associated with data breaches, including legal fees, regulatory fines, and reputational damage, can be substantial. Implementing strong protections helps mitigate these financial risks by preventing breaches and reducing the potential impact of successful attacks.

**Regulatory Compliance:** Many industries are subject to regulations that mandate specific cybersecurity measures, including protections for email and web browsers. Compliance with standards such as GDPR, HIPAA, and others often requires organizations to implement comprehensive security protocols. Adhering to these regulations helps avoid penalties and ensures a higher level of security and trustworthiness.

**Data Protection:** Email and web browsers often handle sensitive information, including personal data, financial details, and proprietary business information. Protecting these channels is crucial for safeguarding this data from unauthorized access and theft. Adequate security measures help maintain critical information's confidentiality, integrity, and availability.

**Operational Continuity:** Cyber attacks can disrupt business operations, leading to downtime and productivity losses. Ensuring robust email and web browser protections helps maintain operational continuity by preventing disruptions caused by malware infections, phishing attacks, and other cyber threats. This reliability is essential for sustaining business activities and customer trust.

**Reputation Management:** A security breach can damage an organization's reputation, eroding customer and stakeholder trust. Organizations demonstrate their commitment to cybersecurity and proactive risk management by implementing strong email and web browser protections. This proactive stance helps build and maintain a positive reputation in the eyes of clients, partners, and the public.

**Incident Response:** Effective email and web browser protections are integral to a comprehensive incident response strategy. By detecting and mitigating threats early, these measures can reduce the impact and scope of cyber incidents. A robust security framework enables quicker recovery and minimizes the long-term consequences of an attack.

**Integration with Other Security Measures:** Email and web browser protections are part of a broader cybersecurity ecosystem. Integrating these measures with other controls, such as network security and endpoint protection, creates a more cohesive and effective defense strategy. This holistic approach enhances the overall security posture of the organization.

**User Empowerment:** Empowering users with the knowledge and tools to recognize and respond to threats is key to email and web browser security. Training programs that educate employees about phishing, safe browsing practices, and reporting mechanisms foster a security-conscious culture. This collective vigilance strengthens the organization's defenses and reduces the likelihood of successful attacks.

# Risks of Not Implementing the Control

Failing to implement robust email and web browser protections exposes an organization to numerous cyber threats and vulnerabilities. These multifaceted risks affect the technical aspects of the organization's infrastructure and its financial stability, reputation, and operational continuity. The following points highlight the critical dangers of inadequate protection in these key areas. Each risk is interconnected, emphasizing the importance of a comprehensive and proactive approach to cybersecurity. Organizations must understand these risks to effectively prioritize and address their email and web browser security measures.

**Data Breach:** A data breach is one of the most severe consequences of inadequate email and web browser protections. Attackers can exploit vulnerabilities to gain unauthorized access to sensitive information, such as personal data, financial records, and proprietary business information. This can lead to significant financial losses, legal liabilities, and damage to an organization's reputation. The aftermath of a data breach often involves costly remediation efforts and can have long-lasting impacts on customer trust and business relationships.

**Malware Infection:** Email and web browsers are prime channels for malware infections without proper protections. Malware can disrupt operations, steal sensitive information, and cause extensive damage to systems and networks. Common malware types include ransomware, which can encrypt critical data and demand ransom payments for its release, and spyware, which can covertly collect information. The costs associated with malware infections include system recovery, data restoration, and potential ransom payments, all of which can be substantial.

**Phishing Attacks:** Phishing attacks are a prevalent threat that leverages email to deceive users into revealing confidential information or installing malware. These attacks can bypass basic security measures and exploit human vulnerabilities. Successful phishing attacks can lead to credential theft, unauthorized access to systems, and further spread of malware. The impact of phishing can be extensive, affecting both individual users and the broader organizational network.

**Business Email Compromise (BEC):** Business Email Compromise (BEC) is a sophisticated scam where attackers impersonate trusted contacts to manipulate employees into transferring funds or sensitive information. The financial and operational repercussions of BEC incidents can be devastating. Organizations can suffer significant monetary losses, business operations disruption, and stakeholder trust erosion. BEC schemes often go undetected until the damage is done, making preventative measures critical.

**Reputational Damage:** A security incident involving email or web browsers can severely damage an organization's reputation. Customers, partners, and stakeholders may lose confidence in the organization's ability to protect sensitive information. Rebuilding trust after a security breach is a long and challenging process, often accompanied by financial and operational costs. Reputational damage can also lead to lost business opportunities and a decline in customer loyalty.

CHAPTER 9   EMAIL AND BROWSER PROTECTIONS

**Regulatory Non-Compliance:** Many industries are subject to stringent regulations that mandate specific cybersecurity measures. Failing to implement adequate email and web browser protections can result in non-compliance with these regulations, leading to legal penalties and fines. Regulatory bodies such as GDPR, HIPAA, and others have strict data protection and breach notification requirements. Non-compliance incurs financial penalties, increases scrutiny from regulators, and damages the organization's reputation.

**Financial Loss:** Cyber attacks facilitated through email and web browsers can lead to significant financial losses. These losses may stem from direct costs, such as remediation efforts, legal fees, and regulatory fines, as well as indirect costs, such as reputational damage and lost business opportunities. The financial impact of a security breach can be long-lasting, affecting an organization's bottom line and overall financial health.

**Operational Disruption:** Security incidents can disrupt business operations, leading to downtime and productivity losses. Malware infections, data breaches, and other cyber threats can incapacitate critical systems and require extensive recovery efforts. Operational disruption affects day-to-day activities and can have long-term consequences for business continuity and service delivery. Ensuring robust email and web browser protections helps maintain operational stability.

**Loss of Intellectual Property:** Inadequate protections can lead to intellectual property theft, including proprietary technologies, business plans, and trade secrets. Intellectual property theft can have severe competitive and financial implications, as stolen information may be used to gain an unfair advantage or sold to competitors. Protecting intellectual property is essential for maintaining a competitive edge and safeguarding business innovations.

**Decreased Customer Trust:** Customers expect organizations to protect their personal and financial information. A security breach involving email or web browsers can erode customer trust and lead to customer attrition. Maintaining strong security measures is crucial for retaining customer confidence and loyalty. Decreased trust can also impact brand reputation and overall market perception.

**Increased Insurance Costs:** Organizations with adequate cybersecurity measures may face higher insurance premiums or need help to obtain coverage. Cyber insurance providers assess the level of risk based on the organization's security posture. Please implement the necessary protections to avoid increased costs or denial of coverage. Investing in robust email and web browser security measures can help mitigate these financial burdens.

**Legal Liabilities:** Security breaches can result in significant legal liabilities, including lawsuits from affected parties and penalties from regulatory bodies. Organizations may be held accountable for failing to protect sensitive information and may face class-action lawsuits or regulatory enforcement actions. Legal liabilities can result in substantial financial penalties and long-term damage to the organization's reputation and financial standing.

# What Questions Should You Ask?

To effectively implement email and web browser protections, cybersecurity leaders must ask critical questions that address the various aspects of these security measures. These questions help identify potential vulnerabilities, assess the current security posture, and guide the development of robust strategies to defend against threats. Each question targets a specific area of concern, ensuring that all facets of email and web browser security are considered. By thoroughly exploring these questions, cybersecurity leaders can form a comprehensive understanding of their organization's needs and the steps required to enhance protection.

CHAPTER 9   EMAIL AND BROWSER PROTECTIONS

**Have our email and web browser systems been updated with the latest security patches?** Ensuring that email and web browser systems are regularly updated with the latest security patches is crucial. Attackers can easily exploit vulnerabilities in outdated software to gain unauthorized access or execute malicious code. Regular updates and patch management practices help close these security gaps, reducing the risk of exploitation. Cybersecurity leaders need to verify that policies and procedures are in place for timely updates. This question highlights the importance of staying current with software maintenance to maintain a secure environment.

**What anti-phishing measures do we have in place?** Phishing is a prevalent and effective attack vector that targets email users. Implementing robust anti-phishing measures, such as email filtering, authentication protocols, and user training, is essential. Cybersecurity leaders should assess the effectiveness of these measures in detecting and preventing phishing attempts. This includes evaluating tools like DMARC, SPF, and DKIM and the frequency and quality of user education programs. Understanding the anti-phishing strategy is key to enhancing defenses against these deceptive attacks.

**How do we handle suspicious emails and web activity?** Establishing clear protocols for handling suspicious emails and web activity is vital for incident response. Cybersecurity leaders should ask how their organization identifies, reports, and responds to potential threats. This includes examining the procedures for quarantining suspicious emails, blocking malicious websites, and alerting IT security teams. Having well-defined processes ensures a swift and effective response to mitigate potential damage. This question underscores the importance of preparedness and clarity in addressing security incidents.

**What training programs do we have for educating employees about email and web security?** User education is critical to cybersecurity, especially regarding email and web security. Cybersecurity leaders should evaluate the comprehensiveness and frequency of training programs designed to educate employees about recognizing and avoiding threats. Effective training can significantly reduce the likelihood of successful phishing attacks and other social engineering tactics. This question helps ensure that employees are well-informed and capable of contributing to the organization's security posture.

**Are we using secure email protocols and encryption?** Securing email communications through encryption and secure protocols is essential for protecting sensitive information. Cybersecurity leaders must verify that their organization employs encryption methods like SSL/TLS for email transmission and storage. Secure protocols prevent unauthorized access and eavesdropping on email communications. This question emphasizes the importance of protecting data in transit and at rest, enhancing the confidentiality and integrity of email communications.

**What are our policies for web browser security?** Web browsers are common targets for cyber attacks, and robust security policies are necessary to mitigate these risks. Cybersecurity leaders should review the organization's policies regarding browser configuration, plugin use, and content filtering. It is critical to ensure that browsers are configured to block pop-ups, prevent automatic execution of potentially harmful content, and restrict plugin installations. This question helps establish the framework for maintaining a secure browsing environment.

**How do we monitor and respond to email and web-based threats?** Continuous monitoring and rapid response are essential for mitigating email and web-based threats. Cybersecurity leaders should assess the tools and processes for detecting and responding to these threats in real time. This includes evaluating the effectiveness of threat detection systems, incident response plans, and the use of threat intelligence. Monitoring and response capabilities are crucial for maintaining a proactive security posture. This question highlights the importance of being vigilant and prepared for potential threats.

CHAPTER 9   EMAIL AND BROWSER PROTECTIONS

**What are the procedures for managing third-party plugins and extensions?** Third-party plugins and extensions can introduce significant security risks if not properly managed. Cybersecurity leaders should inquire about the procedures for evaluating, approving, and regularly reviewing these add-ons. Ensuring that only trusted and necessary plugins are installed and up-to-date reduces the attack surface. This question underscores the need for strict control and oversight of third-party software integrated with web browsers.

**How do we enforce email and web browser usage policies?** Effective enforcement of email and web browser usage policies is crucial for maintaining security. Cybersecurity leaders need to understand how their organization ensures compliance with these policies among employees. This includes examining the tools and methods used for policy enforcement, such as automated monitoring, user access controls, and disciplinary measures for non-compliance. Ensuring adherence to security policies helps maintain a consistent and secure operational environment.

**Are we utilizing DNS filtering to block malicious domains?** DNS filtering is a proactive measure that helps block access to known malicious domains at the network level. Cybersecurity leaders should evaluate whether their organization is leveraging DNS filtering services to prevent users from accessing harmful websites. This technology can significantly reduce the risk of malware infections and phishing attacks. This question highlights the importance of network-level defenses in complementing endpoint security measures.

**What is our approach to securing mobile and remote email access?** With the rise of mobile and remote work, securing email access on these devices is critical. Cybersecurity leaders should assess the measures to protect mobile and remote email access, such as VPNs, mobile device management (MDM) solutions, and secure email apps. Ensuring remote access is as safe as on-premises is vital for protecting organizational data. This question addresses the challenges of securing a mobile and distributed workforce.

**How do we assess and improve our email and web security posture?** Regular assessment and continuous improvement are essential for maintaining robust email and web security. Cybersecurity leaders should ask about the methods and frequency of security assessments, including vulnerability scans, penetration tests, and audits. Understanding the current security posture and identifying areas for improvement helps ensure that defenses evolve with emerging threats. This question underscores the importance of ongoing evaluation and enhancement of security measures.

# Recommended Training

Effective cybersecurity training is essential for IT/Cyber staff and all other employees within an organization. Proper training helps ensure everyone understands the importance of security measures and their role in maintaining a secure environment. This section outlines recommended training programs to equip staff with the knowledge and skills to protect against threats targeting email and web browsers. By addressing various aspects of cybersecurity, these training sessions can significantly reduce the risk of successful attacks and enhance the organization's overall security posture.

**Phishing Awareness Training:** Phishing Awareness Training should be mandatory for all employees, focusing on recognizing and responding to phishing attempts. This training includes identifying suspicious emails, understanding common phishing tactics, and knowing the procedures for reporting suspected phishing. The outcome of this training is a more vigilant workforce capable of identifying and avoiding phishing scams. Reducing the risk of phishing attacks directly protects against credential theft and unauthorized access.

CHAPTER 9   EMAIL AND BROWSER PROTECTIONS

**Secure Email Usage Training:** Secure Email Usage Training is designed for all employees, teaching them best practices for email security. This includes using strong, unique passwords, enabling multi-factor authentication, recognizing secure email protocols, and handling sensitive information securely. The outcome is a workforce understanding of how to use email securely, reducing the risk of email-based attacks. Proper email usage training mitigates risks associated with email spoofing and unauthorized access.

**Web Browser Security Training:** Web Browser Security Training targets all employees, focusing on safe browsing practices. This training covers recognizing secure websites, avoiding malicious downloads, understanding the dangers of browser extensions, and configuring browser security settings. The outcome is a workforce that can safely navigate the Internet, reducing the risk of malware infections and data breaches. Enhancing browser security awareness prevents exposure to web-based threats.

**Incident Response Training:** Incident Response Training is essential for IT/Cyber staff and administrators, providing them with the skills to manage security incidents effectively. This training includes identifying incidents, containing threats, eradicating malicious elements, and recovering systems. The outcome is a well-prepared incident response team capable of minimizing damage during a security breach. A robust incident response capability reduces the overall impact of cyber attacks.

**Email Encryption Training:** Email Encryption Training is aimed at IT/Cyber staff and employees who handle sensitive information. This training covers the principles of email encryption, how to use encryption tools and the importance of securing email communications. The outcome is a workforce that can protect sensitive information from unauthorized access during email transmission. Implementing email encryption reduces the risk of data breaches.

**Social Engineering Defense Training:** Social Engineering Defense Training should be provided to all employees, teaching them to recognize and respond to social engineering tactics. This training includes understanding different types of social engineering, such as pretexting and baiting, and how to report suspicious interactions. The outcome is a more aware workforce that can identify and thwart social engineering attempts. Increasing awareness of social engineering reduces the likelihood of successful attacks.

**Cybersecurity Policy Training:** Cybersecurity Policy Training is designed for all employees, ensuring they understand the organization's cybersecurity policies and responsibilities. This training covers the acceptable use of email and web browsers, data protection policies, and incident reporting procedures. The outcome is a workforce that adheres to established security policies, reducing the risk of policy violations. A clear understanding of cybersecurity policies strengthens overall security compliance.

**Malware Prevention Training:** Malware Prevention Training targets all employees, focusing on preventing malware infections. This training includes recognizing signs of malware, avoiding suspicious downloads, and understanding the importance of antivirus software. The outcome is a workforce that can prevent actions leading to malware infections, reducing the risk of system compromise. Educating employees on malware prevention enhances endpoint security.

**Advanced Threat Detection Training:** Advanced Threat Detection Training is aimed at IT/Cyber staff, equipping them with skills to detect and respond to sophisticated threats. This training covers using advanced threat detection tools, analyzing intelligence, and responding to detected threats. The outcome is a skilled cybersecurity team capable of identifying and mitigating advanced threats. Improving threat detection capabilities strengthens the organization's defense mechanisms.

**DNS Filtering Implementation Training:** DNS Filtering Implementation Training is designed for IT/Cyber staff, focusing on deploying and managing DNS filtering solutions. This training includes configuring DNS filters, monitoring for malicious domains, and responding to DNS filtering alerts. The outcome is an IT team that can effectively use DNS filtering to block access to harmful websites, reducing the risk of web-based attacks. Implementing DNS filtering enhances network-level security.

**Mobile Security Training:** Mobile Security Training targets all employees, particularly those using mobile devices. This training covers securing mobile devices, using VPNs, recognizing mobile phishing, and the importance of regular updates. The outcome is a workforce understanding of securing mobile devices, reducing the risk of mobile-based threats. Enhancing mobile security protects against data breaches from lost or compromised devices.

**Continuous Security Education:** Continuous Security Education is essential for all employees, providing ongoing training to keep up with evolving threats. This training includes regular updates on new security threats, refresher courses on existing practices, and advanced training as needed. The outcome is a workforce that stays informed about the latest cybersecurity challenges and defenses. Ongoing education ensures that security practices remain effective and relevant.

# Actionable Recommendations

Implementing effective email and web browser protections requires a combination of technical measures, policy enforcement, and user education. These recommendations provide a comprehensive approach to safeguarding these critical vectors against cyber threats. Each recommendation addresses a specific aspect of email and web browser security, offering practical steps organizations can take to enhance their defenses. By following these recommendations, organizations can significantly reduce their vulnerability to attacks and improve their overall cybersecurity posture.

**Regularly Update Software:** Ensuring that all email and web browser software is regularly updated is crucial for maintaining security. Updates often include patches for known vulnerabilities that attackers could exploit. Organizations should implement automated update processes to ensure the timely application of patches. This reduces the risk of exploitation through unpatched software vulnerabilities. Keeping software up-to-date is fundamental for maintaining a secure environment.

**Implement Multi-Factor Authentication (MFA):** Multi-factor authentication (MFA) adds an extra layer of security by requiring users to provide two or more verification factors to access their accounts. This significantly reduces the risk of unauthorized access due to compromised credentials. Organizations should enforce MFA for all email accounts and any web services that support it. By doing so, they enhance the security of user accounts and protect sensitive information. MFA is a critical component of a strong authentication strategy.

**Use Secure Email Gateways:** Deploying secure email gateways helps filter out malicious emails before they reach users' inboxes. These gateways can block spam, phishing attempts, and emails containing malware. Organizations should choose gateways that offer advanced threat protection capabilities. This reduces the likelihood of successful email-based attacks by preventing harmful content from entering the network. Secure email gateways are an essential tool for protecting email communication.

**Conduct Regular Phishing Simulations:** Regular phishing simulations help train employees to recognize and respond to phishing attempts. These simulations mimic real-world phishing attacks and provide feedback to users on their performance. Organizations should conduct these simulations frequently and vary the scenarios to cover different phishing tactics. Continuous training improves user awareness and reduces the risk of successful phishing attacks. Phishing simulations are a practical method for reinforcing security training.

**Enable DNS Filtering:** DNS filtering blocks access to known malicious domains at the network level. DNS filtering adds a layer of protection by intercepting DNS requests and preventing connections to harmful sites. Organizations should subscribe to a reputable DNS filtering service and ensure it is properly configured. This reduces the risk of users inadvertently accessing phishing sites or downloading malware. DNS filtering enhances network security by preventing access to dangerous content.

**Restrict Browser Extensions:** Restricting the installation of browser extensions to those that are vetted and approved helps prevent the introduction of malicious software. Organizations should implement policies that limit extensions to those necessary for business functions. Regular reviews and updates of allowed extensions ensure that they remain secure. This reduces the attack surface and prevents exploitation through malicious or vulnerable extensions. Controlled use of browser extensions enhances overall browser security.

**Educate Users on Safe Browsing Practices:** User education on safe browsing practices is essential for reducing the risk of web-based threats. Training should cover recognizing secure websites, avoiding suspicious downloads, and understanding browser security settings. Organizations should provide regular training sessions and resources to keep users informed. This empowers users to make safer choices while browsing the Internet. Educated users are a critical line of defense against web-based attacks.

**Implement Advanced Threat Protection (ATP):** Advanced Threat Protection (ATP) solutions comprehensively defend against sophisticated email and web threats. ATP uses machine learning, behavior analysis, and other advanced techniques to detect and block threats. Organizations should deploy ATP for their email systems and web traffic. This enhances

CHAPTER 9   EMAIL AND BROWSER PROTECTIONS

their ability to identify and mitigate advanced attacks that traditional defenses might miss. ATP solutions are crucial for staying ahead of evolving cyber threats.

**Enforce Strong Password Policies:** Strong password policies ensure that users create passwords that are difficult to guess or crack. Policies should require complex passwords regular changes, and discourage reuse across different accounts. Organizations should use tools that enforce these policies and educate users on creating strong passwords. This reduces the risk of account compromise due to weak or reused passwords. Strong password policies are a fundamental aspect of account security.

**Monitor and Audit Email and Web Activity:** Continuous monitoring and auditing of email and web activity help detect unusual or suspicious behavior. Organizations should implement tools that provide real-time tracking and generate alerts for potential security incidents. Regular audits of activity logs can identify patterns indicative of a breach. This proactive approach allows for early detection and response to threats. Monitoring and auditing are essential for maintaining ongoing security vigilance.

**Develop Incident Response Plans:** Developing and regularly updating incident response plans ensures that the organization can quickly and effectively respond to security incidents. These plans should outline steps for identifying, containing, and eradicating threats and recovering systems. Regular drills and updates to the plans ensure preparedness, reducing the impact of incidents and speeding up recovery. Well-defined incident response plans are critical for effective breach management.

**Foster a Security-Conscious Culture:** Fostering a security-conscious culture involves promoting cybersecurity awareness and best practices throughout the organization. Leadership should emphasize the importance of security and encourage reporting of suspicious activities. Regular communication, training, and recognition of good security practices help build this culture. This collective effort enhances the organization's overall security posture. A security-conscious culture ensures that everyone plays a part in maintaining cybersecurity.

CHAPTER 9   EMAIL AND BROWSER PROTECTIONS

# Simplified Security Controls (SSC)

Security controls are essential for any organization seeking to protect its digital and physical assets from cyber threats. Tailoring these controls to fit the specific needs of your business environment is crucial, as it ensures that the protection mechanisms are relevant and effective against the specific risks your organization faces. There are numerous sources to draw these controls from, including the well-regarded CIS Top 18, which provides a robust framework for crafting defensive strategies. The recommendations presented in this book are based on the CIS controls, among others, offering a comprehensive guide that can be adapted to serve a wide range of security needs. Before implementing these controls, it is vital to thoroughly review their design to ensure they align with your strategic objectives and operational practices. Additionally, after deployment, it is imperative to regularly test the controls to verify their effectiveness and to make necessary adjustments. This ensures that the controls continue functioning as intended, safeguarding your organization against emerging threats and changing conditions.

## CONTROL 1: EMAIL AND WEB BROWSER PROTECTIONS

**Control 1:** Ensure Use of Only Fully Supported Browsers and Email Clients

**Control Objective:** Ensure that only fully supported browsers and email clients are used within the enterprise, employing the latest versions provided by vendors to minimize vulnerabilities.

**Implementation Steps:**

**1.1. Inventory and Assessment:** Conduct an inventory of all browsers and email clients across the enterprise. Assess each for support status and update compliance.

## CHAPTER 9   EMAIL AND BROWSER PROTECTIONS

**1.2. Vendor Communication:** Regularly communicate with browser and email client vendors to stay informed about the latest versions and support status.

**1.3. Update Policy:** Develop and enforce a policy that mandates the use of only fully supported browsers and email clients. Implement automatic updates where possible.

**1.4. Compliance Monitoring:** Implement tools to monitor compliance with the policy, ensuring that only supported versions are in use. Regularly review compliance reports and take corrective action as necessary.

**1.5. User Training:** Educate users on the importance of using fully supported browsers and email clients and provide guidance on updating their software.

**Expected Outcome:** Ensuring the use of fully supported and updated browsers and email clients reduces the risk of security vulnerabilities and exploits, enhancing the overall security posture of the enterprise.

## CONTROL 2: USE DNS FILTERING SERVICES

**Control Objective:** DNS filtering services block access to known malicious domains, protecting enterprise assets from potential threats.

**Implementation Steps:**

**2.1. DNS Filtering Service Selection:** Evaluate and select a reputable DNS filtering service that offers robust protection against known malicious domains.

**2.2. Configuration and Deployment:** Configure the DNS filtering service across all enterprise assets, ensuring proper integration with existing network infrastructure.

**2.3. Policy Enforcement:** Develop and enforce policies that mandate the use of the DNS filtering service on all devices connected to the enterprise network.

**2.4. Monitoring and Reporting:** Implement monitoring tools to track DNS filtering activity and generate reports on blocked access attempts. Regularly review these reports to identify trends and potential issues.

**2.5. User Awareness:** Inform users about the DNS filtering service and how it helps protect them from malicious websites. Guide what to do if they encounter a blocked site notification.

**Expected Outcome:** Implementing DNS filtering services helps prevent access to malicious domains, reducing the risk of malware infections and phishing attacks.

## CONTROL 3: MAINTAIN AND ENFORCE NETWORK-BASED URL FILTERS

**Control Objective:** Enforce and update network-based URL filters to limit access to potentially malicious or unapproved websites, enhancing network security.

**Implementation Steps:**

**3.1. Filter Selection:** Choose network-based URL filtering solutions offering category, reputation, and block list filtering capabilities.

**3.2. Policy Development:** Develop policies that define acceptable use and specify the types of websites that should be blocked. Include criteria for categorization and exceptions.

**3.3. Configuration and Deployment:** Configure the URL filtering solution according to the developed policies and deploy it across the enterprise network.

**3.4. Regular Updates:** The URL filtering solution should be updated to include new malicious or unapproved websites based on the latest threat intelligence.

CHAPTER 9  EMAIL AND BROWSER PROTECTIONS

**3.5. Monitoring and Adjustment:** Monitor the effectiveness of URL filters and adjust policies as needed based on user feedback and security incident analysis.

**Expected Outcome:** Network-based URL filters reduce the risk of accessing harmful websites, protecting the enterprise from web-based threats and improving overall network security.

## CONTROL 4: RESTRICT UNNECESSARY OR UNAUTHORIZED BROWSER AND EMAIL CLIENT EXTENSIONS

**Control Objective:** To minimize security risks, restrict unauthorized or unnecessary browser and email client plugins, extensions, and add-ons.

**Implementation Steps:**

**4.1. Inventory and Assessment:** Identify all browser and email client extensions currently used within the enterprise and assess their necessity and security.

**4.2. Policy Development:** Develop policies that specify which extensions are authorized for use and under what conditions. Include criteria for approval and periodic review.

**4.3. Configuration and Enforcement:** Configure browsers and email clients to prevent the installation of unauthorized extensions and to disable or remove unnecessary ones.

**4.4. User Education:** Educate users on the risks associated with unauthorized extensions and provide instructions on complying with the new policies.

**4.5. Regular Review:** Conduct regular reviews of installed extensions to ensure compliance with policies and to address any new security concerns.

**Expected Outcome:** Restricting unauthorized or unnecessary extensions reduces the attack surface and prevents potential exploitation through malicious add-ons.

CHAPTER 9   EMAIL AND BROWSER PROTECTIONS

## CONTROL 5: IMPLEMENT DMARC

**Control Objective:** Implement DMARC policies and verification to reduce the risk of spoofed or modified emails from valid domains.

**Implementation Steps:**

**5.1. Domain Assessment:** Assess all domains the organization uses to determine the current email authentication status and identify those needing DMARC implementation.

**5.2. SPF and DKIM Setup:** Implement Sender Policy Framework (SPF) and DomainKeys Identified Mail (DKIM) standards for each domain to enable DMARC.

**5.3. DMARC Policy Development:** Develop and publish DMARC policies that specify how to handle emails that fail authentication checks.

**5.4. Monitoring and Adjustment:** Monitor DMARC reports to identify issues and adjust policies to improve email authentication effectiveness.

**5.5. Awareness and Training:** Inform stakeholders about DMARC implementation and train relevant personnel on interpreting DMARC reports and maintaining the policies.

**Expected Outcome:** Implementing DMARC reduces the likelihood of email spoofing and enhances the security of email communications by ensuring authenticity.

CHAPTER 9   EMAIL AND BROWSER PROTECTIONS

## CONTROL 6: BLOCK UNNECESSARY FILE TYPES

**Control Objective:** Block unnecessary file types at the email gateway to reduce the risk of malicious attachments entering the enterprise network.

**Implementation Steps:**

**6.1. File Type Assessment:** Identify and categorize file types necessary for business operations and those not required.

**6.2. Policy Development:** Develop policies to block unnecessary file types at the email gateway, considering potential security risks and business needs.

**6.3. Configuration and Enforcement:** Configure email gateway solutions to block or quarantine emails containing unauthorized file types based on the policies.

**6.4. Monitoring and Reporting:** Implement monitoring tools to track and report on blocked file types, ensuring visibility and accountability.

**6.5. User Communication:** Inform users about the policy on blocked file types and guide how to exchange necessary files securely.

**Expected Outcome:** Blocking unnecessary file types reduces the risk of malware and other malicious content being delivered via email attachments.

CHAPTER 9  EMAIL AND BROWSER PROTECTIONS

## CONTROL 7: DEPLOY AND MAINTAIN EMAIL SERVER ANTI-MALWARE PROTECTIONS

**Control Objective:** Deploy and maintain robust anti-malware protections on email servers to detect and mitigate email-based threats.

**Implementation Steps:**

**7.1. Solution Selection:** Evaluate and select anti-malware solutions that offer comprehensive protection, including attachment scanning and sandboxing capabilities.

**7.2. Configuration and Deployment:** Configure the selected anti-malware solutions to scan all incoming and outgoing emails and attachments for threats.

**7.3. Regular Updates:** Ensure that anti-malware definitions and scanning engines are regularly updated to detect the latest threats.

**7.4. Monitoring and Reporting:** Implement monitoring and reporting tools to track the performance of anti-malware protections and identify any detected threats.

**7.5. Incident Response Integration:** Integrate anti-malware protections with the organization's incident response processes to ensure rapid response to detected threats.

**Expected Outcome:** Deploying and maintaining email server anti-malware protections enhances the organization's ability to detect and mitigate email-based threats, reducing the risk of malware infections.

# CHAPTER 10

# Malware Defenses

Malicious software, commonly known as malware, presents one of the most formidable threats in the digital landscape. Malware's evolution over the years has seen it transform from simple viruses to sophisticated threats like ransomware, spyware, and advanced persistent threats (APTs). This malicious code infiltrates systems through various vectors, including email attachments, compromised websites, and even legitimate software vulnerabilities. The repercussions of a malware infection can be severe, ranging from data theft and financial loss to significant operational disruptions. The increasing sophistication of malware underscores the necessity for robust, comprehensive malware defenses within any cybersecurity framework.

The primary objective of malware defenses is to prevent the installation, spread, and execution of malicious code across enterprise assets. This requires a multifaceted approach, encompassing endpoint protection, network security measures, and user education. Each component is crucial in fortifying an organization's defenses against malware. Effective malware defenses protect sensitive data and ensure the integrity and availability of critical systems and services. This holistic strategy is essential for maintaining a secure and resilient cyber environment.

## CHAPTER 10   MALWARE DEFENSES

Malware's entry points into an enterprise are diverse and often exploit human vulnerabilities. End-users, usually seen as the weakest link in cybersecurity, can inadvertently introduce malware by clicking on malicious links, opening infected email attachments, or using compromised USB drives. Cybercriminals leverage social engineering tactics to exploit these behaviors, making it imperative for organizations to implement comprehensive user training programs. Educating employees about the dangers of malware and the importance of safe online practices is a critical aspect of a robust malware defense strategy.

The dynamic nature of malware requires defenses that are equally adaptive and responsive. Traditional signature-based detection methods, while still relevant, are increasingly supplemented by advanced techniques such as machine learning and behavioral analysis. These modern approaches enhance detecting and responding to previously unknown threats in real time. Automation is key in this context, enabling rapid updates and responses to emerging threats. By integrating these advanced technologies, organizations can enhance their malware defenses and stay ahead of evolving threats.

Integration with other cybersecurity processes, such as vulnerability management and incident response, is essential for effective malware defenses. Vulnerability management helps identify and remediate weaknesses that malware could exploit, while incident response ensures swift action when an infection occurs. This integrated approach ensures that malware defenses are not isolated but are part of a cohesive cybersecurity strategy. Such synergy enhances the overall security posture and improves the organization's ability to mitigate and recover from malware incidents.

Centralized management of malware defenses ensures consistency and efficiency across the entire enterprise. This includes deploying and managing endpoint protection solutions, firewall configurations, and intrusion detection systems. Centralized logging and monitoring are also crucial, providing visibility into potential threats and enabling timely responses. This approach simplifies the management of defenses and enhances their effectiveness by ensuring that all components work together seamlessly.

The concept of "living off the land" (LotL) has emerged as a significant challenge in the fight against malware. This tactic involves cybercriminals using legitimate tools and processes within the target environment to carry out malicious activities. By blending in with normal operations, they reduce the likelihood of detection. Effective malware defenses must, therefore, include capabilities to detect and respond to such tactics. This involves monitoring the usage of legitimate tools and identifying unusual or unauthorized activities that may indicate a LotL attack.

Logging and monitoring play a pivotal role in detecting and analyzing malware incidents. Organizations can identify patterns and anomalies indicating malware infection by collecting and analyzing logs from various sources. This capability is enhanced by centralized logging solutions, which consolidate logs across the enterprise into a single location for analysis. Effective logging not only aids in detecting malware but also supports incident response efforts by providing a detailed record of events leading up to and following an incident.

The ever-evolving nature of malware means that defenses must be continuously updated and improved. This involves staying informed about the latest threats and trends in malware development and ensuring that defenses are updated accordingly. Threat intelligence feeds and automated update mechanisms are invaluable in providing timely information about new threats and enabling rapid deployment of countermeasures. Continuous improvement of malware defenses is essential to maintain their effectiveness in the face of evolving threats.

User behavior remains a critical factor in the success of malware defenses. Despite technological advancements, human actions can undermine even the most robust defenses. Organizations must, therefore, focus on fostering a security-aware culture where employees understand the importance of cybersecurity and their role in maintaining it. Regular training and awareness programs can help employees recognize and respond to threats.

Integrating artificial intelligence (AI) and machine learning (ML) into malware defenses represents a significant advancement in the field. These technologies enhance the ability to detect and respond to new and unknown threats by analyzing vast amounts of data and identifying patterns that may indicate malicious activity. AI and ML can also automate routine tasks, freeing up cybersecurity professionals to focus on more complex and strategic issues. Incorporating these technologies into malware defenses is critical in staying ahead of sophisticated cyber threats.

Malware defenses are a crucial component of any cybersecurity strategy, designed to protect against malicious software's diverse and evolving threats. By combining advanced technologies, centralized management, and user education, organizations can build robust defenses that protect their assets and ensure the integrity and availability of their systems. Continuous improvement and adaptation are key to maintaining the effectiveness of these defenses in the face of ever-changing threats.

# Key Concepts and Terms

Understanding malware defenses' fundamental concepts and terms is crucial for effectively implementing and managing these protective measures. This section provides an in-depth exploration of essential terminology that will help readers comprehend the strategies and tools used to combat malicious software.

**Malware:** Malware, short for malicious software, encompasses a variety of harmful programs designed to damage, disrupt, or gain unauthorized access to computer systems. This includes viruses, worms, Trojans, ransomware, and spyware. Malware can infiltrate systems through various vectors, such as email attachments, infected websites, and

## CHAPTER 10  MALWARE DEFENSES

removable media. Its impact ranges from data theft and financial loss to severe operational disruptions. Recognizing the different types of malware is essential for implementing effective defense mechanisms.

**Endpoint Protection:** Endpoint protection refers to security solutions that safeguard individual devices such as computers, mobile phones, and other network-connected devices from malware and other threats. These solutions include antivirus software, firewalls, and intrusion detection systems. Endpoint protection is vital because it represents the first line of defense against malware attempting to enter an organization's network. Effective endpoint protection solutions are continuously updated to address new threats and vulnerabilities.

**Behavioral Analysis:** Behavioral analysis is a technique used to detect malware by monitoring the behavior of software and applications within a system. Unlike traditional signature-based detection, which relies on known malware signatures, behavioral analysis identifies anomalies and suspicious activities that could indicate the presence of malware. This approach is particularly practical against new and unknown threats, as it focuses on what the malware does rather than what it looks like.

**Signature-Based Detection:** Antivirus software uses Signature-based detection Endpoint protection to identify malware based on known patterns or signatures. These signatures are unique strings of data that match known malware samples. While effective against known threats, this method has limitations in detecting new or polymorphic malware, which can alter its signature to avoid detection. Regular updates of malware signatures are necessary to maintain the effectiveness of signature-based detection.

**Living-Off-the-Land (LotL) Tactics:** Living-off-the-land (LotL) tactics involve cybercriminals using legitimate tools and processes within the target environment to carry out their malicious activities. Attackers can blend in with normal operations by utilizing built-in tools and scripts already in the system, making detection more challenging. Understanding LotL tactics is crucial for developing advanced detection methods to identify when legitimate tools are being used for malicious purposes.

## CHAPTER 10  MALWARE DEFENSES

**Ransomware:** Ransomware is a type of malware that encrypts the victim's data and demands a ransom payment for the decryption key. This type of malware can cause significant disruptions by rendering critical data and systems inaccessible. Ransomware attacks have become increasingly common and sophisticated, often targeting organizations with weak defenses. Preventing ransomware requires a combination of robust backups, regular updates, and user education to avoid phishing attacks that often deliver ransomware.

**Intrusion Detection Systems (IDS):** Intrusion detection systems (IDS) are security tools designed to detect unauthorized access or attacks on a network or system. IDS can be signature-based, detect known attack patterns, or be anomaly-based, identifying deviations from normal behavior. Effective IDS implementation is crucial for early detection of malware and other security incidents, allowing for prompt response and mitigation.

**Phishing:** Phishing is a social engineering tactic cybercriminals use to trick individuals into providing sensitive information or installing malware. This is often achieved through deceptive emails or messages that appear to come from trusted sources. Phishing is a common method for delivering malware, highlighting the importance of user education and awareness in preventing malware infections. Training employees to recognize phishing attempts is critical to a comprehensive cybersecurity strategy.

**Zero-Day Exploit:** A zero-day exploit refers to a vulnerability in software that is unknown to the software vendor and, therefore, has not been patched. Cybercriminals exploit these vulnerabilities to install malware before the vendor can release a fix. Zero-day exploits are highly dangerous due to the lack of defenses against them during the attack. Keeping software up-to-date and implementing advanced threat detection techniques are essential for mitigating the risks associated with zero-day exploits.

**Incident Response:** Incident response identifies, manages, and mitigates the impact of a cybersecurity incident, such as a malware infection. An effective incident response plan includes preparation, detection, containment, eradication, recovery, and lessons learned. Incident response is crucial for minimizing the damage caused by malware and restoring normal operations as quickly as possible. Organizations must regularly update and test their incident response plans to ensure they are ready for potential incidents.

**Threat Intelligence:** Threat intelligence involves collecting and analyzing information about current and emerging threats to inform defensive strategies. This information can include data on new malware variants, attack methods, and vulnerabilities. Integrating threat intelligence into malware defenses helps organizations stay ahead of cybercriminals by anticipating and preparing for new threats. Automated threat intelligence feeds can provide real-time updates, enhancing the effectiveness of malware detection and prevention efforts.

**Automated Updates:** Automated updates automatically apply the latest security patches and updates to software and systems. This is essential for maintaining defenses against malware, as cybercriminals continuously exploit new vulnerabilities. Automated updates ensure that security measures are always current, reducing the window of opportunity for attackers. Implementing a robust automated update mechanism is a key component of a comprehensive malware defense strategy.

# Importance and Relevance

In today's rapidly evolving digital landscape, the threat posed by malicious software cannot be overstated. Malware defenses are a cornerstone of any robust cybersecurity strategy, essential for safeguarding enterprise assets and maintaining operational integrity. This section outlines the importance and relevance of implementing comprehensive malware defenses, emphasizing how they contribute to a secure and resilient cyber environment.

# CHAPTER 10   MALWARE DEFENSES

**Protecting Sensitive Data:** Malware often aims to exfiltrate sensitive information, including personal data, financial records, and intellectual property. Organizations can prevent unauthorized access and data breaches by implementing robust malware defenses. Protecting sensitive data not only safeguards the privacy of individuals but also maintains the trust and reputation of the organization. Data breaches can lead to severe financial penalties and legal consequences, making it imperative to have strong malware defenses in place. Ensuring data integrity is critical to maintaining compliance with various regulatory requirements.

**Maintaining Operational Continuity:** Malware can disrupt business operations by compromising critical systems and services. Effective malware defenses help ensure the continuous availability of essential operations, preventing downtime and financial losses. Operational continuity is vital for maintaining customer trust and meeting contractual obligations. In sectors such as healthcare and finance, uninterrupted access to systems is crucial for delivering timely and effective services. Robust defenses against malware contribute to the overall resilience and reliability of the organization.

**Mitigating Financial Losses:** The financial impact of a malware attack can be substantial, encompassing direct costs such as ransom payments and indirect costs like lost productivity and reputational damage. By preventing malware infections, organizations can avoid these significant financial burdens. Investing in malware defenses is a cost-effective strategy, as the cost of implementing security measures is often far less than the potential losses from an attack. Cyber insurance premiums may also be lower for organizations with strong malware defenses, providing additional financial benefits. Effective malware defenses help protect the bottom line and ensure long-term financial stability.

**Enhancing Incident Response:** Comprehensive malware defenses include mechanisms for detecting, responding to, and recovering from malware incidents. These capabilities are crucial for minimizing the impact of an attack and restoring normal operations swiftly. An effective incident response plan includes containment, eradication, and recovery steps supported by detailed logs and forensic analysis. Quick and effective incident response can significantly reduce the damage caused by a malware infection. Organizations can improve their security posture and resilience by enhancing incident response capabilities.

**Supporting Regulatory Compliance:** Many industries are subject to strict regulatory requirements regarding data protection and cybersecurity. Implementing robust malware defenses is often key to achieving and maintaining compliance with these regulations. Failure to comply with regulatory standards can result in severe penalties and legal actions. By adhering to best practices for malware defense, organizations can demonstrate their commitment to protecting sensitive information and complying with industry standards. Regulatory compliance also enhances the organization's reputation and trustworthiness.

**Preserving Brand Reputation:** A malware attack can damage an organization's reputation, eroding customer trust and loyalty. Strong malware defenses help preserve and enhance the brand's reputation by preventing such attacks. Customers and partners are more likely to engage with organizations that demonstrate robust cybersecurity practices. Reputation recovery after a malware attack can be lengthy and challenging, highlighting the importance of proactive defense measures. Maintaining a positive reputation is critical for business success and growth in a competitive market.

**Protecting Against Advanced Threats:** Modern malware is increasingly sophisticated, often employing advanced techniques such as polymorphism and encryption to evade detection. Effective malware defenses utilize advanced technologies like machine learning and behavioral analysis to identify and mitigate these threats. Staying ahead of advanced threats requires continuous monitoring and updating of defense mechanisms. By leveraging cutting-edge technologies, organizations can enhance their ability to detect and respond to new and emerging malware. Protecting against advanced threats is essential for maintaining a robust cybersecurity posture.

**Reducing Human Error:** Human error is a significant factor in many malware infections, often resulting from phishing attacks or unsafe online behaviors. Implementing comprehensive malware defenses, including user education and awareness programs, can significantly reduce the risk of human error. Training employees to recognize and respond appropriately to potential threats is critical to a holistic security strategy. User education helps create a security-aware culture where individuals understand their role in maintaining cybersecurity. Reducing human error enhances the overall effectiveness of malware defenses.

**Facilitating Business Growth:** Strong malware defenses enable organizations to pursue growth opportunities, knowing their assets are protected confidently. Effective security measures are essential to mitigate associated risks as businesses expand and adopt new technologies. By securing their digital infrastructure, organizations can focus on innovation and growth without being hindered by security concerns. Trustworthy cybersecurity practices also attract customers and partners, facilitating new business relationships. Ensuring robust malware defenses supports sustainable business growth and development.

**Integrating with Other Security Measures:** Malware defenses are most effective when integrated with other cybersecurity processes, such as vulnerability management and incident response. This holistic approach ensures that all aspects of the security strategy work together seamlessly to protect the organization. Integration enhances detecting and responding to threats, providing a more comprehensive defense. Organizations can achieve a more cohesive and effective security posture by aligning malware defenses with broader cybersecurity initiatives. This integration also simplifies management and improves overall efficiency.

**Adapting to Evolving Threats:** The threat landscape constantly changes, with new malware variants and attack methods emerging regularly. Effective malware defenses must be adaptable, incorporating the latest threat intelligence and updates to stay ahead of cybercriminals. Continuous improvement and adaptation are essential for maintaining the effectiveness of security measures. Organizations can proactively adjust their defenses by staying informed about the latest threats and trends. Adapting to evolving threats ensures that malware defenses remain robust and relevant.

**Promoting a Security Culture:** Implementing strong malware defenses helps foster a culture of security within the organization. Employees become more aware of cybersecurity risks and the importance of following best practices. A security-conscious culture reduces the likelihood of successful malware attacks and enhances overall resilience. Encouraging a proactive approach to security among all staff members contributes to a more secure and vigilant organization. Promoting a security culture is an essential element of a comprehensive cybersecurity strategy.

# Risks of Not Implementing the Control

Failure to implement robust malware defenses can expose organizations to a myriad of significant risks. These risks threaten the security of sensitive data and impact financial stability, operational continuity, and regulatory compliance. Organizations become vulnerable to cyber threats without effective malware defenses that can have long-lasting repercussions. The following sections highlight twelve critical risks associated with inadequate malware protection, emphasizing the necessity of proactive cybersecurity measures to mitigate these threats.

**Data Breach:** A data breach occurs when unauthorized individuals access or steal sensitive information. Without robust malware defenses, organizations are highly susceptible to such breaches, leading to the loss of confidential data, including personal information, financial records, and proprietary business information. The fallout from a data breach can include legal penalties, loss of customer trust, and significant financial costs associated with remediation and notification efforts. Effective malware defenses are essential to safeguard against unauthorized access and protect sensitive information. Failing to implement these defenses significantly increases the risk of data breaches.

**Operational Disruption:** Malware can severely disrupt business operations by infecting critical systems and networks. This disruption can result in downtime, loss of productivity, and the inability to deliver services to customers. Operational disruptions can have dire consequences for organizations that rely heavily on continuous operations, such as healthcare providers and financial institutions. The financial impact of downtime can be substantial, affecting the bottom line and overall business viability. Ensuring robust malware defenses helps maintain operational continuity and prevents costly disruptions.

**Financial Loss:** The financial implications of a malware attack can be extensive, encompassing direct costs such as ransom payments and indirect costs like lost revenue and damage to the organization's reputation. Organizations may also incur expenses related to incident response, system recovery, and legal fees. Insurance premiums may increase for companies that fail to demonstrate adequate cybersecurity measures. Implementing strong malware defenses is a cost-effective strategy to mitigate these financial risks and protect the organization's economic stability. Failure to do so can result in significant financial losses that could be detrimental to the business.

**Reputational Damage:** A malware attack can significantly harm an organization's reputation, eroding customer trust and loyalty. Adverse publicity resulting from an attack can deter potential customers and partners, impacting business relationships and market position. Rebuilding a damaged reputation can be long and challenging, requiring substantial effort and resources. Organizations with a history of security breaches may also need help attracting and retaining talent, as employees may hesitate to join a company with known vulnerabilities. Maintaining a strong security posture with robust malware defenses is critical to preserving and enhancing the organization's reputation.

**Legal and Regulatory Consequences:** Non-compliance with data protection regulations and industry standards can result in severe legal and regulatory consequences. Organizations must implement adequate security measures to protect sensitive information and maintain compliance with laws such as GDPR, HIPAA, and CCPA. Failure to do so can lead to hefty fines, legal actions, and increased scrutiny from regulatory bodies. Additionally, non-compliance can result in losing certifications and accreditations, which may be essential for operating in specific industries. Implementing effective malware defenses is crucial to ensure regulatory compliance and avoid legal repercussions.

**Intellectual Property Theft:** Malware can steal valuable intellectual property (IP), including trade secrets, patents, and proprietary technologies. The loss of IP can have a devastating impact on an organization's competitive advantage and market position. Competitors or malicious actors who gain access to IP can use it to replicate products, innovate faster, or undermine the victim's market share. Protecting intellectual property is essential for maintaining innovation and business growth. Robust malware defenses help prevent IP theft and protect the organization's valuable assets from cyber threats.

**Customer Trust Erosion:** Trust is fundamental to a business's customer relationship. A malware attack that compromises customer data can quickly erode this trust, leading to customer churn and decreased loyalty. Customers expect organizations to protect their personal and financial information; failure can drive them to competitors. Rebuilding trust after a security breach is a challenging endeavor that requires transparent communication and significant investment in enhanced security measures. By implementing strong malware defenses, organizations can maintain customer trust and loyalty.

CHAPTER 10   MALWARE DEFENSES

**Increased Insurance Premiums:** Cybersecurity insurance is an important safeguard for organizations, providing financial protection against the costs associated with cyber incidents. However, insurance providers may increase premiums or deny coverage for organizations that fail to demonstrate adequate cybersecurity practices, including robust malware defenses. High premiums can strain financial resources, making investing in other critical business areas more challenging. Demonstrating strong cybersecurity measures can help reduce insurance costs and ensure adequate coverage. Failing to implement effective malware defenses can lead to increased financial burdens due to higher insurance premiums.

**Intensified Attack Efforts:** Cybercriminals often target organizations with weak security measures, knowing they are more likely to succeed in their attacks. Inadequate malware defenses can make an organization an attractive target, leading to repeated and intensified attack efforts. These persistent attacks can overwhelm the organization's security team and resources, increasing the likelihood of a successful breach. Implementing robust malware defenses can deter attackers and reduce the frequency and severity of attack attempts. Organizations with solid security postures are less likely to be targeted by cybercriminals.

**Loss of Competitive Advantage:** A malware attack can result in the loss of critical business information, including strategic plans, financial data, and customer insights. This loss can undermine an organization's competitive advantage, as competitors may gain access to valuable information. The inability to protect sensitive data can also affect partnerships and collaborations, as stakeholders may question the organization's ability to safeguard shared information. Maintaining robust malware defenses is essential to protect competitive advantage and ensure long-term business success. With adequate protection, organizations can stay caught up in the market.

**Impact on Employee Productivity:** Malware infections can significantly impact employee productivity by disrupting access to systems and data. Employees may be unable to perform their duties, leading to delays in project timelines and decreased overall efficiency. In addition, the stress and uncertainty caused by a cyber attack can affect employee morale and job satisfaction. Implementing strong malware defenses helps ensure that employees can work without interruption and maintain high productivity levels. Protecting the work environment from cyber threats is essential for supporting employee performance and well-being.

**Disruption of Supply Chain:** Malware attacks can have a cascading effect on the supply chain, impacting suppliers, partners, and customers. A compromised system can disrupt the flow of goods and services, leading to delays and financial losses for all parties involved. Organizations may also face reputational damage if their security weaknesses negatively affect their supply chain partners. Ensuring robust malware defenses protects the organization and helps maintain the integrity and reliability of the entire supply chain. Strong cybersecurity measures are essential for preventing disruptions and maintaining business continuity.

# What Questions Should You Ask?

Formulating the right questions is crucial for cybersecurity leaders aiming to implement effective malware defenses. These questions help identify gaps, assess current capabilities, and guide the development of a comprehensive strategy to combat malware threats. The following questions are designed to provoke critical thinking and ensure a thorough evaluation of an organization's preparedness against malware. Each question delves into different aspects of malware defense, highlighting their importance and the actions needed to address potential vulnerabilities.

**How are we currently detecting and responding to malware threats?** Understanding the existing malware detection and response mechanisms is essential for identifying gaps and areas for improvement. This includes evaluating the tools and technologies in place and the effectiveness of the incident response plan. Effective detection and response capabilities are crucial for minimizing the impact of malware incidents. Assessing the current state helps prioritize areas that need enhancement. Ensuring robust detection and response mechanisms is foundational to a strong cybersecurity posture.

**What are our primary vectors for malware entry?** Identifying the main entry points for malware within the organization allows for targeted defenses. These vectors include email attachments, web downloads, USB devices, and network vulnerabilities. Knowing the primary entry points helps implement specific controls to block these paths. Regularly assessing and updating the understanding of these vectors ensures the organization stays ahead of evolving threats. Protecting these entry points is crucial for preventing malware infiltration.

**Do we have a centralized logging system for monitoring suspicious activities?** Centralized logging is critical for tracking and analyzing events across the network. It enables the timely identification of anomalies that may indicate malware activity. A robust logging system supports incident response by providing detailed records of activities before, during, and after a malware attack. Ensuring centralized logging helps correlate events and detect patterns indicative of malicious behavior. Implementing comprehensive logging capabilities is key to effective threat monitoring.

**How often are our malware signatures and detection tools updated?** Keeping malware detection tools and signatures up-to-date is essential for protecting against the latest threats. Cybercriminals continuously develop new malware variants, making regular updates critical for maintaining effective defenses. Automated update mechanisms can ensure that the latest protections are always in place. Evaluating the frequency and reliability of updates helps ensure that defenses remain robust. Staying current with updates is vital for defending against emerging threats.

**What training and awareness programs do we have in place for employees?** User education is critical to malware defense, as human error often facilitates malware infections. Training programs should cover safe online practices, recognizing phishing attempts, and properly handling suspicious emails and attachments. Regularly updating and reinforcing these programs helps maintain a security-aware culture. Assessing the effectiveness of training programs ensures they meet the organization's needs. Educating employees reduces the risk of malware incidents significantly.

**How do we handle and secure removable media?** Removable media, such as USB drives, can be a significant vector for malware introduction. Establishing strict policies for the use of removable media helps mitigate this risk. This includes controlling access, using encrypted devices, and scanning media before use. Evaluating current practices and policies around removable media ensures they are adequate and enforced. Securing removable media is essential for preventing malware from entering the network.

**What is our patch management process?** Regular patching of software and systems is crucial for closing vulnerabilities that malware can exploit. An effective patch management process ensures that updates are applied promptly and consistently across all devices. Evaluating the current patch management strategy helps identify any delays or gaps that could expose the organization to risk. Implementing a robust process for timely patching strengthens the overall security posture. Staying diligent with patch management is key to reducing vulnerabilities.

**Do we conduct regular vulnerability assessments and penetration testing?** Regular vulnerability assessments and penetration testing help identify and remediate security weaknesses. These activities provide insights into potential entry points for malware and test the effectiveness of existing defenses. Assessing the frequency and scope of these evaluations ensures they are comprehensive and up-to-date. Incorporating findings from these assessments into the security strategy enhances protection. Conducting regular assessments is essential for maintaining a proactive security stance.

**How do we manage access controls and user privileges?** Properly managed access controls and user privileges are vital for limiting the potential spread of malware. Ensuring that users have the minimum necessary access reduces the risk of malware gaining elevated privileges. Regularly reviewing and updating access controls helps maintain security. Implementing strong authentication measures further enhances protection. Effective management of access controls is a key defense against malware propagation.

**What backup and recovery procedures do we have in place?** Robust backup and recovery procedures are critical for minimizing the impact of a malware attack, especially ransomware. Ensuring that backups are regular, comprehensive, and stored securely helps protect against data loss. Testing recovery procedures regularly ensures they work effectively when needed. Assessing the current backup strategy helps identify any gaps or weaknesses. Implementing strong backup and recovery processes is essential for resilience against malware.

**How do we integrate threat intelligence into our defenses?** Leveraging threat intelligence helps anticipate and defend against emerging malware threats. Integrating real-time threat intelligence into security operations enhances the ability to detect and respond to new threats. Assessing how threat intelligence is used within the organization helps identify areas for improvement. Regularly updating threat intelligence sources ensures they remain relevant and effective. Utilizing threat intelligence is crucial for proactive defense.

**What incident response capabilities do we have, and how are they tested?** Effective incident response is critical for minimizing the damage caused by a malware attack. Regularly testing incident response plans through drills and simulations ensures readiness. Assessing the comprehensiveness of the incident response plan helps identify any gaps or weaknesses. Ensuring that all relevant personnel are trained and aware of their roles enhances the effectiveness of the response. Implementing and regularly testing incident response capabilities is key to a strong security posture.

# Recommended Training

Effective training is a cornerstone of a robust cybersecurity strategy, ensuring that IT/Cyber staff and employees are well-equipped to recognize and respond to potential threats. Training programs must be comprehensive, covering technical aspects for specialized staff and general security awareness for the broader workforce. This multifaceted approach enhances the overall security posture and helps mitigate risks associated with human error, which is a common factor in cybersecurity incidents. The following recommendations outline essential training initiatives that can be implemented to strengthen an organization's defenses against malware and other cyber threats.

**Phishing Awareness Training:** All employees should attend phishing awareness training focusing on identifying and avoiding phishing attacks. The training should include examples of phishing emails, techniques used by attackers, and best practices for verifying the authenticity of messages. The outcome is an increased ability to recognize phishing attempts, reducing the likelihood of successful attacks. Educating employees on spotting and handling suspicious emails can significantly lower the risk of malware infections. Regular refreshers should be provided to keep the knowledge up-to-date.

**Incident Response Training:** IT and Cyber staff should undergo incident response training covering the procedures and tools necessary to respond to a cybersecurity incident. The training should include scenario-based exercises, identification of incident types, and steps for containment, eradication, and recovery. The outcome is a well-prepared team capable of effectively managing and mitigating incidents. This training reduces risk by ensuring the organization can quickly and efficiently address threats, minimizing damage and downtime. Continuous improvement and periodic drills are essential components of this training.

## CHAPTER 10   MALWARE DEFENSES

**Secure Coding Practices:** Developers and software engineers should receive training on secure coding practices to prevent vulnerabilities in software applications. The training should cover common security flaws, such as SQL injection and cross-site scripting, and how to mitigate them. The outcome is the development of more secure software, reducing the risk of exploitation by malware. This training helps ensure that applications are built with security, addressing potential threats during the development phase. Regular code reviews and updates to training materials are important to keep up with evolving threats.

**Endpoint Security Training:** IT staff and system administrators should be trained on endpoint security measures, including the configuration and management of antivirus software, firewalls, and intrusion detection systems. The training should cover best practices for deploying and maintaining these tools to ensure they provide maximum protection. The outcome is a well-secured network of devices, reducing the risk of malware spreading through the organization. By equipping IT staff with the knowledge to manage endpoint security effectively, the organization can prevent many common entry points for malware. Ongoing training and updates are necessary as technology and threats evolve.

**Data Protection and Privacy Training:** All employees should attend data protection and privacy training, focusing on safeguarding sensitive information. The training should include best practices for handling and sharing data and compliance with relevant regulations such as GDPR and HIPAA. The outcome is a workforce that understands the importance of data security and takes steps to protect it. This training reduces the risk of data breaches and ensures that employees are aware of their responsibilities regarding data protection. Regular updates and assessments should be conducted to reinforce these practices.

**Network Security Fundamentals:** Network administrators and IT staff should receive training on network security fundamentals, including designing and implementing secure networks. The training should cover topics such as network segmentation, secure configuration of network devices, and monitoring for suspicious activity. The outcome is a robust and secure network infrastructure, reducing the risk of malware propagation and unauthorized access. This training ensures network administrators can build and maintain secure networks that protect the organization's assets. Periodic reviews and updates to network security practices are necessary to address new threats.

**Social Engineering Awareness:** All employees should be trained in social engineering awareness, focusing on recognizing and responding to manipulation attempts by attackers. The training should include examples of common social engineering tactics, such as pretexting, baiting, and tailgating. The outcome is an increased awareness of these threats and the ability to respond appropriately. By educating employees on identifying and avoiding social engineering attacks, the organization can prevent unauthorized access and reduce the risk of malware. Regular reinforcement and updates to the training content are essential to keep it practical.

**Mobile Device Security:** Employees who use mobile devices for work should receive training on security, including best practices for securing their devices. The training should cover strong passwords, encryption, and the risks of downloading unverified apps. The outcome is a workforce that understands how to secure mobile devices, reducing the risk of malware infections and data breaches. This training helps ensure that mobile devices do not become a weak point in the organization's security defenses. Continuous updates and reminders are necessary as mobile security threats evolve.

**Cloud Security Training:** IT staff and administrators should receive training on cloud security, focusing on the secure configuration and management of cloud services. The training should cover topics such as identity and access management, data encryption, and monitoring for unusual activity. The outcome is a secure cloud environment that protects the organization's data and applications. By equipping staff with

## CHAPTER 10   MALWARE DEFENSES

the knowledge to manage cloud security effectively, the organization can mitigate risks associated with cloud computing. Ongoing training and updates are essential to address new cloud security challenges.

**Password Management Training:** All employees should attend password management training covering the importance of strong passwords and best practices for creating and managing them. The training should include guidance on using password managers and implementing multi-factor authentication (MFA). The outcome is a workforce that uses strong, unique passwords, reducing the risk of account compromise. This training helps prevent unauthorized access to systems and data, enhancing the overall security posture. Regular reminders and updates are necessary to reinforce good password hygiene.

**Vulnerability Management Training:** IT staff and security teams should receive training on vulnerability management, including the identification, assessment, and remediation of security vulnerabilities. The training should cover vulnerability scanning tools and the process for prioritizing and addressing vulnerabilities. The outcome is a proactive approach to identifying and mitigating potential security weaknesses. This training ensures the organization stays ahead of threats by regularly assessing and improving its security posture. Continuous improvement and updates to vulnerability management practices are essential.

**Compliance and Regulatory Training:** All employees should be trained on the importance of compliance with industry regulations and standards related to cybersecurity. The training should cover relevant laws, such as GDPR, HIPAA, and CCPA, and the organization's policies for meeting these requirements. The outcome is a workforce that understands its legal obligations and follows best practices to ensure compliance. This training reduces the risk of regulatory fines and legal actions resulting from non-compliance. Regular updates and assessments should be conducted to inform employees of any regulation changes.

# Actionable Recommendations

Implementing effective malware defenses requires a strategic approach encompassing technology, processes, and people. The following recommendations provide a comprehensive framework for organizations to build robust defenses against malware threats. Each recommendation addresses malware prevention, detection, and response, ensuring a holistic approach to cybersecurity. These actionable steps will help organizations strengthen their security posture, minimize risks, and enhance their resilience against cyber threats.

**Implement Multi-Layered Defense:** Deploying a multi-layered defense strategy is crucial for protecting against various types of malware. This approach includes endpoint protection, network security measures, and advanced threat detection technologies. Each layer provides a different level of protection, making it more difficult for malware to penetrate and spread. Combining these layers creates a robust defense-in-depth strategy that addresses multiple attack vectors. Regularly updating and testing each layer ensures continued effectiveness against evolving threats.

**Automate Updates and Patches:** Keeping systems and software up-to-date with the latest patches and updates is essential for closing security vulnerabilities that malware can exploit. Implement automated patch management processes to ensure timely application of security updates across all devices and systems. Regularly review and verify that updates are successfully applied to avoid potential gaps. Automation reduces the risk of human error and ensures that critical updates are not missed. Maintaining up-to-date systems significantly reduces the risk of malware infections.

**Deploy Advanced Threat Detection Tools:** Utilize advanced threat detection tools, such as intrusion detection systems (IDS), intrusion prevention systems (IPS), and behavioral analysis solutions. These tools can identify and respond to unusual activities that may indicate the presence of malware. Implementing machine learning and AI-powered solutions enhances the ability to detect unknown or emerging threats. Regularly review and update detection rules and algorithms to keep pace with evolving threats. Advanced detection tools are essential for identifying and mitigating sophisticated malware attacks.

**Conduct Regular Security Assessments:** Perform regular security assessments, including vulnerability scans and penetration testing, to identify and remediate potential weaknesses. These assessments provide insights into the organization's security posture and highlight areas that require improvement. Scheduling periodic assessments ensures that vulnerabilities are identified and addressed promptly. Use the findings to enhance existing security measures and develop new strategies. Regular security assessments help maintain a proactive approach to threat management.

**Implement Strong Access Controls:** Establish strict access controls to limit user privileges and prevent unauthorized access to sensitive systems and data. Use the principle of least privilege to ensure that users have only the access necessary to perform their roles. Implement multi-factor authentication (MFA) to add an extra layer of security. Regularly review and update access controls to reflect changes in roles and responsibilities. Strong access controls prevent malware from spreading and accessing critical assets.

**Educate Employees on Cyber Hygiene:** Conduct regular training sessions for all employees on best practices for cyber hygiene, including recognizing phishing attempts and avoiding suspicious downloads. Educate staff on the importance of strong passwords, safe browsing habits, and properly handling sensitive information. Provide ongoing training and updates to inform employees about new threats and evolving attack techniques. Encouraging a culture of cybersecurity awareness reduces the risk of human error leading to malware infections. Employee education is a vital component of an organization's overall security strategy.

**Establish Incident Response Procedures:** Develop and implement comprehensive procedures to address malware infections and other security incidents. These procedures should include detection, containment, eradication, and recovery steps. Conduct regular drills and simulations to ensure all relevant personnel know their roles and responsibilities. Continuously update the incident response plan based on lessons learned from past incidents and emerging threats. Effective incident response procedures minimize the impact of malware attacks and facilitate rapid recovery.

**Use Endpoint Detection and Response (EDR):** Implement Endpoint Detection and Response (EDR) solutions to continuously monitor and analyze endpoint activities. EDR provides real-time visibility into endpoint behavior, enabling the rapid detection and investigation of suspicious activities. Integrate EDR with other security tools to enhance threat detection and response capabilities. Regularly update EDR solutions to keep pace with new threat vectors. EDR is crucial for identifying and mitigating malware threats at the endpoint level.

**Encrypt Sensitive Data:** Implement encryption for sensitive data at rest and in transit to protect it from unauthorized access. Use strong encryption standards and ensure that encryption keys are securely managed. Review and update encryption practices regularly to align with current best practices and regulatory requirements. Encryption provides an additional layer of security, making it more difficult for attackers to access and exploit sensitive information. Protecting data through encryption is a fundamental aspect of a robust security strategy.

**Deploy Network Segmentation:** Utilize network segmentation to isolate critical systems and data from the rest of the network. This approach limits the ability of malware to move laterally across the network, reducing the potential impact of an infection. Implement strict access controls and monitoring between segmented network areas. Regularly review and adjust network segmentation to reflect changes in the network architecture and emerging threats. Network segmentation enhances the overall security posture by containing potential threats.

**Backup and Recovery Planning:** Establish and maintain comprehensive backup and recovery plans to ensure data integrity and availability during a malware attack. Regularly backup critical data and systems and store backups securely, preferably offsite or in the cloud. Test recovery procedures regularly to ensure they work effectively and can be executed quickly when needed. Implementing a robust backup strategy reduces the risk of data loss and enables rapid restoration of operations. Backup and recovery planning is essential for resilience against ransomware and other destructive malware.

**Integrate Threat Intelligence:** Incorporate threat intelligence into your security operations to stay informed about the latest threats and attack vectors. Use threat intelligence feeds to update detection tools, inform risk assessments, and guide incident response efforts. Collaborate with industry peers and threat intelligence-sharing communities to gain insights into emerging threats. Regularly review and act on threat intelligence to enhance your security posture. Leveraging threat intelligence helps organizations anticipate and defend against new and evolving malware threats.

## Simplified Security Controls (SSC)

Security controls are essential for any organization seeking to protect its digital and physical assets from cyber threats. Tailoring these controls to fit the specific needs of your business environment is crucial, as it ensures that the protection mechanisms are relevant and effective against the specific risks your organization faces. There are numerous sources to draw these controls from, including the well-regarded CIS Top 18, which provides a robust framework for crafting defensive strategies. The recommendations presented in this book are based on the CIS controls, among others, offering a comprehensive guide that can be adapted to

CHAPTER 10   MALWARE DEFENSES

serve a wide range of security needs. Before implementing these controls, it is vital to thoroughly review their design to ensure they align with your strategic objectives and operational practices. Additionally, after deployment, it is imperative to regularly test the controls to verify their effectiveness and to make necessary adjustments. This ensures that the controls continue to function as intended, safeguarding your organization against emerging threats and changing conditions.

## CONTROL 1: DEPLOY AND MAINTAIN ANTI-MALWARE SOFTWARE

**Control Objective:** To ensure comprehensive protection against malicious software by deploying and maintaining anti-malware software on all enterprise assets.

**Implementation Steps:**

**1.1. Asset Inventory:** Conduct an inventory of all enterprise assets to identify devices that require anti-malware software installation.

**1.2. Selection of Anti-Malware Software:** Choose reputable and effective anti-malware software solutions compatible with the organization's operating systems and applications.

**1.3. Deployment:** Install the selected anti-malware software on all identified assets, ensuring coverage across desktops, laptops, servers, and mobile devices.

**1.4. Regular Maintenance:** Schedule regular maintenance activities, including software updates and system scans, to ensure the software remains effective against new and emerging threats.

**1.5. Monitoring and Reporting:** Implement a system for monitoring the status and effectiveness of the anti-malware software, generating regular reports to inform management of the security posture.

**Expected Outcome:** The deployment and maintenance of anti-malware software across all enterprise assets provide a foundational layer of defense against malware, reducing the risk of infections and enhancing overall security.

## CONTROL 2: CONFIGURE AUTOMATIC ANTI-MALWARE SIGNATURE UPDATES

**Control Objective:** To ensure anti-malware software remains effective against the latest threats by configuring automatic updates for anti-malware signature files on all enterprise assets.

**Implementation Steps:**

**2.1. Enable Automatic Updates:** Configure anti-malware software on all enterprise assets to automatically receive and apply signature updates.

**2.2. Update Frequency:** Set the update frequency to the highest possible setting to ensure timely protection against new threats.

**2.3. Verification:** Regularly verify that updates are being received and applied correctly, addressing any issues that may arise.

**2.4. Update Monitoring:** Implement monitoring tools to track the status of anti-malware updates and alert IT staff if updates fail.

**2.5. Reporting:** Generate regular reports on the status of anti-malware signature updates to assure management.

**Expected Outcome:** Automatic updates of anti-malware signature files ensure that enterprise assets are continuously protected against the latest malware threats, reducing the risk of successful attacks.

CHAPTER 10   MALWARE DEFENSES

## CONTROL 3: DISABLE AUTORUN AND AUTOPLAY FOR REMOVABLE MEDIA

**Control Objective:** To prevent the automatic execution of potentially malicious code from removable media by turning off autorun and autoplay features.

**Implementation Steps:**

**3.1. Policy Development:** Develop and implement a policy to turn off autorun and autoplay features on all enterprise devices.

**3.2. Configuration:** Configure operating systems and software settings to turn off autorun and autoplay functionality.

**3.3. Testing:** Test the configuration changes on a subset of devices to ensure they do not disrupt normal operations.

**3.4. Deployment:** Roll out the configuration changes across all enterprise devices.

**3.5. User Education:** Educate users on the reasons for turning off these features and how to manually access files on removable media safely.

**Expected Outcome:** Disabling autorun and autoplay features significantly reduces the risk of malware spreading through removable media by preventing the automatic execution of malicious code.

## CONTROL 4: CONFIGURE AUTOMATIC ANTI-MALWARE SCANNING OF REMOVABLE MEDIA

**Control Objective:** To prevent malware infections from removable media by configuring anti-malware software to scan all removable media upon insertion automatically.

## CHAPTER 10  MALWARE DEFENSES

**Implementation Steps:**

**4.1. Policy Development:** Establish a policy requiring automatic scanning of all removable media.

**4.2. Configuration:** Configure anti-malware software to automatically scan removable media when connected to any enterprise device.

**4.3. Testing:** Conduct tests to ensure the scanning process is effective and does not interfere with normal device operations.

**4.4. Deployment:** Implement the configuration changes across all enterprise devices.

**4.5. Monitoring:** Regularly monitor the scanning logs to identify and address any detected threats.

**Expected Outcome:** Automatic scanning of removable media ensures that any potential malware is detected and mitigated before it can infect enterprise systems, thereby enhancing security.

## CONTROL 5: ENABLE ANTI-EXPLOITATION FEATURES

**Control Objective:** Protect enterprise assets and software from exploitation by enabling anti-exploitation features such as Data Execution Prevention (DEP) and Windows Defender Exploit Guard (WDEG).

**Implementation Steps:**

**5.1. Feature Identification:** Identify and document all available anti-exploitation features for the operating systems and applications.

**5.2. Configuration:** Enable anti-exploitation features on all applicable systems, ensuring compatibility with existing software and operations.

**5.3. Testing:** Test the enabled features in a controlled environment to ensure they do not cause disruptions.

CHAPTER 10   MALWARE DEFENSES

**5.4. Deployment:** Roll out the configurations across the enterprise, prioritizing high-risk assets first.

**5.5. Monitoring and Updating:** Continuously monitor the effectiveness of these features and update configurations as necessary to address new vulnerabilities.

**Expected Outcome:** Enabling anti-exploitation features significantly reduces the risk of successfully exploiting vulnerabilities within enterprise systems, enhancing overall security.

## CONTROL 6: CENTRALLY MANAGE ANTI-MALWARE SOFTWARE

**Control Objective:** To ensure consistent and effective management of anti-malware software across the organization by implementing centralized management.

**Implementation Steps:**

**6.1. Centralized Management Tool:** Select and deploy a centralized management tool for overseeing anti-malware software across all enterprise assets.

**6.2. Configuration:** Configure the tool to enforce standardized policies, manage updates, and monitor compliance across the network.

**6.3. Training:** Provide training for IT staff on using the centralized management tool effectively.

**6.4. Monitoring and Reporting:** Use the tool to continuously monitor the status of anti-malware installations, updates, and scans, generating regular compliance reports.

**6.5. Continuous Improvement:** Regularly review the effectiveness of the centralized management approach and make improvements as needed.

**Expected Outcome:** Centralized management of anti-malware software ensures consistent application of security policies, improves oversight, and enhances the overall effectiveness of malware defenses.

## CONTROL 7: USE BEHAVIOR-BASED ANTI-MALWARE SOFTWARE

**Control Objective:** To enhance malware detection and response capabilities by utilizing behavior-based anti-malware software that identifies threats based on their behavior rather than signatures.

**Implementation Steps:**

**7.1. Software Selection:** Identify and select behavior-based anti-malware solutions compatible with the organization's systems.

**7.2. Deployment:** Deploy the behavior-based anti-malware software across all enterprise assets.

**7.3. Configuration:** Configure the software to integrate with existing security tools and processes, ensuring comprehensive coverage.

**7.4. Monitoring and Tuning:** Monitor the software's performance and adjust detection rules to minimize false positives and maximize threat detection.

**7.5. Training:** Train IT staff on managing and interpreting alerts from behavior-based anti-malware software to ensure timely and accurate responses.

**Expected Outcome:** Using behavior-based anti-malware software enhances the organization's ability to detect and respond to sophisticated malware threats that may evade traditional signature-based detection methods.

# CHAPTER 11

# Data Recovery

Establishing and maintaining robust data recovery practices is essential for ensuring that enterprise assets can be restored to a pre-incident and trusted state. In cybersecurity, the triad of Confidentiality, Integrity, and Availability (CIA) underlines the importance of data recovery. While the confidentiality and integrity of data are critical, availability can be equally, if not more, crucial in certain scenarios. Enterprises rely heavily on the accessibility of data to make informed business decisions. For instance, transportation companies depend on real-time weather data to manage their operations efficiently. When data is unavailable or untrusted, it can severely impact business continuity and decision-making processes.

The need for reliable data recovery mechanisms is amplified when considering the potential impact of cyber attacks. Attackers often target enterprise assets, making unauthorized changes to configurations, adding malicious accounts, and installing harmful software or scripts. These changes can be subtle and difficult to detect, as attackers might disguise their actions to appear legitimate. For example, they might corrupt or replace trusted applications with malicious versions, alter registry entries, open unauthorized ports, disable security services, delete logs, or perform other actions compromising system security. Not all such actions are malicious; human errors can also result in significant system disruptions, highlighting the importance of having recent backups or mirrors to restore systems to a known, trusted state.

# CHAPTER 11   DATA RECOVERY

The rise of ransomware over recent years has further underscored the necessity of effective data recovery practices. Ransomware, although not a new threat, has evolved into a sophisticated and organized method for attackers to extort money from victims. Attackers encrypt an enterprise's data and demand ransom for its decryption. Recent backups allow organizations to recover their data without succumbing to extortion demands. However, ransomware tactics have also evolved to include data exfiltration, where attackers steal data before encrypting it and threaten to sell or publicize it unless a ransom is paid. In such cases, data recovery helps restore systems to a trusted state, allowing business operations to continue, although it does not address the risk of data exposure.

Implementing data recovery procedures requires a systematic approach to ensure backups are reliable and effective. These procedures should be integrated into the broader data management processes, as outlined in comprehensive data protection frameworks. Backups should be based on data value, sensitivity, and retention requirements, helping to determine the appropriate backup frequency and type, whether full or incremental. Regular testing of backups is crucial to verify their integrity and functionality. A testing team should evaluate a random sampling of backups at least once per quarter or whenever new backup technologies are introduced. Testing involves restoring backups in a controlled environment to ensure the operating system, applications, and data are intact and functional.

In the event of a malware infection, it is critical to use a version of the backup that predates the original infection. This ensures that restored systems are free from malicious code or unauthorized changes. Developing a comprehensive data recovery strategy involves understanding the different types of backups and their respective advantages. Full backups, which include copying all data, provide a complete snapshot of the system but can be time-consuming and require significant storage. On the other hand, incremental backups only capture changes since the last backup, making them faster and more storage-efficient but potentially more complex to manage.

Data recovery is not just about having backups; it also involves planning for various scenarios and ensuring recovery procedures are well-documented and practiced. Organizations should clearly understand their Recovery Time Objectives (RTOs) and Recovery Point Objectives (RPOs). RTOs define the maximum acceptable downtime after a disruption, while RPOs specify the maximum acceptable data loss. These metrics guide the development of recovery strategies and help prioritize resources to minimize operational impact. Regularly reviewing and updating data recovery plans ensure they remain effective and aligned with evolving business needs and technological advancements.

Another critical aspect of data recovery is ensuring that backups are stored securely and separately from the primary data. This prevents attackers from accessing and compromising the live data and the backups simultaneously. Offline or air-gapped backups, which are disconnected from the network, provide an additional layer of security. Cloud-based backup solutions offer scalability and redundancy but require careful management to ensure data privacy and compliance with regulatory requirements. Encryption of backup data, both in transit and at rest, further enhances security by protecting against unauthorized access.

Training and awareness programs are essential to ensure all stakeholders understand their roles and responsibilities in data recovery. Employees should be educated about the importance of following data management and backup procedures and recognizing potential threats that could compromise data integrity. Incident response teams must be well-versed in executing recovery plans under pressure, often during high-stress situations. Conducting regular drills and simulations helps prepare teams for real-world incidents, ensuring a swift and effective response when needed.

The ever-evolving threat landscape necessitates a proactive approach to data recovery. Monitoring systems and networks for signs of compromise allows for early detection and swift action to mitigate potential damage. Implementing advanced threat detection tools and integrating threat intelligence into security operations enhances an organization's ability to anticipate and respond to attacks. Collaboration with industry peers and participation in information-sharing networks further strengthens defenses by providing insights into emerging threats and best practices.

Effective data recovery is a cornerstone of resilient cybersecurity practices. It ensures business continuity and strengthens an organization's overall security posture. By establishing robust data recovery protocols, organizations can minimize the impact of cyber incidents, maintain the trust of their stakeholders, and safeguard their valuable assets. In an increasingly digital world, where cyber threats are a constant concern, the ability to recover data quickly and reliably is a critical component of a comprehensive cybersecurity strategy.

Data recovery is an ongoing process requiring constant vigilance and adaptation. As technology evolves and cyber threats become more sophisticated, organizations must continually refine their data recovery practices to stay ahead of potential risks. By embracing a culture of continuous improvement and leveraging the latest advancements in data protection and recovery technologies, organizations can ensure they are well-prepared to face the challenges of the digital age.

# Key Concepts and Terms

Understanding data recovery's fundamental concepts and terms is essential for implementing effective cybersecurity strategies. This section provides a comprehensive overview of crucial terminology associated with data recovery practices, helping IT professionals, cybersecurity experts, and organizational leaders navigate the intricacies of restoring enterprise assets to a pre-incident and trusted state. By familiarizing themselves with these concepts, stakeholders can better prepare for and respond to data-related incidents, ensuring business continuity and maintaining trust in their systems.

**Data Recovery:** Data recovery refers to restoring lost, accidentally deleted, corrupted, or inaccessible data from backup copies. This process is critical in the aftermath of data loss incidents, including cyber attacks, hardware failures, or human errors. Effective data recovery practices ensure organizations can quickly return to normal operations with minimal data loss. It involves various techniques and tools tailored to recover data from different types of storage media, including hard drives, solid-state drives, and cloud storage.

**Backup:** A backup is a copy of data created to restore the original in the event of data loss. Backups can be full, capturing all data, or incremental, capturing only data that has changed since the last backup. They are essential to data recovery strategies, safeguarding against data loss due to cyber incidents, system failures, or accidental deletions. Regularly scheduled backups ensure that the most recent data can be recovered, minimizing the impact of data loss on business operations.

**Ransomware:** Ransomware is malicious software designed to block access to a computer system or data, usually by encrypting the data until a ransom is paid. It has become a prevalent and lucrative method for cybercriminals to extort money from organizations. Ransomware attacks can be devastating, leading to significant downtime and potential data loss. Effective data recovery practices, including maintaining up-to-date backups, are crucial for mitigating ransomware attacks and restoring affected systems.

**Recovery Point Objective (RPO):** The Recovery Point Objective (RPO) measures the maximum acceptable amount of data loss during a disaster or data loss event. It represents the point in time to which data must be recovered to resume normal operations. RPO is a critical metric in data recovery planning, helping organizations determine the frequency of backups needed to meet their data recovery goals. A lower RPO indicates a need for more frequent backups to minimize data loss.

**Recovery Time Objective (RTO):** The Recovery Time Objective (RTO) is the maximum acceptable time that a computer, system, network, or application can be down after a failure or disaster occurs. It defines the target time frame for recovering and restoring data to ensure minimal disruption to business operations. Effective data recovery strategies aim to achieve RTOs that align with the organization's operational needs and continuity plans, ensuring rapid restoration of services.

**Incremental Backup:** Incremental backups involve copying only the data that has changed since the last backup operation. This method is efficient in terms of storage space and backup time, making it a popular choice for organizations with large volumes of data. Incremental backups require a series of backup sets to restore the data, starting from the last full backup. This approach is integral to maintaining up-to-date data recovery capabilities while optimizing resource usage.

**Full Backup:** A full backup is a complete copy of all data at a specific time. While it is more time-consuming and requires more storage than incremental backups, a full backup provides a comprehensive system snapshot, simplifying the data recovery. Organizations often use a combination of full and incremental backups to balance the need for comprehensive data protection with efficiency.

**Data Exfiltration:** Data exfiltration is the unauthorized data transfer from an organization's network to an external location. This tactic is often employed in advanced ransomware attacks, where attackers steal data before encrypting it and demanding a ransom. Data exfiltration poses significant risks, including data breaches and exposure to sensitive information. Effective data recovery plans must address the potential for data exfiltration by implementing robust security measures and ensuring that backups are secure and uncompromised.

**Disaster Recovery Plan (DRP):** A Disaster Recovery Plan (DRP) is a documented process or set of procedures to recover and protect a business IT infrastructure during a disaster. DRPs include strategies for data recovery, system restoration, and maintaining operations during disruptions. Developing and regularly testing a DRP is essential for ensuring an organization can quickly and effectively respond to data loss incidents and other emergencies.

**Business Continuity Plan (BCP):** A Business Continuity Plan (BCP) outlines procedures and instructions an organization must follow in the face of disaster, covering business processes, assets, human resources, and business partners. BCPs are designed to ensure that essential functions can continue during and after a disaster. Data recovery is a critical component of BCPs, providing the foundation for restoring data and resuming operations.

**Air-Gapped Backup:** An air-gapped backup is a backup copy stored offline and physically isolated from the network, making it inaccessible to attackers. This method effectively protects against ransomware and other cyber threats that target online backup repositories. Air-gapped backups ensure that a secure and unaltered copy of data is always available for recovery, providing a crucial layer of defense in data recovery strategies.

**Backup Verification:** Backup verification tests backup copies to ensure they can be successfully restored and are free from corruption. Regular verification is essential to validate the integrity and reliability of backups, ensuring that data recovery efforts will be effective when needed. This practice involves restoring a sample of backups in a test environment and checking for completeness and functionality, reinforcing confidence in the data recovery process.

CHAPTER 11   DATA RECOVERY

# Importance and Relevance

Data recovery practices are a cornerstone of effective cybersecurity. In today's digital landscape, where cyber threats are continually evolving and becoming more sophisticated, having robust data recovery strategies is vital for organizations. These strategies help restore data after incidents and play a crucial role in maintaining business continuity, protecting sensitive information, and ensuring regulatory compliance. This section highlights twelve key reasons why data recovery is critically important and relevant to cybersecurity today.

**Ensuring Business Continuity:** Data recovery is essential for maintaining business continuity during data loss incidents. Cyber attacks, such as ransomware, can cripple operations by encrypting vital data and rendering systems unusable. Organizations can quickly restore their operations using reliable data recovery practices and minimizing downtime and financial losses. This ensures critical business functions can continue without significant disruption, preserving the organization's reputation and customer trust.

**Mitigating the Impact of Ransomware:** The rise of ransomware has made data recovery more critical. Attackers increasingly target organizations with sophisticated ransomware attacks, encrypting data and demanding hefty ransoms for decryption keys. Effective data recovery strategies, including regular and secure backups, allow organizations to restore their data without paying ransoms. This not only saves money but also discourages the proliferation of ransomware by reducing its profitability.

**Protecting Against Data Loss:** Data loss can occur for various reasons, including hardware failures, software glitches, human error, and malicious attacks. Data recovery practices ensure that lost data can be retrieved, safeguarding the organization's valuable information assets. This protection is crucial for maintaining the integrity and availability of data, which are fundamental aspects of a robust cybersecurity posture.

**Supporting Regulatory Compliance:** Many industries are subject to stringent data protection regulations that mandate the safeguarding and recoverability of data. Compliance with laws such as GDPR, HIPAA, and CCPA requires organizations to have effective data recovery plans. Failure to comply can result in severe penalties and legal repercussions. By implementing robust data recovery practices, organizations can meet regulatory requirements and avoid consequences of non-compliance.

**Reducing Downtime:** In the event of a cyber incident, the ability to quickly recover data is paramount to reducing downtime. Extended periods of downtime can have catastrophic effects on productivity, revenue, and customer satisfaction. Data recovery practices ensure systems can be restored swiftly, allowing normal operations to resume with minimal interruption. This rapid recovery is vital for maintaining competitive advantage and operational efficiency.

**Preserving Data Integrity:** Cyber attacks and system failures can compromise data integrity, leading to corruption or unauthorized modifications. Data recovery practices help restore data to its original, unaltered state, ensuring its accuracy and reliability. This preservation of data integrity is essential for making informed business decisions and maintaining the trust of stakeholders.

**Enhancing Incident Response:** Effective data recovery is critical to a comprehensive incident response plan. It enables organizations to quickly restore affected systems and data, facilitating a swift return to normal operations. This capability is crucial for minimizing the impact of cyber incidents and reducing the overall recovery time. A well-prepared incident response plan with robust data recovery practices enhances the organization's resilience to cyber threats.

**Ensuring Data Availability:** Data availability is a key aspect of the cybersecurity triad, alongside confidentiality and integrity. Ensuring data is available when needed is crucial for operational continuity and decision-making. Data recovery practices guarantee that even in the face of incidents, data remains accessible and usable. This availability is vital for maintaining the flow of information and supporting ongoing business activities.

**Safeguarding Against Human Error:** Human error is a common cause of data loss and system disruptions. Mistakes such as accidental deletions, misconfigurations, and improper data handling can have significant consequences. Data recovery practices provide a safety net that allows organizations to recover from these errors without major setbacks. This safeguard is essential for mitigating the risks associated with human fallibility.

**Supporting Disaster Recovery Plans:** Data recovery is a fundamental component of disaster recovery planning. It ensures that data can be restored in natural disasters, cyber attacks, or other catastrophic events, and operations can resume. Effective disaster recovery plans with robust data recovery strategies are crucial for organizational resilience. They enable organizations to withstand and recover from significant disruptions, ensuring long-term sustainability.

**Building Customer Trust:** Organizations demonstrating effective data recovery practices are more likely to gain and retain customer trust. Customers expect their data to be protected and recoverable during incidents. Organizations can reassure customers that their information is safe and secure by implementing and maintaining robust data recovery strategies. This trust is essential for building strong customer relationships and maintaining a positive reputation.

**Enhancing Cyber Resilience:** Cyber resilience refers to an organization's ability to withstand, respond to, and recover from cyber threats. Data recovery is critical to cyber resilience, enabling organizations to bounce back quickly from incidents. By incorporating effective data recovery practices into their cybersecurity strategies, organizations can enhance their overall resilience to cyber threats. This resilience is vital for maintaining operational stability and protecting against the evolving landscape of cyber risks.

# Risks of Not Implementing the Control

If organizations fail to establish and maintain effective data recovery practices, they face numerous risks. These risks range from operational disruptions and financial losses to reputational damage and legal consequences. In a world where cyber threats are becoming more sophisticated and frequent, the inability to recover data swiftly and efficiently can have devastating impacts. This section explores twelve critical risks associated with neglecting data recovery practices, highlighting the importance of proactive measures to safeguard data integrity and availability.

**Operational Disruptions:** Organizations are vulnerable to significant disruptions without robust data recovery practices. Cyber incidents like ransomware attacks or system failures can render critical data inaccessible, halting business operations. The inability to recover data promptly can lead to prolonged downtime, negatively impacting productivity and service delivery. This disruption can cascade across various departments, compounding the adverse effects on overall business performance.

**Financial Losses:** The financial implications of inadequate data recovery practices are profound. Extended downtime and the inability to access critical data can lead to lost revenue, increased operational costs, and potential penalties for failing to meet contractual obligations. Moreover, paying ransoms to cybercriminals desperately to recover data can be financially draining. The cumulative financial impact of these factors can be devastating for any organization, affecting profitability and long-term viability.

**Reputational Damage:** Trust is a cornerstone of any business relationship, and the inability to recover data after a cyber incident can severely damage an organization's reputation. Customers, partners, and stakeholders expect organizations to safeguard their data and ensure its availability. Failure to meet these expectations can result in a loss of trust, diminished brand reputation, and customer attrition. The long-term repercussions of reputational damage can be more severe than the immediate financial losses.

**Legal and Regulatory Penalties:** Many industries are governed by strict data protection regulations that mandate the availability and recoverability of data. Non-compliance with these regulations can result in hefty fines and legal penalties. In addition, organizations may face lawsuits from affected parties whose data was compromised or lost. The legal and regulatory risks of inadequate data recovery practices underscore the importance of adhering to industry standards and guidelines.

**Loss of Competitive Advantage:** Data is a key competitive asset in today's fast-paced business environment. The inability to recover data quickly can hinder an organization's ability to innovate, respond to market changes, and make informed decisions. This loss of agility can erode a company's competitive advantage, allowing rivals to capitalize on the disruption. Ensuring data recoverability is essential for maintaining a strategic edge in the market.

**Increased Vulnerability to Future Attacks:** Organizations that fail to implement effective data recovery practices remain vulnerable to repeated cyber attacks. Cybercriminals often target organizations with known weaknesses, exploiting their inability to recover from previous incidents. Each attack can have compounded effects without robust recovery mechanisms, making it increasingly difficult for the organization to regain stability. Proactive data recovery practices are crucial for breaking this cycle and strengthening cybersecurity resilience.

**Customer Attrition:** Customers expect their data to be protected and readily available. An organization failing to recover customer data after a cyber incident breaches this trust. Customers may seek alternatives, leading to increased attrition rates. The cost of acquiring new customers is significantly higher than retaining existing ones, making customer attrition a serious risk with long-term financial implications.

**Intellectual Property Loss:** Intellectual property (IP) is valuable for many organizations, driving innovation and competitive advantage. The loss or compromise of IP due to inadequate data recovery practices can have severe consequences. Cyber incidents that result in the theft or irretrievable loss of IP can hinder research and development efforts, stifle innovation, and erode market position. Protecting IP through robust data recovery strategies is essential for safeguarding an organization's future.

**Interruption of Critical Services:** For organizations that provide critical services, such as healthcare, finance, and utilities, the inability to recover data can have life-threatening or catastrophic consequences. Service interruptions can affect public safety, disrupt essential services, and lead to significant public outcry. Data recoverability is vital for continuously delivering critical services and protecting public welfare.

**Loss of Historical Data:** Historical data is invaluable for trend analysis, strategic planning, and regulatory compliance. The inability to recover historical data can disrupt these activities, leaving organizations without essential insights into their operations and performance. This loss can impede long-term planning and decision-making processes, affecting the organization's ability to adapt and thrive in a changing business environment.

**Negative Impact on Employee Morale:** Frequent disruptions and the inability to recover data can negatively impact employee morale and productivity. Employees rely on data to perform their tasks effectively, and repeated data loss incidents can create a stressful and demoralizing work environment. This can lead to decreased job satisfaction, higher turnover rates, and reduced productivity.

**Supply Chain Disruptions:** Modern organizations are heavily interconnected with their supply chains, relying on seamless data exchange for efficient operations. Inadequate data recovery practices can disrupt this flow, causing delays and inefficiencies in the supply chain. These disruptions can ripple through the entire supply network, affecting suppliers, partners, and customers, ultimately leading to financial losses and reputational damage.

CHAPTER 11   DATA RECOVERY

# What Questions Should You Ask?

For cybersecurity leaders, forming a robust strategy for data recovery involves asking critical questions that address the core aspects of data protection and recovery. These questions guide the development of comprehensive data recovery plans, ensuring all potential risks and operational needs are considered. Addressing these questions helps identify vulnerabilities, establish effective recovery procedures, and prepare the organization for various data loss scenarios. The following are twelve essential questions that should form the basis of work when implementing data recovery practices.

**What are our most critical data assets?** Understanding which data assets are most critical to the organization is the first step in developing a data recovery strategy. Identifying these assets allows cybersecurity leaders to prioritize recovery efforts and allocate resources effectively. This prioritization ensures that the most vital data is protected and can be recovered quickly during a cyber incident. Knowing the importance of each data asset helps to tailor backup and recovery procedures to meet specific business needs.

**What is our current backup frequency, and is it sufficient?** Evaluating the frequency of backups is crucial to ensure data can be restored with minimal loss. This question helps determine whether the backup schedule aligns with the organization's Recovery Point Objectives (RPOs). Regular and timely backups are necessary to protect against data loss due to cyber attacks, system failures, or human error. Ensuring adequate backup frequency supports the organization's recovery of recent data and business continuity.

**Where are our backups stored, and are they secure?** The location and security of backup storage are fundamental to data recovery. Backups should be stored in a secure, offsite location to protect against physical and cyber threats. This question helps assess whether current storage practices are sufficient and if additional measures, such as encryption or air-gapped storage, are needed. Secure storage ensures that backup data is protected from unauthorized access and tampering.

**How often do we test our backups?** Regular testing of backups is essential to verify their integrity and functionality. This question addresses the frequency and thoroughness of backup testing procedures. Testing ensures that backups can be restored and data recovery processes work as intended. Identifying issues during testing allows for timely remediation, providing reliable data recovery when needed.

**What are our Recovery Time Objectives (RTOs) and Recovery Point Objectives (RPOs)?** Defining RTOs and RPOs is crucial for setting realistic and achievable recovery goals. RTOs determine the acceptable downtime after an incident, while RPOs define the maximum acceptable data loss. This question helps align data recovery efforts with business requirements, ensuring recovery plans meet operational needs. Clear RTOs and RPOs guide the development of effective backup and recovery strategies.

**Do we have a disaster recovery plan in place?** A comprehensive disaster recovery plan outlines the procedures for restoring data and systems after a catastrophic event. This question ensures that the organization has a well-documented and regularly updated plan. The plan should include detailed steps for data recovery, roles and responsibilities, and communication protocols. Having a disaster recovery plan is essential for coordinated and efficient recovery efforts.

**Are our backup and recovery procedures documented and accessible?** Proper documentation of backup and recovery procedures is critical for ensuring they can be followed accurately during an incident. This question addresses whether all procedures are well-documented, easily accessible, and understood by relevant personnel. Clear documentation helps streamline recovery processes, reducing the risk of errors and delays. Ensuring accessibility and clarity of procedures enhances the organization's readiness to respond to data loss events.

## CHAPTER 11   DATA RECOVERY

**What backups do we use (full, incremental, differential)?** Understanding the types of backups in use helps assess their effectiveness and efficiency. Full backups provide a complete copy of data, while incremental and differential backups offer faster, more storage-efficient options. This question helps determine whether the backup strategy suits the organization's needs. Choosing the suitable backup types ensures a balance between comprehensive data protection and resource utilization.

**How do we ensure the integrity of our backups?** Ensuring the integrity of backups is vital to guarantee that data can be restored without corruption. This question addresses the measures in place to verify the accuracy and completeness of backup data. Techniques such as checksum verification and regular integrity checks help maintain the reliability of backups. Protecting backup integrity ensures that recovered data is accurate and usable.

**What is our process for restoring data in case of a malware infection?** A clear process for restoring data after a malware infection is essential for timely and effective recovery. This question examines whether the organization has defined steps to identify and restore clean backup versions. Ensuring that backup data predates the infection minimizes the risk of reintroducing malware. A well-defined restoration process helps quickly return systems to a trusted state.

**Are our employees trained in data recovery procedures?** Employee training is crucial for effective data recovery. This question addresses whether staff are adequately trained on recovery procedures and understand their roles during an incident. Regular exercise and drills ensure that employees can execute recovery plans efficiently. Well-trained personnel are better prepared to handle data loss events and contribute to swift recovery efforts.

**Do we collaborate with external partners for data recovery?** Collaboration with external partners, such as backup service providers or cybersecurity consultants, can enhance data recovery capabilities. This question examines the extent of such collaborations and the benefits they bring. External partners can offer additional expertise, resources, and support during recovery. Leveraging these partnerships can improve the organization's overall data recovery strategy.

# Recommended Training

Effective data recovery practices hinge on technology and the preparedness and proficiency of the organization's personnel. Training is critical in ensuring that IT/cyber staff and all other employees understand their roles and responsibilities in a data loss incident. Comprehensive training programs tailored to different employee groups help build a culture of cybersecurity awareness and resilience. This section outlines twelve essential training programs organizations should implement to enhance their data recovery capabilities and security posture.

**Data Recovery Procedures Training:** This training should be mandatory for all IT and cyber staff, including system administrators and backup operators. The program should cover detailed procedures for backing up data, verifying backup integrity, and restoring data from backups. Participants will learn to use data recovery tools and execute recovery plans effectively. The outcome is a well-prepared team capable of swiftly and accurately recovering data, thus minimizing downtime and operational disruptions. This training significantly reduces the risk of data loss and ensures that recovery efforts are efficient and effective.

**Incident Response Training:** Aimed at the IT and cybersecurity teams, this training focuses on the steps to take during a cyber incident, including data recovery. The curriculum should include identifying the type of incident, isolating affected systems, and coordinating with relevant stakeholders. By understanding the incident response lifecycle, staff can better manage and mitigate the impact of cyber attacks. The primary outcome is a faster, more coordinated response that limits data loss and operational implications. This training ensures that incident response efforts are comprehensive and well-executed.

**Backup Management Training:** This program is essential for IT personnel managing backups. Training should cover best practices for backup scheduling, types of backups (full, incremental, differential), and secure storage solutions. Participants will also learn how to test backups for integrity and reliability. The outcome is a robust backup strategy that ensures data can be restored when needed. This training reduces the risk of backup failures and data loss, providing confidence in the organization's backup systems.

**Disaster Recovery Planning:** This training is crucial for IT managers, cybersecurity leaders, and business continuity planners. It involves developing and maintaining a disaster recovery plan with data recovery procedures. Training should encompass risk assessment, defining RTOs and RPOs, and coordinating recovery efforts across departments. The primary outcome is a comprehensive disaster recovery plan that is regularly updated and tested. This training ensures that organizations are prepared for various disaster scenarios, minimizing data loss and downtime.

**Phishing Awareness Training:** All employees should undergo regular phishing awareness training to recognize and avoid phishing attempts. Training should include identifying phishing emails, understanding the risks of malicious links and attachments, and reporting suspicious activities. Reducing the likelihood of successful phishing attacks minimizes the risk of data breaches and subsequent data loss. The primary outcome is a vigilant workforce knowledgeable about phishing threats. This training enhances the overall security posture of the organization.

**Data Handling and Protection Training:** This program should be mandatory for all employees, focusing on adequately handling and protecting sensitive data. Training should include data classification, secure storage practices, and guidelines for sharing information. Employees will learn to recognize the importance of data protection and the potential consequences of data breaches. The outcome is a workforce that understands how to safeguard data, reducing the risk of accidental or intentional data loss. This training fosters a culture of data security and responsibility.

**Secure Configuration Training:** Aimed at IT and cybersecurity staff, this training covers best practices for securely configuring systems and applications. Topics should include hardening operating systems, managing user permissions, and securing network devices. Proper configuration reduces vulnerabilities that could be exploited in a cyber attack, thereby protecting data integrity and availability. The primary outcome is a more secure IT environment that supports reliable data recovery. This training ensures that systems are resilient against cyber threats.

**Cybersecurity Awareness Training:** This training should be mandatory for all employees to create a baseline understanding of cybersecurity principles. Topics include recognizing common cyber threats, understanding the importance of strong passwords, and following company security policies. By raising overall cybersecurity awareness, employees become the first line of defense against cyber incidents. The outcome is a security-conscious workforce actively contributing to the organization's cybersecurity efforts. This training builds a strong foundation of cybersecurity knowledge and practices.

**Access Control Training:** This program is essential for both IT staff and general employees. It focuses on the principles of access control and should cover the importance of least privilege, proper account management, and secure authentication methods. Understanding access control helps prevent unauthorized access to sensitive data and systems. The primary outcome is improved security through controlled access to information. This training mitigates the risk of data breaches caused by improper access controls.

**Malware Detection and Prevention Training:** IT and cybersecurity staff should undergo specialized training in detecting and preventing malware infections. The curriculum should include recognizing signs of malware, using anti-malware tools, and implementing proactive security measures. By enhancing their ability to detect and respond to malware, staff can prevent data loss and maintain system integrity. The outcome is a more resilient IT environment capable of withstanding malware attacks. This training ensures that staff are equipped to handle malware threats effectively.

**Data Privacy Training:** All employees, especially those handling sensitive or personal data, should receive training on privacy principles and regulations. Training should include understanding data privacy laws, implementing privacy controls, and respecting customer data. Organizations can avoid legal penalties and maintain customer trust by adhering to privacy standards. The primary outcome is a compliant and ethical approach to data handling. This training promotes a culture of privacy and responsibility.

**Tabletop Exercises and Simulations:** IT, cybersecurity staff, and key stakeholders should regularly participate in tabletop exercises and simulations. These exercises simulate real-world cyber incidents, including data breaches and ransomware attacks, to test the organization's response and recovery procedures. Participants will gain practical experience in executing recovery plans and coordinating efforts. The outcome is improved readiness and confidence in handling actual incidents. This training ensures that the organization is prepared for various cyber threats.

# Actionable Recommendations

Implementing effective data recovery practices requires a strategic approach that addresses an organization's unique needs and challenges. By following actionable recommendations, cybersecurity leaders can ensure that their data recovery processes are robust, efficient, and aligned with best practices. This section outlines twelve key recommendations to help organizations develop and maintain a resilient data recovery strategy. These recommendations cover various topics, from backup frequency to employee training, ensuring a comprehensive data protection and recovery approach.

**Conduct a Data Inventory:** Start by thoroughly inventorying all data assets within the organization. This inventory should categorize data based on its importance, sensitivity, and regulatory requirements. Understanding what data exists and where it is stored helps prioritize backup and recovery efforts. Regularly updating the inventory ensures that all critical data is accounted for and protected. This foundational step supports informed decision-making in developing data recovery strategies.

**Define Recovery Objectives:** Recovery Time Objectives (RTOs) and Recovery Point Objectives (RPOs) for different data assets. RTOs determine how quickly data needs to be restored after an incident, while RPOs specify the maximum acceptable amount of data loss. Establishing these objectives helps set realistic and achievable recovery goals. Aligning recovery objectives with business requirements ensures that critical data can be restored within acceptable time frames. This clarity guides the development and implementation of effective backup and recovery plans.

**Implement Regular Backups:** Establish a regular backup schedule, including full and incremental backups. Full backups provide a complete copy of all data, while incremental backups capture only the changes since the last backup. This combination ensures comprehensive data protection while optimizing storage and backup times. Automate backups where possible to reduce the risk of human error and ensure consistency. Regular backups are essential for maintaining up-to-date and recoverable data.

**Utilize Offsite and Cloud Storage:** Store backups in multiple locations, including offsite and cloud storage. Offsite storage protects against physical damage or loss at the primary site, such as in the case of natural disasters. Cloud storage offers scalability, redundancy, and accessibility, ensuring backups are available even if compromised on-premises systems.

Implement strong encryption for data at rest and in transit to protect backup integrity. Diversified storage locations enhance data security and recovery capabilities.

**Regularly Test Backup Integrity:** Conduct regular tests to verify the integrity and recoverability of backups. Testing should include restoring a random sample of backups in a controlled environment to ensure they are complete and functional. Regular testing helps identify and address any backup procedures or storage media issues. Document the results of these tests to track performance and improvements over time. This practice ensures that backups are reliable and recovery processes work as intended.

**Develop a Comprehensive Disaster Recovery Plan:** Create a detailed disaster recovery plan with specific data recovery procedures. The plan should outline restoring data, roles and responsibilities, and communication protocols. Regularly review and update the plan to reflect changes in the organization's data environment and threat landscape. Conduct drills and simulations to ensure all stakeholders know and can execute the plan effectively. A well-prepared disaster recovery plan is crucial for minimizing the impact of data loss incidents.

**Implement Secure Configuration Management:** Ensure that all systems and applications are securely configured to prevent unauthorized access and vulnerabilities. Use configuration management tools to automate and enforce security policies. Regularly review and update configurations to address new threats and compliance requirements. Secure configurations reduce the risk of data breaches and enhance the overall security of the data environment. This proactive approach supports reliable data recovery by protecting the integrity of systems.

**Train Employees on Data Recovery Procedures:** Provide regular training on data recovery procedures and their roles during an incident. Training should cover the importance of backups, how to report data loss incidents, and the steps to take during recovery efforts. Ensure that IT and cybersecurity staff receive specialized training on recovery tools

CHAPTER 11   DATA RECOVERY

and techniques. Well-trained employees are better prepared to respond to data loss incidents, reducing the risk of errors and delays. Continuous education fosters a culture of awareness and preparedness.

**Establish Clear Access Controls:** Implement strict access controls to limit who can access and modify critical data and backups. Use role-based access control (RBAC) to ensure that employees only have access to the data they need for their roles. Regularly review and update access permissions to reflect changes in job functions or organizational structure. Robust access controls protect against unauthorized data access and tampering. This security measure is essential for safeguarding backup integrity.

**Monitor and Audit Backup Activities:** Monitor and audit backup activities to ensure policy compliance and identify anomalies. Automated monitoring tools track backup operations, storage usage, and access attempts. Regular audits help identify potential issues and areas for improvement in backup procedures. Documenting and reviewing audit findings supports accountability and transparency. Ongoing monitoring enhances the reliability and security of backup systems.

**Implement Data Encryption:** Encrypt backup data at rest and in transit to protect it from unauthorized access and breaches. Use strong encryption standards and regularly update encryption keys. Ensure that encryption is applied consistently across all backup locations and media. Encryption safeguards sensitive data and ensures its confidentiality during storage and transmission. This security measure is critical for protecting data integrity and compliance with regulatory requirements.

**Collaborate with External Experts:** Engage with external experts, such as cybersecurity consultants or managed service providers, to enhance data recovery capabilities. External partners can provide specialized knowledge, resources, and support for backup and recovery efforts. Collaborating with experts helps identify best practices, assess risks, and implement effective recovery strategies. Regularly review and update partnerships to ensure they meet organizational needs. Leveraging external expertise strengthens the overall data recovery strategy.

## Simplified Security Controls (SSC)

Security controls are essential for any organization seeking to protect its digital and physical assets from cyber threats. Tailoring these controls to fit the specific needs of your business environment is crucial, as it ensures that the protection mechanisms are relevant and effective against the specific risks your organization faces. There are numerous sources to draw these controls from, including the well-regarded CIS Top 18, which provides a robust framework for crafting defensive strategies. The recommendations presented in this book are based on the CIS controls, among others, offering a comprehensive guide that can be adapted to serve a wide range of security needs. Before implementing these controls, it is vital to thoroughly review their design to ensure they align with your strategic objectives and operational practices. Additionally, after deployment, it is imperative to regularly test the controls to verify their effectiveness and to make necessary adjustments. This ensures the controls continue functioning as intended, safeguarding your organization against emerging threats and changing conditions.

### CONTROL 1: ESTABLISH AND MAINTAIN A DATA RECOVERY PROCESS

**Control Objective:** To develop and maintain a comprehensive data recovery process that ensures the prompt and secure recovery of data in the event of an incident while addressing recovery scope, prioritization, and backup data security.

**Implementation Steps:**

**1.1. Define Recovery Scope and Activities:** Identify all enterprise assets and data that require backup and recovery. Determine the specific activities involved in the data recovery process, including data collection, storage, and restoration procedures.

**1.2. Prioritize Recovery Efforts:** Establish criteria for prioritizing recovery efforts based on the criticality and sensitivity of data. Create a prioritization matrix to guide recovery efforts during an incident.

**1.3. Secure Backup Data:** Implement security measures to protect backup data, including encryption and secure access controls. Ensure that backup data security is equivalent to that of the original data.

**1.4. Document Recovery Procedures:** Create detailed documentation of the data recovery process, including roles, responsibilities, and step-by-step instructions. Review and update this documentation annually or whenever significant changes occur.

**1.5. Train Personnel:** Provide training for all relevant personnel on the data recovery process. Ensure staff know their roles and responsibilities during a data recovery scenario.

**Expected Outcome:** Establishing a well-defined and secure data recovery process ensures that the organization can quickly and effectively restore data following an incident. This process minimizes downtime, protects sensitive information, and supports business continuity.

CHAPTER 11   DATA RECOVERY

## CONTROL 2: PERFORM AUTOMATED BACKUPS

**Control Objective:** To ensure that automated backups of in-scope enterprise assets are performed regularly, based on the sensitivity of the data, to protect against data loss and facilitate timely recovery.

**Implementation Steps:**

**2.1. Identify Critical Assets:** Identify and categorize all in-scope enterprise assets that require automated backups, prioritizing based on data sensitivity and criticality.

**2.2. Implement Backup Automation Tools:** Deploy automated backup tools and solutions that support scheduled and consistent backups. Configure these tools to perform backups weekly or more frequently as needed.

**2.3. Monitor Backup Processes:** Establish monitoring mechanisms to ensure backups are completed successfully. Set up alerts for backup failures or inconsistencies.

**2.4. Verify Backup Completeness:** Regularly verify that backups are complete and data is recoverable. Perform spot checks and automated verification routines to ensure integrity.

**2.5. Review and Adjust Backup Schedules:** Periodically review backup schedules and adjust them based on data sensitivity, volume, or regulatory requirements changes.

**Expected Outcome:** Regular automated backups ensure critical data is consistently protected against loss, enabling swift recovery and minimizing operational disruptions.

## CONTROL 3: PROTECT RECOVERY DATA

**Control Objective:** To protect recovery data with controls equivalent to those applied to the original data, ensuring its security during storage and transit.

**Implementation Steps:**

**3.1. Implement Encryption:** Encrypt recovery data at rest and in transit to protect it from unauthorized access and breaches. Use strong encryption standards and regularly update encryption keys.

**3.2. Enforce Access Controls:** Apply strict access controls to recovery data, ensuring only authorized personnel can access it. Implement role-based access controls and regular access reviews.

**3.3. Secure Backup Storage:** Store recovery data in secure locations, such as physically protected offsite facilities or secure cloud environments. Implement multi-factor authentication for access to backup storage.

**3.4. Regular Security Audits:** Conduct regular security audits of backup and recovery processes to identify and address potential vulnerabilities. Document and remediate any findings promptly.

**3.5. Data Separation Techniques:** Data separation techniques, such as air-gapped or isolated networks, are used to protect recovery data from potential threats further.

**Expected Outcome:** Enhanced protection of recovery data ensures its integrity and confidentiality, reducing the risk of data breaches and ensuring reliable data recovery.

CHAPTER 11   DATA RECOVERY

## CONTROL 4: ESTABLISH AND MAINTAIN AN ISOLATED INSTANCE OF RECOVERY DATA

**Control Objective:** To create and maintain an isolated instance of recovery data protected from primary system vulnerabilities, ensuring its availability for recovery.

**Implementation Steps:**

**4.1. Identify Backup Destinations:** Determine appropriate destinations for isolated recovery data, including offline, cloud-based, or offsite storage solutions.

**4.2. Implement Isolation Mechanisms:** Use isolation mechanisms such as air-gapping, network segmentation, or dedicated secure environments to keep recovery data separate from primary systems.

**4.3. Version Control:** Implement version control for backups to ensure multiple recovery points are available. Regularly update and verify these versions.

**4.4. Test Isolated Recovery:** Regularly test the recovery process from isolated instances to ensure data can be restored quickly and accurately. Document test results and make improvements as needed.

**4.5. Maintain Redundancy:** Ensure isolated recovery data is replicated across multiple locations to provide redundancy and enhance data availability.

**Expected Outcome:** Isolated recovery data provides a secure and reliable fallback option in the event of a primary system failure, ensuring continuity and data integrity.

CHAPTER 11    DATA RECOVERY

## CONTROL 5: TEST DATA RECOVERY

**Control Objective:** To regularly test data recovery procedures to ensure that backups are functional and data can be restored as needed, minimizing downtime and ensuring data integrity.

**Implementation Steps:**

**5.1. Develop a Testing Schedule:** Establish a regular testing schedule for data recovery, with tests conducted quarterly or more frequently based on data criticality and regulatory requirements.

**5.2. Select Test Samples:** For each recovery test, choose a representative sample of in-scope enterprise assets, ensuring a comprehensive assessment of recovery capabilities.

**5.3. Simulate Recovery Scenarios:** Conduct recovery tests by simulating various data loss scenarios, including cyber attacks, system failures, and accidental deletions. Document the process and results.

**5.4. Evaluate Recovery Performance:** Assess the performance of recovery procedures, identifying any issues or delays. Use metrics such as recovery time and data integrity to evaluate success.

**5.5. Implement Improvements:** Based on test results, improve recovery processes, tools, and documentation. Ensure continuous enhancement of recovery capabilities.

**Expected Outcome:** Regular testing of data recovery procedures ensures that backups are reliable and that the organization can quickly restore data, minimizing the impact of data loss incidents.

# CHAPTER 12

# Network Infrastructure Management

Establishing a secure network infrastructure is fundamental to an organization's cybersecurity posture. Network infrastructure, comprising gateways, firewalls, routers, switches, and wireless access points, forms the backbone of any digital enterprise. These devices manage data flow, enforce security policies, and act as the first defense against cyber threats. Ensuring their proper management and configuration is critical to preventing attackers from exploiting vulnerabilities. This necessity is underscored by the evolving landscape of cyber threats and the increasing complexity of network environments.

Network devices often come with default configurations, prioritizing ease of use over security. These default settings may include open services and ports, default accounts and passwords, and support for outdated protocols. Such configurations can leave the network vulnerable to exploitation. Attackers frequently scan for these vulnerabilities to gain unauthorized access, redirect network traffic, or intercept sensitive data. Addressing these risks requires diligent management, continuous network device settings, and configuration monitoring.

A comprehensive network security strategy involves more than just securing individual devices; it requires a holistic approach to managing the entire network infrastructure. This includes regularly updating network architecture diagrams and configurations, monitoring for changes, and reassessing access controls. Such proactive management helps identify and mitigate potential security gaps before attackers can exploit them. Maintaining an up-to-date inventory of network devices and their configurations is essential for effective vulnerability management.

Vendor support for network devices is crucial for maintaining a secure infrastructure. End-of-Life (EOL) components, which no longer receive security updates and patches, pose significant risks. Organizations must plan for timely upgrades of these components or implement mitigating controls to isolate them from critical network segments. This ensures that the network remains resilient against known vulnerabilities and emerging threats. Regular vendor communication can also provide insights into the latest security features and best practices.

The dynamic nature of network security necessitates continuous evaluation and adaptation. Network configurations that were secure at one point may become vulnerable over time due to evolving threats and changing business needs. Regularly reviewing and updating network architecture diagrams, access controls, and allowed traffic flows is essential to maintaining a robust security posture. This ongoing process helps identify and address potential weaknesses attackers could exploit.

Effective account management is a cornerstone of network security. This involves controlling who has access to network devices and ensuring that access is logged and monitored. Strong authentication mechanisms, such as multi-factor authentication (MFA), are critical for securing administrative access to network devices. Additionally, infrastructure administration should be conducted over secure protocols and from dedicated administrative devices or out-of-band networks to minimize the risk of unauthorized access.

Commercial tools can significantly enhance network security management by automating the evaluation of rule sets and access control lists (ACLs). These tools can identify inconsistencies or conflicts in network filtering devices, providing an automated sanity check that helps ensure the intended security policies are enforced. Running these tools after significant changes to firewall rule sets, router ACLs, or other filtering technologies is a best practice that helps maintain the integrity of network security controls.

The complexity of modern network environments and the increasing sophistication of cyber threats underscores the importance of robust network infrastructure management. Organizations must adopt a proactive approach, continuously monitoring and updating their network configurations to stay ahead of potential threats. This involves addressing technical vulnerabilities and implementing strong policies and procedures for managing network security. Comprehensive documentation and regular audits of network devices and configurations are essential to this strategy.

Network security is not a one-time effort but an ongoing process that requires constant vigilance. As business needs evolve, so must the network configurations that support them. This dynamic nature of network security requires a flexible approach that can adapt to changing conditions and emerging threats. Regular training and awareness programs for IT staff and network administrators are crucial for keeping up with the latest security trends and best practices.

The rise of remote work and cloud-based technologies has added new dimensions to network security challenges. Organizations must now secure their on-premises infrastructure, remote connections, and cloud environments. This requires a comprehensive approach that integrates network security across all facets of the enterprise. Implementing secure remote access solutions, monitoring cloud configurations, and ensuring consistent security policies across all environments are critical for protecting the network infrastructure in this new paradigm.

Network infrastructure management also involves ensuring compliance with relevant regulations and standards. Many industries have specific requirements for network security that organizations must adhere to. Regularly reviewing these requirements and ensuring that network configurations meet or exceed them is important to maintaining a compliant and secure network. This can also involve regular third-party assessments and audits to validate the effectiveness of network security measures.

Effective network infrastructure management is critical to an organization's cybersecurity strategy. It involves a combination of technical controls, policies, and procedures to secure the network from potential threats. Organizations can significantly enhance their network security posture by maintaining up-to-date configurations, managing access controls, leveraging commercial tools for automated checks, and continuously adapting to evolving threats. This proactive approach is essential for safeguarding sensitive data and ensuring the integrity of the network infrastructure in an increasingly connected world.

Network infrastructure management is protecting against known threats and anticipating and mitigating potential risks. As cyber threats evolve, organizations must remain vigilant and proactive in their approach to network security. This involves continuous learning, adaptation, and improvement of network security practices to stay ahead of attackers. By fostering a security culture and ensuring that network infrastructure management is a top priority, organizations can build a resilient defense against the ever-changing landscape of cyber threats.

# Key Concepts and Terms

In understanding Network Infrastructure Management, several key concepts and terms are essential for grasping the intricacies of this critical area in cybersecurity. Each term provides a foundational element

## CHAPTER 12   NETWORK INFRASTRUCTURE MANAGEMENT

that contributes to the overall security and management of network infrastructures. This section elucidates these terms to offer clarity and depth to readers, ensuring a comprehensive understanding of the critical components of securing network infrastructures.

**Network Infrastructure:** Network infrastructure refers to an entire network's hardware and software resources that enable network connectivity, communication, operations, and management. It includes physical devices like routers, switches, firewalls, wireless access points, and the software necessary to run them. The infrastructure also encompasses network services such as DNS, DHCP, and VPNs that facilitate the management and delivery of data across the network. Maintaining network infrastructure ensures data flows efficiently and securely between devices. Maintaining a secure network infrastructure helps prevent unauthorized access and cyber threats.

**Default Configurations:** Default configurations are the pre-set settings that come with network devices from the manufacturer. These configurations are typically designed for ease of use and rapid deployment, often at the expense of security. Default settings may include open ports, default usernames and passwords, and enabled services that might not be necessary for the device's intended use. Attackers often exploit these default settings to gain unauthorized access to networks. Changing default configurations to secure settings is critical to protect network devices from potential threats.

**Vulnerability Management:** Vulnerability management identifies, evaluates, treats, and reports security vulnerabilities in systems and the software that runs on them. This process is essential for maintaining the security and integrity of network infrastructures. It involves regular scans to detect vulnerabilities, prioritizing them based on their potential impact, and applying patches or other remediation methods to address them. Effective vulnerability management helps prevent attackers from exploiting weaknesses in the network. Keeping systems up-to-date with the latest security patches is fundamental to this practice.

CHAPTER 12   NETWORK INFRASTRUCTURE MANAGEMENT

**Patch Management:** Patch management distributes and applies updates to software and hardware to fix vulnerabilities and improve functionality. This practice is crucial in maintaining the security of network devices as it addresses known security flaws that attackers could exploit. Vendors typically provide patches that must be applied promptly to ensure the network remains secure. Effective patch management requires a systematic approach to track, test, and deploy patches across the network. Keeping all devices up-to-date with the latest patches is vital for protecting against cyber threats.

**Access Control Lists (ACLs):** Access Control Lists (ACLs) are rules used to control network traffic and enforce security policies. ACLs are implemented on network devices like routers and firewalls to permit or deny traffic based on predefined criteria, such as IP addresses, port numbers, and protocols. They are critical in managing network access and ensuring that only authorized users and devices can access network resources. Properly configured ACLs help prevent unauthorized access and mitigate the risk of cyber attacks. Regularly reviewing and updating ACLs is essential to maintaining their effectiveness.

**Multi-Factor Authentication (MFA):** Multi-factor authentication (MFA) is a security mechanism requiring users to provide two or more verification factors to access a network or system. MFA enhances security by adding an extra layer of protection beyond just a username and password. Common factors include something you know (password), something you have (security token), and something you are (biometric verification). Implementing MFA for administrative access to network devices significantly reduces the risk of unauthorized access. This practice is a critical component of a robust network security strategy.

**Secure Protocols:** Secure protocols are communication protocols that provide security for data transmission over a network. These protocols include HTTPS, SSH, and SSL/TLS, which encrypt data and ensure its integrity and confidentiality. Using secure protocols for network administration and data transfer is essential to protect sensitive information from being intercepted by attackers. Secure protocols help prevent eavesdropping, man-in-the-middle attacks, and other cyber threats. Ensuring that all network communications are conducted over secure protocols is a fundamental security practice.

**End-of-Life (EOL) Components:** End-of-life (EOL) components are hardware or software products that have reached the end of their useful life as defined by the manufacturer. These components no longer receive updates, including security patches, making them vulnerable to exploitation. Organizations must plan to replace or upgrade EOL components to maintain a secure network infrastructure. Failing to address EOL components can leave significant security gaps in the network. Isolating EOL components or implementing mitigating controls is necessary until they can be properly replaced.

**Network Segmentation:** Network segmentation divides a network into smaller, isolated segments to enhance security and improve performance. This approach limits the spread of cyber attacks by containing them within a specific segment, preventing them from affecting the entire network. Segmentation can be achieved through VLANs, subnets, and firewalls, which control traffic flow between segments. Proper network segmentation reduces the attack surface and helps protect sensitive data. It is an effective strategy for managing complex network environments.

**Network Monitoring:** Network monitoring involves continuously observing network activity to detect and respond to real-time security incidents. This practice uses tools and techniques to analyze traffic patterns, identify anomalies, and alert administrators to potential threats. Effective network monitoring helps ensure network infrastructure availability, performance, and security. It provides visibility into network operations and supports proactive threat detection. Implementing robust network monitoring is essential for maintaining a secure and resilient network.

**Configuration Management:** Configuration management systematically manages network device and software changes to ensure consistency and security. This practice involves maintaining an inventory of network assets, documenting configurations, and tracking changes. Configuration management helps prevent unauthorized changes, reduces the risk of configuration errors, and ensures compliance with security policies. Regularly reviewing and validating configurations is critical for maintaining a secure network environment. Proper configuration management supports effective vulnerability and patch management.

**Administrative Devices:** Administrative devices are dedicated hardware or virtual machines used solely for managing network infrastructure. These devices are configured with enhanced security measures and restricted access to minimize the risk of compromise. Using administrative devices ensures network management activities are conducted in a controlled and secure environment. They often employ secure protocols, strong authentication, and isolation from general network traffic. Implementing dedicated administrative devices is a best practice for secure network infrastructure management.

# Importance and Relevance

Network infrastructure management is a cornerstone of modern cybersecurity practices. As cyber threats evolve and become more sophisticated, maintaining a secure and well-managed network infrastructure cannot be overstated. Effective network infrastructure management ensures that organizations are well-prepared to defend against attacks, mitigate risks, and maintain the integrity and availability of their systems and data. This section explores the critical reasons why robust network infrastructure management is essential for cybersecurity today.

# CHAPTER 12   NETWORK INFRASTRUCTURE MANAGEMENT

**Protection Against Evolving Threats:** Cyber threats constantly evolve, with attackers developing new methods to exploit vulnerabilities. Proper network infrastructure management ensures that all devices are up-to-date with the latest security patches, making it harder for attackers to exploit known vulnerabilities. Regular updates and proactive vulnerability management are key to avoiding potential threats. Organizations can better defend against the latest cyber threats by continuously monitoring and updating network infrastructure. This proactive approach is crucial in the ever-changing landscape of cybersecurity.

**Minimizing Attack Surfaces:** A well-managed network infrastructure helps minimize attack surfaces by ensuring that unnecessary services and ports are disabled and default configurations are changed. Attackers often target these weak points to gain unauthorized access to networks. Network segmentation, secure configurations, and regular audits help reduce these vulnerabilities. Organizations can significantly lower the risk of successful cyber attacks by minimizing attack surfaces. This focused effort on reducing entry points is fundamental to a strong security posture.

**Enhancing Incident Response:** Effective network infrastructure management improves an organization's ability to detect and respond to security incidents. With proper monitoring and logging in place, suspicious activities can be identified and addressed quickly. Detailed network documentation and architecture diagrams aid in understanding the network layout, making isolating and mitigating incidents easier. A well-prepared incident response plan, supported by comprehensive network management, ensures timely and effective responses to security breaches. This capability is essential for minimizing the impact of incidents.

**Ensuring Regulatory Compliance:** Many industries are subject to strict regulatory requirements regarding data protection and network security. Proper network infrastructure management helps organizations comply with these regulations by implementing security controls and maintaining detailed documentation. Regular audits and assessments ensure the network meets compliance standards, avoiding fines and legal issues. Compliance with rules protects the organization and builds trust with customers and partners. Meeting regulatory standards is a critical aspect of modern cybersecurity.

**Safeguarding Sensitive Data:** Sensitive data, such as personal information and intellectual property, must be protected from unauthorized access and breaches. Effective network infrastructure management ensures data is securely transmitted and stored within the network. Secure protocols, encryption, and access controls help protect data from interception and unauthorized access. By safeguarding sensitive data, organizations can prevent breaches and maintain customer trust. Data protection is a fundamental responsibility in the digital age.

**Supporting Business Continuity:** Network infrastructure management is vital for maintaining business continuity in the face of cyber threats. Ensuring high availability and redundancy of critical systems prevents disruptions caused by cyber attacks or hardware failures. Proper planning and regular testing of disaster recovery plans ensure that the organization can quickly recover from incidents. By supporting business continuity, network management helps maintain operations and minimize downtime. This resilience is crucial for sustaining business functions and customer satisfaction.

**Enabling Secure Remote Work:** The rise of remote work has introduced new challenges for network security. Effective network infrastructure management ensures that remote access is secure, using VPNs and strong authentication methods. Securely managing remote connections protects against potential vulnerabilities introduced by remote work environments. Organizations can maintain productivity by enabling secure remote work while protecting their network from threats. This capability has become increasingly important in today's flexible work environment.

# CHAPTER 12   NETWORK INFRASTRUCTURE MANAGEMENT

**Facilitating Scalability and Growth:** As organizations grow, their network infrastructure must scale to support increased demands. Proper management ensures the network can handle additional devices and users without compromising security. Planning for scalability includes updating architecture diagrams and ensuring that new components are securely integrated. Network management supports the organization's growth by facilitating scalability while maintaining a strong security posture. This proactive approach ensures that security evolves alongside the organization.

**Enhancing Visibility and Control:** Effective network infrastructure management provides comprehensive visibility into network activities and configurations. This visibility is essential for detecting anomalies, managing access, and identifying potential security issues. Advanced monitoring tools and centralized management systems help maintain control over the network. Enhanced visibility and control enable organizations to respond quickly to threats and manage their network more efficiently. Maintaining visibility is a key aspect of proactive cybersecurity management.

**Reducing Operational Costs:** Proper network infrastructure management can help reduce operational costs by preventing costly security incidents and optimizing network performance. Regular maintenance, updates, and proactive management prevent issues that could lead to downtime and expensive remediation efforts. Efficient management practices also reduce the need for emergency fixes and improve overall network efficiency. By reducing operational costs, organizations can allocate resources more effectively and support long-term growth. Cost savings are a significant benefit of proactive network management.

**Building Customer Trust:** Customers expect organizations to protect their data and maintain secure operations. Effective network infrastructure management demonstrates a commitment to security and builds trust with customers and partners. Meeting security standards and protecting sensitive information enhances the organization's reputation. Trust is a valuable asset in today's competitive market, and strong network management practices help maintain it. Organizations can strengthen their market position and foster long-term relationships by building customer trust.

**Supporting Technological Advancements:** Network infrastructure must evolve to support new tools and capabilities as technology advances. Proper management ensures that the network can integrate new technologies securely and efficiently. This includes adopting cloud services, IoT devices, and advanced analytics tools. Network management helps organizations stay competitive and leverage new opportunities by supporting technological advancements. Keeping pace with technology is essential for innovation and growth in the digital era.

# Risks of Not Implementing the Control

Failing to implement robust network infrastructure management poses significant risks to any organization. Without proper management, vulnerabilities in network devices can go unnoticed and unaddressed, leading to severe security breaches. These risks are compounded by the increasing complexity of network environments and the evolving nature of cyber threats. Organizations may face data breaches, financial losses, and damage to their reputation, among other consequences. Understanding these risks is crucial for recognizing the importance of proactive network infrastructure management.

**Unpatched Vulnerabilities:** When network devices are not regularly updated with the latest patches, they become susceptible to known vulnerabilities. Attackers can exploit these vulnerabilities to gain unauthorized access, disrupt services, or steal sensitive data. The longer a vulnerability remains unpatched, the greater the risk of exploitation. Regular patch management is essential to close these security gaps and protect the network from attacks. Neglecting this can lead to significant security incidents and financial losses.

**Unauthorized Access:** Inadequate access controls can result in unauthorized individuals accessing network devices and sensitive data. Without proper authentication mechanisms, such as multi-factor authentication, the risk of compromised credentials increases. Attackers can exploit weak or default passwords to infiltrate the network, potentially leading to data breaches or system disruptions. Implementing strong access controls and regularly reviewing access permissions are critical for preventing unauthorized access. Failure to do so can expose the organization to significant security threats.

**Data Interception:** Without secure protocols, data transmitted across the network can be intercepted by malicious actors. This can result in the exposure of sensitive information, including personal data and confidential business communications. Encrypting data in transit using secure protocols like SSL/TLS helps protect against interception and eavesdropping. Organizations that fail to implement these measures risk compromising the confidentiality and integrity of their data. This can lead to regulatory penalties and loss of customer trust.

**Network Downtime:** Poorly managed network infrastructure can lead to frequent outages and downtime. Network devices not adequately maintained or configured are more prone to failures and disruptions. Downtime can severely impact business operations, resulting in lost productivity and revenue. Ensuring network devices are regularly updated and configured correctly is essential for maintaining continuous operations. Organizations that neglect this aspect of network management may face significant operational challenges.

**Regulatory Non-Compliance:** Many industries are subject to regulations that mandate specific security measures for network infrastructure. Failure to comply with these regulations can result in substantial fines and legal consequences. Regular audits and network security assessments are necessary to ensure compliance with relevant standards and regulations. Organizations not prioritizing network infrastructure management risk falling short of these requirements. This can lead to financial penalties and damage to the organization's reputation.

**Increased Attack Surface:** Neglecting network segmentation and proper configuration increases the attack surface of the network. An unsegmented network allows attackers to move laterally and access multiple systems once they breach a single entry point. Proper network segmentation restricts this lateral movement and contains potential breaches. Failing to implement segmentation can lead to widespread network compromises and data loss. Reducing the attack surface through effective segmentation is critical to network security.

**Ineffective Incident Response:** Detecting and responding to security incidents becomes challenging without comprehensive network monitoring and management. A lack of visibility into network activities can delay the identification of breaches and compromise the effectiveness of incident response efforts. Implementing robust monitoring tools and processes is essential for timely detection and response to security threats. Organizations not investing in these capabilities may find themselves unprepared for handling security incidents. This can exacerbate the impact of attacks and prolong recovery times.

**Data Breaches:** Inadequate network infrastructure management significantly increases the risk of data breaches. Poorly configured devices, unpatched vulnerabilities, and weak access controls create multiple entry points for attackers. Data breaches can lead to the loss of sensitive information, financial losses, and reputational damage. Ensuring proper configuration, regular updates, and strong security measures are critical for preventing data breaches. Organizations that overlook these practices are more likely to experience significant security incidents.

**Financial Losses:** The financial impact of poor network infrastructure management can be substantial. Costs associated with data breaches, regulatory fines, and operational disruptions can add up quickly.

Additionally, the cost of remediation and recovery efforts following a security incident can be significant. Investing in robust network infrastructure management practices helps mitigate these financial risks. Organizations that fail to do so may face severe financial consequences.

**Reputational Damage:** Security breaches and network disruptions can severely damage an organization's reputation. Customers and partners lose trust in an organization that cannot protect its network and data. Rebuilding a damaged reputation can be challenging and time-consuming. Effective network infrastructure management is essential for maintaining customer trust and business relationships. Neglecting this aspect of security can lead to long-term reputational harm.

**Loss of Competitive Advantage:** A secure and reliable network infrastructure is crucial for maintaining a competitive edge in the market. Frequent security incidents and network disruptions can hinder an organization's ability to innovate and deliver services effectively. Competitors with more robust security practices may gain an advantage. Prioritizing network infrastructure management helps ensure that an organization remains resilient and competitive. Organizations that overlook this, risk falling behind in the market.

**Operational Inefficiency:** Inefficient network management can lead to operational challenges and inefficiencies. Network issues can disrupt workflows, impact employee productivity, and delay project timelines. Ensuring network devices are properly managed and maintained is essential for smooth operations. Organizations that neglect network infrastructure management may struggle with operational inefficiencies. This can affect overall business performance and growth.

# What Questions Should You Ask?

Implementing effective network infrastructure management requires a strategic approach guided by insightful questions. Cybersecurity leaders must evaluate current practices, identify gaps, and develop comprehensive plans to address vulnerabilities. By asking the right questions, they can ensure that their network infrastructure is resilient, secure, and capable of supporting organizational objectives. These questions cover various aspects of network security, from configuration management to monitoring and compliance. Here are twelve critical questions cybersecurity leaders should ask to form the foundation of their implementation strategy.

**Are all network devices and configurations documented?** Thorough documentation of all network devices and configurations is essential for effective management and troubleshooting. This includes physical and virtual devices, as well as detailed network diagrams. Proper documentation helps maintain an up-to-date inventory, crucial for vulnerability management and incident response. It becomes challenging to identify outdated components and potential security gaps without accurate records. Regularly updating this documentation ensures the network's current state is always known.

**Are we regularly reviewing and updating our network architecture diagrams?** Regular review and updating of network architecture diagrams are necessary to reflect changes in the network environment. This practice ensures that all components are accurately represented and any modifications, such as new devices or configuration changes, are documented. They are keeping these diagrams current to aid in vulnerability assessments and planning for future upgrades. It also helps identify potential weaknesses in the network design. Accurate diagrams are vital for effective communication and coordination among IT and security teams.

**How are we managing the end-of-life (EOL) components in our network?** Managing end-of-life components involves planning for their timely replacement or isolation. EOL devices no longer receive security updates, making them vulnerable to exploitation. Identifying these components and prioritizing their upgrade is crucial to maintaining a

## CHAPTER 12  NETWORK INFRASTRUCTURE MANAGEMENT

secure network. Organizations should also implement mitigating controls if immediate replacement is not possible. Proactively addressing EOL components helps prevent potential security breaches.

**Do we have a robust patch management process in place?** A robust patch management process ensures that all network devices receive timely updates to address known vulnerabilities. This process involves tracking available patches, testing them in a controlled environment, and deploying them across the network. Regular patching is critical for maintaining security and functionality. Without an effective patch management strategy, networks remain exposed to exploits and attacks. Ensuring patches are applied promptly helps safeguard the network against emerging threats.

**Are our access controls and authentication mechanisms adequate?** Adequate access controls and authentication mechanisms are essential to prevent unauthorized access to network devices and data. This includes implementing multi-factor authentication (MFA) and regularly reviewing access permissions. Robust access controls minimize the risk of credential compromise and unauthorized activities. Organizations must ensure that only authorized personnel can access critical network infrastructure. Regular audits and updates to access policies help maintain robust security.

**How do we monitor and respond to network anomalies?** Effective monitoring and response to network anomalies are crucial for detecting and mitigating security incidents. Organizations should implement comprehensive monitoring tools that provide real-time visibility into network activities. These tools help identify suspicious behavior and potential threats. An established incident response plan ensures that detected anomalies are addressed promptly. Continuous monitoring and quick response are key to minimizing the impact of security incidents.

**Are we using secure protocols for network communication?** Using secure protocols for network communication helps protect data in transit from interception and tampering. Protocols like HTTPS, SSH, and SSL/

CHAPTER 12   NETWORK INFRASTRUCTURE MANAGEMENT

TLS ensure that information is encrypted and secure. Implementing these protocols is essential for maintaining data confidentiality and integrity. Organizations must regularly review and update their network configurations to ensure secure protocols are used. This practice reduces the risk of data breaches and unauthorized access.

**Do we conduct regular vulnerability assessments?** Regular vulnerability assessments are necessary to identify and address security weaknesses in the network infrastructure. These assessments involve scanning the network for known vulnerabilities and evaluating the effectiveness of existing security measures. Addressing identified vulnerabilities helps mitigate potential risks. Organizations should conduct these assessments periodically and after significant changes to the network. Proactive vulnerability management is critical for maintaining a secure network environment.

**How do we ensure compliance with relevant regulations and standards?** Ensuring compliance with relevant regulations and standards involves implementing and maintaining security practices that meet or exceed regulatory requirements. This includes conducting regular audits and assessments to verify compliance. Organizations must stay informed about changes in regulations and update their practices accordingly. Compliance helps avoid legal penalties and enhances the organization's security posture. It also builds trust with customers and partners by demonstrating a commitment to security.

**Are our network segmentation practices effective?** Effective network segmentation limits the spread of cyber attacks by isolating different network segments. This practice involves dividing the network into smaller, manageable sections, each with its security controls. Proper segmentation helps contain breaches and prevent attackers from moving laterally across the network. Organizations should regularly review and update their segmentation strategies to ensure effectiveness. This approach enhances overall network security and resilience.

**How do we train and educate our staff on network security?**
Training and educating staff on network security are vital for building a security-conscious culture within the organization. This involves regular training sessions, awareness programs, and hands-on exercises to ensure employees understand security best practices. Educated staff are better equipped to identify and respond to security threats. Organizations should foster an environment where security is a shared responsibility. Continuous education helps keep staff informed about the latest threats and mitigation strategies.

**What tools and technologies are we using to automate network security?** Using tools and technologies to automate network security helps streamline processes and reduce the risk of human error. Automation can be applied to various aspects of network security, including monitoring, patch management, and access control. Automated solutions enhance efficiency and allow security teams to focus on more strategic tasks. Organizations should evaluate and adopt tools that best fit their security needs. Automation is key to maintaining a proactive and resilient security posture.

# Recommended Training

Effective training is essential for equipping IT/Cyber staff and employees with the knowledge and skills to protect an organization's network infrastructure. This training should cover a range of topics, from technical skills for IT professionals to general cybersecurity awareness for all staff. By providing comprehensive training programs, organizations can ensure that everyone understands their role in maintaining security and can recognize potential threats. This section outlines key training recommendations to help reduce risks and strengthen the overall cybersecurity posture.

## CHAPTER 12   NETWORK INFRASTRUCTURE MANAGEMENT

**Network Security Fundamentals:** All IT and cybersecurity staff should attend Network Security Fundamentals training. This training covers the basics of network security, including common threats, security protocols, and best practices for configuring and managing network devices. Participants will learn how to identify vulnerabilities and implement measures to mitigate risks. The outcome is a foundational understanding of network security principles, essential for building more advanced skills. This training reduces risk by ensuring all IT staff have a solid grasp of essential security concepts.

**Advanced Configuration and Management:** Advanced Configuration and Management training is designed for network administrators and senior IT staff. The training focuses on advanced techniques for configuring and managing network devices, including routers, switches, and firewalls. Topics include secure device configurations, advanced firewall rule sets, and network segmentation. The outcome is the ability to implement and maintain complex network security measures effectively. This training reduces risk by ensuring network administrators can securely and efficiently manage infrastructure.

**Vulnerability Assessment and Management:** The training covers methodologies for conducting vulnerability assessments, using tools to scan for weaknesses, and prioritizing remediation efforts. Participants will learn how to create and implement effective vulnerability management programs. The outcome is an improved capability to identify and address vulnerabilities promptly. This training reduces risk by ensuring that vulnerabilities are discovered and mitigated before they can be exploited.

**Incident Response and Management:** Incident Response and Management training is essential for IT and cybersecurity staff responding to security incidents. This training covers developing and implementing incident response plans, including detection, analysis, containment, eradication, and recovery processes. Participants will engage in simulated incident scenarios to practice their skills. The outcome is a well-prepared incident response team capable of handling security breaches effectively. This training reduces risk by ensuring rapid and coordinated responses to security incidents.

**Secure Coding Practices:** Secure Coding Practices training is aimed at software developers and application engineers. The training focuses on writing secure code, identifying common coding vulnerabilities, and using tools to test code for security flaws. Participants will learn how to integrate security into the software development lifecycle. The outcome is the production of secure software less vulnerable to attacks. This training reduces risk by preventing security issues at the source during development.

**Cybersecurity Awareness for All Employees:** Cybersecurity Awareness training should be mandatory for all employees, regardless of their role. This training covers basic cybersecurity principles, including recognizing phishing attacks, using strong passwords, and reporting suspicious activities. The training aims to build a security-conscious culture within the organization. The outcome is a vigilant workforce aware of common cyber threats. This training reduces risk by empowering employees to act as the first defense against cyber attacks.

**Phishing Simulation and Training:** Phishing Simulation and Training is targeted at all employees to educate them about phishing threats. The training involves simulated phishing attacks to test employees' ability to recognize and respond to phishing attempts. Participants receive feedback and additional training based on their performance. The outcome is improved awareness and detection of phishing attempts. This training reduces risk by reducing the likelihood of successful phishing attacks.

**Compliance and Regulatory Training:** Compliance and Regulatory Training is essential for IT, cybersecurity staff, and compliance officers. This training covers relevant regulations and standards, such as GDPR, HIPAA, and PCI DSS, and how to ensure compliance. Participants will learn about the legal and regulatory requirements affecting their organization. The outcome is a clear understanding of compliance obligations and how to meet them. This training reduces risk by ensuring the organization adheres to legal and regulatory standards, avoiding penalties, and enhancing security.

**Secure Remote Work Practices:** Secure Remote Work Practices training is vital for employees who work remotely. The training covers secure practices for remote work, including using VPNs, securing home networks, and protecting sensitive data. Participants will learn how to maintain security while working outside the office. The outcome is a secure remote workforce that follows best practices for protecting organizational data. This training reduces risk by addressing the unique security challenges of remote work.

**Multi-Factor Authentication (MFA) Implementation:** Multi-factor authentication (MFA) Implementation training is aimed at IT administrators and security teams. This training covers implementing and managing MFA systems, including best practices for deployment and user education. Participants will learn how to configure and troubleshoot MFA solutions. The outcome is a robust MFA implementation that enhances security. This training reduces risk by adding an extra layer of protection against unauthorized access.

**Network Monitoring and Threat Detection:** It should attend Network Monitoring and Threat Detection training, and cybersecurity staff should be responsible for monitoring network activities. The training covers tools and techniques for real-time network monitoring, detecting anomalies, and responding to threats. Participants will learn how to use monitoring solutions to gain visibility into network traffic. The outcome is an enhanced ability to quickly detect and respond to potential threats. This training reduces risk by improving threat detection and response capabilities.

**Physical Security for IT Assets:** Physical Security for IT Assets training is essential for facilities management and IT staff. This training covers best practices for securing physical IT assets, including access control, surveillance, and environmental controls. Participants will learn how to protect data centers, server rooms, and other critical infrastructure. The outcome is a secure physical environment that complements cybersecurity measures. This training reduces risk by preventing physical breaches and protecting sensitive equipment.

# Actionable Recommendations

Effective implementation of network infrastructure management requires a series of strategic actions tailored to an organization's unique needs. These recommendations provide a practical roadmap for enhancing network operations' security, reliability, and efficiency. By following these guidelines, organizations can mitigate risks, improve compliance, and ensure robust defenses against cyber threats. Twelve actionable recommendations are designed to help organizations optimize their network infrastructure management efforts.

**Regularly Update Network Devices:** Keeping network devices up-to-date is crucial for maintaining security and performance. Regularly check for firmware and software updates from device manufacturers and apply them promptly. This practice helps address known vulnerabilities and enhances device functionality. Scheduling updates during planned maintenance windows minimizes disruptions to network services. Staying current with updates ensures your network devices are protected against emerging threats.

**Implement Strong Access Controls:** Robust access controls prevent unauthorized access to network devices and sensitive data. Use multi-factor authentication (MFA) for administrative access to critical network components. Regularly review and update access permissions to align with current roles and responsibilities. Implement least privilege principles to limit access to only what is necessary for job functions. Strong access controls help reduce the risk of credential compromise and unauthorized activities.

**Conduct Regular Network Audits:** Regular network audits help identify and address security gaps and configuration issues. Perform comprehensive audits that include device configurations, access controls, and network architecture. Use automated tools to assist in identifying vulnerabilities and misconfigurations. Document findings and create action plans to remediate identified issues. Regular audits ensure the network remains secure and compliant with best practices and regulatory requirements.

**Use Secure Communication Protocols:** Secure communication protocols protect data in transit from interception and tampering. Implement protocols such as HTTPS, SSH, and SSL/TLS for all network communications. Regularly review and update configurations to ensure that only secure protocols are used. Educate staff on the importance of using secure communication methods. Secure protocols help maintain the confidentiality and integrity of sensitive information.

**Implement Network Segmentation:** Network segmentation limits the spread of cyber attacks by isolating different network segments. Use VLANs, subnets, and firewalls to create secure zones within the network. Regularly review and adjust segmentation strategies to reflect changes in the network environment. Ensure that critical assets are isolated from less secure segments. Effective segmentation reduces the attack surface and enhances overall network security.

**Develop and Test Incident Response Plans:** An effective incident response plan is critical for minimizing the impact of security breaches. Develop a comprehensive plan that includes detection, analysis, containment, eradication, and recovery steps. Conduct regular drills and simulations to test the plan and ensure staff are prepared to respond to incidents. Update the plan based on lessons learned from exercises and actual incidents. A well-practiced incident response plan helps ensure a quick and coordinated reaction to security threats.

**Automate Network Monitoring:** Automating network monitoring helps detect and respond to threats in real time. Use advanced monitoring tools to observe network traffic and identify anomalies continuously. Set up automated alerts to notify security teams of potential issues. Integrate monitoring solutions with other security tools for a comprehensive view of network activity. Automation enhances visibility and allows for faster detection and mitigation of threats.

**Maintain Comprehensive Documentation:** Comprehensive documentation of network infrastructure is essential for effective management and troubleshooting. Document all network devices, configurations, and architecture diagrams. Keep documentation up-to-date to reflect any changes in the network environment. Use centralized documentation systems to ensure easy access and sharing of information. Accurate documentation supports efficient operations and quick resolution of issues.

**Train Staff on Network Security:** Regular training ensures that staff know network security best practices and emerging threats. Provide specialized training for IT and cybersecurity staff and general awareness training for all employees. Include topics such as secure configurations, incident response, and recognizing phishing attacks. Use a variety of training methods, including hands-on exercises and simulations. Well-trained staff contribute to a stronger security posture and are better equipped to handle security challenges.

**Plan for End-of-Life Components:** Proactively managing end-of-life components helps prevent security vulnerabilities. Identify and track devices approaching end-of-life and plan for their replacement or upgrade. Implement mitigating controls for components that cannot be immediately replaced. Communicate with vendors to stay informed about product lifecycles and support timelines. Proper planning ensures that end-of-life components do not pose a security risk to the network.

**Utilize Advanced Configuration Management Tools:** Advanced configuration management tools help maintain consistent and secure device configurations. Use these tools to automate configuration changes, backups, and compliance checks. Regularly review and validate configurations against security baselines and best practices. Implement version control to track changes and roll back configurations if needed. Effective configuration management reduces the risk of misconfigurations and enhances overall network stability.

**Ensure Regulatory Compliance:** Ensuring compliance with relevant regulations and standards is critical for avoiding legal penalties and enhancing security. Regularly review regulatory requirements and align network security practices accordingly. Conduct periodic compliance audits and address any identified gaps. Maintain documentation to demonstrate compliance efforts and readiness for inspections. Compliance efforts help build trust with customers and partners and ensure the organization meets legal obligations.

# Simplified Security Controls (SSC)

Security controls are essential tools in the arsenal of any organization seeking to protect its digital and physical assets from various cyber threats. Tailoring these controls to fit the specific needs of your business environment is crucial, as it ensures that the protection mechanisms are relevant and effective against the specific risks your organization faces. There are numerous sources to draw these controls from, including the well-regarded CIS Top 18, which provides a robust framework for crafting defensive strategies. The recommendations presented in this book are based on the CIS controls, among others, offering a comprehensive guide that can be adapted to serve a wide range of security needs. Before implementing these controls, it is vital to thoroughly review their design to ensure they align with your strategic objectives and operational practices. Additionally, after deployment, it is imperative to regularly test the controls to verify their effectiveness and to make necessary adjustments. This ensures that the controls continue to function as intended, safeguarding your organization against emerging threats and changing conditions.

CHAPTER 12  NETWORK INFRASTRUCTURE MANAGEMENT

## CONTROL 1: ENSURE NETWORK INFRASTRUCTURE IS UP-TO-DATE

**Control Objective:** Ensure network infrastructure is kept current with the latest stable software releases and supported network-as-a-service (NaaS) offerings to mitigate vulnerabilities and enhance security.

**Implementation Steps:**

**1.1. Inventory Network Devices:** Conduct a comprehensive inventory of all network devices and their respective software versions. This should include routers, switches, firewalls, and wireless access points.

**1.2. Schedule Regular Updates:** Establish a schedule for reviewing and updating software versions on all network devices. This review should occur monthly or more frequently to ensure all devices run the latest stable releases.

**1.3. Vendor Communication:** Regularly communicate with network device vendors to stay informed about the latest updates and patches. Implement a process for prompt application of these updates.

**1.4. Automate Update Processes:** Where possible, automate the update process to ensure the timely application of patches and minimize the risk of human error.

**Expected Outcome:** Regularly updating network infrastructure reduces the risk of exploitation of known vulnerabilities, thereby enhancing the overall security and reliability of the network.

CHAPTER 12   NETWORK INFRASTRUCTURE MANAGEMENT

## CONTROL 2: ESTABLISH AND MAINTAIN A SECURE NETWORK ARCHITECTURE

**Control Objective:** Develop and sustain a network architecture that ensures segmentation, least privilege, and high availability to protect organizational assets.

**Implementation Steps:**

**2.1. Network Segmentation:** Implement network segmentation to isolate critical systems and sensitive data. Use VLANs and firewalls to enforce segmentation policies.

**2.2. Apply Least Privilege:** Ensure access controls are based on the principle of least privilege. Only grant users and devices the minimum access necessary for their roles.

**2.3. Redundancy and Availability:** Design the network architecture to include redundant systems and failover mechanisms to ensure high availability and business continuity.

**2.4. Regular Assessments:** Conduct regular security assessments of the network architecture to identify and mitigate potential vulnerabilities.

**Expected Outcome:** A secure network architecture reduces the risk of unauthorized access and ensures that critical systems remain available and resilient in the face of disruptions.

## CONTROL 3: SECURELY MANAGE NETWORK INFRASTRUCTURE

**Control Objective:** Implement secure management practices for network infrastructure, including version-controlled infrastructure-as-code and secure protocols.

**Implementation Steps:**

**3.1. Version-Controlled Infrastructure:** Use infrastructure-as-code (IaC) tools with version control to manage network configurations. This ensures consistency and enables rollback capabilities.

**3.2. Secure Protocols:** Enforce using secure management protocols such as SSH and HTTPS for all network device management activities.

**3.3. Access Control:** Restrict management access to network devices to authorized personnel only, using strong authentication methods.

**3.4. Monitor Management Activities:** Implement logging and monitoring of all management activities to detect and respond to unauthorized access attempts.

**Expected Outcome:** Securely managing network infrastructure protects against unauthorized changes and enhances the overall security posture by ensuring that only authorized, secure methods are used for network management.

## CONTROL 4: ESTABLISH AND MAINTAIN ARCHITECTURE DIAGRAM(S)

**Control Objective:** Create and maintain up-to-date architecture diagrams and network documentation to reflect current configurations and changes.

**Implementation Steps:**

**4.1. Create Initial Diagrams:** Develop detailed architecture diagrams that represent the current state of the network, including all devices, connections, and configurations.

**4.2. Regular Updates:** Review and update the diagrams annually or whenever significant changes occur within the network.

**4.3. Centralized Documentation:** Store all diagrams and network documentation in a centralized, accessible location for use by relevant stakeholders.

**4.4. Documentation Review Process:** Implement a formal process for periodically reviewing and validating the accuracy of the network documentation.

**Expected Outcome:** Maintaining accurate architecture diagrams and documentation enhances network management, troubleshooting, and security planning by providing a clear, up-to-date view of the network infrastructure.

## CONTROL 5: CENTRALIZE NETWORK AUTHENTICATION, AUTHORIZATION, AND AUDITING (AAA)

**Control Objective:** Implement centralized AAA mechanisms to streamline and secure access control across the network.

**Implementation Steps:**

**5.1. Implement Centralized AAA Systems:** Deploy centralized authentication, authorization, and auditing systems such as RADIUS or TACACS+ to manage network access.

**5.2. Integrate with Directory Services:** Integrate AAA systems with existing directory services (e.g., Active Directory) to streamline user management.

**5.3. Define Access Policies:** Establish clear access policies that define user roles and permissions based on the principle of least privilege.

**5.4. Monitor and Audit Access:** Continuously monitor and audit access attempts to detect and respond to unauthorized activities.

**Expected Outcome:** Centralized AAA systems enhance security by ensuring consistent access control policies and providing comprehensive auditing capabilities.

CHAPTER 12   NETWORK INFRASTRUCTURE MANAGEMENT

## CONTROL 6: USE OF SECURE NETWORK MANAGEMENT AND COMMUNICATION PROTOCOLS

**Control Objective:** Ensure secure network management and communication protocols are used to protect data integrity and confidentiality.

**Implementation Steps:**

**6.1. Enforce Secure Protocols:** Mandate using secure protocols such as 802.1X for network access control and WPA2 Enterprise for wireless networks.

**6.2. Regular Protocol Reviews:** Review and update protocol configurations to meet current security standards.

**6.3. Training for IT Staff:** Provide training for IT staff on implementing and managing secure network protocols.

**6.4. Monitor Network Traffic:** Use monitoring tools to ensure that only authorized, secure protocols are used within the network.

**Expected Outcome:** Using secure network management and communication protocols protects data in transit and prevents unauthorized access, enhancing overall network security.

## CONTROL 7: ENSURE REMOTE DEVICES UTILIZE A VPN AND ARE CONNECTING TO AN ENTERPRISE'S AAA INFRASTRUCTURE

**Control Objective:** Remote devices must use a VPN and authenticate through the enterprise's AAA infrastructure before accessing network resources.

**Implementation Steps:**

**7.1. Deploy VPN Solutions:** Implement VPN solutions to provide secure remote access to the network for all remote devices.

**7.2. Mandatory VPN Use:** Enforce policies requiring all remote devices to use the VPN when accessing enterprise resources.

**7.3. Integrate VPN with AAA:** Ensure VPN authentication is integrated with the enterprise's AAA infrastructure for consistent access control.

**7.4. Monitor Remote Access:** Continuously monitor and log remote access attempts to detect and respond to unauthorized access.

**Expected Outcome:** Ensuring remote devices use a VPN and authenticate through the AAA infrastructure secures remote access and protects enterprise resources from unauthorized access.

---

## CONTROL 8: ESTABLISH AND MAINTAIN DEDICATED COMPUTING RESOURCES FOR ALL ADMINISTRATIVE WORK

**Control Objective:** Provide dedicated computing resources for administrative tasks, segregated from the primary network and isolated from the Internet.

**Implementation Steps:**

**8.1. Dedicated Admin Workstations:** Establish dedicated workstations or virtual machines for administrative tasks, separate from regular user devices.

**8.2. Network Segmentation:** Segment the administrative network from the primary network to limit exposure to potential threats.

**8.3. No Internet Access:** Restrict access on administrative devices to prevent external threats from compromising administrative tasks.

**8.4. Strong Authentication:** Implement strong authentication measures on administrative devices to ensure only authorized personnel can access them.

**Expected Outcome:** Dedicated, isolated computing resources for administrative work enhance security by reducing the risk of compromised administrative credentials through general network or Internet exposure.

# CHAPTER 13

# Network Monitoring and Defense

Understanding and implementing effective network monitoring and defense strategies is essential for any organization aiming to protect its digital assets. Cyber threats continuously evolve, and adversaries are becoming more sophisticated in their methods. This necessitates a robust approach to network security that goes beyond traditional defenses. By focusing on continuous monitoring and defense, organizations can be better prepared to detect, respond to, and mitigate security incidents swiftly.

One of the key challenges in network security is the inherent imperfection of network defenses. Despite advanced security tools and systems, adversaries constantly develop new exploits and techniques to bypass these defenses. This evolving threat landscape means no single tool or solution can guarantee complete security. Therefore, organizations must adopt a comprehensive strategy that includes continuous monitoring and human expertise to identify and respond to threats effectively.

The role of human expertise in network monitoring must be balanced. While technology plays a crucial role in detecting and analyzing potential threats, the human element provides the necessary context and intuition to understand and address these threats. Security professionals must be able to interpret data, recognize patterns, and make informed decisions quickly. This combination of technology and human insight is vital for maintaining a robust security posture.

One common issue that organizations face is the misconfiguration of security tools. Human error or a lack of understanding of the tools' capabilities can lead to gaps in security, providing adversaries with opportunities to exploit. To mitigate this risk, it is essential to have well-trained personnel who understand how to configure and manage these tools effectively. Regular training and updates on the latest security trends and techniques can help maintain a high level of expertise within the organization.

In addition to human expertise, continuous monitoring is critical to effective network defense. This involves regularly collecting and analyzing data from various sources within the network to identify any unusual or suspicious activity. Tools such as Security Information and Event Management (SIEM) systems can aggregate and correlate data from multiple sources, providing a comprehensive view of the network's security status. However, these tools are not a substitute for skilled security personnel who can interpret the data and respond to incidents appropriately.

Visibility into all threat vectors is another essential aspect of network monitoring and defense. Organizations must have insight into every part of their infrastructure, including on-premises systems, cloud platforms, and remote endpoints. This holistic view allows security teams to identify potential threats from any source and take appropriate action. Ensuring comprehensive visibility requires integrating various monitoring tools and practices across the entire network.

The speed of detection and response is crucial in minimizing the impact of security incidents. The longer a threat goes undetected, the more damage it can cause. Organizations can detect threats early and respond quickly by establishing a robust situational awareness program,

## CHAPTER 13  NETWORK MONITORING AND DEFENSE

reducing the potential impact. This involves having the right tools in place and ensuring that security teams are prepared to act swiftly and effectively when an incident occurs.

Developing an internal threat intelligence capability can significantly enhance an organization's ability to anticipate and respond to cyber threats. This involves collecting and analyzing data on the tactics, techniques, and procedures (TTPs) used by attackers and their indicators of compromise (IOCs). By understanding these elements, security teams can develop proactive strategies to identify and mitigate potential threats before they can cause harm. This proactive approach is essential for staying ahead of adversaries in the constantly evolving cyber threat landscape.

Implementing a comprehensive network monitoring and defense strategy also supports regulatory compliance. Many industries have specific requirements for data protection and incident response, and adhering to these regulations is crucial for maintaining trust and avoiding penalties. By adopting best practices in network monitoring and defense, organizations can ensure they meet these requirements and demonstrate their commitment to cybersecurity.

The importance of situational awareness in network security cannot be overstated. This concept involves clearly understanding the network's current state, including any potential threats and vulnerabilities. Situational awareness allows security teams to make informed decisions and respond to incidents effectively. Achieving this requires continuous monitoring, regular assessments, and quickly adapting to new information and changing circumstances.

In conclusion, network monitoring and defense are fundamental components of a robust cybersecurity strategy. Organizations must recognize the limitations of technology alone and incorporate human expertise and continuous monitoring into their security practices. By doing so, they can enhance their ability to detect, respond to, and mitigate cyber threats, ultimately protecting their digital assets and maintaining the trust of their stakeholders. The ongoing evolution of cyber threats makes organizations need to remain vigilant and proactive in their approach to network security.

Investing in training and resources for security personnel is essential for building a resilient network defense strategy. Skilled professionals who understand the intricacies of network security tools and techniques can significantly enhance an organization's ability to protect itself against cyber threats. Regularly updating and refining security policies and procedures based on the latest threat intelligence and industry best practices is also crucial for maintaining a solid security posture.

Lastly, fostering a culture of cybersecurity awareness within the organization can help ensure that all employees understand the importance of network monitoring and defense. This includes regular training sessions, awareness campaigns, and encouraging a proactive approach to security among all staff members. By promoting a security-conscious culture, organizations can reduce the risk of human error and improve their overall cybersecurity resilience.

# Key Concepts and Terms

Understanding network monitoring and defense's foundational concepts and terms is crucial for effectively implementing cybersecurity strategies. This section outlines key concepts and terms for establishing and maintaining robust network defenses.

**Network Monitoring:** Network monitoring involves continuously observing a network for slow or failing components and ensuring the network is functioning optimally. This process includes using specialized software tools to track and analyze network traffic, detect anomalies, and identify potential security threats. Effective network monitoring helps maintain the network's health and ensures quick detection and response to any issues that may arise. Organizations can proactively monitor network activity to prevent small issues from escalating into significant problems.

**Security Information and Event Management (SIEM):** SIEM systems are tools that provide real-time analysis of security alerts generated by network hardware and applications. These systems collect, store, and analyze log data from various sources, allowing security teams to detect suspicious activities and respond to potential threats promptly. SIEM solutions are critical for correlating different types of log data to provide a comprehensive view of an organization's security posture. They help identify patterns that may indicate a security breach or vulnerability, thus enabling a quicker and more coordinated response.

**Indicators of Compromise (IOCs):** IOCs are pieces of forensic data, such as data found in system log entries or files, that identify potentially malicious activity on a system or network. These indicators help cybersecurity professionals detect potential breaches and assess the extent of a security incident. Common IOCs include unusual network traffic, file metadata changes, and unexpected files or code on a system. Identifying IOCs is essential for understanding and mitigating the impact of security threats.

**Tactics, Techniques, and Procedures (TTPs):** TTPs refer to the behavior patterns of cyber adversaries, including the methods they use to plan and execute attacks. Tactics describe an attacker's overall goals, techniques are the methods used to achieve those goals, and procedures are the specific steps taken during an attack. Understanding TTPs is vital for developing proactive defense strategies and anticipating future threats. By studying and cataloging TTPs, organizations can better prepare for and defend against sophisticated cyber attacks.

**Incident Response:** Incident response is a structured approach to handling and managing the aftermath of a security breach or cyber attack. The goal is to handle the situation in a way that limits damage and reduces recovery time and costs. An effective incident response plan includes preparation, detection and analysis, containment, eradication, recovery, and post-incident activities. This process ensures that the organization can quickly and efficiently respond to incidents, minimizing their impact and preventing future occurrences.

**Threat Intelligence:** Threat intelligence involves collecting and analyzing information about current and potential threats to an organization. This intelligence helps organizations understand attackers' tactics, techniques, and procedures and provides actionable insights to enhance their defense mechanisms. By leveraging threat intelligence, organizations can proactively identify and mitigate threats before they can cause significant harm. This intelligence can be gathered from various sources, including security vendors, threat-sharing communities, and internal data analysis.

**False Positives:** In network security, false positives are alerts or notifications that incorrectly indicate the presence of a threat. These can lead to unnecessary investigations and overwhelm security teams, potentially causing them to miss actual threats. Managing false positives involves tuning security systems and continuously updating rules and algorithms to improve accuracy. Reducing the number of false positives is essential for maintaining the efficiency and effectiveness of security operations.

**Cloud Security:** As organizations increasingly adopt cloud technologies, securing cloud environments becomes critical to network defense. Cloud security protects data, applications, and infrastructures from threats. This includes implementing access controls, encryption, and continuous monitoring of cloud resources. Ensuring visibility and control over cloud environments is crucial for detecting and responding to threats that may not be visible through traditional on-premises security measures.

**Log Management:** Log management collects, stores, and analyzes log data from various sources within an IT environment. Effective log management helps detect anomalies, understand system behavior, and conduct forensic analysis during a security incident. Logs can provide detailed insights into the activities occurring within a network, making them invaluable for identifying and responding to threats. Regular review and analysis of logs are essential for maintaining a secure and compliant IT infrastructure.

**Anomaly Detection:** Anomaly detection involves identifying patterns in data that do not conform to expected behavior. In network security, anomaly detection is used to identify unusual activities that may indicate a security threat. This can include deviations in network traffic, unusual login attempts, or unexpected changes in system configurations. Implementing robust anomaly detection mechanisms helps in the early identification of potential threats, enabling quicker response and mitigation.

**Security Operations Center (SOC):** A SOC is a centralized unit that deals with security issues on an organizational and technical level. It comprises a dedicated team of security experts who monitor, detect, and respond to cybersecurity incidents in real time. The SOC is responsible for continuously monitoring network and system activities, incident management, and implementing defensive measures. Having a SOC enhances an organization's ability to defend against and respond to cyber threats effectively.

**Threat Hunting:** Threat hunting is the proactive search for cyber threats lurking undetected within a network. Unlike traditional security measures that rely on automated alerts, threat hunting involves security experts manually analyzing data to identify signs of compromise. This practice helps uncover advanced threats that may bypass conventional defenses and provides deeper insights into potential vulnerabilities. By regularly conducting threat-hunting exercises, organizations can improve their security posture and resilience against sophisticated cyber attacks.

CHAPTER 13  NETWORK MONITORING AND DEFENSE

# Importance and Relevance

Network monitoring and defense have become critical components of effective cybersecurity strategies in today's rapidly evolving digital landscape. The sophistication and frequency of cyber threats continue to rise, making organizations need to adopt comprehensive measures to protect their digital infrastructure. This section outlines the key reasons network monitoring and defense are essential for maintaining robust cybersecurity. By understanding these factors, organizations can better appreciate the necessity of implementing and adhering to effective network defense practices.

**Rapidly Evolving Threat Landscape:** Cyber threats are constantly changing, with new vulnerabilities and attack methods emerging regularly. Adversaries are becoming more sophisticated, sharing information within their communities to develop new exploits and bypass security measures. This dynamic threat environment necessitates continuous network monitoring to detect and respond to threats in real time. Without ongoing vigilance, organizations risk falling victim to advanced persistent threats that can cause significant damage.

**Human Error and Misconfigurations:** Even the most advanced security tools can be rendered ineffective by human error and misconfigurations. Employees may inadvertently leave vulnerabilities open or fail to properly configure security settings, providing opportunities for attackers to exploit. Continuous monitoring helps identify and rectify these issues before they can be exploited. Regular training and awareness programs for staff also play a crucial role in minimizing the risk of human error.

**Speed of Detection and Response:** The ability to detect and respond to threats quickly is crucial for minimizing the impact of a security incident. Delayed responses can lead to prolonged exposure and more significant damage. Comprehensive network monitoring provides the visibility needed to detect anomalies and respond swiftly to potential threats. Organizations can significantly mitigate cyber attacks' effects by reducing detection and response time.

**Compliance and Regulatory Requirements:** Many industries are subject to stringent regulatory requirements regarding data protection and incident response. Compliance with these regulations is a legal obligation and essential for maintaining customer trust and protecting sensitive information. Effective network monitoring and defense practices ensure that organizations meet these requirements, avoiding penalties and reputational damage. Regular audits and assessments can help maintain compliance and improve overall security posture.

**Proactive Threat Management:** Reactive approaches to cybersecurity are no longer sufficient in the face of modern threats. Proactive threat management involves identifying potential vulnerabilities and threats before exploitation. Network monitoring enables organizations to detect unusual activity and take preemptive action to prevent breaches. This proactive stance helps build a more resilient security framework capable of withstanding sophisticated attacks.

**Enhanced Situational Awareness:** Situational awareness involves having a comprehensive understanding of the current security state of the network, including all potential threats and vulnerabilities. This awareness is achieved through continuous monitoring and analysis of network activity. With enhanced situational awareness, security teams can make informed decisions and respond effectively to incidents. This level of understanding is critical for maintaining a solid defense against cyber threats.

**Reduction of False Positives:** Security tools often generate numerous alerts, many of which can be false positives. These false alarms can overwhelm security teams and obscure genuine threats. Effective network monitoring involves tuning and refining security tools to reduce the occurrence of false positives. This ensures that security personnel can focus on actual threats, improving the efficiency and effectiveness of the security operations center (SOC).

CHAPTER 13   NETWORK MONITORING AND DEFENSE

**Visibility Across All Network Components:** Modern networks are complex, comprising on-premises systems, cloud environments, and remote endpoints. Comprehensive network monitoring provides visibility into all network components, ensuring that no part of the infrastructure is left unchecked. This holistic view is essential for detecting threats from any part of the network. Ensuring complete visibility helps maintain a robust security posture.

**Support for Incident Response and Forensics:** In the event of a security breach, thorough incident response and forensic investigation are necessary to understand the scope and impact of the attack. Network monitoring provides the data needed for these activities, including logs and records of network activity. This information is crucial for identifying the cause of the breach and implementing measures to prevent future incidents. Effective incident response relies heavily on the insights gained from continuous network monitoring.

**Building Internal Threat Intelligence:** Threat intelligence involves gathering information about potential threats and using it to strengthen security measures. Network monitoring plays a crucial role in creating this intelligence by identifying patterns and indicators of compromise (IOCs). Organizations can develop more effective defense strategies by understanding attackers' tactics, techniques, and procedures (TTPs). This internal threat intelligence is vital for staying ahead of evolving threats.

**Facilitating Collaboration and Information Sharing:** Effective cybersecurity often involves collaboration and sharing among different teams and organizations. Network monitoring provides the data for such collaboration, enabling teams to identify and mitigate threats. Sharing threat intelligence and best practices can help improve the security posture of all involved parties. This collective effort is essential for combating the sophisticated nature of modern cyber threats.

**Maintaining Business Continuity:** Cyber attacks can disrupt business operations, leading to significant financial and reputational damage. Continuous network monitoring and defense help ensure that organizations can maintain business continuity despite cyber threats. By quickly identifying and responding to incidents, businesses can minimize downtime and continue to operate effectively. This resilience is critical for maintaining customer trust and achieving long-term success in a digital world.

## Risks of Not Implementing the Control

Effective network monitoring and defense measures can leave an organization vulnerable to cyber threats. The absence of these crucial protections can result in severe financial, operational, and reputational damage. Without continuous monitoring and defense, companies cannot promptly detect and respond to threats, increasing the likelihood of significant breaches. These vulnerabilities can lead to data loss, regulatory penalties, and a loss of customer trust. Understanding the specific risks associated with not implementing network monitoring and defense highlights the importance of these measures in maintaining a robust cybersecurity posture.

**Data Breaches:** Data breaches are among the most significant risks for companies that do not implement network monitoring and defense. Without these measures, malicious actors can infiltrate the network and exfiltrate sensitive data without detection. This can include customer information, intellectual property, and financial records, leading to severe financial and reputational harm. Companies may face legal penalties and loss of customer trust, which can be difficult to recover. Effective monitoring is essential to detect and mitigate breaches before they cause substantial damage.

**Financial Loss:** Cyber attacks can result in substantial financial losses for organizations. These losses stem from various sources, including theft of sensitive data, ransomware attacks, and the costs associated with responding to and recovering from incidents. Companies may also incur fines for non-compliance with regulatory requirements and suffer from lost revenue due to downtime and disrupted operations. The financial impact of a cyber attack can be devastating, underscoring the importance of proactive network defense.

**Operational Disruption:** Operational disruption is a significant risk associated with inadequate network defense. Cyber attacks can cripple an organization's infrastructure, leading to extended downtime and interrupted services. This can affect production lines, supply chains, and customer-facing services, causing widespread disruption. The longer it takes to identify and resolve the issue, the greater the operational impact. Ensuring continuous network monitoring helps minimize downtime and maintain business continuity.

**Reputational Damage:** Reputational damage is a critical consequence of failing to protect a company's network. Customers and partners expect their data to be handled securely; breaches can damage trust. Adverse publicity and loss of customer confidence can have long-term effects on a company's market position and profitability. Rebuilding a damaged reputation requires significant effort and resources, making prevention through robust network defense essential.

**Legal and Regulatory Penalties:** Non-compliance with data protection regulations can lead to substantial legal and regulatory penalties. Laws such as the GDPR and CCPA impose strict requirements on organizations' handling and protecting personal data. Failure to implement adequate network monitoring and defense measures can result in non-compliance, leading to fines and legal action. Maintaining compliance through effective cybersecurity practices is essential to avoid these penalties and protect the organization.

**Intellectual Property Theft:** Intellectual property (IP) theft is a significant risk for companies that do not secure their networks effectively. Cybercriminals and state-sponsored actors target valuable IP, including trade secrets, product designs, and proprietary technology. The loss of intellectual property can erode competitive advantage and result in significant financial loss. Implementing robust network monitoring and defense helps protect these critical assets from unauthorized access and theft.

**Ransomware Attacks:** Ransomware attacks pose a significant threat to organizations, encrypting critical data and demanding payment for its release. These attacks can go undetected without adequate monitoring until the damage is done. The financial and operational impact of ransomware can be severe, and paying the ransom does not guarantee data recovery. Preventing ransomware through proactive network defense is crucial to safeguarding the organization's data and resources.

**Insider Threats:** Insider threats, whether malicious or accidental, are a considerable risk to network security. Employees with access to sensitive information can misuse their privileges, intentionally or unintentionally compromising data. Without monitoring, detecting these threats is challenging, leaving the organization vulnerable to internal attacks. Implementing network monitoring helps identify suspicious behavior and mitigate insider threats effectively.

**Advanced Persistent Threats (APTs):** Advanced Persistent Threats (APTs) are sophisticated, long-term attacks aimed at stealing information or disrupting operations. These threats often go undetected for extended periods due to their stealthy nature. Without continuous monitoring, organizations are at a higher risk of falling victim to APTs, which can cause significant and prolonged damage. Proactive monitoring is essential to identify and respond to these threats promptly.

**Loss of Competitive Advantage:** Cyber attacks can lead to losing competitive advantage by exposing sensitive business strategies, research and development efforts, and proprietary information. Competitors or malicious actors accessing this information can undermine the organization's market position. Protecting this information through effective network defense is crucial to maintaining competitive advantage. Continuous monitoring ensures that attempts to access sensitive information are detected and thwarted.

**Customer Trust Erosion:** Organizations that fail to secure their networks face a significant risk of eroded customer trust. Customers expect their data to be protected, and breaches can lead to loss of confidence and loyalty. The impact on customer relationships can be long-lasting, affecting the organization's reputation and revenue. Effective network monitoring and defense are essential to maintaining customer trust and safeguarding business relationships.

**Cyber Espionage:** Cyber espionage involves unauthorized access to an organization's network to steal confidential information for strategic advantage. This can include government, corporate, or personal data. The absence of robust network defenses makes organizations vulnerable to espionage activities, which can compromise national security, business interests, and individual privacy. Continuous monitoring and defense are critical to detect and prevent espionage activities and protect sensitive information.

# What Questions Should You Ask?

Formulating the right questions is essential for cybersecurity leaders aiming to implement effective network monitoring and defense. These questions help to uncover critical aspects of the network, identify potential vulnerabilities, and ensure that the appropriate measures are in place to detect and respond to threats. By addressing these questions, leaders can comprehensively understand their network's security posture and take informed steps to enhance it. This proactive approach is crucial for safeguarding the organization against the ever-evolving landscape of cyber threats.

**What critical assets need to be protected?** Identifying critical assets is the first step in any security strategy. These assets can include sensitive data, intellectual property, critical infrastructure, and key business applications. Understanding what needs to be protected helps prioritize

## CHAPTER 13   NETWORK MONITORING AND DEFENSE

resources and efforts to ensure these assets are adequately secured. This focus ensures that the most valuable components of the organization are shielded from potential threats.

**How is network traffic monitored and analyzed?** Continuous monitoring and analysis of network traffic are essential for detecting anomalies and potential threats. Understanding the current methods and tools used for monitoring helps identify gaps and areas for improvement. Effective traffic analysis can reveal unusual patterns that may indicate malicious activity. Ensuring robust monitoring mechanisms are in place is critical for maintaining network security.

**What logging and reporting mechanisms are currently implemented?** Logging and reporting are vital for maintaining visibility into network activities. Comprehensive logging ensures that all significant events are recorded and can be analyzed for signs of compromise. Regular reporting helps identify trends and unusual activities that require further investigation. Evaluating existing logging practices is necessary to ensure they provide the required level of detail and accuracy.

**Who is responsible for monitoring and responding to security incidents?** Clearly defined roles and responsibilities are crucial for an effective incident response. Identifying who is responsible ensures accountability and facilitates a swift response to security incidents. This clarity helps coordinate efforts and ensure that incidents are handled efficiently and effectively. A well-defined incident response team is essential for minimizing the impact of security breaches.

**What is the current state of our incident response plan?** An incident response plan outlines the steps to be taken during a security breach. Understanding this plan's current state helps identify weaknesses and areas for improvement. Regularly updating and testing the plan ensures that it remains effective and relevant. A robust incident response plan is critical for mitigating the effects of security incidents.

CHAPTER 13   NETWORK MONITORING AND DEFENSE

**How are threats and vulnerabilities identified and managed?** Identifying and managing threats and vulnerabilities is a continuous process that involves regular assessments and updates. Understanding current processes helps identify and address all potential risks promptly. Effective threat and vulnerability management is crucial for preventing security incidents. Regular assessments and updates are necessary to keep up with the evolving threat landscape.

**What tools and technologies are used for network defense?** The tools and technologies used for network defense play a significant role in determining the effectiveness of the security strategy. Understanding these tools' capabilities and limitations helps identify gaps and areas for improvement. Ensuring the right tools are in place is essential for maintaining robust network security. These tools are regularly evaluated to ensure they meet the organization's needs.

**How is user access to network resources controlled?** Controlling user access is essential for preventing unauthorized access to sensitive information and critical systems. Understanding the current access control mechanisms helps identify weaknesses and areas for improvement. Effective access control ensures that only authorized users can access the network resources they need to perform their duties. Implementing strict access controls is crucial for maintaining network security.

**What measures are in place to protect against insider threats?** Whether malicious or accidental, insider threats pose a significant risk to network security. Understanding the current measures helps identify gaps and areas for improvement. Effective monitoring and controls are necessary to detect and prevent insider threats. Regular training and awareness programs can also help in mitigating this risk.

**How is threat intelligence gathered and utilized?** Threat intelligence involves collecting and analyzing information about potential threats to enhance security measures. Understanding the current processes helps identify gaps and areas for improvement. Effective threat intelligence can provide valuable insights into attackers' tactics, techniques, and procedures. Utilizing this intelligence is crucial for staying ahead of evolving threats.

**What training and awareness programs are in place for staff?** Training and awareness programs are essential for ensuring staff understand their role in maintaining network security. Understanding the current programs helps identify gaps and areas for improvement. Regular training ensures staff know the latest threats and best practices for preventing security incidents. A well-informed staff is crucial for maintaining a solid security posture.

**How is the effectiveness of security measures evaluated?** Regular evaluation of security measures is essential for ensuring their effectiveness. Understanding the current processes helps identify gaps and areas for improvement. Regular assessments and audits can provide valuable insights into the effectiveness of the security strategy. Continuous evaluation is necessary to ensure that security measures remain effective and relevant.

# Recommended Training

Effective cybersecurity training is crucial for IT and cybersecurity staff and all other employees within an organization. This training ensures that everyone understands their role in protecting the network and can recognize and respond to potential threats. Tailored training programs can address the specific needs of different employee groups, providing them with the knowledge and skills required to maintain a secure environment. By implementing comprehensive training initiatives, organizations can significantly reduce the risk of cyber incidents and enhance their overall security posture. The following training recommendations cover various aspects of cybersecurity, each designed to address unique challenges and requirements.

# CHAPTER 13  NETWORK MONITORING AND DEFENSE

**Phishing Awareness Training:** Phishing attacks are among the most common cyber threats. All employees should attend phishing awareness training to recognize and respond to phishing emails and messages. The training should include examples of phishing attempts, techniques used by attackers, and best practices for avoiding phishing scams. By raising awareness, employees will be less likely to fall victim to phishing attacks, reducing the risk of data breaches and other security incidents.

**Incident Response Training:** It is essential for IT and cybersecurity staff responsible for managing and responding to security incidents. This training should cover the steps involved in identifying, containing, eradicating, and recovering from incidents. Participants should also learn how to document and report incidents effectively. With proper incident response training, staff can quickly and efficiently handle security breaches, minimizing their impact on the organization.

**Security Policy and Procedures Training:** All employees should know the organization's security policies and procedures. This training should cover the critical policies, their importance, and how employees must comply. Understanding these policies helps ensure that everyone follows best practices and contributes to maintaining a secure environment. Regular updates and refresher courses can keep employees informed about any policy changes.

**Data Protection and Privacy Training:** Data protection and privacy training is vital for all employees, especially those handling sensitive information. This training should cover data handling best practices, the importance of data privacy, and compliance with relevant regulations such as GDPR or CCPA. Employees should learn to store, transmit, and dispose of data securely. Proper data protection training helps prevent data breaches and ensures compliance with legal requirements.

**Network Security Fundamentals Training:** IT and cybersecurity staff should receive training on network security fundamentals. This training should cover network architecture basics, common vulnerabilities, and best practices for securing network components. Participants should also learn about network monitoring and defense tools. Understanding these fundamentals helps staff implement adequate security measures and protect the organization's network from threats.

**Secure Coding Practices Training:** Developers and IT staff involved in software development should attend secure coding practices training. This training should focus on common coding vulnerabilities, secure coding standards, and techniques for writing secure code. By following secure coding practices, developers can reduce the risk of introducing application vulnerabilities. This training helps ensure that the software developed by the organization is robust and secure.

**Access Control Management Training:** Access control management training is essential for IT staff managing user access to network resources. This training should cover the principles of access control, methods for implementing and enforcing access controls, and best practices for managing user permissions. Proper access control management helps prevent unauthorized access to sensitive information and systems, and it ensures that access controls are effectively implemented and maintained.

**Social Engineering Awareness Training:** Social engineering attacks exploit human psychology to gain access to sensitive information. All employees should receive social engineering awareness training to recognize and resist these attacks. The training should cover common social engineering techniques, such as pretexting, baiting, and tailgating, and provide strategies for responding. Organizations can reduce the risk of falling victim to these manipulative attacks by educating employees about social engineering.

**Cybersecurity Best Practices Training:** All employees should receive cybersecurity best practices training to ensure they understand how to protect themselves and the organization from cyber threats. This training should cover password management, secure browsing, and recognizing suspicious activity. By following best practices, employees can contribute to a safer work environment. Regular training sessions can help reinforce these practices and keep security in mind.

**Mobile Device Security Training:** With the increasing use of mobile devices for work, mobile device security training is crucial for all employees. This training should cover the risks of mobile device usage, such as data theft and malware, and best practices for securing mobile devices. Employees should learn how to use security features like encryption and remote wiping. Proper mobile device security training helps protect organizational data and reduces the risk of mobile-related security incidents.

**Cloud Security Training:** As more organizations move to cloud-based services, cloud security training becomes essential for IT and cybersecurity staff. This training should cover cloud security principles, risks, and best practices for securing cloud environments. Participants should learn about cloud-specific security tools and techniques. Understanding cloud security helps protect the organization's cloud infrastructure from threats.

**Regular Security Drills and Simulations:** Conducting regular security drills and simulations is important for testing the effectiveness of the organization's security measures and incident response plans. These exercises should involve all relevant staff and cover various scenarios, such as phishing attacks, data breaches, and ransomware incidents. Employees can improve their readiness and effectiveness by practicing their response to security incidents. Regular drills help identify weaknesses and areas for improvement in the organization's security posture.

# Actionable Recommendations

Implementing effective network monitoring and defense measures requires a strategic approach encompassing various best practices and technologies. These recommendations provide practical steps organizations can take to enhance their cybersecurity posture. By following these guidelines, organizations can ensure that their network

CHAPTER 13   NETWORK MONITORING AND DEFENSE

defenses are robust, capable of detecting and responding to threats in real time, and aligned with industry best practices. Each recommendation focuses on a specific aspect of network security, offering actionable insights to help organizations protect their digital assets and maintain operational integrity.

**Develop a Comprehensive Network Monitoring Strategy:** A well-defined network monitoring strategy is essential for identifying and responding to potential threats. This strategy should outline the goals, tools, processes, and personnel involved in monitoring activities. It is crucial to include all network components, including on-premises systems, cloud environments, and remote endpoints. Regularly review and update the strategy to ensure it adapts to evolving threats and organizational changes. A comprehensive plan provides a clear framework for effective network monitoring.

**Implement Security Information and Event Management (SIEM):** Deploying an SIEM system is critical in centralizing and analyzing log data across the network. SIEM solutions can aggregate data from multiple sources, correlate events, and generate alerts for suspicious activities. Ensure the SIEM is configured to cover all relevant data sources and is tuned to minimize false positives. Regularly review and update SIEM rules and configurations to keep up with emerging threats. A well-implemented SIEM enhances visibility and response capabilities.

**Conduct Regular Vulnerability Assessments and Penetration Testing:** Regular vulnerability assessments and penetration tests are essential for identifying and addressing security weaknesses. These activities help uncover vulnerabilities that attackers could exploit and provide insights into the effectiveness of existing security measures. Schedule assessments and tests periodically and after significant changes to the network or applications. Address identified vulnerabilities promptly and track remediation efforts. Ongoing evaluations and testing ensure the network remains secure against new threats.

CHAPTER 13    NETWORK MONITORING AND DEFENSE

**Establish a Dedicated Security Operations Center (SOC):** A dedicated SOC provides a centralized hub for monitoring, detecting, and responding to security incidents. Staff the SOC with skilled security professionals who can analyze alerts, investigate incidents, and coordinate response efforts. Equip the SOC with advanced tools and technologies to enhance its capabilities. Define clear procedures for incident handling and ensure continuous training for SOC personnel. A dedicated SOC improves the organization's ability to manage and mitigate cyber threats effectively.

**Implement Network Segmentation:** Network segmentation involves dividing the network into smaller, isolated segments to limit the spread of threats. Use firewalls, VLANs, and access control lists to enforce segmentation and restrict access between segments. Regularly review and update segmentation policies to reflect network and business requirements changes. Monitor traffic between segments to detect and respond to suspicious activities. Network segmentation reduces the attack surface and contains potential breaches.

**Utilize Endpoint Detection and Response (EDR) Solutions:** EDR solutions provide visibility into endpoint activities and enable rapid detection and response to threats. Deploy EDR tools on all endpoints, including desktops, laptops, and servers, to monitor for signs of compromise. Configure EDR solutions to automatically respond to detected threats, such as isolating affected devices. Regularly review EDR alerts and investigate incidents to improve threat detection and response processes. EDR solutions enhance the organization's ability to detect and mitigate endpoint threats.

**Regularly Review and Update Security Policies:** Security policies provide the foundation for an organization's security practices and controls. Please periodically review and update these policies to reflect current threats, technologies, and regulatory requirements. Engage stakeholders across the organization in the policy review process to ensure comprehensive coverage and buy-in. Communicate policy updates to all employees and provide training to ensure understanding and compliance. Up-to-date security policies are critical for maintaining a solid security posture.

# CHAPTER 13   NETWORK MONITORING AND DEFENSE

**Implement Robust Access Control Measures:** Access control measures are essential for preventing unauthorized access to network resources. Implement role-based access control (RBAC) to ensure that users have access only to the resources they need for their job functions. Multi-factor authentication (MFA) adds an extra layer of security for accessing sensitive systems and data. Regularly review access controls and adjust permissions as needed to maintain security. Robust access control measures help protect sensitive information and critical systems.

**Enhance User Training and Awareness Programs:** User training and awareness programs are vital for educating employees about cybersecurity best practices and emerging threats. Develop and deliver regular training sessions covering phishing, social engineering, and secure data handling. Use simulated phishing campaigns to test and reinforce training effectiveness. Encourage a culture of security awareness and make it easy for employees to report suspicious activities. Effective training programs reduce the risk of human error and enhance overall security.

**Deploy Advanced Threat Detection Technologies:** Advanced threat detection technologies, such as intrusion detection systems (IDS) and intrusion prevention systems (IPS), are essential for identifying and mitigating sophisticated threats. Deploy these technologies at critical points in the network, such as perimeter and internal segments. Configure IDS/IPS to detect known and unknown threats and respond automatically to prevent or contain attacks. Regularly update detection signatures and rules to keep up with the latest threats. Advanced threat detection technologies enhance the organization's ability to detect and respond to cyberattacks.

**Establish a Comprehensive Incident Response Plan:** A comprehensive incident response plan outlines the steps to be taken in the event of a security breach. Develop the plan to include roles and responsibilities, communication protocols, and procedures for containing and recovering from incidents. Regularly test the plan through tabletop exercises and simulated incidents to ensure effectiveness. Update the

CHAPTER 13   NETWORK MONITORING AND DEFENSE

plan as needed to reflect organizational and threat landscape changes. A well-defined incident response plan is crucial for minimizing the impact of security incidents.

**Leverage Threat Intelligence Services:** These services provide valuable insights into emerging threats and attacker tactics. Subscribe to reputable threat intelligence feeds and integrate this information into security monitoring and response processes. Use threat intelligence to proactively identify and mitigate potential threats before they impact the organization. Share threat intelligence with industry peers and participate in intelligence communities to stay informed about the latest threats. Leveraging threat intelligence services enhances the organization's ability to stay ahead of evolving cyber threats.

# Simplified Security Controls (SSC)

Security controls are essential for any organization seeking to protect its digital and physical assets from cyber threats. Tailoring these controls to fit the specific needs of your business environment is crucial, as it ensures that the protection mechanisms are relevant and effective against the specific risks your organization faces. There are numerous sources to draw these controls from, including the well-regarded CIS Top 18, which provides a robust framework for crafting defensive strategies. The recommendations presented in this book are based on the CIS controls, among others, offering a comprehensive guide that can be adapted to serve a wide range of security needs. Before implementing these controls, it is vital to thoroughly review their design to ensure they align with your strategic objectives and operational practices. Additionally, after deployment, it is imperative to regularly test the controls to verify their effectiveness and to make necessary adjustments. This ensures that the controls continue to function as intended, safeguarding your organization against emerging threats and changing conditions.

CHAPTER 13   NETWORK MONITORING AND DEFENSE

## CONTROL 1: CENTRALIZE SECURITY EVENT ALERTING

**Control Objective:** To centralize security event alerting across all enterprise assets, enabling comprehensive log correlation and analysis for timely threat detection and response.

**Implementation Steps:**

**1.1. Deploy a SIEM Solution:** Implement a Security Information and Event Management (SIEM) solution that centralizes logs from all critical assets. Ensure the SIEM is capable of correlating security events based on vendor-defined alerts.

**1.2. Configure Log Analytics Platform:** Set up a log analytics platform with security-relevant correlation alerts. This platform should be capable of analyzing logs from various sources and generating actionable alerts.

**1.3. Integrate Enterprise Assets:** Ensure all enterprise assets, including servers, endpoints, and network devices, are configured to forward logs to the centralized SIEM or log analytics platform.

**1.4. Regularly Update Correlation Rules:** Continuously update and refine correlation rules within the SIEM to keep pace with emerging threats and changes in the IT environment.

**1.5. Monitor and Respond:** Establish a dedicated team to monitor alerts from the SIEM and log analytics platform. Ensure they have clear procedures for investigating and responding to security incidents.

**Expected Outcome:** Centralized security event alerting provides a holistic view of the organization's security posture, enabling faster detection and response to threats. This approach enhances the ability to correlate events across different assets and reduces the likelihood of missed alerts due to decentralized logging.

## CHAPTER 13  NETWORK MONITORING AND DEFENSE

## CONTROL 2: DEPLOY A HOST-BASED INTRUSION DETECTION SOLUTION

**Control Objective:** To detect potential security breaches at the host level by deploying host-based intrusion detection solutions (HIDS) across enterprise assets.

**Implementation Steps:**

**2.1. Select HIDS Software:** Choose a reputable host-based intrusion detection software compatible with your enterprise assets.

**2.2. Deploy on Critical Assets:** Install HIDS on critical servers, endpoints, and other enterprise assets where appropriate. Ensure that all deployed instances are configured correctly.

**2.3. Configure Detection Rules:** Customize detection rules within the HIDS to match the organization's specific needs and threat landscape. Include rules for common attack vectors and behaviors.

**2.4. Regular Updates:** Regularly update the HIDS software and detection rules to incorporate the latest threat intelligence and security patches.

**2.5. Monitor Alerts:** Establish a process for continuously monitoring alerts generated by HIDS. Ensure that alerts are investigated promptly and that appropriate response actions are taken.

**Expected Outcome:** Deploying host-based intrusion detection solutions enhances the organization's ability to detect and respond to potential threats at the host level, providing an additional layer of security against breaches.

CHAPTER 13   NETWORK MONITORING AND DEFENSE

## CONTROL 3: DEPLOY A NETWORK INTRUSION DETECTION SOLUTION

**Control Objective:** To monitor network traffic for signs of malicious activity by deploying network intrusion detection systems (NIDS) or equivalent cloud service provider (CSP) services.

**Implementation Steps:**

**3.1. Select NIDS Technology:** Choose a network intrusion detection system that fits the organization's needs and can monitor traffic across different network segments.

**3.2. Deploy NIDS Sensors:** Install NIDS sensors at strategic points within the network, such as at the network perimeter and key internal segments.

**3.3. Configure Detection Rules:** Customize detection rules and signatures to align with the organization's threat profile and security policies.

**3.4. Integrate with SIEM:** Ensure NIDS alerts are integrated with the centralized SIEM for comprehensive correlation and analysis.

**3.5. Continuous Monitoring:** Establish a team responsible for continuously monitoring NIDS alerts and responding to potential threats.

**Expected Outcome:** Network intrusion detection solutions enhance visibility into network traffic, allowing the organization to detect and respond to malicious activities more effectively.

## CONTROL 4: PERFORM TRAFFIC FILTERING BETWEEN NETWORK SEGMENTS

**Control Objective:** To enhance network security by filtering traffic between different network segments, thereby limiting the spread of potential threats.

**Implementation Steps:**

**4.1. Define Segmentation Policy:** Develop a network segmentation policy that outlines how different segments should be isolated based on sensitivity and function.

**4.2. Implement Filtering Rules:** Configure firewalls and routers to enforce traffic filtering rules between network segments. Ensure that only necessary traffic is allowed between segments.

**4.3. Regularly Review Rules:** Review and update traffic filtering rules to ensure they remain effective and aligned with changing network requirements.

**4.4. Monitor Inter-Segment Traffic:** Use monitoring tools to continuously analyze traffic between segments for signs of unauthorized access or anomalous activity.

**4.5. Respond to Violations:** Establish procedures for responding to violations of traffic filtering rules, including investigation and remediation actions.

**Expected Outcome:** Effective traffic filtering between network segments limits the spread of threats within the network, reducing the risk of widespread compromise.

CHAPTER 13   NETWORK MONITORING AND DEFENSE

## CONTROL 5: MANAGE ACCESS CONTROL FOR REMOTE ASSETS

**Control Objective:** To ensure secure access for remote assets connecting to enterprise resources by enforcing strict access control measures.

**Implementation Steps:**

**5.1. Define Access Control Policies:** Develop policies that specify the security requirements for remote access, including up-to-date anti-malware software, secure configurations, and regular updates.

**5.2. Implement Access Controls:** Use VPNs, multi-factor authentication (MFA), and other technologies to enforce access control policies for remote assets.

**5.3. Monitor Remote Access:** Monitor remote access sessions for signs of unauthorized access or anomalous behavior.

**5.4. Regular Compliance Checks:** Conduct regular compliance checks to ensure remote assets adhere to security policies and configurations.

**5.5. Respond to Non-Compliance:** Establish procedures for addressing non-compliance, including remediation steps and potential access revocation.

**Expected Outcome:** Managing access control for remote assets ensures that only secure and compliant devices can access enterprise resources, reducing the risk of unauthorized access and potential breaches.

CHAPTER 13  NETWORK MONITORING AND DEFENSE

## CONTROL 6: COLLECT NETWORK TRAFFIC FLOW LOGS

**Control Objective:** To enhance visibility and analysis capabilities by collecting and reviewing network traffic flow logs from network devices.

**Implementation Steps:**

**6.1. Enable Traffic Flow Logging:** Configure network devices such as routers and switches to collect traffic flow logs (e.g., NetFlow, sFlow).

**6.2. Centralize Log Collection:** Set up a centralized log collection system to aggregate traffic flow logs from all relevant network devices.

**6.3. Configure Alerts:** Implement alerting mechanisms to notify security teams of unusual traffic patterns or potential threats.

**6.4. Regular Log Analysis:** Regularly analyze traffic flow logs to identify trends, anomalies, and potential security incidents.

**6.5. Integrate with SIEM:** Ensure traffic flow logs are integrated for comprehensive analysis and correlation with other security events.

**Expected Outcome:** Collecting and analyzing network traffic flow logs provides valuable insights into network activity, enabling proactive detection and response to potential threats.

## CONTROL 7: DEPLOY A HOST-BASED INTRUSION PREVENTION SOLUTION

**Control Objective:** To prevent security breaches at the host level by deploying host-based intrusion prevention solutions (HIPS) on enterprise assets.

**Implementation Steps:**

**7.1. Select HIPS Technology:** Choose a reputable host-based intrusion prevention solution that fits the organization's needs.

CHAPTER 13  NETWORK MONITORING AND DEFENSE

**7.2. Deploy on Critical Assets:** Install HIPS on critical servers, endpoints, and other enterprise assets where appropriate.

**7.3. Configure Prevention Rules:** Customize prevention rules within the HIPS to match the organization's specific needs and threat landscape.

**7.4. Regular Updates:** Regularly update the HIPS software and prevention rules to incorporate the latest threat intelligence and security patches.

**7.5. Monitor and Respond:** Establish a process for continuously monitoring HIPS alerts and ensuring timely response to potential threats.

**Expected Outcome:** Deploying host-based intrusion prevention solutions enhances the organization's ability to prevent and mitigate potential threats at the host level, providing a proactive layer of defense.

## CONTROL 8: DEPLOY A NETWORK INTRUSION PREVENTION SOLUTION

**Control Objective:** To protect the network from malicious activities by deploying intrusion prevention systems (NIPS) or equivalent CSP services.

**Implementation Steps:**

**8.1. Select NIPS Technology:** Choose a network intrusion prevention system suitable for the organization's architecture and security needs.

**8.2. Deploy NIPS Sensors:** Install NIPS sensors at strategic points within the network to monitor and analyze traffic for malicious activity.

**8.3. Configure Prevention Rules:** Customize prevention rules and signatures to align with the organization's threat profile and security policies.

**8.4. Integrate with SIEM:** Ensure NIPS alerts are integrated with the centralized SIEM for comprehensive correlation and analysis.

**8.5. Continuous Monitoring:** Establish a team responsible for continuously monitoring NIPS alerts and responding to potential threats.

**Expected Outcome:** Network intrusion prevention solutions enhance the organization's ability to detect and prevent malicious activities at the network level, providing an additional layer of security.

## CONTROL 9: DEPLOY PORT-LEVEL ACCESS CONTROL

**Control Objective:** To control access to network ports and ensure that only authorized devices can connect to the network by deploying port-level access control mechanisms.

**Implementation Steps:**

**9.1. Implement 802.1x:** Deploy 802.1x authentication on network switches and access points to enforce port-level access control.

**9.2. Use Certificates and Authentication:** Utilize certificates, user authentication, and device authentication to validate access requests.

**9.3. Configure Access Policies:** Develop and implement access control policies that define the criteria for allowing or denying access to network ports.

**9.4. Monitor Access Attempts:** Monitor access attempts and log all successful and unsuccessful connection attempts.

**9.5. Respond to Unauthorized Access:** Establish procedures for responding to unauthorized access attempts, including investigation and remediation actions.

**Expected Outcome:** Deploying port-level access control ensures that only authorized devices can connect to the network, reducing the risk of unauthorized access and potential security breaches.

CHAPTER 13   NETWORK MONITORING AND DEFENSE

## CONTROL 10: PERFORM APPLICATION LAYER FILTERING

**Control Objective:** To enhance network security by filtering traffic at the application layer, preventing malicious activities and unauthorized access.

**Implementation Steps:**

**10.1. Deploy Filtering Solutions:** Implement application layer filtering solutions such as filtering proxies, firewalls, or gateways.

**10.2. Define Filtering Policies:** Develop and enforce policies that specify allowed and disallowed application traffic based on organizational needs and security requirements.

**10.3. Regularly Update Rules:** Continuously update filtering rules to reflect the latest threat intelligence and changes in application usage.

**10.4. Monitor Application Traffic:** Use monitoring tools to analyze application layer traffic for signs of malicious activity or policy violations.

**10.5. Respond to Incidents:** Establish procedures for investigating and responding to incidents detected by application layer filtering mechanisms.

**Expected Outcome:** Performing application layer filtering enhances the organization's ability to control and secure application traffic, reducing the risk of malicious activities and unauthorized access.

## CHAPTER 13  NETWORK MONITORING AND DEFENSE

## CONTROL 11: TUNE SECURITY EVENT ALERTING THRESHOLDS

**Control Objective:** To ensure the effectiveness and relevance of security event alerting by regularly tuning alerting thresholds.

**Implementation Steps:**

**11.1. Establish Baseline Thresholds:** Define initial alerting thresholds based on historical data and security policies.

**11.2. Monthly Review:** Conduct monthly reviews of alerting thresholds to ensure they remain effective and aligned with current threat landscapes.

**11.3. Adjust Based on Analysis:** Adjust thresholds based on analysis of false positives, false negatives, and actual security incidents.

**11.4. Document Changes:** Document all changes to alerting thresholds and the rationale behind them to maintain a clear record of adjustments.

**11.5. Continuous Improvement:** Implement a process for continuous improvement, incorporating feedback from security teams and lessons learned from incidents.

**Expected Outcome:** Regularly tuning security event alerting thresholds ensures that alerts remain relevant and actionable, reducing the number of false positives and improving the organization's ability to detect and respond to genuine threats.

# CHAPTER 14

# Security Awareness and Skills Training

In the modern digital landscape, the human element remains a pivotal aspect of cybersecurity. While advanced technological defenses are essential, the actions and behaviors of individuals within an organization can significantly influence its security posture. A robust security awareness and skills training program is fundamental to cultivating a security-conscious workforce capable of recognizing and mitigating cyber threats. This approach empowers employees with the knowledge and skills to protect sensitive information and fosters a culture of vigilance and accountability across all enterprise levels.

The primary rationale behind security awareness and skills training is recognizing that human error is often the weakest link in the cybersecurity chain. Cyber attackers frequently exploit this vulnerability, using phishing, social engineering, and malware-laden emails to bypass technical defenses. Intentionally or unintentionally, employees can become vectors for cyber incidents by mishandling data, using weak passwords, or falling prey to deceptive tactics. Organizations can significantly reduce the risk of successful cyber attacks by educating the workforce on these threats and appropriate countermeasures.

## CHAPTER 14  SECURITY AWARENESS AND SKILLS TRAINING

A comprehensive security awareness program is not a one-time event but an ongoing process that adapts to the evolving threat landscape. Regular updates and training sessions ensure that employees remain informed about the latest cyber threats and best practices for mitigating them. This continuous education approach is crucial, reinforcing security concepts and keeping them fresh in employees' minds. Additionally, it allows organizations to address specific threats that may arise due to changes in the operational environment or the emergence of new vulnerabilities.

Different roles within an organization are exposed to varying levels of risk and types of threats, necessitating tailored training programs. Executives, for instance, handle highly sensitive information and are prime targets for spear-phishing and business email compromise (BEC) attacks. System administrators have access to critical systems and applications, making them potential targets for attacks aimed at gaining control over the network infrastructure. By providing role-specific training, organizations can equip their employees with the knowledge and skills pertinent to their responsibilities and the threats they are most likely to encounter.

The effectiveness of a security awareness program hinges on its ability to engage employees and make the training content relevant and relatable. This can be achieved through real-world scenarios, interactive training modules, and regular phishing simulations. These methods help to reinforce the training material and enable employees to apply what they have learned in practical situations. Employees are more likely to retain engaging training programs, leading to better compliance with security policies and procedures.

In addition to regular training sessions, timely and topical security messages can significantly enhance employees' awareness. For instance, reminding employees about the importance of solid passwords after a major data breach reported in the media can reinforce the need for good password hygiene. Similarly, alerts about the rise of phishing attempts during tax season or the holidays can prepare employees to be extra vigilant during these periods. These contextual messages keep security top-of-mind and encourage proactive behavior.

Organizations must also consider their specific regulatory and threat environments when designing security awareness programs. Financial institutions, for example, may need to focus on compliance-related training for data handling and fraud prevention. Healthcare organizations must prioritize protecting patient data and compliance with regulations such as HIPAA. By aligning training programs with industry-specific requirements and threats, organizations can ensure their employees are well-prepared to meet their unique challenges.

Social engineering tactics are among the most effective methods cyber attackers use, making training particularly important. Phishing simulations, for example, can help employees recognize and respond appropriately to deceptive emails and messages. Training should also cover more sophisticated tactics, such as pretexting and baiting, which may be used to manipulate employees into divulging sensitive information or performing unauthorized actions. By understanding these tactics, employees can better protect themselves and the organization from social engineering attacks.

A key component of any security awareness program is ensuring employees know how to report potential security incidents. Prompt reporting of suspicious activities, such as receiving a phishing email or noticing unusual system behavior, can enable the security team to respond quickly and mitigate potential threats. Training programs should emphasize the importance of reporting and provide clear instructions on how to do so. This helps to create a proactive security culture where employees act as the first line of defense.

The rise of remote work and using personal devices for business purposes have introduced new security challenges that must be addressed through training. Employees must understand the risks of connecting to

## CHAPTER 14   SECURITY AWARENESS AND SKILLS TRAINING

insecure networks and the importance of using secure configurations for their home network infrastructure. Training should cover best practices for remote work security, such as using virtual private networks (VPNs), strong Wi-Fi passwords, and regular software updates. This ensures employees maintain a secure working environment, even when working from home.

Effective security awareness training also involves preparing employees for specific threats they may encounter in their roles. For IT professionals, this might include training on secure system administration practices and awareness of common vulnerabilities. Understanding the OWASP Top 10 vulnerabilities and how to prevent them is crucial for web application developers. High-profile roles, such as executives and financial officers, may require advanced training in social engineering and other targeted attack methods. Organizations can enhance the overall security posture by tailoring training to the needs of different roles.

Measuring the effectiveness of a security awareness program is essential for continuous improvement. Organizations should implement metrics to assess the impact of training on employee behavior and security outcomes. This might include tracking the number of reported phishing attempts, the rate of compliance with security policies, and the results of regular security assessments. By analyzing these metrics, organizations can identify areas for improvement and adjust their training programs accordingly.

Security awareness and skills training is critical to a comprehensive cybersecurity strategy. It addresses the human element of cyber risk by educating employees about threats and best practices for mitigating them. By fostering a culture of security awareness, organizations can enhance their resilience to cyber attacks and protect their sensitive data and systems. Regular updates, role-specific training, and continuous engagement are key to maintaining an effective security awareness program that adapts to the evolving threat landscape.

# Key Concepts and Terms

Understanding key concepts and terms is essential for effectively implementing and managing a security awareness and skills training program. This section delves into fundamental concepts and terminology relevant to this area, providing a comprehensive foundation for IT professionals and organizational leaders.

**Security Awareness Program:** A structured initiative to educate employees about cybersecurity threats and best practices to mitigate them. This program involves regular training sessions, updates, and reminders to keep security knowledge fresh in the minds of the workforce. The goal is to foster a security culture within the organization, where employees understand their role in protecting sensitive information and systems.

**Phishing:** A cyberattack technique where attackers send fraudulent messages, often via email, to trick recipients into revealing sensitive information or downloading malware. Phishing is one of the most common and effective methods cybercriminals use due to its reliance on social engineering. Training employees to recognize and report phishing attempts is crucial in preventing such attacks from succeeding.

**Social Engineering:** The psychological manipulation of people into performing actions or divulging confidential information. Social engineering attacks exploit human behavior and trust to gain unauthorized access to systems or data. Awareness training helps employees recognize these tactics and respond appropriately to protect themselves and the organization.

**Role-Specific Training:** Tailored training programs to address the unique security risks of different organizational roles. For example, executives, IT administrators, and finance personnel each face distinct threats and require specialized training to handle them effectively. This approach ensures that all employees know what is relevant to their responsibilities.

**Business Email Compromise (BEC):** A type of cyber attack where attackers spoof email accounts to impersonate executives or trusted partners, often to initiate fraudulent financial transactions. BEC attacks target high-level employees who can authorize significant financial decisions. Training employees to verify requests for sensitive actions or information through additional communication channels can prevent these attacks.

**Security Culture:** The collective mindset and behaviors regarding security within an organization. A strong security culture means that employees at all levels are aware of security policies, understand their importance, and actively participate in protecting the organization's assets. Building this culture involves continuous education, clear communication, and leadership commitment to security.

**Incident Reporting:** The process by which employees notify IT or security teams about potential security incidents or suspicious activities. Prompt incident reporting is critical for timely response and mitigation of threats. Training programs should emphasize the importance of reporting and provide clear guidelines on how to do so effectively.

**Remote Work Security:** Measures and best practices to secure remote work environments, mainly when employees use personal devices and home networks. Remote work security includes VPNs, strong passwords, regular software updates, and secure Wi-Fi configurations. As remote work becomes more prevalent, ensuring that employees can work securely from any location is essential.

**Password Hygiene:** Creating and managing strong, unique passwords for different accounts and systems. Good password hygiene includes using complex passwords, changing them regularly, and not reusing passwords across multiple sites. Educating employees on these practices helps prevent unauthorized access due to compromised credentials.

**Data Handling and Protection:** Properly managing sensitive information to prevent unauthorized access, disclosure, or loss. This includes understanding data classification, using encryption, and following regulatory compliance requirements. Training employees on data handling protocols protect the organization's critical information assets.

**Phishing Simulation:** A training exercise where employees are sent simulated phishing emails to test their ability to recognize and respond to phishing attempts. These simulations help identify vulnerabilities in employee awareness and provide opportunities for targeted training. Regular phishing simulations can significantly improve an organization's defense against phishing attacks.

**Regulatory Compliance Training:** Education on the legal and regulatory requirements for data protection and cybersecurity specific to an industry. Compliance training ensures employees understand and adhere to GDPR, HIPAA, or PCI-DSS laws. This type of training is crucial for avoiding legal penalties and protecting sensitive information in regulated industries.

**Security Updates and Patches:** Regular updates and patches are critical for maintaining the security of software and systems. Training employees to recognize the importance of promptly applying these updates helps prevent attackers from exploiting vulnerabilities. Employees should also know how to report issues with automated update processes to ensure continuous protection.

# Importance and Relevance

The significance of a robust security awareness and skills training program in today's cybersecurity landscape cannot be overstated. With the increasing sophistication of cyber threats and the prevalence of remote work, organizations must equip their workforce with the necessary knowledge and skills to identify and mitigate potential risks. The following points outline why this control is essential and should be diligently implemented across all organizations.

# CHAPTER 14   SECURITY AWARENESS AND SKILLS TRAINING

**Human Error Reduction:** Human error remains a primary cause of cybersecurity incidents. Employees might unintentionally click on malicious links, use weak passwords, or mishandle sensitive information. By implementing comprehensive security awareness training, organizations can significantly reduce the likelihood of such errors. Educated employees are better equipped to recognize and avoid common threats, thereby minimizing the risk of incidents caused by human mistakes.

**Phishing Attack Mitigation:** Phishing attacks are one of the most common methods cybercriminals use to gain unauthorized access to systems. It is crucial to train employees to identify phishing emails and other social engineering tactics. Regular phishing simulations and awareness campaigns help reinforce this training, making employees more vigilant and less likely to fall victim to these attacks. This proactive approach can prevent many security breaches.

**Enhanced Incident Response:** Prompt and effective incident response is vital in mitigating the damage caused by cybersecurity incidents. When employees are trained to recognize and report suspicious activities or potential breaches, the organization's security team can respond more quickly. This reduces the window of opportunity for attackers and limits the impact of security incidents. A well-informed workforce acts as an early warning system, enhancing the overall security posture.

**Compliance with Regulations:** Many industries are subject to stringent data protection regulations, such as GDPR, HIPAA, and PCI-DSS. Security awareness training helps employees understand and adhere to these regulatory requirements. This not only helps avoid legal penalties but also promotes the responsible handling of sensitive information. Compliance training is a critical component of maintaining trust with customers and stakeholders.

**Protection of Sensitive Data:** Different roles within an organization handle various types of sensitive data, from financial records to personal health information. Training programs tailored to these specific roles ensure that employees know how to protect the data they work with. This targeted approach minimizes the risk of data breaches and ensures that all sensitive information is adequately safeguarded.

**Adaptation to Evolving Threats:** The cybersecurity threat landscape constantly evolves, with new attack vectors and techniques emerging regularly. Continuous security awareness training informs employees about the latest threats and best practices for mitigating them. This adaptability is crucial in maintaining an effective defense against evolving cyber threats. Regular updates and refreshers help maintain a high level of vigilance.

**Reduction of Insider Threats:** Insider threats, whether intentional or accidental, pose significant risks to organizations. Security awareness training educates employees about the potential consequences of their actions and the importance of following security protocols. This awareness helps reduce the likelihood of malicious insider activities and unintentional breaches. A culture of security can deter insiders from engaging in harmful behavior.

**Strengthened Security Culture:** Building a strong security culture within an organization is essential for long-term cybersecurity resilience. When employees at all levels understand and prioritize security, it becomes ingrained in the organizational ethos. This cultural shift encourages everyone to take responsibility for protecting the organization's assets. A strong security culture leads to more consistent and effective adherence to security policies and procedures.

**Support for Remote Work:** The rise of remote work has introduced new security challenges, such as insecure home networks and personal device usage. Security awareness training addresses these challenges by educating employees on best practices for securing their remote work environments. This includes using VPNs, securing home Wi-Fi networks, and being cautious about public Wi-Fi. Proper training ensures that employees can work securely from any location.

**Cost-Effective Risk Management:** Investing in security awareness training is a cost-effective way to manage cyber risk. Preventing security incidents through education is often less expensive than dealing with the aftermath of a breach. Training reduces the likelihood of incidents, saving the organization from costly data breaches, legal fees, and reputational damage. It is a proactive measure that provides significant long-term benefits.

**Employee Empowerment:** Empowering employees with knowledge about cybersecurity threats and defenses fosters a sense of ownership and responsibility. When employees understand how their actions impact the organization's security, they are more likely to take proactive steps to protect it. This empowerment leads to more engaged and security-conscious employees. An empowered workforce is a critical asset in the fight against cyber threats.

**Improved Vendor and Partner Security:** Organizations often rely on a network of vendors and partners, which can introduce additional security risks. Training employees to recognize potential threats from third-party interactions helps mitigate these risks. Employees can apply their knowledge to assess the security practices of vendors and partners, ensuring that they meet the organization's security standards. This vigilance extends the security perimeter beyond the organization's immediate boundaries.

# Risks of Not Implementing the Control

Neglecting to establish a comprehensive security awareness and skills training program exposes organizations to many cybersecurity risks. Without proper education and training, employees are likelier to fall victim to cyber attacks, mishandling sensitive information, and failing to recognize and report suspicious activities. This lack of awareness can lead to increased incidents of data breaches, financial losses, and reputational damage. Furthermore, non-compliance with regulatory requirements can result in legal penalties and financial repercussions. The following points highlight the risks of failing to implement effective security awareness and skills training.

**Increased Susceptibility to Phishing Attacks:** Employees without adequate training are likelier to fall prey to phishing scams. These attacks can compromise sensitive information, allow unauthorized access to systems, and install malware. Phishing is one of the most prevalent and effective attack vectors because it exploits human behavior. A lack of awareness and preparedness makes an organization a prime target for such attacks, increasing the risk of significant security breaches.

**Higher Likelihood of Data Breaches:** Mishandling of sensitive data by untrained employees can result in data breaches. This includes sending confidential information to the wrong recipients, failing to encrypt sensitive data, or improperly disposing of documents. Data breaches can lead to the exposure of personal information, financial losses, and legal ramifications. Organizations needing to prioritize security training are more vulnerable to these costly and damaging incidents.

**Insufficient Incident Response:** Employees may not know how to recognize or report potential security incidents without proper training. This delay in reporting can give attackers more time to exploit vulnerabilities and cause extensive damage. An effective incident response requires immediate action, which can only be achieved if employees are well-informed and vigilant. Failure to train employees adequately on incident response procedures can result in prolonged and more severe security incidents.

**Regulatory Non-Compliance:** Many industries have strict regulations regarding data protection and cybersecurity. Failure to comply with these regulations can result in hefty fines, legal action, and loss of business. Security awareness training ensures that employees understand and adhere to these regulatory requirements. Organizations that neglect this aspect risk facing severe legal and financial consequences.

**Loss of Customer Trust:** Customers expect organizations to protect their personal and financial information. A data breach resulting from inadequate security training can damage customer trust and loyalty. Rebuilding this trust is challenging and can take years, during which the organization may suffer from reduced business and negative publicity. Protecting customer information through proper training is essential for maintaining a positive reputation.

**Increased Financial Losses:** Cybersecurity incidents can result in significant financial losses due to operational downtime, remediation costs, and legal fees. Training employees on security best practices helps prevent these incidents, reducing the likelihood of financial repercussions. Without such training, organizations are more vulnerable to attacks that can disrupt business operations and incur substantial recovery costs.

**Intellectual Property Theft:** Organizations possess valuable intellectual property that cybercriminals can target. Employees not trained to recognize and prevent social engineering attacks may inadvertently disclose proprietary information. This can lead to competitive disadvantages and financial losses. Protecting intellectual property requires employees to be vigilant and knowledgeable about potential threats.

**Operational Disruptions:** Cyber attacks can cause significant disruptions to business operations. Employees not trained to maintain secure systems and networks can inadvertently create vulnerabilities that attackers exploit. This can lead to system downtime, loss of productivity, and delayed business processes. Training employees to follow security protocols ensures smooth and uninterrupted operations.

**Increased Risk of Insider Threats:** Insider threats, whether malicious or accidental, pose a significant risk to organizations. Employees unaware of the potential consequences of their actions or who do not follow security policies can unintentionally cause security breaches. Proper training helps mitigate this risk by educating employees about the importance of adhering to security protocols and recognizing suspicious behavior.

**Damage to Business Partnerships:** Business partners and vendors expect a certain level of security from the organizations they work with. A security incident resulting from inadequate employee training can damage these relationships and cause the loss of valuable partnerships. Ensuring employees are well-trained in cybersecurity practices is crucial for maintaining trust and collaboration with business partners.

**Increased Vulnerability to Emerging Threats:** The cybersecurity landscape constantly evolves, with new threats emerging regularly. Employees not updated with the latest security trends and threats are less capable of protecting the organization. Regular and continuous training ensures that employees know current threats and how to respond effectively. Neglecting this aspect leaves the organization vulnerable to novel and sophisticated attacks.

**Reduced Overall Security Posture:** An organization's security posture is only as strong as its weakest link. Attackers can exploit employees who lack proper training, a significant weakness. Comprehensive security awareness and skills training strengthen the overall security posture by ensuring all employees are knowledgeable and vigilant. This holistic approach is essential for protecting the organization from various cyber threats.

# What Questions Should You Ask?

When implementing a security awareness and skills training program, cybersecurity leaders must ask the right questions to ensure the program's effectiveness. These questions help identify the organization's specific needs, assess current capabilities, and determine the best strategies for fostering a security-conscious workforce. By thoroughly evaluating these aspects, leaders can design a tailored program that addresses their organization's unique risks and challenges. The following questions provide a comprehensive framework for developing and implementing a robust security awareness and skills training program.

**What are the specific security threats our organization faces?** Understanding the threats relevant to your organization is essential for tailoring the training program to address these risks. Different industries and business models encounter distinct cyber threats, such as phishing, ransomware, or insider threats. Identifying these threats helps design targeted training that equips employees with the knowledge and skills to counteract these specific dangers effectively.

**Who are the key stakeholders involved in the training program?** Identifying and involving key stakeholders, such as IT staff, HR, and executive leadership, ensures the training program has the necessary support and resources. Stakeholder involvement is crucial for gaining buy-in, allocating budgets, and integrating security awareness into the organizational culture. Their input can also provide valuable insights into training needs and potential resistance areas.

**What are the regulatory and compliance requirements we must meet?** Compliance with industry regulations and standards is often a primary driver for security training programs. Understanding these requirements ensures that the training covers all necessary topics and helps avoid legal penalties. It also reinforces the importance of security practices among employees, highlighting the consequences of non-compliance for the organization.

**How will we measure the effectiveness of the training program?** Establishing metrics and evaluation methods is crucial for assessing the training program's impact. This might include tracking the number of reported phishing attempts, evaluating changes in employee behavior, or measuring improvements in compliance rates. Regular evaluation helps identify areas for improvement and demonstrates the value of the training to stakeholders.

## CHAPTER 14  SECURITY AWARENESS AND SKILLS TRAINING

**What are the different roles and responsibilities within the organization?** Different roles within the organization face varying levels of risk and require specific training content. For example, executives might need training on avoiding spear-phishing attacks, while IT staff require technical training on securing systems. Tailoring the training to address the needs of different roles ensures that all employees receive relevant and applicable information.

**How frequently should training sessions be conducted?** Determining the frequency of training sessions is essential for maintaining awareness and keeping security practices top-of-mind. While annual training might be the minimum requirement, more frequent sessions, such as quarterly or monthly, can reinforce learning and adapt to emerging threats. Regular training helps ensure that employees remain vigilant and up-to-date on the latest security trends.

**What methods will we use to deliver the training?** Choosing the right delivery methods, such as online courses, in-person workshops, or interactive simulations, can significantly impact the effectiveness of the training program. Different formats can cater to various learning styles and preferences, enhancing engagement and retention. Blended learning approaches that combine multiple methods can provide a more comprehensive and flexible training experience.

**How will we ensure ongoing engagement and reinforcement?** Keeping employees engaged with security training requires continuous effort and reinforcement. This might include sending regular security tips, conducting surprise phishing simulations, or integrating security topics into team meetings. Ongoing engagement helps maintain a security culture and ensures that employees consistently apply what they have learned.

**What resources and tools will we provide to support the training?** Resources such as guides, cheat sheets, and access to security tools can enhance the training program's effectiveness. These resources are reference materials that employees can consult when needed, reinforcing the training content. Ensuring employees have the tools to apply security best practices in their daily work is critical for long-term success.

**How will we address and incorporate feedback from employees?** Gathering and incorporating employee feedback can help improve the training program and make it more relevant to their needs. Feedback can highlight areas where employees feel uncertain or identify topics that require more in-depth coverage. Regularly seeking and acting on feedback demonstrates that the organization values employee input and is committed to continuous improvement.

**What incentives and recognition will we offer for participation?** Encouraging participation in security training through incentives and recognition can boost engagement and motivation. This might include rewards for completing training modules, recognition in company communications, or integrating security awareness into performance evaluations. Positive reinforcement can help create a more enthusiastic and proactive approach to security among employees.

**How will we address and mitigate resistance to the training?** Anticipating and addressing potential resistance to security training is crucial for achieving widespread participation. This might involve communicating the importance of the training, addressing common misconceptions, and providing support for employees who struggle with the content. Understanding and mitigating resistance helps ensure that all employees buy into and take the program seriously.

# Recommended Training

Effective security awareness and skills training should be tailored to meet the needs of IT/Cyber staff, administrators, and all other employees within the organization. This dual approach ensures that technical staff have the advanced knowledge to protect systems and networks. At the same time, all employees have the fundamental skills to recognize and respond to security threats. By implementing comprehensive training programs across different levels of the organization, businesses can significantly enhance their overall security posture and reduce the risk of cyber incidents. The following training recommendations provide a framework for developing a robust and effective security training program.

**Phishing Awareness Training:** This training is essential for all employees, focusing on recognizing and responding to phishing attempts. It should cover common phishing tactics, such as deceptive emails, links, and attachments. Employees will learn to identify and report suspicious emails to the IT department. The outcome is a workforce that is vigilant against phishing attacks, reducing the risk of credential theft and malware infections.

**Password Management Training:** All employees should attend training on creating and managing strong, unique passwords. The training should include best practices for password creation, the use of password managers, and the importance of not reusing passwords across multiple sites. Employees can help prevent unauthorized access to systems and sensitive information by adopting strong password practices. This reduces the risk of breaches due to compromised credentials.

**Incident Response Training:** IT/Cyber staff and administrators need specialized training on incident response procedures. This training should include identifying, containing, eradicating, and recovering from cyber incidents. Participants will learn to coordinate effectively during an incident, minimizing damage and ensuring a swift recovery. Well-prepared incident response teams can reduce the impact of security breaches and restore normal operations quickly.

**Data Protection and Privacy Training:** This training is crucial for employees who handle sensitive data, such as those in HR, finance, and legal departments. It should cover data classification, handling procedures, and regulatory compliance requirements. Employees will understand how to protect personal and sensitive information, reducing the risk of data breaches and ensuring compliance with legal standards. Proper data protection practices safeguard the organization's most valuable information assets.

**Secure Configuration Training:** IT/Cyber staff should receive training on secure configuration practices for hardware and software. This includes setting firewalls, implementing secure baseline configurations, and maintaining system integrity. Organizations can reduce vulnerabilities that attackers might exploit by ensuring that systems are securely configured. Secure configurations form the foundation of a robust cybersecurity posture.

**Remote Work Security Training:** As remote work becomes more prevalent, all employees should be trained on securing their home office environments. This training should cover using VPNs, securing home Wi-Fi networks, and recognizing the risks of public Wi-Fi. Employees will learn to maintain security standards outside the office, reducing the risk of breaches in remote work. Secure remote work practices protect the organization's data regardless of employees' location.

**Social Engineering Awareness Training:** All employees must be aware of social engineering tactics that attackers use to manipulate them into divulging sensitive information. This training includes recognizing pretexting, baiting, and other social engineering techniques. Employees will be better equipped to question unusual requests and verify identities before providing information. Awareness of social engineering tactics helps prevent breaches caused by human manipulation.

**Compliance and Regulatory Training:** In regulated industries, such as healthcare and finance, employees should receive training on relevant compliance and regulatory requirements. This training should cover specific laws and standards, such as GDPR, HIPAA, and PCI-DSS. Understanding these regulations helps employees handle data appropriately and avoid legal penalties. Compliance training ensures that the organization meets legal obligations and protects sensitive information.

**Secure Software Development Training:** This training is essential for developers and IT/Cyber staff involved in software development. It should cover secure coding practices, code review processes, and awareness of common vulnerabilities, such as those listed in the OWASP Top 10. Developers will learn to build security into their applications from the ground up, reducing the risk of vulnerabilities in the software. Secure software development practices prevent exploitable weaknesses in applications.

**Mobile Device Security Training:** As mobile devices are increasingly used for business purposes, all employees should be trained on mobile device security best practices. This training should cover device encryption, app security, and safe usage practices. Employees will understand how to protect sensitive data on their mobile devices, reducing the risk of data breaches through lost or compromised devices. Secure mobile device usage protects organizational data on the go.

**Network Security Training:** IT/Cyber staff and administrators should receive training on maintaining secure network infrastructure. This includes implementing network segmentation, intrusion detection systems, and regular network monitoring. Participants will learn to identify and mitigate network vulnerabilities, ensuring robust security. Secure network practices protect against unauthorized access and cyber attacks on the network.

**Advanced Threat Detection Training:** IT/Cyber staff should be trained on advanced threat detection techniques, including threat intelligence and behavioral analysis. This training should cover identifying indicators of compromise and responding to sophisticated attacks. By staying ahead of emerging threats, cybersecurity teams can detect and mitigate attacks before they cause significant damage. Advanced threat detection capabilities enhance the organization's overall security posture.

# Actionable Recommendations

Implementing a comprehensive security awareness and skills training program requires a strategic approach tailored to the organization's specific needs and risk profile. The following recommendations provide actionable steps for establishing and maintaining a robust training program. By following these guidelines, organizations can ensure that their employees are well-equipped to recognize and respond to cyber threats, fostering a security culture and reducing the overall risk of cybersecurity incidents. These recommendations cover various aspects of program development, from initial planning to continuous improvement.

**Conduct a Risk Assessment:** Conduct a thorough risk assessment to identify your organization's specific threats and vulnerabilities. This assessment should consider factors such as industry-specific risks, the organization's technological infrastructure, and the potential impact of different types of cyber attacks. Understanding these risks helps prioritize training topics and ensures the program addresses the most relevant threats. A comprehensive risk assessment lays the foundation for a targeted and effective training program.

**Define Clear Objectives:** Establish clear and measurable objectives for the security awareness and skills training program. These objectives should align with the organization's overall cybersecurity strategy and address specific risk areas identified in the risk assessment. Objectives might include reducing the number of successful phishing attacks, improving incident reporting rates, or increasing compliance with security policies. Clear objectives provide a framework for designing and measuring the training program's success.

**Develop Role-Based Training Modules:** Create training modules tailored to the specific roles and responsibilities within the organization. Different roles encounter different types of threats and require distinct security practices. For example, training for IT staff should cover advanced technical topics, while training for general employees should focus on recognizing and reporting phishing attempts. Role-based training ensures that all employees receive relevant and applicable information.

**Leverage Multiple Training Formats:** Utilize a variety of training formats to cater to different learning styles and preferences. This might include online courses, in-person workshops, interactive simulations, and regular security newsletters. Blended learning approaches can enhance engagement and retention by providing multiple ways for employees to absorb and apply the training material. Diverse training formats make the program more accessible and effective.

**Integrate Real-World Scenarios:** Incorporate real-world scenarios and examples into the training content to make it more relatable and impactful. Simulated phishing attacks, case studies of security breaches, and interactive exercises can help employees understand the practical implications of cybersecurity threats. Real-world scenarios enhance the training experience by demonstrating the relevance of security practices in everyday work situations.

**Schedule Regular Training Sessions:** Establish a schedule for regular training sessions to reinforce security concepts and keep employees up-to-date on emerging threats. While annual training might be the minimum requirement, consider more frequent sessions, such as quarterly or monthly, to maintain a high level of awareness. Regular training ensures that employees remain vigilant and knowledgeable about current security trends and best practices.

**Provide Continuous Updates and Reminders:** Keep security top-of-mind by providing continuous updates and reminders about key security practices. This might include sending security tips, updates on recent cyber threats, and reminders to complete training modules. Continuous engagement helps reinforce the training material and encourages employees to stay proactive about security. Regular updates and reminders create a culture of ongoing security awareness.

**Encourage Active Participation:** Foster a culture of active participation by encouraging employees to share their experiences and insights related to cybersecurity. This can be done through discussion forums, feedback surveys, and team meetings focused on security topics. Active participation helps employees internalize and apply the training material in their daily work. Engaging employees in the conversation about security enhances their commitment to protecting the organization.

**Implement Phishing Simulations:** Conduct regular phishing simulations to test employees' ability to recognize and respond to phishing attempts. These simulations provide valuable feedback on the effectiveness of the training program and highlight areas where additional education is needed. Organizations can better prepare employees to handle actual threats by simulating real phishing attacks. Phishing simulations are a practical tool for reinforcing security awareness.

**Measure Training Effectiveness:** Establish metrics and evaluation methods to measure the effectiveness of the training program. This might include tracking the number of reported phishing attempts, assessing changes in employee behavior, and conducting pre-and post-training assessments. Measuring effectiveness helps identify areas for improvement and demonstrates the value of the training to stakeholders. Regular evaluation ensures that the training program remains relevant and impactful.

**Incorporate Feedback and Continuous Improvement:** Regularly gather employee feedback about the training program and use it to improve continuously. Feedback can highlight areas where employees feel uncertain or identify topics that require more in-depth coverage. Actively seeking and incorporating feedback demonstrates a commitment to providing valuable and practical training. Continuous improvement keeps the training program aligned with the organization's evolving needs.

**Recognize and Reward Participation:** Encourage participation in the training program by recognizing and rewarding employees who complete training modules and demonstrate strong security practices. This might include certificates, public recognition, or incentives such as gift cards or extra time off. Positive reinforcement helps motivate employees to engage with the training program and apply what they have learned. Recognizing and rewarding participation fosters a positive security culture.

## Simplified Security Controls (SSC)

Security controls are essential for any organization seeking to protect its digital and physical assets from cyber threats. Tailoring these controls to fit the specific needs of your business environment is crucial, as it ensures that the protection mechanisms are relevant and effective against the specific risks your organization faces. There are numerous sources to draw these controls from, including the well-regarded CIS Top 18, which provides a robust framework for crafting defensive strategies. The recommendations presented in this book are based on the CIS controls, among others, offering a comprehensive guide that can be adapted to serve a wide range of security needs. Before implementing these controls, it is vital to thoroughly review their design to ensure they align with your strategic objectives and operational practices. Additionally, after deployment, it is imperative to regularly test the controls to verify their effectiveness and to make necessary adjustments. This ensures that the controls continue to function as intended, safeguarding your organization against emerging threats and changing conditions.

## CHAPTER 14 SECURITY AWARENESS AND SKILLS TRAINING

## CONTROL 1: ESTABLISH AND MAINTAIN A SECURITY AWARENESS PROGRAM

**Control Objective:** To create and sustain a comprehensive security awareness program that educates employees on cybersecurity best practices and reduces the risk of security breaches due to human error.

**Implementation Steps:**

**1.1. Program Development:** Create a detailed security awareness program outlining the objectives, scope, and critical topics to be covered.

**1.2. Initial Training:** Conduct mandatory training for all new hires on secure interaction with enterprise assets and data.

**1.3. Annual Training:** Implement annual security training sessions for all employees, ensuring content is current and relevant.

**1.4. Content Review and Update:** Review and update the training content annually or whenever significant changes occur within the enterprise that impact security practices.

**Expected Outcome:** A well-informed workforce that understands the importance of cybersecurity and adheres to best practices, reducing the risk of security breaches due to human error.

## CONTROL 2: TRAIN WORKFORCE MEMBERS TO RECOGNIZE SOCIAL ENGINEERING ATTACKS

**Control Objective:** To equip employees with the knowledge and skills to recognize and thwart social engineering attacks, thereby significantly reducing the risk of successful breaches.

## CHAPTER 14  SECURITY AWARENESS AND SKILLS TRAINING

**Implementation Steps:**

**2.1. Training Content:** Develop training modules on identifying and responding to social engineering attacks, including phishing, pretexting, and tailgating.

**2.2. Simulation Exercises:** Conduct regular phishing simulations and social engineering tests to reinforce learning and assess employee vigilance.

**2.3. Reporting Mechanisms:** Establish clear procedures for reporting suspected social engineering attempts.

**2.4. Feedback and Improvement:** Collect employee feedback on the training and make necessary adjustments to improve effectiveness.

**Expected Outcome:** Employees with the knowledge and skills to recognize and thwart social engineering attacks significantly reduce the risk of successful breaches.

### CONTROL 3: TRAIN WORKFORCE MEMBERS ON AUTHENTICATION BEST PRACTICES

**Control Objective:** To enhance user account security by adopting strong authentication practices, mitigating the risk of unauthorized access.

**Implementation Steps:**

**3.1. Training Topics:** Cover topics such as multi-factor authentication (MFA), strong password creation, and credential management.

**3.2. Practical Demonstrations:** Provide hands-on demonstrations on setting up and using MFA and password managers.

**3.3. Policy Communication:** Ensure all employees know and adhere to the organization's authentication policies.

**3.4. Regular Updates:** Keep the workforce informed about new authentication methods and emerging threats.

**Expected Outcome:** Enhanced user account security by adopting strong authentication practices, mitigating the risk of unauthorized access.

## CONTROL 4: TRAIN WORKFORCE ON DATA HANDLING BEST PRACTICES

**Control Objective:** To ensure proper data handling and disposal practices that prevent unauthorized access and data breaches.

**Implementation Steps:**

**4.1. Data Classification:** Educate employees on the organization's data classification system and handling procedures for different data types.

**4.2. Secure Storage and Transfer:** Train on secure methods for storing, transferring, and archiving sensitive data.

**4.3. Clear Desk and Screen Policies:** Implement and reinforce clear desk and screen policies to protect sensitive information.

**4.4. Data Disposal:** Provide guidelines on the secure disposal of both physical and digital data.

**Expected Outcome:** Proper data handling and disposal practices that prevent unauthorized access and data breaches.

## CONTROL 5: TRAIN WORKFORCE MEMBERS ON CAUSES OF UNINTENTIONAL DATA EXPOSURE

**Control Objective:** To increase awareness and reduce incidents of unintentional data exposure through informed employee behavior.

**Implementation Steps:**

**5.1. Common Causes:** Highlight common causes of unintentional data exposure, such as misdelivery of sensitive information and loss of devices.

**5.2. Real-World Examples:** Use case studies and examples to illustrate the impact of data exposure incidents.

**5.3. Prevention Strategies:** Provide strategies and best practices to prevent unintentional data exposure.

**5.4. Incident Reporting:** Establish clear protocols for reporting accidental data exposure.

**Expected Outcome:** Increased awareness and reduction in incidents of unintentional data exposure through informed employee behavior.

## CONTROL 6: TRAIN WORKFORCE MEMBERS ON RECOGNIZING AND REPORTING SECURITY INCIDENTS

**Control Objective:** To ensure prompt and effective reporting and response to security incidents, minimizing potential damage and recovery time.

**Implementation Steps:**

**6.1. Incident Identification:** Teach employees to recognize signs of potential security incidents, such as unusual system behavior or unauthorized access attempts.

**6.2. Reporting Procedures:** Clearly define the procedures for reporting security incidents, including points of contact and reporting channels.

**6.3. Incident Response Training:** Conduct training sessions on initial response actions employees should take when they suspect a security incident.

**6.4. Continuous Improvement:** Regularly review and update incident reporting and response protocols based on feedback and evolving threats.

**Expected Outcome:** Prompt and effective reporting and response to security incidents, minimizing potential damage and recovery time.

---

## CONTROL 7: TRAIN WORKFORCE ON HOW TO IDENTIFY AND REPORT IF THEIR ENTERPRISE ASSETS ARE MISSING SECURITY UPDATES

**Control Objective:** To ensure timely identification and resolution of software update issues, ensuring systems remain protected against known vulnerabilities.

**Implementation Steps:**

**7.1. Update Verification:** Educate employees on how to check if their software and systems are up-to-date.

**7.2. Reporting Mechanisms:** Establish clear reporting channels for employees to notify IT personnel of outdated software or failed updates.

**7.3. Automated Tools:** Train employees on using automated tools for update management and monitoring.

**7.4. Follow-Up Actions:** Ensure IT personnel promptly address reported issues and communicate resolutions to employees.

**Expected Outcome:** Timely identification and resolution of software update issues, ensuring systems remain protected against known vulnerabilities.

## CONTROL 8: TRAIN WORKFORCE ON THE DANGERS OF CONNECTING TO AND TRANSMITTING ENTERPRISE DATA OVER INSECURE NETWORKS

**Control Objective:** To reduce the risk of data breaches and unauthorized access due to insecure network connections, particularly for remote and mobile workers.

**Implementation Steps:**

**8.1. Network Security Risks:** Inform employees about the risks of using insecure networks, such as public Wi-Fi.

**8.2. Secure Practices:** Provide guidelines on secure methods for connecting to networks, including using VPNs.

**8.3. Remote Work Policies:** Ensure remote workers are trained on securing their home network infrastructure.

**8.4. Regular Reminders:** Send periodic reminders about the importance of secure network practices.

**Expected Outcome:** Reduced risk of data breaches and unauthorized access due to insecure network connections, particularly for remote and mobile workers.

CHAPTER 14   SECURITY AWARENESS AND SKILLS TRAINING

## CONTROL 9: CONDUCT ROLE-SPECIFIC SECURITY AWARENESS AND SKILLS TRAINING

**Control Objective:** To equip employees with specialized knowledge and skills pertinent to their roles, enhancing the organization's overall security posture.

**Implementation Steps:**

**9.1. Needs Assessment:** Conduct a needs assessment to identify specific security training requirements for different organizational roles.

**9.2. Customized Training:** Develop customized training modules for various roles, such as IT professionals, web developers, and high-profile executives.

**9.3. Advanced Topics:** Include advanced security topics relevant to specific roles, such as secure coding practices and advanced threat detection.

**9.4. Regular Updates:** Update role-specific training content regularly to address new threats and changes in job responsibilities.

**Expected Outcome:** Employees equipped with specialized knowledge and skills pertinent to their roles, enhancing the organization's overall security posture.

# CHAPTER 15

# Service Provider Management

In today's interconnected digital landscape, organizations increasingly rely on third-party service providers for essential functions. These external partners, often managing critical data and I.T. platforms, play a pivotal role in businesses' operational success. However, this reliance introduces a significant dimension of risk, necessitating robust processes to ensure these service providers adhere to stringent security measures. Effective service provider management is crucial for safeguarding sensitive data and maintaining the integrity of enterprise operations.

The importance of scrutinizing third-party service providers cannot be overstated. Historical incidents highlight the vulnerabilities that can be exploited through these external relationships. For example, breaches in the late 2000s, where payment card information was compromised through smaller third-party vendors, are a stark reminder of the potential repercussions. More recently, ransomware attacks have illustrated how disruptions at a service provider can cascade, affecting the primary enterprise and causing substantial operational disruptions. This interconnected risk landscape demands vigilant oversight and comprehensive management strategies.

Regulatory frameworks have recognized the critical nature of third-party risk, integrating specific requirements for service provider management. Regulations like the Health Insurance Portability and

# CHAPTER 15  SERVICE PROVIDER MANAGEMENT

Accountability Act (HIPAA) in healthcare, the Federal Financial Institutions Examination Council (FFIEC) guidelines for financial institutions, and the U.K. Cyber Essentials emphasize the need for extending data protection mandates to third-party service providers. Compliance with these regulations ensures legal adherence and fortifies the organization's defense mechanisms against potential breaches originating from external partners.

Developing a systematic approach to service provider management involves several key components. Firstly, establishing a detailed inventory of all service providers is fundamental. This inventory should list these providers and classify them based on various criteria, such as data sensitivity, data volume, and the criticality of their services. Regular reviews and updates to this inventory are essential to reflect any significant changes in the enterprise's operational landscape.

Another cornerstone of this approach is a comprehensive service provider management policy. Such a policy should encompass the entire lifecycle of service provider relationships, from initial assessment and onboarding to ongoing monitoring and eventual decommissioning. Ensuring this policy is regularly reviewed and updated helps maintain its relevance and effectiveness in the face of evolving threats and changes in the business environment.

Classification of service providers based on risk factors is critical in this process. Factors to consider include the sensitivity of the data handled, the volume of data, the regulatory landscape, and the potential impact of a service disruption. This classification aids in prioritizing resources and efforts toward managing the most critical relationships, thereby optimizing the overall risk management strategy.

Monitoring and assessment of service providers are essential to ensure continuous compliance and security. Utilizing third-party assessment platforms can provide a dynamic risk score for service providers, enabling enterprises to make informed decisions based on comprehensive and up-to-date risk assessments. These platforms often leverage passive technical assessments and aggregated data from other organizations to present a holistic view of the service provider's security posture.

Contractual agreements with service providers should include specific clauses addressing security expectations and accountability. These contracts must stipulate the measures service providers need to implement to protect the enterprise's data and systems. Additionally, they should outline the consequences and responsibilities in the event of a security incident, ensuring there is a clear framework for managing breaches and mitigating their impact.

The decommissioning of service providers is an often overlooked aspect of service provider management. When a contract is terminated, it is crucial to ensure all access is revoked, data flows are halted, and any enterprise data residing within the service provider's systems is securely disposed of. This prevents potential misuse or unauthorized access to sensitive information after the relationship ends.

The proliferation of service providers in the business ecosystem has increased reliance on standardized assessment frameworks. Tools like the Shared Assessments program in the financial sector or the Higher Education Community Vendor Assessment Toolkit (HECVAT) in academia provide structured approaches to evaluating third-party risks. These frameworks help streamline the assessment process, reducing the burden on service providers who might otherwise face multiple audits from different clients.

Finally, the dynamic nature of the digital landscape necessitates a proactive stance in service provider management. Enterprises must stay abreast of new threats and adjust their risk management strategies accordingly. This includes responding to incidents, anticipating potential vulnerabilities, and addressing them before they can be exploited. Regular training and awareness programs for internal staff and service providers can enhance the overall security posture and foster a culture of vigilance.

## CHAPTER 15   SERVICE PROVIDER MANAGEMENT

The effective management of service providers is a critical aspect of modern cybersecurity strategies. By implementing comprehensive policies, maintaining up-to-date inventories, and continuously monitoring third-party risks, organizations can significantly reduce their exposure to external threats. Ensuring service providers adhere to stringent security standards and contractual obligations is essential for safeguarding sensitive data and maintaining operational integrity in an increasingly interconnected world.

# Key Concepts and Terms

Understanding the critical concepts and terminology associated with service provider management is essential for developing a robust cybersecurity strategy. These terms form the foundation for effectively managing third-party risks, ensuring all stakeholders are aligned in safeguarding sensitive data and critical I.T. systems.

**Service Provider Inventory:** A service provider inventory is a comprehensive list of all third-party vendors and partners an organization engages with. This inventory includes detailed information such as the services provided, the nature of the data handled, and the criticality of the services to the organization. Regularly updating and maintaining this inventory ensures that the organization understands its external dependencies and can effectively manage associated risks.

**Service Provider Classification:** Classification of service providers involves categorizing them based on various risk factors, including the sensitivity of the data they handle, the volume of data, and the criticality of their services. This classification helps prioritize which providers need more stringent security measures and closer monitoring. By understanding the risk profile of each provider, organizations can allocate resources more effectively to mitigate potential threats.

**Risk Assessment:** A risk assessment is a systematic process of evaluating the potential risks involved in a projected activity or undertaking. For service providers, this includes analyzing their security posture, past performance, and potential vulnerabilities. The goal is to identify risks that could impact the organization and to develop strategies to mitigate these risks. Regular risk assessments are crucial for maintaining a proactive security posture.

**Due Diligence:** Due diligence involves thoroughly investigating and evaluating a service provider before entering a contractual relationship. This involves reviewing the provider's security policies, practices, and compliance with relevant regulations. Conducting due diligence ensures that the provider meets the organization's security standards and reduces the risk of future security incidents.

**Contractual Security Clauses:** Contractual security clauses are specific terms included in service provider agreements that outline the security requirements and responsibilities of the provider. These clauses can include requirements for data protection, incident response, and audit rights. Clearly defined security clauses help ensure that service providers are legally obligated to maintain a high-security standard and are accountable for any breaches.

**Ongoing Monitoring:** Ongoing monitoring involves continuously assessing the security posture of service providers throughout the contract. This can include regular security audits, vulnerability assessments, and performance reviews. Continuous tracking helps detect and address security issues promptly, ensuring that the provider maintains compliance with the organization's security standards.

**Third-Party Risk Management Platforms:** Third-party risk management platforms are specialized tools that help organizations manage and assess the risks associated with their service providers. These platforms often provide a centralized view of all third-party relationships, dynamic risk scoring, and automated workflows for assessments and audits. Utilizing these platforms can streamline the management process and enhance the organization's ability to respond to emerging threats.

**Decommissioning Procedures:** Decommissioning procedures are securely terminating a service provider relationship. This includes revoking access, halting data flows, and ensuring the secure disposal of enterprise data within the provider's systems. Proper decommissioning is essential to prevent unauthorized access and ensure that no residual data poses a security risk after the contract ends.

**Regulatory Compliance:** Regulatory compliance involves adhering to laws, regulations, and guidelines that govern data protection and cybersecurity. For service provider management, this means ensuring that third-party providers comply with regulations such as HIPAA, FFIEC, and the U.K. Cyber Essentials. Compliance protects the organization from legal repercussions and enhances its overall security posture.

**Incident Response Plan:** An incident response plan is a set of procedures and guidelines an organization follows in case of a security breach or cyber incident. For service providers, this includes clearly defined roles and responsibilities, communication protocols, and steps for containing and mitigating the impact of the incident. A well-defined incident response plan ensures a coordinated and effective response to security threats.

**Security Audits:** Security audits are comprehensive evaluations of an organization's or a service provider's security practices and controls. These audits can be conducted internally or by external parties and typically involve reviewing policies, procedures, and technical controls. Regular security audits help identify security posture gaps and ensure service providers adhere to agreed-upon security standards.

**Cyber Insurance:** Cyber insurance is designed to help organizations mitigate the financial impact of cyber incidents, including breaches, ransomware attacks, and data theft. For service providers, holding cybersecurity insurance can be a significant risk reduction measure, providing coverage for the provider and the enterprise in case of a security incident. This insurance can cover costs related to incident response, legal fees, and recovery efforts, providing a safety net for both parties.

# Importance and Relevance

The management of service providers has become an indispensable element of modern cybersecurity strategies. As organizations increasingly rely on external partners to manage critical data and I.T. platforms, the potential risks associated with these relationships have grown significantly. Ensuring service providers adhere to robust security measures is crucial for protecting sensitive information and maintaining operational integrity. The following points highlight the importance and relevance of effective service provider management in today's cybersecurity landscape.

**Minimizing Third-Party Breach Risks:** Third-party breaches can devastate an organization's security posture. When a service provider is compromised, attackers may indirectly access the primary organization's data and systems. Organizations can minimize these risks by implementing rigorous service provider management processes, ensuring their external partners have robust security measures to protect against breaches.

**Ensuring Regulatory Compliance:** Many industries are subject to strict data protection and cybersecurity regulations that extend to third-party service providers. Regulations such as HIPAA, FFIEC, and the U.K. Cyber Essentials require organizations to ensure their service providers comply with specific security standards. Adhering to these regulatory requirements not only avoids legal penalties but also strengthens the overall security framework of the organization.

**Protecting Sensitive Data:** Service providers often handle sensitive and critical data for their organizations. This data could include personal information, financial records, or intellectual property. Effective management of service providers ensures that these data are protected through appropriate security controls, reducing the risk of data breaches and unauthorized access.

**Mitigating Operational Disruptions:** A security incident involving a service provider can lead to significant operational disruptions for the primary organization. This can include downtime, loss of productivity, and reputational damage. By carefully assessing and managing the risks associated with service providers, organizations can mitigate the potential impact of such incidents, ensuring continuity of operations.

**Enhancing Incident Response Capabilities:** Having well-defined incident response procedures is crucial in a security breach involving a service provider. This includes clear communication channels, predefined roles and responsibilities, and detailed response plans. Effective service provider management ensures that these elements are in place, facilitating a swift and coordinated response to mitigate the impact of the incident.

**Strengthening Trust and Transparency:** Building trust and transparency with service providers is essential for effective cybersecurity management. Regular assessments, open communication, and collaborative security practices help establish this trust. Organizations can then be confident that their service providers proactively address security risks and maintain high protection standards.

**Reducing Legal and Financial Liabilities:** Security incidents involving service providers can lead to significant legal and financial liabilities for the primary organization. This can include fines, legal fees, and compensation for affected parties. Implementing comprehensive service provider management practices helps reduce these liabilities by ensuring that service providers adhere to contractual security requirements and industry best practices.

**Facilitating Business Continuity Planning:** Business continuity planning involves preparing for disruptions to critical business functions, including those caused by service provider incidents. Effective management of service providers ensures that contingency plans are in place, including alternative providers and backup processes. This helps maintain business operations and reduces the impact of disruptions.

**Improving Security Posture Through Collaboration:** Collaboration with service providers can improve the overall security posture of both parties. Organizations can enhance their defenses by sharing best practices, conducting joint security assessments, and participating in threat intelligence sharing. This collaborative approach fosters a more resilient and secure environment for the organization and its service providers.

**Enabling Proactive Risk Management:** Proactive risk management involves identifying and addressing potential security risks before they materialize. Regular assessments and continuous monitoring of service providers would allow organizations to stay ahead of emerging threats. This proactive stance helps prevent security incidents and ensures that service providers maintain adequate security controls.

**Supporting Strategic Business Goals:** Effective service provider management supports the organization's strategic business goals by ensuring that third-party relationships are secure and reliable. This enables the organization to focus on its core objectives without being hindered by security concerns. Organizations can achieve greater efficiency and success by aligning service provider management with business goals.

**Adapting to Evolving Cyber Threats:** The cybersecurity landscape constantly evolves, with new threats emerging regularly. Service providers must keep pace with these changes to protect the organization's data and systems effectively. Effective management practices ensure service providers continuously update their security measures and stay vigilant against new and emerging threats.

CHAPTER 15   SERVICE PROVIDER MANAGEMENT

# Risks of Not Implementing the Control

Implementing effective service provider management can expose organizations to many cybersecurity risks. The interconnected nature of modern business operations means that vulnerabilities within a service provider's system can directly impact the security posture of the primary organization. This lack of oversight can lead to severe data breaches, regulatory non-compliance, operational disruptions, and significant financial and reputational damage. Understanding these risks is crucial for organizations aiming to protect their critical data and maintain the integrity of their operations. Here are some of the most significant risks of neglecting service provider management.

**Data Breaches:** Service providers may not adhere to the security standards to protect sensitive data without proper oversight. This can result in data breaches where malicious actors access or steal confidential information. Such breaches can have severe consequences, including financial losses, legal liabilities, and damage to the organization's reputation.

**Regulatory Non-Compliance:** Many industries are governed by strict data protection regulations that extend to third-party service providers. Failure to ensure service providers comply with these regulations can result in hefty fines and legal penalties. Additionally, non-compliance can lead to losing trust among customers and partners, further impacting the organization's credibility and market position.

**Operational Disruptions:** Service providers play a critical role in maintaining business operations. If a service provider suffers a security incident, it can disrupt their services, leading to significant operational downtime for the primary organization. This disruption can affect productivity, customer service, and the organization's bottom line.

**Financial Losses:** Security incidents involving service providers can lead to substantial financial losses. These losses can stem from direct costs such as fines, legal fees, and remediation efforts, as well as indirect costs like lost business opportunities and damage to the organization's reputation. The financial impact can be particularly severe for smaller organizations with limited resources.

**Reputational Damage:** Trust is a critical component of any business relationship. A security breach involving a service provider can severely damage an organization's reputation, as customers and partners may lose confidence in its ability to protect sensitive information. Rebuilding trust after such an incident can be long and challenging, often requiring significant investment in public relations and enhanced security measures.

**Legal Liabilities:** In a data breach or other security incident, the primary organization may face legal action from affected parties. This can include lawsuits from customers, partners, and regulatory bodies. Legal battles can be costly and time-consuming, diverting resources from core business activities and further exacerbating financial and reputational damage.

**Intellectual Property Theft:** Service providers often have access to valuable intellectual property (I.P.). If these providers are not properly managed and secured, there is a risk that I.P. could be stolen or misused by malicious actors. This can undermine the organization's competitive advantage and result in significant financial and strategic losses.

**Loss of Competitive Advantage:** Effective service provider management is crucial for maintaining a competitive edge in the market. Organizations that fail to secure their service provider relationships may be disadvantaged compared to competitors with robust cybersecurity measures. This can lead to lost business opportunities and a decline in market share.

**Inadequate Incident Response:** Without proper management, organizations may lack the necessary procedures and protocols to respond effectively to security incidents involving service providers. This can result in delayed or inadequate responses, exacerbating the impact of the incident and prolonging recovery times. An effective incident response plan is essential for minimizing damage and restoring normal operations quickly.

**Supply Chain Vulnerabilities:** Service providers are integral to an organization's supply chain. A security incident affecting a key provider can cause a ripple effect, disrupting the entire supply chain and impacting the organization's ability to deliver products and services. Identifying and mitigating these vulnerabilities is essential for maintaining supply chain resilience.

**Exposure to Advanced Threats:** Cybercriminals often target service providers to gain access to larger organizations. Without effective management, organizations may be exposed to advanced threats that exploit vulnerabilities in the service provider's systems. This can include sophisticated attacks such as ransomware, which can have devastating consequences for the primary organization.

**Compromised Business Continuity:** Business continuity planning relies on the availability and reliability of service providers. A security incident involving a service provider can compromise business continuity, leading to prolonged disruptions and an inability to meet customer and partner expectations. Ensuring that service providers have robust security measures is critical for maintaining business continuity and resilience.

# What Questions Should You Ask?

When implementing effective service provider management, cybersecurity leaders must ask critical questions to ensure all aspects of third-party risk are adequately addressed. These questions help identify potential vulnerabilities, ensure regulation compliance, and establish clear protocols for monitoring and managing service providers. Cybersecurity leaders can create a robust framework that protects their organization's data and systems from external threats by asking the right questions. The following questions are a foundation for developing a comprehensive service provider management strategy.

**What is the scope of services provided by each vendor?**
Understanding the exact services each vendor offers is crucial for assessing the potential risks associated with those services. This includes knowing what data the vendor can access, how it is processed, and the criticality of these services to the organization's operations. Defining the scope helps in tailoring security measures to the specific risks posed by each service provider.

**How are service providers classified based on risk?** Classifying service providers based on risk factors such as data sensitivity, volume, and regulatory requirements allows for prioritizing security efforts. High-risk providers handling sensitive data may require more stringent security controls and frequent audits. Establishing a risk classification system ensures that resources are allocated efficiently and effectively to mitigate potential threats.

**What regulatory requirements apply to service providers?** Service providers must comply with different industries' specific regulatory requirements, such as HIPAA for healthcare or FFIEC for financial institutions. Ensuring service providers meet these regulatory standards is critical for legal compliance and protecting sensitive data. Understanding these requirements helps select and manage service providers who can uphold these standards.

**What security measures are in place at the service provider?** Evaluating the security measures implemented by service providers is essential for ensuring they align with the organization's security policies. This includes encryption practices, access controls, and incident response procedures. A thorough assessment of these measures helps identify gaps and areas for improvement in the service provider's security posture.

**How is the service provider's security posture assessed and monitored?** Continuous assessment and monitoring of a service provider's security posture are crucial for identifying and addressing emerging threats. This can involve regular audits, vulnerability assessments, and leveraging third-party risk management platforms. Ongoing monitoring ensures that the service provider maintains robust security practices throughout the contract.

**What are the incident response protocols for service providers?** Clearly defined incident response protocols are vital for ensuring a coordinated and efficient response to security incidents involving service providers. This includes roles and responsibilities, communication channels, and steps for containment and remediation. Having these protocols in place minimizes the impact of security incidents and facilitates rapid recovery.

**How is data handled and protected by the service provider?** Understanding how service providers handle and protect data is fundamental for ensuring data security and privacy. This includes data storage practices, encryption methods, and data transmission security. Ensuring these practices meet the organization's standards helps protect sensitive information from unauthorized access and breaches.

**What contractual obligations and security clauses are included in service agreements?** Including specific security clauses and obligations in service agreements ensures that service providers are contractually bound to maintain high-security standards. These clauses cover data protection, incident reporting, and compliance with relevant regulations. Clearly defined contractual obligations hold service providers accountable for their security practices.

**What is the process for onboarding new service providers?** A structured onboarding process is essential for ensuring new service providers meet the organization's security requirements before they are integrated into the system. This process can include initial risk assessments, security audits, and background checks. A thorough onboarding process helps identify potential risks early and ensures that only trusted providers are engaged.

**How is the termination and decommissioning of service providers managed?** Securely terminating and decommissioning service providers is crucial for preventing unauthorized access to data after the contract ends. This includes revoking access, halting data flows, and securely disposing of residual data. Proper decommissioning procedures protect the organization from post-termination security risks.

**What are the insurance and liability considerations for service providers?** Understanding the insurance coverage and liability considerations for service providers helps mitigate financial risks associated with security incidents. This includes ensuring that service providers have adequate cybersecurity insurance and understanding the scope of their coverage. Clear liability terms in contracts ensure that service providers are accountable for any damages resulting from security breaches.

**How are service provider performance and compliance tracked and reported?** Regular tracking and reporting on service provider performance and compliance are essential for maintaining oversight and ensuring continuous improvement. This can include performance metrics, compliance reports, and security audit results. Consistent tracking and reporting provide visibility into the service provider's adherence to security standards, and help make informed decisions.

# Recommended Training

Effective training is essential for ensuring that I.T./cybersecurity staff and all other employees are equipped to manage and mitigate risks associated with service provider management. This training should encompass a broad range of topics tailored to the specific roles and responsibilities within the organization. By providing comprehensive training programs, organizations can foster a culture of security awareness, ensuring that everyone understands their role in protecting sensitive data and maintaining the integrity of I.T. systems. The following recommended training programs are designed to enhance the skills and knowledge of all employees, ultimately reducing the risk of security incidents.

**Service Provider Risk Assessment Training:** I.T. and cybersecurity staff should attend this training, which covers the methodologies and tools used to assess risks associated with service providers. The training should include practical exercises on risk assessment, evaluating security controls, and using third-party risk management platforms. The outcome is a team capable of identifying and mitigating risks posed by service providers, thereby enhancing the overall security posture.

**Data Protection and Privacy Training:** This training is crucial for all employees, especially those handling sensitive data. It should cover data classification, data handling best practices, and compliance with privacy regulations such as GDPR and HIPAA. By understanding the importance of data protection, employees can minimize the risk of data breaches and ensure that personal and confidential information is handled securely.

**Incident Response and Reporting Training:** Both IT staff and general employees should participate in this training to understand their roles in the event of a security incident. The training should include incident detection, response protocols, communication channels, and reporting procedures. The outcome is a coordinated and efficient response to incidents, reducing the impact of security breaches and facilitating quicker recovery.

**Contract Management and Legal Compliance Training:** This training is designed for I.T. staff, legal teams, and procurement officers. It should cover the inclusion of security clauses in contracts, legal obligations, and compliance with relevant regulations. The organization can hold providers accountable and mitigate legal risks by ensuring that contracts with service providers include robust security requirements.

**Phishing and Social Engineering Awareness Training:** All employees should receive this training to recognize and respond to phishing attempts and social engineering attacks. The training should include real-world examples, identification techniques, and best practices for reporting suspicious activities. This training reduces the risk of successful attacks by increasing employee vigilance and promoting a security-aware culture.

**Security Auditing and Monitoring Training:** I.T. and cybersecurity staff should be trained to conduct security audits and continuously monitor service providers. The training should cover audit methodologies and tools for monitoring and interpreting security reports. This ensures that the organization can constantly assess the security posture of service providers and address vulnerabilities proactively.

**Secure Software Development Training:** This training is essential for developers and I.T. staff involved in software development. It should include secure coding practices, vulnerability assessment tools, and application security testing. By integrating security into the development lifecycle, the organization can reduce the risk of vulnerabilities in software used by or provided to service providers.

**Access Control and Identity Management Training:** I.T. staff and administrators should be trained on implementing and managing access control systems and identity management solutions. The training should cover best practices for user authentication, authorization, and monitoring access to sensitive systems. Effective access control reduces the risk of unauthorized access and data breaches.

**Business Continuity and Disaster Recovery Training:** This training is important for I.T. staff, management, and key business units. It should cover developing and implementing business continuity plans and disaster recovery strategies. By preparing for disruptions, the organization can ensure that critical functions continue and recover quickly from incidents affecting service providers.

**Compliance and Regulatory Update Training:** Regular training sessions should be conducted for I.T. staff, legal teams, and compliance officers to stay updated on changing regulations and compliance requirements. This training should include updates on data protection laws, industry standards, and regulatory changes. Staying informed about regulatory updates ensures that the organization remains compliant and avoids legal penalties.

**Vendor Management Best Practices Training:** Procurement officers, I.T. staff, and management should attend this training, which covers best practices for selecting and managing vendors. The training should include vendor evaluation criteria, performance monitoring, and contract negotiation strategies. Effective vendor management reduces risks associated with third-party services and ensures that providers meet security expectations.

**Cybersecurity Awareness and Culture Training:** All employees should participate in regular cybersecurity awareness training to foster a security culture within the organization. The training should cover basic cybersecurity principles, the current threat landscape, and the importance of personal responsibility in protecting the organization's assets. A strong security culture reduces the risk of human error and promotes proactive security behaviors.

# Actionable Recommendations

Effective service provider management is crucial for maintaining a strong cybersecurity posture and protecting sensitive data. Organizations must adopt a strategic approach, incorporating best practices and leveraging appropriate tools to manage third-party risks. The following recommendations provide actionable steps to enhance service provider management, ensuring all external partners adhere to robust security standards and contribute to the organization's security.

**Establish a Comprehensive Inventory:** Create and maintain a detailed inventory of all service providers, including the services they provide and the data they handle. This inventory should be regularly updated to reflect any changes in relationships or services. Organizations can better assess and manage associated risks by having a clear view of all service providers.

**Develop a Risk Classification Framework:** Implement a framework to classify service providers based on the sensitivity of the data they handle, the criticality of their services, and their compliance with regulatory requirements. This classification helps prioritize security efforts and allocate resources effectively. High-risk providers should be subject to more stringent controls and frequent assessments.

**Conduct Thorough Due Diligence:** Perform comprehensive due diligence before engaging with any service provider. This includes reviewing their security policies, past performance, and compliance with relevant regulations. Thorough due diligence ensures that only trustworthy providers are selected, reducing the risk of future security incidents.

**Include Security Clauses in Contracts:** Ensure all contracts with service providers include specific security clauses that outline their responsibilities and the required security measures. These clauses should cover data protection, incident response, and compliance with relevant regulations. Clearly defined contractual obligations hold service providers accountable and ensure they adhere to the organization's security standards.

**Implement Continuous Monitoring:** Establish continuous monitoring of service providers to assess their security posture continuously. This can involve regular security audits, vulnerability assessments, and leveraging third-party risk management platforms. Continuous monitoring helps detect and address security issues promptly, maintaining a strong security posture.

**Develop Incident Response Protocols:** Create detailed incident response protocols that define the roles and responsibilities of the organization and the service provider during a security incident. These protocols should include communication channels, containment measures, and recovery steps. Effective incident response protocols minimize the impact of security incidents and facilitate rapid recovery.

**Enforce Data Handling Standards:** Implement strict data handling standards for service providers to ensure that sensitive data is always protected. This includes data encryption, secure data transmission, and controlled access to data. Enforcing these standards reduces the risk of data breaches and unauthorized access.

**Regularly Review and Update Policies:** Continuously review and update service provider management policies to reflect changes in the threat landscape, regulatory requirements, and business operations. Regular updates ensure that policies remain effective and relevant. This proactive approach helps organizations stay ahead of emerging threats and maintain compliance.

**Provide Training and Awareness Programs:** Offer regular training and awareness programs for employees and service providers to promote a security culture. Training should cover data protection best practices, incident response, and the importance of adhering to security policies. Well-informed employees and service providers can better identify and mitigate security risks.

**Utilize Third-Party Risk Management Tools** Leverage third-party risk management tools to streamline the assessment and monitoring of service providers. These tools provide a centralized view of third-party risks, dynamic risk scoring, and automated workflows for assessments and audits. Utilizing these tools enhances efficiency and effectiveness in managing third-party risks.

**Secure Decommissioning Procedures:** Implement secure decommissioning procedures for terminating service provider relationships. This includes revoking access, halting data flows, and ensuring the safe disposal of any residual data. Proper decommissioning prevents unauthorized access to data after the contract ends and protects the organization from post-termination security risks.

**Engage in Collaborative Security Practices:** Foster collaboration with service providers to improve overall security. This includes sharing threat intelligence, conducting joint security assessments, and participating in industry forums. Collaborative security practices help build a stronger security posture and promote mutual trust and transparency.

## Simplified Security Controls (SSC)

Security controls are essential for any organization seeking to protect its digital and physical assets from cyber threats. Tailoring these controls to fit the specific needs of your business environment is crucial, as it ensures that the protection mechanisms are relevant and effective against the specific risks your organization faces. There are numerous sources to draw these controls from, including the well-regarded CIS Top 18, which provides a robust framework for crafting defensive strategies. The recommendations presented in this book are based on the CIS controls, among others, offering a comprehensive guide that can be adapted to serve a wide range of security needs. Before implementing these controls, it is vital to thoroughly review their design to ensure they align with your strategic objectives and operational practices. Additionally, after deployment, it is imperative to regularly test the controls to verify their effectiveness and to make necessary adjustments. This ensures that the controls continue to function as intended, safeguarding your organization against emerging threats and changing conditions.

## CHAPTER 15  SERVICE PROVIDER MANAGEMENT

# CONTROL 1: ESTABLISH AND MAINTAIN AN INVENTORY OF SERVICE PROVIDERS

**Control Objective:** To develop and maintain a comprehensive inventory of all service providers, including classification, enterprise contacts, and relevant details, ensuring it is regularly reviewed and updated to reflect significant changes within the enterprise.

**Implementation Steps:**

**1.1. Identify Service Providers:** Compile a list of all service providers currently engaged by the organization, detailing their services.

**1.2. Classify Service Providers:** Classify each service provider based on data sensitivity, service criticality, and regulatory requirements.

**1.3. Assign Enterprise Contacts:** Designate an internal enterprise contact responsible for managing the relationship with each service provider.

**1.4. Annual Review:** Review and update the inventory annually or when significant enterprise changes occur, ensuring it remains current and accurate.

**1.5. Documentation:** Maintain detailed documentation for each service provider, including classification criteria and the contact information of the enterprise representative.

**Expected Outcome:** A well-maintained inventory of service providers ensures the organization has a clear and up-to-date understanding of all external dependencies, facilitating effective management and risk mitigation.

CHAPTER 15   SERVICE PROVIDER MANAGEMENT

## CONTROL 2: ESTABLISH AND MAINTAIN A SERVICE PROVIDER MANAGEMENT POLICY

**Control Objective:** To create and sustain a comprehensive service provider management policy that addresses classification, inventory, assessment, monitoring, and decommissioning and ensures regular review and updates.

**Implementation Steps:**

**2.1. Policy Development:** Develop a detailed service provider management policy covering all service provider engagement and oversight aspects.

**2.2. Define Classification Criteria:** Include specific criteria for classifying service providers based on data sensitivity, service criticality, and other relevant factors.

**2.3. Assessment Procedures:** Outline procedures for service providers' initial and ongoing assessment, including risk assessments and security audits.

**2.4. Monitoring Requirements:** Specify the requirements for continuous monitoring of service provider compliance and performance.

**2.5. Decommissioning Protocols:** Establish protocols for securely decommissioning service providers, ensuring the safe termination of services and data disposal.

**2.6. Regular Review:** Review and update the policy annually or when significant changes occur within the enterprise, ensuring it remains effective and relevant.

**Expected Outcome:** A robust service provider management policy ensures consistent and effective oversight of all service providers, aligning their operations with the organization's security requirements and reducing associated risks.

CHAPTER 15   SERVICE PROVIDER MANAGEMENT

## CONTROL 3: CLASSIFY SERVICE PROVIDERS

**Control Objective:** To classify service providers based on data sensitivity, volume, availability requirements, applicable regulations, inherent risk, and mitigated risk, ensuring regular review and updates.

**Implementation Steps:**

**3.1. Define Classification Criteria:** Establish clear criteria for classifying service providers, considering various risk factors and regulatory requirements.

**3.2. Initial Classification:** Apply the defined criteria to classify all current service providers, documenting the classification process and outcomes.

**3.3. Annual Review:** Conduct an annual review of all service provider classifications, updating them as necessary based on changes in the service provider's operations or the organization's requirements.

**3.4. Dynamic Adjustment:** Adjust classifications promptly in response to significant changes such as new service engagements, regulatory updates, or security incidents.

**3.5. Communication:** Ensure that all relevant stakeholders are informed of the classification criteria and the classification status of each service provider.

**Expected Outcome:** Accurate and up-to-date classification of service providers allows for tailored risk management strategies, ensuring that higher-risk providers receive appropriate levels of scrutiny and control.

## CHAPTER 15   SERVICE PROVIDER MANAGEMENT

## CONTROL 4: ENSURE SERVICE PROVIDER CONTRACTS INCLUDE SECURITY REQUIREMENTS

**Control Objective:** To ensure that all service provider contracts include comprehensive security requirements that align with the organization's service provider management policy.

**Implementation Steps:**

**4.1. Define Security Requirements:** Develop a set of minimum security requirements to include all service provider contracts, covering aspects such as data protection, incident response, and data disposal.

**4.2. Contract Review:** Review all existing service provider contracts to identify and rectify any missing or inadequate security requirements.

**4.3. Standard Contract Templates:** Create standard contract templates incorporating the defined security requirements for future engagements with service providers.

**4.4. Annual Contract Audit:** Conduct an annual audit of service provider contracts to ensure ongoing compliance with security requirements.

**4.5. Enforcement Mechanisms:** Establish mechanisms for enforcing contractual security requirements, including penalties for non-compliance and regular performance reviews.

**Expected Outcome:** Including robust security requirements in service provider contracts ensures that service providers are contractually obligated to maintain high-security standards, reducing the risk of data breaches and other security incidents.

CHAPTER 15  SERVICE PROVIDER MANAGEMENT

## CONTROL 5: ASSESS SERVICE PROVIDERS

**Control Objective:** To conduct regular assessments of service providers consistent with the organization's service provider management policy, ensuring they meet security and compliance standards.

**Implementation Steps:**

**5.1. Initial Assessment:** Perform a comprehensive initial assessment of all service providers, evaluating their security controls, compliance with regulations, and overall risk profile.

**5.2. Assessment Tools:** Utilize standardized assessment tools and frameworks, such as SOC 2 reports, PCI AoC, and customized questionnaires.

**5.3. Annual Reassessments:** Conduct annual reassessments of all service providers, or more frequently for high-risk providers, or when contracts are renewed.

**5.4. Documentation and Reporting:** Document all assessment findings and provide detailed reports to relevant stakeholders, including recommendations for remediation.

**5.5. Continuous Improvement:** Use assessment results to continuously improve service provider security practices, providing feedback and support as needed.

**Expected Outcome:** Regular assessments ensure that service providers maintain adequate security controls and compliance, mitigating risks associated with third-party services.

CHAPTER 15   SERVICE PROVIDER MANAGEMENT

## CONTROL 6: MONITOR SERVICE PROVIDERS

**Control Objective:** To continuously monitor service providers per the organization's service provider management policy, ensuring ongoing compliance and security.

**Implementation Steps:**

**6.1. Monitoring Framework:** Develop a comprehensive monitoring framework that outlines the methods and tools used to monitor service provider compliance and security.

**6.2. Periodic Reassessments:** Conduct periodic reassessments of service providers to evaluate their compliance with security requirements and identify any emerging risks.

**6.3. Real-Time Monitoring:** Implement real-time monitoring tools to track service provider activities, including release notes, security updates, and potential security incidents.

**6.4. Dark Web Monitoring:** Monitor dark web activity to identify any compromised data or credentials associated with service providers.

**6.5. Reporting and Alerts:** Establish a reporting system for monitoring results and alerts, ensuring that relevant stakeholders are promptly informed of any issues or anomalies.

**Expected Outcome:** Continuous monitoring ensures that service providers consistently adhere to security standards and allows for the early detection and mitigation of potential security threats.

CHAPTER 15   SERVICE PROVIDER MANAGEMENT

## CONTROL 7: SECURELY DECOMMISSION SERVICE PROVIDERS

**Control Objective:** To ensure the secure decommissioning of service providers, including the deactivation of accounts, termination of data flows, and secure disposal of enterprise data.

**Implementation Steps:**

**7.1. Decommissioning Plan:** Develop a detailed plan for the secure decommissioning of service providers, outlining the steps and responsibilities involved.

**7.2. Account Deactivation:** Ensure the deactivation of all user and service accounts associated with the decommissioned service provider.

**7.3. Terminate Data Flows:** Safely terminate all data flows between the organization and the service provider, ensuring no residual access remains.

**7.4. Data Disposal:** Implement procedures for the secure disposal of any enterprise data stored within the service provider's systems, following industry best practices.

**7.5. Audit and Verification:** Conduct an audit to verify the completion of all decommissioning activities and ensure that no data or access remains with the former service provider.

**Expected Outcome:** Secure decommissioning processes prevent unauthorized access and data breaches post-termination, ensuring that all data and access are effectively controlled and disposed of.

# CHAPTER 16

# Application Software Security

Managing the security lifecycle of application software is essential to modern cybersecurity practices. Applications are the primary interfaces through which users interact with complex data and system resources, making them prime targets for cyber attackers. By focusing on application software security, organizations can proactively prevent, detect, and remediate security weaknesses before they impact the enterprise. Given the complexities of today's development environments and the integration of third-party components, a robust application security program is beneficial and necessary.

Applications serve as a bridge between users and the data they need to perform their tasks. They simplify access to complex system functions and manage sensitive information, so their security is paramount. Attackers frequently target applications to exploit vulnerabilities, leading to unauthorized data access or system control. The evolving nature of application architectures—from traditional client-server models to modern web, mobile, and cloud-based platforms—adds complexity to securing these applications. This complexity necessitates a comprehensive application software security approach that addresses the potential vulnerabilities.

# CHAPTER 16   APPLICATION SOFTWARE SECURITY

The rapid evolution of development methodologies, such as the shift from waterfall to DevOps, has shortened development lifecycles. This acceleration means that code changes frequently, increasing the risk of introducing security flaws. Applications today are rarely built from scratch; they often incorporate a mix of development frameworks, libraries, and pre-existing code. This assembly-line approach to software creation can introduce vulnerabilities if the components used are not adequately vetted for security. Consequently, maintaining a secure development process that includes rigorous testing and validation is crucial.

One significant challenge in application software security is managing third-party components. Many applications rely on external libraries and frameworks, which, if not properly managed, can introduce significant security risks. Enterprises must maintain an updated inventory of these components and ensure they come from trusted sources. Regularly evaluating and updating this inventory helps mitigate the risks associated with third-party Software. Additionally, organizations should have a clear process for addressing vulnerabilities in these components to ensure they do not compromise the application's overall security.

Training developers in secure coding is another vital aspect of application software security. Developers must understand the principles of secure application design and be equipped to identify and mitigate potential security issues in their code. Regular training sessions help foster a culture of security within development teams, ensuring that security is considered at every stage of the software development lifecycle. By embedding security into the development process, organizations can reduce the likelihood of vulnerabilities being introduced in the first place.

Threat modeling is a proactive approach that can significantly enhance application security. This process involves identifying potential security threats during the design phase, allowing developers to address these issues before any code is written. Threat modeling requires a deep understanding of the application's technical and business aspects, and it is most effective when conducted by individuals with specialized training.

CHAPTER 16   APPLICATION SOFTWARE SECURITY

Integrating threat modeling into the development lifecycle helps ensure that security considerations are built into the application's architecture from the ground up.

Application penetration testing is essential for identifying vulnerabilities that might not be apparent through automated testing alone. Penetration testing involves simulating attacks on the application to uncover weaknesses that real-world attackers could exploit. This type of testing is particularly effective for identifying business logic flaws and other complex vulnerabilities that automated tools might miss. Regular penetration testing and automated code analysis provide a comprehensive approach to identifying and addressing security issues.

The use of standardized, vetted modules and services for critical application functions, such as identity management and encryption, can help reduce the risk of security vulnerabilities. Experts typically develop and maintain these modules, and they are extensively tested for security. By leveraging these trusted components, developers can focus on their application's unique aspects without reinventing the wheel for common security functions. This approach not only enhances security but also streamlines the development process.

Implementing a vulnerability management process that integrates with the development lifecycle is critical for maintaining application security. This process should include mechanisms for tracking, prioritizing, and addressing vulnerabilities as they are discovered. By treating security vulnerabilities like any other bug, organizations can ensure they are fixed promptly and not pose a long-term risk to the application. A well-defined vulnerability management process also helps organizations prioritize remediation efforts based on each vulnerability's severity and potential impact.

The infrastructure that supports applications is another critical area that must be secured to ensure overall application security. This includes the servers, databases, and other components the application relies on. Standard hardening configurations for these infrastructure

## CHAPTER 16   APPLICATION SOFTWARE SECURITY

components can help minimize their attack surface and reduce the risk of vulnerabilities. Regularly updating and patching these components is essential to protect against known security threats and ensure they do not become a weak link in the application's security chain.

A severity rating system for application vulnerabilities can help organizations prioritize their remediation efforts. This system assigns a severity level to each vulnerability based on its potential impact and likelihood of exploitation. By focusing on the most severe vulnerabilities first, organizations can effectively manage their risk and promptly address critical issues. Regularly reviewing and updating the severity rating system helps ensure it remains relevant and effective in the face of evolving security threats.

The rise of Software as a Service (SaaS) platforms introduces unique challenges for application security. Organizations must understand the risks of using third-party SaaS solutions and ensure that these platforms adhere to robust security practices. When customizing SaaS applications, following the same security principles as in-house development is essential. Establishing clear security requirements and conducting regular security assessments of SaaS providers can help mitigate the risks associated with using these platforms.

Application software security is a multifaceted discipline requiring a comprehensive approach to address modern applications' diverse and evolving threats. By integrating security into every stage of the development lifecycle, training developers in secure coding practices, and implementing robust vulnerability management processes, organizations can significantly enhance the security of their applications. Adopting industry best practices and leveraging trusted components and services further strengthens the security posture, ensuring that applications remain resilient in the face of emerging cyber threats.

CHAPTER 16   APPLICATION SOFTWARE SECURITY

# Key Concepts and Terms

Understanding application software security requires familiarity with several key concepts and terms. These elements are foundational to comprehending the complexities and methodologies involved in managing the security lifecycle of software applications. Each term or concept provides insight into the practices and strategies necessary to protect applications from various vulnerabilities and threats. Here, we will explore twelve essential terms integral to application software security.

**Secure Application Development Process:** This term refers to the comprehensive approach used to ensure that Software is developed with security in mind from the outset. It encompasses practices such as secure coding standards, regular security training for developers, and rigorous testing throughout the development lifecycle. The goal is to integrate security measures at each stage of development rather than treating security as an afterthought. This proactive approach helps identify and mitigate vulnerabilities early, reducing the risk of exploitation.

**Threat Modeling:** Threat modeling is a systematic process used to identify and address potential security threats during the design phase of application development. This involves mapping out the application's architecture, identifying potential entry points for attackers, and assessing the risks associated with each. By understanding the possible threats, developers can design countermeasures to protect against them. Threat modeling is crucial for preventing design-level vulnerabilities, which are often more severe and difficult to fix than code-level issues.

**Vulnerability Management:** This concept involves the processes and tools to identify, assess, and remediate application security vulnerabilities. Effective vulnerability management integrates with the software development lifecycle, ensuring vulnerabilities are tracked and addressed promptly. This includes regular security assessments, automated scanning

CHAPTER 16    APPLICATION SOFTWARE SECURITY

tools, and a system for prioritizing and fixing vulnerabilities based on severity. Proper vulnerability management helps maintain the security of applications over time, even as new threats emerge.

**Static and Dynamic Analysis:** Static analysis refers to examining application code without executing it, typically using automated tools to identify potential security flaws. On the other hand, dynamic analysis involves testing the application in a running state to identify vulnerabilities that might not be evident from the code alone. Both methods are essential for a comprehensive security testing strategy. Static analysis helps catch issues early in the development process, while dynamic analysis provides a real-world perspective on how the application performs under various conditions.

**Third-Party Components:** Modern applications often rely on third-party components, such as libraries, frameworks, and modules, to speed up development and add functionality. However, these components can introduce significant security risks if not properly managed. It is crucial to maintain an inventory of all third-party components used, regularly evaluate their security, and ensure they are sourced from trusted providers. Managing third-party components effectively helps mitigate the risk of vulnerabilities being introduced through external code.

**Penetration Testing:** This term describes the practice of simulating attacks on an application to identify and exploit vulnerabilities, providing a real-world assessment of the application's security. Penetration testing goes beyond automated scanning, relying on the skill and creativity of the tester to uncover flaws that may not be detected through other means. It is particularly useful for identifying complex issues, such as business logic flaws, that require a deep understanding of the application. Regular penetration testing helps ensure that security measures are effective and up-to-date.

**Secure Coding Practices:** Developers follow guidelines and techniques to create secure Software. Secure coding practices include input validation, proper error handling, and avoiding common vulnerabilities like SQL injection and cross-site scripting. Training developers in these practices is essential to prevent security flaws from being introduced during the coding process. By adhering to secure coding practices, developers can significantly reduce the risk of vulnerabilities in their applications.

**Security Champions:** Security champions are individuals within development teams who take on the responsibility of advocating for and leading security efforts. These champions receive specialized training in application security and serve as the go-to resource for security-related questions and issues. They help integrate security practices into the development process and promote a culture of security awareness. Having security champions ensures that security considerations are consistently addressed throughout the software development lifecycle.

**Software Bill of Materials (SBOM):** An SBOM is a comprehensive list of all components, libraries, and dependencies used in an application. It provides transparency into what third-party elements are included and helps track their security status. Maintaining an up-to-date SBOM is critical for managing the security of third-party components, as it allows organizations to identify and remediate vulnerabilities in these elements quickly. An SBOM is an essential tool for ensuring the integrity and security of complex software applications.

**Severity Rating System:** This system classifies vulnerabilities based on their potential impact and likelihood of exploitation. A well-defined severity rating system helps prioritize remediation efforts, ensuring the most critical vulnerabilities are addressed first. This approach improves risk management by focusing resources on the areas of greatest need. Regularly updating the severity rating system ensures it remains effective as new threats and vulnerabilities emerge.

**Bug Bounty Programs:** Bug bounty programs incentivize external security researchers to find and report application vulnerabilities. These programs can be a valuable supplement to in-house security efforts, providing access to a broader pool of expertise. Organizations can identify

CHAPTER 16   APPLICATION SOFTWARE SECURITY

and fix issues that might otherwise go unnoticed by offering rewards for discovered vulnerabilities. Bug bounty programs enhance the overall security posture by leveraging the skills of the global security community.

**Secure Software Development Framework (SSDF):** The SSDF is a set of practices and guidelines designed to integrate security into the software development process. Developed by NIST, the SSDF consolidates industry best practices and provides a framework for planning, implementing, and evaluating software security activities. Organizations can use the SSDF to ensure their development processes align with industry standards and effectively address security concerns. Implementing the SSDF helps build more secure applications and reduces the risk of vulnerabilities.

# Importance and Relevance

In the rapidly evolving cybersecurity landscape, application software security is critical for protecting organizational assets and sensitive data. As applications become more sophisticated and integral to business operations, the risks associated with their vulnerabilities also escalate. Ensuring robust application security is no longer optional but necessary for any organization aiming to safeguard its digital infrastructure. The following points highlight the importance and relevance of application software security in today's cybersecurity environment.

**Protecting Sensitive Data:** Applications often handle sensitive data, including personal information, financial records, and intellectual property. A breach in application security can lead to unauthorized access and theft of this data, resulting in significant financial and reputational damage. Implementing strong security measures within applications is crucial to protect this data from malicious actors.

**Mitigating Attack Vectors:** Modern applications are frequent targets for cyber attacks due to their complexity and the valuable data they process. Attackers exploit vulnerabilities such as SQL injection, cross-site scripting, and buffer overflows to gain unauthorized access or control over applications. Organizations can mitigate these attack vectors by focusing on application security and reducing the risk of successful exploits.

**Compliance with Regulations:** Various regulations and standards, such as GDPR, HIPAA, and PCI DSS, mandate strict security measures for applications that handle personal and financial data. Non-compliance can result in hefty fines and legal repercussions. Ensuring application security helps organizations comply with these regulations and avoid legal and financial penalties.

**Preventing Financial Loss:** Cyber attacks targeting applications can lead to significant financial losses due to data breaches, service disruptions, and the cost of remediation. Investing in application security can prevent these costly incidents by identifying and addressing vulnerabilities before they can be exploited. This proactive approach helps safeguard the organization's financial health.

**Maintaining Customer Trust:** Customers expect their personal and financial information to be secure when using an organization's applications. A security breach can erode customer trust and damage the organization's reputation. Strong application security measures demonstrate a commitment to protecting customer data and helping to maintain and build trust.

**Supporting Business Continuity:** Applications are critical to business operations, and security breaches can disrupt services, leading to downtime and loss of productivity. Ensuring application security helps maintain business continuity by preventing disruptions caused by cyber attacks. This reliability is essential for sustaining day-to-day operations and achieving long-term business goals.

**Adapting to Technological Advancements:** The rise of cloud computing, mobile applications, and IoT devices has expanded the attack surface for applications. Securing these diverse and interconnected

## CHAPTER 16   APPLICATION SOFTWARE SECURITY

environments requires robust application security practices. Staying ahead of technological advancements and associated risks is crucial for maintaining a strong security posture.

**Reducing Remediation Costs:** Identifying and fixing security vulnerabilities during the development phase is significantly cheaper than addressing them after deployment. Application security practices such as secure coding, regular testing, and vulnerability management help detect and remediate issues early. This proactive approach reduces the overall cost of security management.

**Encouraging Secure Development Practices:** Implementing application security measures promotes a culture of security awareness among developers. Regular training in secure coding practices and integrating security into the development lifecycle ensure that security is a fundamental consideration in every project. This culture shift leads to the creation of more secure applications.

**Enhancing Competitive Advantage:** Organizations prioritizing application security can differentiate themselves from competitors by offering more secure products and services. This competitive advantage can attract customers who prioritize security and data protection. Demonstrating a solid commitment to application security can also enhance the organization's reputation in the market.

**Leveraging Industry Best Practices:** Adopting established application security frameworks and best practices, such as those outlined by NIST and CIS, helps organizations stay aligned with industry standards. This alignment ensures that security measures are comprehensive and up-to-date with the latest threats and mitigation techniques. Utilizing these resources strengthens the overall security posture.

**Facilitating Secure Integration:** Modern applications often integrate with third-party services, APIs, and other external components. Ensuring the security of these integrations is crucial to prevent vulnerabilities from external sources. Robust application security practices help manage and secure these interactions, reducing the risk of external threats compromising the application.

# Risks of Not Implementing the Control

Failing to implement robust application software security can expose an organization to a myriad of risks, each with the potential to cause significant harm. These risks range from data breaches and financial losses to regulatory penalties and reputational damage. As applications increasingly become the backbone of business operations, ensuring their security is critical to protecting sensitive information and maintaining trust with customers and stakeholders. The following points highlight the specific risks organizations face when they neglect application software security.

**Data Breaches:** A lack of application security can lead to data breaches, where unauthorized parties access sensitive information. This can include personal data, financial records, and proprietary business information. Data breaches often result in severe financial and reputational damage, eroding customer trust and potentially leading to legal action. Protecting applications from vulnerabilities that can be exploited to access this data is crucial to avoid such breaches.

**Financial Loss:** Cyber attacks targeting insecure applications can result in substantial financial losses. These losses may stem from direct theft of funds, costs associated with incident response and remediation, and loss of business due to service disruptions. Additionally, organizations may face fines and legal fees if found non-compliant with data protection regulations. Investing in application security is a cost-effective measure to prevent these potentially devastating financial consequences.

**Regulatory Penalties:** Non-compliance with industry regulations and standards, such as GDPR, HIPAA, and PCI DSS, can result in significant penalties. These regulations often mandate specific security measures for applications that handle sensitive data. Failure to meet these requirements can lead to fines, legal challenges, and increased scrutiny from regulatory bodies. Ensuring application security helps organizations comply with these mandates and avoid the associated penalties.

**Reputational Damage:** Security breaches and data leaks can damage an organization's reputation. Customers, partners, and stakeholders lose trust in an organization's ability to protect their information. This loss of trust can result in decreased business, negative publicity, and long-term harm to the organization's brand. Maintaining strong application security practices is essential to preserving and enhancing an organization's reputation.

**Intellectual Property Theft:** Insecure applications can be exploited to steal intellectual property, including trade secrets, proprietary algorithms, and confidential business strategies. This theft can undermine an organization's competitive advantage and result in significant economic losses. Protecting applications through robust security measures helps safeguard valuable intellectual property from cybercriminals and competitors.

**Service Disruption:** Cyber attacks on applications can lead to disruptions, preventing customers and employees from accessing critical services. These disruptions can result in lost revenue, decreased productivity, and damaged customer relationships. Ensuring the security of applications minimizes the risk of service interruptions caused by cyber incidents, maintaining business continuity.

**Malware Infections:** Insecure applications can serve as entry points for malware, which can then spread throughout an organization's network. Malware infections can lead to data loss, system outages, and costly remediation efforts. Implementing strong application security measures helps prevent malware from infiltrating the network through vulnerable applications.

**Credential Harvesting:** Attackers often target applications to harvest user credentials, which can then be used to gain unauthorized access to other systems and data. This can lead to further breaches and exploitation of sensitive information. Protecting applications with secure authentication and authorization mechanisms is critical to preventing credential theft and ensuring overall system security.

**Increased Attack Surface:** Modern applications often integrate with various third-party services and components, expanding the attack surface. These integrations can introduce vulnerabilities that attackers can exploit without proper security measures. Ensuring comprehensive application security helps manage and mitigate the risks associated with an expanded attack surface.

**Operational Inefficiency:** Dealing with security breaches and their aftermath can drain significant resources and divert attention from core business activities. The time and effort required to respond to incidents, fix vulnerabilities, and restore services can negatively impact operational efficiency. Proactive application security measures help prevent such disruptions, allowing organizations to focus on their primary objectives.

**Legal Liability:** Organizations may be liable if a security breach harms customers, partners, or other stakeholders. This liability can lead to costly lawsuits, settlements, and long-term financial burdens. Implementing robust application security practices reduces the risk of breaches and the associated legal consequences.

**Loss of Competitive Edge:** Security incidents can erode an organization's competitive edge by damaging its reputation, incurring financial losses, and diverting resources from innovation to remediation. Competitors prioritizing application security can leverage their resilience as a selling point, attracting customers and partners. Maintaining strong application security is essential to sustaining and enhancing an organization's competitive position in the market.

CHAPTER 16   APPLICATION SOFTWARE SECURITY

# What Questions Should You Ask?

To effectively implement a robust application software security program, cybersecurity leaders must ask critical questions that address various aspects of application development, deployment, and maintenance. These questions are designed to uncover potential vulnerabilities, ensure compliance with best practices, and foster a culture of security awareness within development teams. By systematically addressing these questions, leaders can form a comprehensive strategy to safeguard their applications against evolving cyber threats. The following questions serve as a foundation for this essential process.

**What are the security requirements for our applications?**
Identifying and defining security requirements is the first step in ensuring that applications are designed and developed with security in mind. These requirements should be based on industry standards, regulatory compliance needs, and specific organizational risk assessments. Understanding what security measures must be implemented helps create a clear roadmap for the development and testing phases.

**How are we integrating security into the development lifecycle?**
Security should be an integral part of the software development lifecycle (SDLC) rather than an afterthought. This question emphasizes the importance of embedding security practices, such as secure coding, regular code reviews, and security testing, into every stage of the development process. Ensuring security is considered from the outset reduces the risk of introducing vulnerabilities.

**What training do our developers need to write secure code?**
Continuous education and training in secure coding practices are vital for developers. This question addresses the need for regular training sessions to keep developers updated on the latest security threats, best practices, and compliance requirements. Well-trained developers are better equipped to recognize and mitigate potential security issues in their code.

**How are we managing third-party components and libraries?**
Modern applications often rely on third-party components, which can introduce vulnerabilities if not properly managed. This question highlights the need to maintain an inventory of all third-party components, regularly assess their security, and ensure they are sourced from reputable providers. Proper management of third-party components helps mitigate risks associated with external code.

**What processes do we have for identifying and remediating vulnerabilities?** Effective vulnerability management involves continuous monitoring, assessment, and remediation of security flaws. This question focuses on the processes in place to identify, prioritize, and fix vulnerabilities in a timely manner. A systematic approach to vulnerability management helps maintain the security integrity of applications over time.

**Are we conducting regular security assessments and penetration testing?** Regular security assessments and penetration testing are crucial for uncovering vulnerabilities that are not apparent through standard testing procedures. This question ensures that comprehensive testing is performed to identify weaknesses that attackers could exploit. These assessments provide valuable insights into the security posture of applications.

**What is our process for handling security incidents and breaches?**
Having a well-defined incident response plan is essential for effectively managing security breaches when they occur. This question addresses the need for a clear process that includes identification, containment, eradication, and recovery steps. A robust incident response plan helps minimize the impact of security incidents on the organization.

**How do we ensure compliance with relevant regulations and standards?** Compliance with industry regulations and standards, such as GDPR, HIPAA, and PCI DSS, is critical for legal and operational reasons. This question emphasizes the importance of aligning application security practices with regulatory requirements. Ensuring compliance helps avoid legal penalties and enhances the overall security posture.

**How do we monitor and log application activities for security purposes?** Effective monitoring and logging are essential for detecting and responding to security incidents. This question focuses on implementing comprehensive logging mechanisms that capture relevant security events and activities. Monitoring and logging provide visibility into the application's behavior, aiding in the early detection of suspicious activities.

**What role does threat modeling play in our security strategy?** Threat modeling helps identify potential security threats during the design phase, allowing for proactive mitigation. This question highlights the importance of incorporating threat modeling into the development process. Understanding and addressing security threats early in the design phase can prevent vulnerabilities from being introduced into the application.

**How do we handle the security of cloud-based applications and services?** As organizations increasingly rely on cloud services, securing these environments becomes paramount. This question addresses the unique security challenges associated with cloud-based applications and services. Ensuring that security measures are tailored to the cloud environment helps protect against specific threats and vulnerabilities.

**What measures are in place to protect against insider threats?** Whether malicious or unintentional, insider threats pose a significant risk to application security. This question focuses on the policies and practices to detect and prevent insider threats. Implementing strong access controls, monitoring employee activities, and fostering a culture of security awareness are key strategies for mitigating insider risks.

# Recommended Training

Training is a crucial component of a comprehensive application software security strategy. It ensures that all members of an organization, from IT and cybersecurity staff to administrators and general employees, are equipped with the knowledge and skills needed to protect against security threats. Effective training programs focus on technical aspects and foster a culture of security awareness throughout the organization. The following recommendations outline essential training topics and their importance in reducing risks associated with application software security.

**Secure Coding Practices Training:** This training should be mandatory for all developers and IT staff involved in application development. It covers best practices for writing secure code, including input validation, proper error handling, and avoiding common vulnerabilities such as SQL injection and cross-site scripting. By learning these practices, developers can reduce the likelihood of introducing security flaws into their applications. The outcome is more robust and secure Software, significantly lowering the risk of exploitation by attackers.

**Threat Modeling Workshops:** Designed for development teams and security professionals, these workshops teach participants how to identify and mitigate potential security threats during the design phase of application development. The training includes hands-on exercises and case studies to illustrate the threat modeling process. By integrating threat modeling into the development lifecycle, organizations can proactively address security issues before they become vulnerabilities. This approach helps prevent design-level flaws that are often more severe and harder to fix.

**Vulnerability Management Training:** This training is essential for IT and cybersecurity staff responsible for identifying, assessing, and remediating application vulnerabilities. It covers the use of automated tools for vulnerability scanning, techniques for prioritizing vulnerabilities based on severity, and best practices for remediation. Participants will learn how to integrate vulnerability management into the development process, ensuring that security flaws are promptly addressed. Effective vulnerability management reduces the risk of exploitation and enhances overall application security.

**Incident Response Training:** Incident response training should be provided to all IT and cybersecurity personnel to prepare them for effectively handling security breaches. The training includes developing and practicing incident response plans, identifying indicators of compromise, and performing forensic analysis. By being well-prepared for incidents, organizations can minimize the impact of breaches and recover more quickly. This training ensures that security teams respond efficiently and effectively to any security incidents.

**Security Awareness Training for All Employees:** All employees should receive regular security awareness training regardless of their role. This training covers topics such as recognizing phishing attempts, creating strong passwords, and understanding the importance of security policies. Educating employees on these basics helps create a security-conscious culture and reduces the risk of human error leading to security breaches. By fostering security awareness, organizations can mitigate the threat of social engineering attacks.

**Third-Party Component Management Training:** This training targets developers and IT staff who manage third-party application components and libraries. It includes best practices for sourcing, evaluating, and maintaining these components to ensure they do not introduce security vulnerabilities. Participants will learn how to create and maintain a software bill of materials (SBOM) to track third-party components. Proper management of third-party components helps prevent vulnerabilities from external sources.

**Penetration Testing Training:** Cybersecurity professionals and advanced developers should undergo penetration testing training to identify and exploit application vulnerabilities. This training includes both automated and manual testing techniques and understanding the tools used for penetration testing. Organizations can uncover and fix vulnerabilities before attackers exploit them by conducting regular penetration tests. This proactive approach enhances the security of applications.

**Compliance and Regulatory Training:** This training ensures that all relevant staff understand the legal and regulatory requirements for application security. It covers standards such as GDPR, HIPAA, and PCI DSS, and their implications for application development and data protection. By understanding these requirements, staff can ensure that applications comply with relevant regulations, avoiding legal penalties and enhancing overall security. Compliance training helps integrate regulatory considerations into the security strategy.

**Security Logging and Monitoring Training:** IT and cybersecurity staff should receive training on implementing and maintaining effective logging and monitoring systems. This includes setting up logging mechanisms, understanding what activities to monitor, and using tools to analyze log data. Effective logging and monitoring are crucial for detecting and responding to real-time security incidents. This training helps organizations quickly identify and address suspicious activities.

**Cloud Security Training:** With the increasing use of cloud services, IT and cybersecurity staff need to be trained in cloud-specific security practices. This training covers securing cloud environments, managing cloud-based applications, and understanding the shared responsibility model. Participants will learn how to protect data and applications in the cloud, reducing the risk of cloud-specific threats. Cloud security training ensures that staff are equipped to manage the unique challenges of cloud security.

**Insider Threat Detection Training:** This training is aimed at IT staff and general employees to help them recognize and respond to potential insider threats. It includes understanding the signs of insider threats, implementing access controls, and fostering a culture of accountability. By being vigilant against insider threats, organizations can protect against risks posed by malicious or negligent insiders. Insider threat training helps create a secure internal environment.

**Continuous Security Education Programs:** Establishing ongoing security education programs for all staff ensures that security knowledge remains current. These programs can include regular updates on emerging threats, refresher courses on security best practices, and advanced training for IT and cybersecurity professionals. Continuous education helps maintain a high level of security awareness and competency across the organization. Organizations can better adapt to the evolving threat landscape by keeping security knowledge up-to-date.

## Actionable Recommendations

Implementing robust application software security measures requires a strategic approach that addresses various aspects of the development and operational lifecycle. Ensuring that applications are secure from inception through deployment and maintenance involves a combination of technical practices, policy development, and ongoing education. The following recommendations provide actionable steps organizations can take to enhance their application security posture effectively.

**Establish a Secure Development Lifecycle (SDLC):** Integrate security practices into every phase of the software development lifecycle. This includes incorporating security requirements during the planning phase, conducting security reviews during design, and performing regular security testing during development and deployment. By embedding security into the SDLC, organizations can identify and address vulnerabilities early, reducing the risk of exploitation.

**Conduct Regular Code Reviews and Audits:** Implement a process for regular code reviews and security audits. Peer reviews help catch security flaws that automated tools might miss, while audits ensure that security policies and practices are followed consistently. Regular reviews and audits improve code quality and help maintain a high-security standard throughout development.

**Implement Continuous Integration/Continuous Deployment (CI/CD) Security Checks:** Integrate security checks into the CI/CD pipeline to automate the detection of vulnerabilities. Use tools that perform static and dynamic analysis, dependency checking, and configuration management. Automated security checks in the CI/CD process ensure that security issues are identified and addressed quickly, reducing the risk of deploying vulnerable applications.

**Develop a Comprehensive Training Program:** Provide ongoing training for developers, IT staff, and other employees on secure coding practices, threat modeling, and security awareness. Tailor training programs to address the specific needs of different organizational roles. Continuous education helps maintain a security culture and ensures all staff are equipped to recognize and mitigate security risks.

**Perform Threat Modeling:** Conduct threat modeling sessions during the design phase of application development. Identify potential threats, vulnerabilities, and attack vectors and design countermeasures to address them. Threat modeling helps create a more secure application architecture and prevents design-level vulnerabilities from being introduced.

**Utilize Static and Dynamic Analysis Tools:** Use static and dynamic analysis tools to identify security vulnerabilities in the application code. Static analysis tools examine the code without executing it, while dynamic analysis tools test the running application. Combining both approaches provides comprehensive coverage and helps identify various security issues.

**Maintain an Updated Inventory of Third-Party Components:** Keep a detailed inventory of all third-party components, libraries, and application frameworks. Regularly update and assess these components for security vulnerabilities and ensure they come from reputable sources. Managing third-party components effectively reduces the risk of introducing vulnerabilities through external code.

## CHAPTER 16   APPLICATION SOFTWARE SECURITY

**Establish a Bug Bounty Program:** Implement a bug bounty program to incentivize external security researchers to find and report vulnerabilities. Offer rewards for valid security flaws discovered in applications. Bug bounty programs supplement internal security efforts and provide an additional layer of defense by leveraging the broader security community.

**Create a Robust Incident Response Plan:** Develop and regularly update an incident response plan outlining security breach procedures. Include steps for identifying, containing, eradicating, and recovering from incidents. A well-defined incident response plan ensures the organization can respond effectively to security incidents, minimizing their impact.

**Use Hardened Configuration Templates:** Apply standard, industry-recommended hardening configurations for application infrastructure components such as servers, databases, and web servers. Ensure these configurations are maintained and updated regularly to protect against new threats. Hardened configurations help reduce the attack surface and improve overall security.

**Implement Access Controls and Least Privilege:** Enforce strict access controls and adhere to the principle of least privilege. Ensure that users and applications have only the permissions they need to perform their functions. Limiting access reduces the risk of unauthorized actions and helps contain potential security breaches.

**Conduct Regular Security Assessments and Penetration Testing:** Schedule regular security assessments and penetration tests to evaluate the security posture of applications. Use both internal and external testers to identify vulnerabilities that might be overlooked. Regular testing ensures that security measures are effective and helps uncover new vulnerabilities that must be addressed.

CHAPTER 16  APPLICATION SOFTWARE SECURITY

# Simplified Security Controls (SSC)

Security controls are essential for any organization seeking to protect its digital and physical assets from cyber threats. Tailoring these controls to fit the specific needs of your business environment is crucial, as it ensures that the protection mechanisms are relevant and effective against the specific risks your organization faces. There are numerous sources to draw these controls from, including the well-regarded CIS Top 18, which provides a robust framework for crafting defensive strategies. The recommendations presented in this book are based on the CIS controls, among others, offering a comprehensive guide that can be adapted to serve a wide range of security needs. Before implementing these controls, it is vital to thoroughly review their design to ensure they align with your strategic objectives and operational practices. Additionally, after deployment, it is imperative to regularly test the controls to verify their effectiveness and to make necessary adjustments. This ensures that the controls continue functioning as intended, safeguarding your organization against emerging threats and changing conditions.

---

**CONTROL 1: ESTABLISH AND MAINTAIN A SECURE APPLICATION DEVELOPMENT PROCESS**

---

**Control Objective:** To develop and sustain a secure application development process incorporating security standards, practices, and regular updates to mitigate vulnerabilities.

**Implementation Steps:**

**1.1. Define Security Standards:** Establish clear security application design standards and secure coding practices that align with industry best practices and regulatory requirements.

## CHAPTER 16   APPLICATION SOFTWARE SECURITY

**1.2. Developer Training:** Implement a comprehensive training program for developers on secure coding practices and vulnerability management.

**1.3. Integrate Security Testing:** Integrate security testing procedures throughout the development lifecycle, including static and dynamic analysis.

**1.4. Third-Party Code Review:** Ensure the security of third-party code by conducting thorough evaluations and testing before integration.

**1.5. Annual Review:** Review and update the secure application development documentation annually or when significant changes occur within the enterprise.

**Expected Outcome:** A secure application development process that minimizes vulnerabilities and incorporates best practices and regular updates, resulting in more secure applications.

---

## CONTROL 2: ESTABLISH AND MAINTAIN A PROCESS TO ACCEPT AND ADDRESS SOFTWARE VULNERABILITIES

**Control Objective:** To create and maintain a robust process for accepting and addressing reports of software vulnerabilities, ensuring timely and effective remediation.

**Implementation Steps:**

**2.1. Define Vulnerability Handling Policy:** Develop a policy outlining the process for reporting, handling, and remediating software vulnerabilities.

**2.2. External Reporting Mechanism:** Provide a clear and accessible means for external entities to report vulnerabilities.

**2.3. Use a Tracking System:** Implement a vulnerability tracking system with severity ratings and metrics for measuring identification, analysis, and remediation timelines.

**2.4. Assign Responsibilities:** Clearly define roles and responsibilities for handling vulnerability reports.

**2.5. Annual Documentation Review:** Review and update the vulnerability handling documentation annually or when significant enterprise changes occur.

**Expected Outcome:** A well-defined and efficient process for managing software vulnerabilities, ensuring that issues are addressed promptly and effectively, reducing the risk of exploitation.

## CONTROL 3: PERFORM ROOT CAUSE ANALYSIS ON SECURITY VULNERABILITIES

**Control Objective:** To identify and address the underlying causes of security vulnerabilities, preventing recurrence and improving overall security.

**Implementation Steps:**

**3.1. Conduct Root Cause Analysis:** To understand their origin, perform a detailed root cause analysis for all identified security vulnerabilities.

**3.2. Document Findings:** Maintain detailed documentation of root cause findings and remediation actions.

**3.3. Implement Preventive Measures:** Develop and implement preventive measures to address the underlying issues that lead to vulnerabilities.

**3.4. Continuous Improvement:** Use root cause analysis findings to improve development and security practices continuously.

**3.5. Train Developers:** Educate development teams on common root causes of vulnerabilities and how to avoid them in future projects.

**Expected Outcome:** Improved security practices and reduced recurrence of vulnerabilities through comprehensive root cause analysis and preventive measures.

## CONTROL 4: ESTABLISH AND MANAGE AN INVENTORY OF THIRD-PARTY COMPONENTS

**Control Objective:** To maintain an updated inventory of third-party components used in application development, assessing and mitigating associated risks.

**Implementation Steps:**

**4.1. Create an Inventory:** Establish a detailed inventory of all third-party components, libraries, and frameworks used in development.

**4.2. Assess Risks:** Evaluate the security risks associated with each third-party component and document these risks.

**4.3. Monthly Evaluation:** Review and update the inventory at least monthly to identify component changes or updates.

**4.4. Ensure Support:** Verify that third-party components are still supported and receive regular security updates.

**4.5. Track Future Use:** Include components slated for future use in the inventory to plan for their evaluation and integration.

**Expected Outcome:** A comprehensive and up-to-date inventory of third-party components, ensuring their security and reducing risks associated with external code.

CHAPTER 16    APPLICATION SOFTWARE SECURITY

## CONTROL 5: USE UP-TO-DATE AND TRUSTED THIRD-PARTY SOFTWARE COMPONENTS

**Control Objective:** To ensure the use of current and reliable third-party software components, reducing the risk of vulnerabilities.

**Implementation Steps:**

**5.1. Choose Proven Frameworks:** Select established and trusted frameworks and libraries that offer adequate security.

**5.2. Source Verification:** Acquire third-party components from reputable sources and verify their authenticity.

**5.3. Conduct Security Evaluations:** Regularly evaluate third-party Software for vulnerabilities before and after integration.

**5.4. Monitor for Updates:** Keep third-party components up-to-date with the latest security patches and updates.

**5.5. Develop a Trust Criteria:** Establish criteria for evaluating and trusting third-party components based on their security track record.

**Expected Outcome:** Using secure, up-to-date third-party software components minimizes vulnerabilities and enhances overall application security.

CHAPTER 16   APPLICATION SOFTWARE SECURITY

## CONTROL 6: ESTABLISH AND MAINTAIN A SEVERITY RATING SYSTEM AND PROCESS FOR APPLICATION VULNERABILITIES

**Control Objective:** To create and maintain a system that prioritizes application vulnerabilities based on their severity, facilitating efficient remediation.

**Implementation Steps:**

**6.1. Define Severity Criteria:** Establish criteria for rating the severity of application vulnerabilities.

**6.2. Implement Rating System:** Develop a system to assign severity ratings to identified vulnerabilities.

**6.3. Prioritize Remediation:** Use the severity ratings to prioritize the order in which vulnerabilities are addressed.

**6.4. Set Security Minimums:** Define a minimum level of security acceptability for releasing code or applications.

**6.5. Annual Review:** Review and update the severity rating system and process annually to ensure relevance and effectiveness.

**Expected Outcome:** A systematic approach to triaging vulnerabilities, improving risk management, and resolving the most severe issues.

## CONTROL 7: USE STANDARD HARDENING CONFIGURATION TEMPLATES FOR APPLICATION INFRASTRUCTURE

**Control Objective:** To apply and maintain standard hardening configurations for application infrastructure components, reducing the attack surface.

**Implementation Steps:**

**7.1. Develop Hardening Templates:** Create standard, industry-recommended hardening configuration templates for servers, databases, and web servers.

CHAPTER 16   APPLICATION SOFTWARE SECURITY

**7.2. Apply Configurations:** Ensure all application infrastructure components are configured using these templates.

**7.3. Regular Updates:** Regularly update the hardening templates to address new vulnerabilities and security threats.

**7.4. Monitor Compliance:** Implement monitoring to ensure infrastructure components comply with hardening standards.

**7.5. Include Cloud and SaaS:** Extend hardening practices to cloud containers, PaaS, and SaaS components.

**Expected Outcome:** Reduced attack surface and enhanced application infrastructure security through standardized hardening configurations.

## CONTROL 8: TRAIN DEVELOPERS IN APPLICATION SECURITY CONCEPTS AND PRACTICES

**Control Objective:** To ensure that all software development personnel are trained in secure coding and application security practices.

**Implementation Steps:**

**8.1. Develop Training Programs:** Create comprehensive training programs focused on secure coding principles and application security practices.

**8.2. Annual Training:** Conduct training sessions at least annually to keep developers updated on the latest security practices.

**8.3. Include All Developers:** Ensure that all software development personnel, regardless of experience level, participate in the training.

**8.4. Promote Security Culture:** Design training to promote a security culture within the development team.

## CHAPTER 16  APPLICATION SOFTWARE SECURITY

**8.5. Assess Training Effectiveness:** Evaluate the effectiveness of training programs through assessments and feedback.

**Expected Outcome:** A well-trained development team with a strong understanding of application security, leading to the creation of more secure Software.

---

### CONTROL 9: APPLY SECURE DESIGN PRINCIPLES IN APPLICATION ARCHITECTURES

**Control Objective:** To incorporate secure design principles into application architectures, minimizing vulnerabilities and enhancing security.

**Implementation Steps:**

**9.1. Define Secure Design Standards:** Establish secure design principles, including least privilege and input validation.

**9.2. Perform Error Checking:** Ensure explicit error checking is performed and documented for all input.

**9.3. Minimize Attack Surface:** Reduce the application infrastructure attack surface by turning off unprotected ports and removing unnecessary programs.

**9.4. Secure Default Accounts:** Rename or remove default accounts to prevent unauthorized access.

**9.5. Document Design Principles:** Maintain thorough documentation of secure design principles and their implementation in application architectures.

**Expected Outcome:** Secure application architectures incorporating best practices and minimizing vulnerabilities, enhancing overall security.

## CONTROL 10: LEVERAGE VETTED MODULES OR SERVICES FOR APPLICATION SECURITY

**Control Objective:** To utilize trusted and thoroughly vetted modules or services for critical security functions, reducing the likelihood of errors.

**Implementation Steps:**

**10.1. Identify Critical Functions:** Determine which security functions, such as identity management and encryption, are critical to the application.

**10.2. Select Vetted Modules:** Choose modules or services that have been extensively reviewed and proven secure for these functions.

**10.3. Use Standardized Algorithms:** Employ only standardized and currently accepted encryption algorithms.

**10.4. Integrate Platform Features:** Leverage identification, authentication, and authorization features to reduce development workload.

**10.5. Maintain Secure Audit Logs:** Utilize operating system mechanisms to create and maintain secure audit logs.

**Expected Outcome:** Enhanced security through vetted modules and services, reducing the risk of design or implementation errors in critical functions.

CHAPTER 16   APPLICATION SOFTWARE SECURITY

## CONTROL 11: IMPLEMENT CODE-LEVEL SECURITY CHECKS

**Control Objective:** To apply comprehensive code-level security checks throughout the application lifecycle, ensuring adherence to secure coding practices.

**Implementation Steps:**

**11.1. Use Static Analysis Tools:** Implement static analysis tools to examine code without executing it, identifying potential security flaws.

**11.2. Employ Dynamic Analysis Tools:** Use dynamic analysis tools to test the running application for vulnerabilities.

**11.3. Integrate Checks into CI/CD:** Incorporate static and dynamic analysis tools into the CI/CD pipeline for continuous security testing.

**11.4. Review Analysis Results:** Regularly review the static and dynamic analysis results and address identified issues.

**11.5. Maintain Secure Code Standards:** Ensure all code adheres to established secure coding standards and practices.

**Expected Outcome:** A thorough and continuous examination of code for security issues leads to the development of more secure applications.

## CONTROL 12: CONDUCT APPLICATION PENETRATION TESTING

**Control Objective:** To perform regular penetration testing on applications to identify and remediate vulnerabilities that may not be detected through automated testing.

**Implementation Steps:**

**12.1. Schedule Regular Testing:** Plan and schedule regular penetration testing for all critical applications.

CHAPTER 16   APPLICATION SOFTWARE SECURITY

**12.2. Use Skilled Testers:** Employ skilled penetration testers who can manually manipulate applications as both authenticated and unauthenticated users.

**12.3. Focus on Business Logic:** Ensure that penetration testing includes an evaluation of business logic vulnerabilities.

**12.4. Document Findings:** Maintain detailed documentation of all findings from penetration tests and remediation actions taken.

**12.5. Integrate with Development:** Integrate penetration testing results into the development process to address vulnerabilities promptly.

**Expected Outcome:** Identification and remediation of complex vulnerabilities through manual testing, enhancing the security of critical applications.

## CONTROL 13: CONDUCT THREAT MODELING

**Control Objective:** To perform threat modeling to identify and address security design flaws before creating code, ensuring a secure application architecture.

**Implementation Steps:**

**13.1. Train Security Champions:** Train selected individuals within development teams to lead threat modeling efforts.

**13.2. Map Application Architecture:** Create detailed maps of application architecture and infrastructure to understand potential weaknesses.

**13.3. Identify Entry Points:** Evaluate each entry point and access level for potential security risks.

CHAPTER 16   APPLICATION SOFTWARE SECURITY

**13.4. Develop Countermeasures:** Design and implement countermeasures to address identified threats.

**13.5. Document Threat Models:** Maintain thorough documentation of threat modeling activities and their outcomes.

**Expected Outcome:** A proactive approach to security that addresses design-level vulnerabilities early in development, leading to more secure applications.

# CHAPTER 17

# Incident Response Management

Incident Response Management is a cornerstone of a robust cybersecurity strategy, crucial for mitigating the impact of cyber incidents on an organization. Establishing a comprehensive incident response program enables enterprises to prepare for, detect, and respond to cyber attacks effectively. This proactive approach is vital where cyber threats are frequent and increasingly sophisticated. A well-developed incident response capability ensures that organizations can swiftly identify threats, contain damage, and recover operations, minimizing downtime and financial losses.

A thorough incident response program encompasses several key components, including policies, plans, procedures, defined roles, training, and communication strategies. These elements collectively form a cohesive framework that guides an organization through the stages of an incident, from initial detection to final recovery. Organizations can avoid the chaos and confusion often accompanying a cyber incident by delineating clear responsibilities and processes. Structured incident response efforts lead to more efficient and effective handling of security breaches, reducing the overall impact on the organization.

# CHAPTER 17    INCIDENT RESPONSE MANAGEMENT

One of the primary objectives of incident response is to curtail the spread of threats within the enterprise infrastructure. Rapid detection and response are essential to prevent attackers from embedding themselves deeper into the network, which can lead to prolonged dwell times and increased damage. Understanding the full scope of an incident is critical, including how it occurred and what can be done to prevent future occurrences. Without this insight, organizations risk falling into a reactive cycle, perpetually addressing symptoms rather than root causes.

The reality is that no cybersecurity defense can guarantee 100% protection against attacks. This underscores the importance of having a documented incident response plan in place. Such a plan outlines the investigative procedures, reporting mechanisms, data collection methods, and management responsibilities to navigate an incident effectively. It also encompasses legal protocols and communication strategies, ensuring that all aspects of incident management are covered comprehensively. This preparation is vital for enabling a coordinated and informed response, even in high-pressure situations.

Communication is a pivotal aspect of incident response management. Effective communication channels ensure that all stakeholders, from leadership to technical teams, are informed and can collaborate efficiently during an incident. Clear communication helps prioritize remediation efforts and make informed business decisions that support the organization's goals. Regulatory compliance, disclosure obligations, service-level agreements, or mission-critical functions might drive these decisions. Ensuring the right information reaches the right people at the right time is fundamental to effectively managing the incident's impact.

Incident response is not a static capability; it requires continuous refinement and improvement. Regular scenario-based training and exercises prepare the response team for real-world incidents. These exercises simulate various attack scenarios, helping team members understand their roles and responsibilities in the incident response process. They also reveal gaps in existing plans and processes, which

CHAPTER 17   INCIDENT RESPONSE MANAGEMENT

can be addressed to strengthen the overall incident response strategy. This iterative approach to training and improvement is essential for maintaining a high level of readiness.

Integrating threat intelligence and threat hunting into the incident response process is a hallmark of more mature cybersecurity programs. Organizations can proactively identify and monitor critical threats relevant to their industry or enterprise by leveraging threat intelligence. Threat hunting involves actively searching for signs of potential threats within the network based on known tactics, techniques, and procedures (TTPs) used by adversaries. This proactive stance enhances the ability to detect and respond to threats more quickly, reducing the window of opportunity for attackers.

Organizations with limited resources can benefit from a structured incident response plan. It is crucial to define sources for protection and detection and establish a network of external contacts for assistance during an incident. This network might include third-party vendors, law enforcement, cyber insurance providers, and relevant government agencies. Having predefined communication plans for engaging these external entities ensures that the organization can mobilize the necessary support swiftly and efficiently during an incident.

The designation of personnel to manage incident handling is critical in building an effective incident response capability. Appointing a key person and a backup ensures that someone is always responsible for coordinating and documenting the response efforts. This role may be filled by internal employees, third-party vendors, or a combination of both. Regular reviews and updates to the designated personnel and their responsibilities ensure that the incident response capability remains aligned with the organization's evolving needs and threat landscape.

Maintaining accurate and up-to-date contact information for all parties involved in incident response is essential. This includes internal staff, external vendors, and various stakeholders who must be informed during a security incident. Regular verification of this information ensures that the organization can quickly reach out to the right contacts, reducing delays in response efforts. Effective communication relies on having this information readily available and accurate, facilitating seamless coordination during an incident.

Another crucial component is a defined process for the workforce to report security incidents. This process should specify the reporting time frame, the personnel to report to, and the mechanisms for reporting incidents. Ensuring this process is publicly available to all employees encourages prompt and accurate reporting of security issues. Regular reviews and updates to the reporting process ensure that it remains effective and aligned with the organization's needs and the evolving threat landscape.

Conducting post-incident reviews is a vital practice for preventing the recurrence of incidents. These reviews involve analyzing the incident to identify lessons learned and areas for improvement. They provide valuable insights into what went well and what could be improved in the incident response process. By incorporating these lessons into plans and training, organizations can continually enhance their incident response capabilities, making them more resilient to future threats.

Establishing and maintaining security incident thresholds is fundamental for distinguishing between different security events. This differentiation helps prioritize response efforts and allocate resources appropriately. Thresholds include abnormal activity, security vulnerabilities, data breaches, and privacy incidents. Regular reviews and updates to these thresholds ensure they remain relevant and effective in guiding incident response efforts.

Managing and responding to cyber incidents effectively is a defining characteristic of a resilient organization. By developing and maintaining a robust incident response capability, organizations can protect themselves against the potentially devastating impacts of cyber attacks. This proactive approach mitigates damage and strengthens the overall security posture, enabling the organization to thrive in an increasingly digital world.

CHAPTER 17   INCIDENT RESPONSE MANAGEMENT

# Key Concepts and Terms

Cybersecurity professionals must understand key concepts and terms in Incident Response Management. These terms provide a foundation for developing and maintaining a robust incident response capability, enabling organizations to handle and recover from cyber incidents effectively. This section delves into twelve critical concepts and terms relevant to Incident Response Management, offering a clear and concise explanation of each to enhance comprehension and application.

**Incident Response Plan (IRP):** An Incident Response Plan (IRP) is a documented strategy outlining the procedures for identifying, managing, and recovering from cybersecurity incidents. It details the steps to be taken when an incident occurs, including detection, containment, eradication, and recovery. The IRP also specifies roles and responsibilities, ensuring everyone knows their tasks during an incident. Regularly updating and testing the IRP is crucial to keep it effective against evolving threats. A well-crafted IRP helps minimize the impact of incidents and ensures a swift return to normal operations.

**Incident Detection:** Incident Detection identifies potential security breaches within an organization's network and systems. This involves monitoring network traffic, system logs, and user activities to spot anomalies that may indicate a cyber attack. Effective detection relies on automated tools and human oversight to recognize unusual patterns and behaviors. Early detection is vital for mitigating the damage caused by cyber incidents, allowing for prompt response and containment. The faster an incident is detected, the quicker an organization can act to prevent further harm.

**Incident Containment:** Incident Containment involves isolating affected systems and networks to prevent the spread of a cyber threat. This step is crucial to limit the scope and impact of an incident, allowing responders to focus on eradicating the threat and restoring normal operations. Containment strategies can vary depending on the nature and severity of the incident, ranging from disconnecting compromised devices to segmenting parts of the network. Effective containment requires clear procedures and rapid decision-making to protect critical assets and data.

**Incident Eradication:** Incident Eradication removes the cause of a cyber incident from the affected environment. This includes eliminating malware, closing vulnerabilities, and ensuring no residual threats remain. Eradication is a critical step that prevents the attacker from regaining access and causing further damage. Thoroughly cleaning and securing systems during this phase ensures that the organization can safely proceed to recovery. It often involves collaboration between different teams to comprehensively address all aspects of the threat.

**Incident Recovery:** Recovery focuses on restoring systems and operations to normal after an incident has been contained and eradicated. This phase includes repairing affected systems, recovering data, and ensuring all business processes are functional. Recovery plans should be well-defined and tested regularly to ensure they can be executed effectively in the event of an incident. The goal of recovery is to minimize downtime and return the organization to a stable state as quickly as possible while ensuring that all security gaps have been addressed.

**Post-Incident Review:** A Post-Incident Review is an evaluation conducted after an incident has been resolved to analyze the response and identify lessons learned. This review helps organizations understand what went well and what areas need improvement in their incident response processes. By documenting findings and updating response plans based on these insights, organizations can enhance their preparedness for future incidents. Post-incident reviews are essential for continuous improvement and a more resilient cybersecurity posture.

**Threat Intelligence:** Threat Intelligence involves collecting and analyzing information about potential or current threats to an organization. This intelligence helps understand attackers' tactics, techniques, and procedures (TTPs), enabling a proactive defense strategy. Integrating threat intelligence into incident response allows organizations

# CHAPTER 17  INCIDENT RESPONSE MANAGEMENT

to anticipate and prepare for specific threats, improving their detection and response capabilities. It also aids in identifying indicators of compromise (IOCs) that can be used to detect similar threats in the future.

**Incident Response Team (IRT):** An Incident Response Team (IRT) is a group of individuals designated to handle and manage cybersecurity incidents. This team typically includes members from various IT, information security, legal, public relations, and human resources departments. The IRT is responsible for executing the incident response plan, coordinating efforts during an incident, and communicating with stakeholders. A dedicated IRT ensures that the organization can respond swiftly and effectively to cyber threats, minimizing damage and disruption.

**Dwell Time:** Dwell Time refers to the duration between a system's initial compromise and the breach's detection. The longer the dwell time, the more opportunity an attacker has to infiltrate deeper into the network, steal data, and establish persistent access. Reducing dwell time is critical for minimizing the impact of cyber incidents. Organizations aim to achieve this by enhancing their detection capabilities and conducting regular threat hunting to identify and address threats before they cause significant harm.

**Communication Plan:** A Communication Plan is a crucial component of incident response, detailing how information about an incident will be communicated to various stakeholders. This includes internal communication within the response team and organization and external communication with customers, partners, regulators, and the media. An effective communication plan ensures that accurate and timely information is disseminated, helping to manage the incident's impact on reputation and trust. It also facilitates coordinated efforts and informed decision-making during the response.

**Incident Classification:** Incident Classification involves categorizing security events based on their severity and impact. This classification helps prioritize response efforts and allocate resources appropriately. Different categories can include data breaches, malware infections, denial-of-service attacks, and insider threats, each requiring different response strategies. Clear classification criteria enable organizations to respond more effectively and ensure that the most critical incidents receive attention. It also aids in reporting and compliance with regulatory requirements.

**Scenario-Based Training:** Scenario-Based Training prepares incident response teams by simulating real-world cyberattack scenarios. These exercises help team members practice their roles and responsibilities in a controlled environment, allowing them to build confidence and improve their skills. Regular training ensures that the response team is familiar with the incident response plan and can execute it efficiently when an actual incident occurs. Scenario-based training also helps identify gaps in the Plan and processes, providing opportunities for improvement and strengthening the organization's overall readiness.

# Importance and Relevance

In today's rapidly evolving digital landscape, the importance and relevance of Incident Response Management in cybersecurity cannot be overstated. As cyber threats grow in sophistication and frequency, organizations must be prepared to detect, respond to, and recover from incidents swiftly and effectively. The following key points highlight why this control is critical and should be fundamental to every organization's cybersecurity strategy.

**Minimizing Impact on Business Operations:** A well-prepared incident response capability helps minimize cyber incidents' impact on business operations. Rapid detection and response reduce downtime and ensure critical systems and processes can continue functioning. This minimizes financial losses and maintains business continuity, vital for maintaining customer trust and meeting regulatory obligations. Organizations can quickly contain and eradicate threats by having a structured approach to incident response, allowing them to resume normal operations with minimal disruption.

**Protecting Sensitive Data:** Incident response is crucial for protecting sensitive data from theft or exposure. Data breaches can result in significant financial penalties, legal ramifications, and damage to an organization's reputation. Effective incident response strategies help identify and contain data breaches early, limiting the amount of data that can be compromised. This proactive approach is essential for safeguarding personal, financial, and proprietary information, which is increasingly targeted by cybercriminals.

**Ensuring Regulatory Compliance:** Many industries are subject to strict regulatory requirements regarding data protection and incident reporting. A robust incident response plan ensures that organizations meet these compliance obligations by providing a clear framework for detecting, managing, and reporting incidents. Failure to comply with regulations can result in severe penalties and legal consequences. By adhering to best practices in incident response, organizations demonstrate their commitment to cybersecurity and regulatory compliance.

**Enhancing Organizational Resilience:** Effectively responding to cyber incidents enhances an organization's overall resilience. Incident response plans provide a structured approach to dealing with unexpected events, ensuring the organization can quickly adapt and recover. This resilience is critical in a business environment where cyber threats constantly evolve. Organizations that can bounce back soon from incidents are better positioned to withstand the long-term impacts of cyber attacks.

**Reducing Financial Losses:** Cyber incidents can have significant financial implications, from direct costs of remediation to indirect costs such as lost revenue and reputational damage. Effective incident response helps reduce these financial losses by swiftly containing and mitigating the incidents' impact. Investing in incident response capabilities can save organizations substantial money in the long run by preventing extensive damage and enabling faster recovery.

**Improving Threat Detection and Response:** Incident response involves continuously monitoring and analyzing network activity to detect potential threats. This ongoing vigilance helps organizations identify and respond to threats more quickly, reducing the window of opportunity for attackers. Enhanced detection and response capabilities are vital for staying ahead of cybercriminals and protecting organizational assets. Regular updates and improvements to incident response processes ensure they remain effective against new and emerging threats.

**Maintaining Customer Trust:** Trust is critical to any business relationship, and cybersecurity incidents can severely damage customer trust. Effective incident response demonstrates an organization's commitment to protecting customers' data and maintaining their trust. Transparent communication during and after an incident helps reassure customers that the organization handles the situation responsibly. This trust is essential for retaining customers and maintaining a positive brand reputation.

**Supporting Business Continuity:** Incident response is key to business continuity planning. Organizations can maintain critical operations despite cyber attacks by ensuring clear procedures for responding to incidents. This preparedness is vital for minimizing downtime and ensuring that essential services remain available to customers and stakeholders. Incident response plans should be integrated with broader business continuity strategies to provide a comprehensive approach to organizational resilience.

**Facilitating Legal and Forensic Investigations:** Incident response includes processes for collecting and preserving evidence that may be needed for legal and forensic investigations. This capability is crucial for understanding the full scope of an incident and identifying the perpetrators. Properly managed incident response helps ensure that evidence is preserved in a manner that is admissible in court, supporting legal actions against cybercriminals. It also aids in identifying weaknesses in the organization's defenses that can be addressed to prevent future incidents.

**Enhancing Collaboration and Coordination:** Incident response requires coordination between various teams within the organization and external partners and stakeholders. Effective incident response plans facilitate this collaboration by defining roles and responsibilities clearly. This coordination is essential for managing incidents efficiently and ensuring that all necessary resources are mobilized quickly. Organizations can improve their overall incident response effectiveness by fostering a collaborative approach.

**Promoting Continuous Improvement:** Post-incident reviews and continuous improvement processes are integral to incident response. These activities help organizations learn from past incidents and enhance their response strategies. Continuous improvement ensures the organization always evolves its defenses and response capabilities to address new threats. By regularly updating and refining their incident response plans, organizations can stay ahead of cyber threats and improve their overall cybersecurity posture.

**Demonstrating Accountability and Transparency:** Effective incident response shows that an organization takes its cybersecurity responsibilities seriously. This accountability and transparency are important for building trust with customers, partners, and regulators. By having clear and effective incident response processes, organizations demonstrate their commitment to protecting their stakeholders and managing cyber risks proactively. This proactive approach is crucial for maintaining credibility and trust in today's interconnected digital world.

# Risks of Not Implementing the Control

Neglecting to implement an effective incident response management strategy can have severe repercussions for any organization. Without a structured approach to handling cyber incidents, companies expose themselves to risks that can significantly impact their operations, finances, and reputation. These risks are multifaceted and often interrelated, compounding the potential damage when a cyber incident occurs. Understanding these risks is crucial for appreciating the importance of a robust incident response capability. The following key risks illustrate the potential consequences of failing to prioritize incident response management.

**Extended Downtime:** Without a proper incident response plan, organizations may experience prolonged downtime during and after a cyber incident. This extended downtime can halt business operations, leading to lost revenue and productivity. The longer it takes to identify, contain, and resolve an incident, the more significant the disruption to normal activities. Prolonged downtime affects immediate business processes and can erode customer trust and loyalty over time.

**Data Breaches:** Failing to implement effective incident response measures increases the risk of data breaches. Cybercriminals can exploit vulnerabilities without timely detection and response, leading to the unauthorized access and exfiltration of sensitive data. Data breaches can have severe financial and legal consequences, including regulatory fines and the cost of notifying affected individuals. Moreover, losing sensitive data can damage an organization's reputation and erode stakeholder trust.

**Financial Losses:** The financial impact of cyber incidents can be devastating, especially without a robust incident response plan. Costs associated with incident recovery, legal fees, regulatory fines, and compensatory payments to affected parties can quickly add up. Additionally, indirect costs such as loss of business opportunities decreased customer confidence, and increased insurance premiums can further strain financial resources. Effective incident response helps mitigate these financial risks by reducing the time and resources needed to recover from an incident.

**Regulatory Non-Compliance:** Many industries are subject to strict data protection and incident reporting regulations. Organizations may struggle to meet these regulatory requirements without an incident response plan, resulting in non-compliance penalties. Regulatory fines can be substantial and, in some cases, may also include mandatory audits and increased scrutiny from regulatory bodies. Non-compliance affects financial stability and damages the organization's reputation and credibility.

**Reputational Damage:** Cyber incidents can severely damage an organization's reputation, especially if not managed effectively. Negative publicity, loss of customer trust, and decreased stakeholder confidence are common consequences of poorly handled incidents. Reputational damage can have long-lasting effects, making it difficult for organizations to regain their standing in the market. Proactive incident response demonstrates a commitment to cybersecurity and helps preserve the organization's reputation in the event of an incident.

**Operational Disruption:** Cyber incidents can disrupt critical business operations, leading to delays, errors, and decreased efficiency. Without an incident response plan, organizations may find it challenging to restore normal operations quickly, exacerbating the disruption. Operational disruption can affect various aspects of the business, from supply chain management to customer service. Ensuring continuity of operations is essential for maintaining business resilience and customer satisfaction.

**Intellectual Property Theft:** Cybercriminals often target valuable intellectual property (IP), such as trade secrets, patents, and proprietary technologies. Without effective incident response, organizations are more vulnerable to IP theft. The loss of intellectual property can undermine competitive advantage and result in significant financial losses. Protecting IP through timely detection and response is crucial for safeguarding the organization's innovation and market position.

**Legal Liability:** Organizations that fail to implement adequate incident response measures may face legal liabilities if they cannot demonstrate due diligence in protecting data and responding to incidents. Legal actions from affected parties, including customers, partners, and employees,

## CHAPTER 17    INCIDENT RESPONSE MANAGEMENT

can result in substantial legal fees and settlements. Effective incident response helps mitigate legal risks by ensuring compliance with legal obligations and demonstrating a proactive approach to cybersecurity.

**Increased Recovery Costs:** Recovering from a cyber incident can escalate without a well-defined incident response plan. Delays in detection and response allow threats to spread and cause more damage, increasing the complexity and cost of remediation. Recovery may involve extensive system repairs, data restoration, and additional security measures. A structured incident response plan helps contain and mitigate threats early, reducing the overall recovery costs.

**Loss of Customer Trust:** Trust is a critical component of customer relationships, and mishandling cyber incidents can erode this trust. Customers expect organizations to protect their data and respond promptly to security breaches. Failure to do so can lead to customer attrition and negative word-of-mouth, impacting future business opportunities. Maintaining customer trust through effective incident response is essential for long-term business success.

**Diminished Competitive Advantage:** Cyber incidents can undermine an organization's competitive advantage, especially if they result in losing sensitive data or intellectual property. Competitors may exploit these vulnerabilities, gaining insights into the organization's strategies and innovations. A robust incident response plan helps protect competitive advantage by minimizing the impact of cyber incidents and ensuring that sensitive information remains secure.

**Psychological Impact on Employees:** Cyber incidents can also psychologically impact employees, causing stress and uncertainty. Without a clear incident response plan, employees may feel unprepared and unsupported in dealing with the aftermath of an incident. This can affect morale, productivity, and overall job satisfaction. Providing employees with the tools and training to respond effectively to cyber incidents helps build a resilient workforce capable of navigating cybersecurity challenges.

CHAPTER 17    INCIDENT RESPONSE MANAGEMENT

# What Questions Should You Ask?

To effectively implement Incident Response Management, cybersecurity leaders must ask critical questions that guide the development and execution of their incident response strategy. These questions help identify gaps, define priorities, and ensure comprehensive coverage of all necessary aspects of incident response. By systematically addressing these questions, leaders can create a robust framework that prepares their organizations to handle cyber incidents efficiently and effectively. The following key questions serve as a foundation for forming a thorough and proactive incident response plan.

**What are the most likely threats to our organization?** Understanding the threats that pose the most significant risk to your organization. This involves analyzing past incidents, current threat landscapes, and industry-specific vulnerabilities. Knowing the most likely threats helps prioritize resources and develop targeted response strategies. It ensures that the incident response plan is tailored to address the most pertinent risks, enhancing its effectiveness.

**Who is responsible for managing the incident response process?** Designating clear roles and responsibilities is critical for a coordinated response to cyber incidents. Identify key personnel who will oversee the process, including primary and backup incident response managers. Clearly defined responsibilities ensure accountability and the streamlining of communication during an incident. This structure helps avoid confusion and ensures that all necessary tasks are covered efficiently.

**What is our process for detecting and reporting incidents?** Establishing a clear process for detecting and reporting incidents is fundamental. This includes defining the tools and technologies used for monitoring and the procedures for employees to report suspicious activities. An effective detection and reporting process enables early identification of incidents, which is crucial for minimizing damage. Ensuring all staff are aware of and trained on this process is also essential for its success.

**How will we contain an incident to prevent further damage?** Containment strategies are essential for limiting the impact of a cyber incident. Determine the methods and technologies that will be used to isolate affected systems and prevent the spread of threats. Effective containment minimizes disruption and protects critical assets from further compromise. Developing and rehearsing containment procedures ensures they can be implemented swiftly.

**What steps will we take to eradicate the threat?** Eradication involves removing the threat from the affected environment and ensuring it does not reoccur. Define the processes and tools used to clean and restore systems. Thorough eradication is necessary to prevent attackers from regaining access and causing additional harm. This step also includes addressing any vulnerabilities that were exploited during the incident.

**How will we recover and restore normal operations?** Recovery plans detail how to return systems to normal operations following an incident. Identify the steps required to restore data, applications, and services to their pre-incident state. Effective recovery minimizes downtime and ensures business continuity. Regular testing and updating of recovery plans are crucial for their reliability.

**What is our communication plan during an incident?** Communication is vital during a cyber incident to ensure all stakeholders are informed and coordinated. Develop a communication plan that includes internal and external communication strategies, identifying who needs to be told and what information should be shared. Clear communication helps manage the incident effectively and maintains transparency with customers, partners, and regulators. It also supports coordinated efforts and informed decision-making.

**How will we document and review incidents?** Documenting incidents and conducting post-incident reviews are essential for continuous improvement. Establish procedures for recording all actions

## CHAPTER 17   INCIDENT RESPONSE MANAGEMENT

taken during an incident and the outcomes. Post-incident reviews help identify lessons learned and areas for improvement. This documentation is also valuable for compliance and reporting purposes.

**What are our criteria for classifying incidents?** Defining criteria for classifying incidents helps prioritize response efforts. Develop a classification scheme that categorizes incidents based on their severity and impact. Precise classification ensures that the most critical incidents receive immediate attention and resources. It also aids communication and reporting, providing a common framework for discussing incidents.

**How will we ensure compliance with relevant regulations?** Compliance with legal and regulatory requirements is a critical aspect of incident response. Identify the regulations that apply to your organization and ensure that your incident response plan addresses these requirements. This includes procedures for reporting incidents to regulatory bodies and maintaining necessary documentation. Compliance helps avoid legal penalties and supports the organization's reputation.

**What training and exercises will we conduct for our incident response team?** Regular training and exercises are essential for keeping the incident response team prepared. Plan and conduct scenario-based exercises that simulate real-world incidents to test the team's readiness. These exercises help identify gaps in the response plan and improve the team's skills. Continuous training ensures that the team remains proficient and confident in their roles.

**How will we incorporate threat intelligence into our incident response?** Integrating threat intelligence into incident response enhances the ability to anticipate and mitigate threats. Identify sources of threat intelligence and determine how this information will be used to inform response strategies. Proactive use of threat intelligence helps detect and respond to incidents more effectively. It also supports a proactive approach to cybersecurity, staying ahead of potential threats.

CHAPTER 17   INCIDENT RESPONSE MANAGEMENT

# Recommended Training

Training is a crucial component of effective Incident Response Management, ensuring that IT/cyber staff and other employees are appropriately prepared to respond to cyber threats. Comprehensive training programs should cover various aspects of incident response, from technical skills and threat detection to awareness and best practices for all employees. Proper training enhances the skills and knowledge of those directly involved in cybersecurity and fosters a security-conscious culture across the organization. The following recommended training programs aim to equip staff at all levels with the necessary tools and understanding to mitigate risks and respond effectively to incidents.

**Incident Response Planning Workshop:** This workshop should be attended by IT/cybersecurity staff and key decision-makers. It includes developing, reviewing, and updating the incident response plan, ensuring all team members understand their roles and responsibilities. Participants will learn to coordinate during an incident, communicate effectively, and execute the Plan efficiently. This training enhances preparedness and ensures a cohesive response during incidents, reducing response time and potential damage.

**Threat Detection and Monitoring Training:** Geared toward IT and cybersecurity personnel, this training focuses on using tools and techniques to detect and monitor threats. It covers log analysis, anomaly detection, and intrusion detection systems. Participants will learn how to identify indicators of compromise and respond swiftly. Enhanced threat detection capabilities lead to quicker identification and mitigation of potential incidents, reducing the risk of widespread damage.

**Phishing Awareness and Prevention:** This training is essential for all employees, as phishing attacks are a common vector for cyber incidents. The program educates employees on recognizing phishing emails, the dangers of clicking on suspicious links, and proper reporting procedures. By increasing awareness, employees become the first line of defense against phishing attempts. This training reduces the likelihood of successful phishing attacks, protecting sensitive information and systems.

**Secure Password Management:** Targeting all employees, this training emphasizes the importance of creating and maintaining strong, unique passwords. It includes guidance on using password managers, understanding multi-factor authentication, and recognizing the risks of password reuse. Proper password management helps prevent unauthorized access to systems and data. Employees can significantly reduce the risk of credential-based attacks by adopting these practices.

**Data Protection and Privacy Training:** This training is relevant for all staff, particularly those handling sensitive data. It covers data classification, handling protocols, and privacy regulations. Employees will learn how to protect data integrity and confidentiality and how to report data breaches. Understanding data protection principles helps ensure compliance with legal requirements and reduces the risk of data breaches.

**Incident Reporting Procedures:** All employees should understand the procedures for reporting suspected security incidents. This training outlines the steps to take when encountering potential security issues, who to contact, and what information to provide. Clear reporting procedures enable swift incident detection and response. By correctly reporting incidents, employees help ensure that potential threats are addressed promptly.

**Network Security Basics:** Aimed at IT staff and network administrators, this training covers fundamental network security principles, including firewall configuration, network segmentation, and secure network design. Participants will learn how to safeguard network infrastructure against common threats. Strengthening network security reduces the attack surface and protects critical systems from unauthorized access and exploitation.

**Social Engineering Defense:** This training educates all employees about the tactics used in social engineering attacks and how to defend against them. It includes recognizing manipulation techniques and understanding the importance of verifying requests for sensitive information. Employees will be better equipped to spot and resist social engineering attempts. Reducing the success rate of social engineering attacks helps protect the organization from breaches and data theft.

**Incident Simulation Exercises:** IT and cybersecurity teams benefit from participating in simulated incident response exercises. These simulations mimic real-world attacks, allowing teams to practice their response in a controlled environment. Exercises help identify weaknesses in the response plan and improve coordination among team members. Regular simulation exercises ensure the team is well-prepared for actual incidents, enhancing overall response effectiveness.

**Endpoint Security Training:** Focused on IT staff, this training covers best practices for securing endpoints, such as laptops, desktops, and mobile devices. It includes configuring antivirus software, applying patches, and managing device security settings. Proper endpoint security helps prevent malware infections and unauthorized access. By securing endpoints, the organization reduces the risk of cyber threats spreading through compromised devices.

**Cybersecurity Policy Awareness:** All employees should know the organization's cybersecurity policies. This training reviews vital policies, such as acceptable use, data protection, and incident reporting. Understanding these policies helps employees align their actions with organizational standards. Awareness of cybersecurity policies ensures consistent adherence to best practices, strengthening the overall security posture.

**Advanced Threat Hunting:** This specialized training is intended for cybersecurity experts within the organization. It involves proactive searching for signs of malicious activity within the network using advanced tools and techniques. Threat hunters learn to identify and mitigate advanced persistent threats (APTs) before they cause significant harm. Advanced threat hunting enhances the organization's ability to detect and respond to sophisticated attacks, reducing dwell time and potential impact.

# Actionable Recommendations

Implementing an effective incident response management strategy requires careful planning, comprehensive preparation, and ongoing refinement. These actionable recommendations provide a structured approach to building a robust incident response capability. By following these guidelines, organizations can enhance their ability to detect, respond to, and recover from cyber incidents efficiently. The following recommendations cover vital areas such as planning, communication, training, and continuous improvement, ensuring a holistic approach to incident response.

**Develop a Comprehensive Incident Response Plan:** Create a detailed incident response plan outlining the steps to take during a cyber incident. This Plan should include detection, containment, eradication, and recovery procedures. Ensure the Plan is regularly reviewed and updated to reflect changes in the threat landscape and organizational structure. A comprehensive plan provides a clear roadmap for responding to incidents, minimizing confusion, and enhancing coordination.

**Establish Clear Roles and Responsibilities:** Define and assign specific roles and responsibilities for incident response within your organization. Identify key personnel, including an incident response manager, team members, and backup contacts. Ensure everyone involved understands their duties and the chain of command during an incident. Clear roles and responsibilities streamline the response process and ensure accountability.

**Implement Robust Detection Mechanisms:** Deploy advanced detection tools and technologies to monitor network traffic, system logs, and user activities. Utilize intrusion detection systems (IDS), security information and event management (SIEM) systems, and endpoint detection and response (EDR) solutions. Regularly update and tune these tools to detect the latest threats. Effective detection mechanisms enable early identification of incidents, allowing for swift response and containment.

**Conduct Regular Training and Drills:** Provide ongoing training for your incident response team and conduct regular drills to test their readiness. Simulate various attack scenarios to practice response procedures and identify areas for improvement. Training should also extend to all employees, educating them on recognizing and reporting potential security incidents. Regular exercise and drills ensure that your team remains proficient and prepared for real-world incidents.

**Develop a Communication Plan:** Create a communication plan that outlines how information about an incident will be shared internally and externally. Identify key stakeholders, including leadership, employees, customers, partners, and regulatory bodies. Determine the communication channels and frequency for updates. A well-defined communication plan ensures transparency and keeps all parties informed during an incident.

**Integrate Threat Intelligence:** Incorporate threat intelligence into your incident response strategy to stay ahead of emerging threats. Use threat intelligence feeds and analysis to understand attackers' tactics, techniques, and procedures (TTPs). This information can help tailor your detection and response efforts to address specific threats relevant to your industry. Integrating threat intelligence enhances your ability to anticipate and mitigate attacks.

**Establish Incident Classification Criteria:** Develop criteria for classifying incidents based on their severity and potential impact. Categories might include data breaches, malware infections, denial-of-service attacks, and insider threats. Clear classification criteria help prioritize response efforts and allocate resources effectively. Incident classification ensures that the most critical threats receive immediate attention.

**Create a Post-Incident Review Process:** Implement a process for conducting post-incident reviews to analyze the response and identify lessons learned. Document the incident timeline, actions taken, and outcomes. Use this information to improve your incident response

## CHAPTER 17  INCIDENT RESPONSE MANAGEMENT

plan and address gaps or weaknesses. Post-incident reviews facilitate continuous improvement and enhance your overall incident response capability.

**Enhance Endpoint Security:** Focus on securing endpoints such as laptops, desktops, and mobile devices, which are common targets for attackers. Implement endpoint protection solutions, apply regular updates and patches, and enforce strong security policies. Properly secured endpoints reduce the risk of malware infections and unauthorized access. Enhancing endpoint security strengthens your overall defense against cyber threats.

**Ensure Compliance with Regulations:** Align your incident response plan with relevant legal and regulatory requirements. Understand the reporting obligations for data breaches and other incidents specific to your industry. Ensure that your response procedures include steps for notifying regulatory bodies and affected individuals. Compliance with regulations helps avoid legal penalties and demonstrates your commitment to cybersecurity.

**Promote a Security-Aware Culture:** Foster a culture of security awareness throughout your organization. Educate employees about the importance of cybersecurity and their role in protecting the organization. Encourage vigilance and proactive reporting of suspicious activities. A security-aware culture enhances the overall effectiveness of your incident response efforts.

**Leverage External Expertise:** Partner with external experts such as managed security service providers (MSSPs) or incident response consultants. These professionals can provide additional resources, expertise, and support during complex incidents. External partners can also offer specialized services such as forensic analysis and advanced threat hunting. Leveraging external expertise can strengthen your incident response capability and provide valuable insights.

CHAPTER 17   INCIDENT RESPONSE MANAGEMENT

# Simplified Security Controls (SSC)

Security controls are essential for any organization seeking to protect its digital and physical assets from cyber threats. Tailoring these controls to fit the specific needs of your business environment is crucial, as it ensures that the protection mechanisms are relevant and effective against the specific risks your organization faces. There are numerous sources to draw these controls from, including the well-regarded CIS Top 18, which provides a robust framework for crafting defensive strategies. The recommendations presented in this book are based on the CIS controls, among others, offering a comprehensive guide that can be adapted to serve a wide range of security needs. Before implementing these controls, it is vital to thoroughly review their design to ensure they align with your strategic objectives and operational practices. Additionally, after deployment, it is imperative to regularly test the controls to verify their effectiveness and to make necessary adjustments. This ensures that the controls continue to function as intended, safeguarding your organization against emerging threats and changing conditions.

## CONTROL 1: DESIGNATE PERSONNEL TO MANAGE INCIDENT HANDLING

**Control Objective:** To ensure that incident handling is coordinated and documented effectively by assigning dedicated personnel.

**Implementation Steps:**

**1.1. Designate Incident Managers:** Designate a primary incident response manager and at least one backup to oversee the incident handling process.

**1.2. Define Responsibilities:** Define responsibilities for internal personnel and any third-party vendors involved in incident response.

**1.3. Annual Review:** Review and update the designated personnel annually or when significant organizational changes occur.

**Expected Outcome:** Clear assignment of incident handling responsibilities ensures coordinated and efficient response efforts, reducing confusion and improving incident management.

## CONTROL 2: ESTABLISH AND MAINTAIN CONTACT INFORMATION FOR REPORTING

**Control Objective:** To facilitate timely and accurate reporting of security incidents by maintaining up-to-date contact information.

**Implementation Steps:**

**2.1. Compile Contact List:** Compile and maintain a contact list of all relevant parties, including internal staff, third-party vendors, law enforcement, cyber insurance providers, and government agencies.

**2.2. Annual Verification:** Verify and update contact information annually to ensure accuracy.

**2.3. Accessibility:** Ensure the contact list is accessible to all relevant personnel during an incident.

**Expected Outcome:** Maintaining accurate contact information ensures that all necessary parties can be promptly informed during a security incident, facilitating swift and coordinated response efforts.

CHAPTER 17    INCIDENT RESPONSE MANAGEMENT

## CONTROL 3: ESTABLISH AND MAINTAIN AN ENTERPRISE PROCESS FOR INCIDENT REPORTING

**Control Objective:** To standardize the process for reporting security incidents across the organization.

**Implementation Steps:**

**3.1. Develop Reporting Process:** Develop a straightforward incident reporting process, including reporting time frames, responsible personnel, and reporting mechanisms.

**3.2. Public Availability:** Ensure the reporting process is publicly available to all employees and relevant stakeholders.

**3.3. Annual Review:** Review and update the reporting process annually or when significant changes occur.

**Expected Outcome:** A standardized incident reporting process ensures that all incidents are reported consistently and promptly, enabling quick response and mitigation.

## CONTROL 4: ESTABLISH AND MAINTAIN AN INCIDENT RESPONSE PROCESS

**Control Objective:** To provide a structured approach for responding to security incidents, including roles, responsibilities, and communication plans.

**Implementation Steps:**

**4.1. Develop Response Process:** Develop a comprehensive incident response process that addresses detection, containment, eradication, and recovery.

**4.2. Define Roles and Responsibilities:** Define roles and responsibilities for all personnel involved in the incident response process.

**4.3. Annual Review:** Review and update the incident response process annually or when significant organizational changes occur.

**Expected Outcome:** A well-defined incident response process ensures that all aspects of incident management are addressed efficiently and effectively, improving the organization's ability to mitigate and recover from incidents.

## CONTROL 5: ASSIGN KEY ROLES AND RESPONSIBILITIES

**Control Objective:** To ensure the incident response team clearly defines and assigns all necessary roles and responsibilities.

**Implementation Steps:**

**5.1. Identify and Assign Roles:** Identify and assign critical roles, including legal, IT, information security, facilities, public relations, human resources, incident responders, and analysts.

**5.2. Document Responsibilities:** Document the responsibilities of each role and ensure all team members are aware of their duties.

**5.3. Annual Review:** Review and update role assignments annually or when significant organizational changes occur.

**Expected Outcome:** Defined roles and responsibilities ensure that all necessary tasks are covered during an incident, improving coordination and efficiency.

CHAPTER 17   INCIDENT RESPONSE MANAGEMENT

## CONTROL 6: DEFINE MECHANISMS FOR COMMUNICATING DURING INCIDENT RESPONSE

**Control Objective:** To ensure effective communication during a security incident through predefined primary and secondary mechanisms.

**Implementation Steps:**

**6.1. Document Communication Mechanisms:** Identify and document primary and secondary communication mechanisms, such as phone calls, emails, and letters.

**6.2. Ensure Backup Methods:** Ensure backup communication methods are available if primary mechanisms are compromised.

**6.3. Annual Review:** Review and update communication mechanisms annually or when significant changes occur.

**Expected Outcome:** Predefined communication mechanisms ensure that all stakeholders can be informed promptly during an incident, even if primary channels are disrupted.

## CONTROL 7: CONDUCT ROUTINE INCIDENT RESPONSE EXERCISES

**Control Objective:** To prepare key personnel for real-world incidents through regular training and simulation exercises.

**Implementation Steps:**

**7.1. Plan and Conduct Exercises:** At least annually, plan and conduct incident response exercises and scenarios for key personnel.

**7.2. Test Communication Channels:** Test communication channels, decision-making processes, and workflows during exercises.

CHAPTER 17   INCIDENT RESPONSE MANAGEMENT

**7.3. Document and Improve:** Document the outcomes of exercises and incorporate lessons learned into the incident response plan.

**Expected Outcome:** Routine exercises ensure the incident response team is well-prepared for actual incidents, improving readiness and effectiveness.

## CONTROL 8: CONDUCT POST-INCIDENT REVIEWS

**Control Objective:** To identify lessons learned and improve incident response processes through post-incident analysis.

**Implementation Steps:**

**8.1. Conduct Review:** Conduct a thorough review of each incident after resolution, documenting the timeline, actions taken, and outcomes.

**8.2. Identify Improvements:** Identify areas for improvement and update the incident response plan accordingly.

**8.3. Share Findings:** Share findings and lessons learned with all relevant personnel to enhance future response efforts.

**Expected Outcome:** Post-incident reviews help prevent the recurrence of similar incidents and improve overall incident response capabilities.

CHAPTER 17    INCIDENT RESPONSE MANAGEMENT

## CONTROL 9: ESTABLISH AND MAINTAIN SECURITY INCIDENT THRESHOLDS

**Control Objective:** To define and maintain thresholds for differentiating between incidents and events, ensuring appropriate response levels.

**Implementation Steps:**

**9.1. Develop Classification Criteria:** Develop criteria for classifying security incidents and events, such as abnormal activity, vulnerabilities, data breaches, and privacy incidents.

**9.2. Communicate Thresholds:** Document and communicate these thresholds to all relevant personnel.

**9.3. Annual Review:** Review and update thresholds annually or when significant organizational changes occur.

**Expected Outcome:** Clearly defined incident thresholds ensure that incidents are classified and responded to appropriately, improving the effectiveness of incident management efforts.

# CHAPTER 18

# Penetration Testing

Penetration testing, often abbreviated as pen testing, is a critical component of a comprehensive cybersecurity strategy. This process involves evaluating the security of an organization's IT infrastructure by simulating attacks from malicious outsiders and insiders. The objective is to identify and exploit system weaknesses, clearly showing the organization's defensive posture. Unlike routine security assessments, penetration testing delves deeper, aiming to mimic the strategies and techniques of actual attackers. Doing so helps organizations understand the potential impact of vulnerabilities and the real-world risks they pose.

One of the primary reasons penetration testing is essential is the ever-evolving nature of technology and the corresponding increase in sophisticated cyber threats. As organizations integrate new technologies and expand their digital footprint, the attack surface for potential threats also grows. Penetration testing helps ensure that security measures keep pace with these advancements. It allows organizations to proactively identify gaps in their defenses before attackers can exploit them. This proactive approach is crucial for maintaining robust security in a dynamic threat landscape.

Penetration testing evaluates technical vulnerabilities and the effectiveness of an organization's policies, procedures, and training programs. Security is not solely a technical issue; it also involves people and processes. For instance, social engineering attacks, which exploit human psychology rather than technical vulnerabilities, are a common vector for cyber threats. Penetration testing often includes simulated social engineering attacks to test employees' awareness and adherence to security protocols. This holistic evaluation helps organizations strengthen their security posture by addressing weaknesses.

The penetration testing scope can vary widely, from testing specific applications and systems to comprehensive assessments of the entire network. It may involve external testing, simulating attacks from outside the organization, or internal testing, which assumes the perspective of an insider threat. The choice of scope depends on the organization's specific needs and the potential impact of identified vulnerabilities. Regardless of the scope, the insights gained from penetration testing are invaluable for understanding and mitigating risks.

A significant benefit of penetration testing is providing tangible evidence of vulnerabilities. This is particularly useful for communicating risks to decision-makers who may not have a technical background. A well-conducted penetration test can demonstrate the potential consequences of security weaknesses, making it easier to justify investments in security improvements. This evidence-based approach ensures that security measures are prioritized and funded appropriately.

In addition to identifying vulnerabilities, penetration testing helps organizations validate the effectiveness of their existing security measures. Organizations can see how well their defenses hold up under pressure by testing the same systems and controls that protect against real-world attacks. This validation process is crucial for ensuring security investments deliver the intended results. It also helps identify areas where additional training or technical enhancements may be needed.

Penetration testing is not a one-time activity but an ongoing process. Cyber threats are constantly evolving, and new vulnerabilities are discovered regularly. Regular penetration testing ensures organizations remain vigilant and adaptive in their security efforts. It provides a continuous feedback loop, enabling organizations to refine their defenses and stay ahead of emerging threats. This iterative approach to security is essential for maintaining resilience in the face of an ever-changing threat landscape.

Conducting penetration tests requires specialized skills and expertise. It is not merely a matter of running automated tools; it involves creative thinking and a deep understanding of attacker methodologies. As such, organizations often engage third-party experts to perform these tests. External testers bring an objective perspective and are more likely to identify overlooked vulnerabilities. Additionally, their findings carry more weight, as they are considered unbiased evaluations of the organization's security posture.

The complexity and potential risks of penetration testing necessitate careful planning and execution. A clear scope and rules of engagement must be established to avoid unintended consequences, such as system outages or data corruption. Only authorized personnel should be aware of the tests to ensure that the results accurately reflect the organization's defensive capabilities. Moreover, the findings from penetration tests should be handled with care, as they provide detailed blueprints for exploiting vulnerabilities.

Penetration testing can reveal process weaknesses that are not immediately apparent through other means. For example, it can uncover issues in configuration management, patching procedures, or incident response protocols. These process-related vulnerabilities can be just as critical as technical flaws, as they often provide attackers with the means to bypass otherwise robust defenses. Addressing these weaknesses is essential for building a resilient security framework.

One of the emerging trends in penetration testing is the integration of red team exercises. Red teaming involves simulating advanced persistent threats (APTs) tailored to specific adversaries. Unlike traditional penetration testing, which may focus on individual vulnerabilities, red team exercises assess the organization's ability to detect and respond to sophisticated attacks. This approach provides a more comprehensive evaluation of the organization's security capabilities and helps identify areas for improvement in threat detection and response.

Penetration testing also plays a crucial role in compliance with regulatory requirements and industry standards. Many regulations mandate regular security assessments, including penetration tests, to ensure that organizations adhere to best practices in cybersecurity. Compliance-driven testing helps organizations avoid legal and financial penalties while demonstrating their commitment to maintaining a secure environment. It also assures customers and partners that the organization takes security seriously.

Penetration testing is an indispensable tool for modern cybersecurity. It provides a thorough and realistic assessment of an organization's defenses, helping to identify and mitigate risks before they can be exploited. By combining technical evaluations with policies, procedures, and employee awareness assessments, penetration testing offers a holistic view of security. Regular testing and promptly remedying identified vulnerabilities ensure organizations remain resilient despite evolving cyber threats. As the digital landscape continues to grow and change, the importance of penetration testing in maintaining robust security cannot be overstated.

# Key Concepts and Terms

Understanding the fundamental concepts and terminology associated with penetration testing is crucial for grasping the depth and breadth of this cybersecurity discipline. This section provides detailed explanations of key terms and concepts that are essential for comprehending the methodologies, objectives, and intricacies of penetration testing. By familiarizing yourself with these terms, you will better understand how penetration testing fits into the broader context of cybersecurity and how it helps identify and mitigate vulnerabilities within an organization's infrastructure.

**Reconnaissance:** Reconnaissance, also known as information gathering, is the initial phase of a penetration test. During this stage, testers collect as much information as possible about the target system to identify potential entry points. This involves network scanning, examining public records, and searching for exposed data online. Effective reconnaissance can uncover critical details such as IP addresses, domain names, and employee information, which can be used to craft more targeted attacks. The goal is to understand the target environment thoroughly before attempting any exploitation.

**Vulnerability Scanning:** Vulnerability scanning involves using automated tools to identify known vulnerabilities in an organization's systems. These scans help detect weaknesses such as unpatched software, misconfigurations, and outdated protocols. Although vulnerability scanning is a preliminary step and less invasive than penetration testing, it provides a foundation for identifying potential targets for deeper investigation. The results from vulnerability scans guide testers in pinpointing areas that require manual analysis and possible exploitation.

**Exploitation:** Exploitation is the phase where identified vulnerabilities are actively targeted to gain unauthorized system access. This step goes beyond identifying vulnerabilities and involves executing attacks to determine their real-world impact. Testers might use various tools and techniques to exploit these weaknesses, simulating how an actual attacker would operate. The objective is to demonstrate how vulnerabilities can be leveraged to breach security controls, access sensitive data, or disrupt operations, providing a clear picture of the potential risks.

**Social Engineering:** Social engineering involves manipulating individuals into divulging confidential information or performing actions to compromise security. This tactic exploits human psychology rather than technical vulnerabilities. Common techniques include phishing emails, pretexting, and baiting. Penetration testers use social engineering to evaluate an organization's human defenses and employee adherence to security policies. Successful social engineering attacks can reveal significant weaknesses in user training and awareness, highlighting areas for improvement in security culture.

**Red Teaming:** Red teaming is a strategy that simulates advanced persistent threats (APTs) to evaluate an organization's security posture. Unlike traditional penetration testing, which might focus on specific vulnerabilities, red teaming assesses the organization's ability to detect, respond to, and mitigate sophisticated attacks. This involves emulating particular adversaries' tactics, techniques, and procedures (TTPs). The insights from red teaming exercises are invaluable for understanding how well an organization can withstand targeted, long-term attacks.

**Rules of Engagement:** The rules of engagement (RoE) outline a penetration test's scope, limitations, and objectives. These guidelines ensure the testing process is controlled and does not disrupt normal operations. RoE specifies what systems are in scope, acceptable testing hours, methods to be used, and the protocol for communication. Clear RoE helps manage risks associated with penetration testing, such as unintentional system outages or data corruption and ensures that the test aligns with organizational goals.

**Command and Control (C2):** Command and Control (C2) refers to the infrastructure and mechanisms used by attackers to maintain communication with compromised systems. During a penetration test, establishing a C2 channel allows testers to simulate how an attacker would remotely control and exfiltrate data from an infiltrated network. Understanding and detecting C2 activities are vital for effective defense against advanced threats. This concept is critical for evaluating an organization's ability to recognize and respond to ongoing intrusions.

**Clear Box and Opaque Box Testing:** Clear box testing, also known as white box testing, involves conducting penetration tests with full knowledge of the target environment, including network diagrams, source code, and access to internal systems. This approach allows testers to conduct a thorough and detailed analysis. In contrast, opaque box testing, or black box testing, simulates an external attacker without prior knowledge of the internal structure. Both methods provide valuable insights, with clear box testing focusing on internal security posture and opaque box testing assessing external defenses.

**Physical Penetration Testing:** Physical penetration testing evaluates the security of an organization's physical premises. Testers attempt to bypass physical security controls, such as locks, badges, and security guards, to gain unauthorized access to facilities. This type of testing can reveal vulnerabilities in physical security measures, such as tailgating, lock picking, or exploiting social engineering tactics to enter restricted areas. The findings help enhance the security of physical assets and protect against real-world threats that could impact cyberinfrastructure.

**Scope of Testing:** The testing scope defines a penetration test's boundaries and focus areas. It determines which systems, applications, and networks are to be tested, ensuring that the assessment aligns with the organization's risk priorities. A well-defined scope helps avoid unnecessary disruptions and thoroughly evaluates critical assets. It also sets expectations for the depth and breadth of the test, guiding the testers in identifying the most relevant vulnerabilities.

**Remediation:** Remediation involves addressing and fixing the vulnerabilities identified during a penetration test. This step is crucial for improving the organization's security posture. Remediation can include applying patches, reconfiguring systems, enhancing security policies, or improving employee training programs. Effective remediation not only mitigates identified risks but also helps prevent future vulnerabilities. The process must be systematic and prioritized based on the severity and potential impact of each finding.

**Legal and Ethical Considerations:** Legal and ethical considerations are paramount in penetration testing to ensure compliance with laws and regulations. Testers must operate within the legal boundaries and adhere to ethical standards, such as obtaining proper authorization before conducting tests. These considerations protect both the organization and the testers from legal repercussions. Maintaining confidentiality and integrity in handling sensitive information obtained during tests is crucial. Legal frameworks, such as data protection laws, must be considered to ensure penetration testing does not violate regulatory requirements.

## Importance and Relevance

Penetration testing is a critical practice in today's cybersecurity landscape. As cyber threats evolve in complexity and frequency, robust security measures become increasingly essential. Penetration testing comprehensively evaluates an organization's defenses, providing insights beyond surface-level assessments. By understanding the importance and relevance of penetration testing, organizations can better prepare for and mitigate the risks posed by cyber adversaries. The following points illustrate why penetration testing is indispensable in modern cybersecurity.

**Identifying Hidden Vulnerabilities:** Penetration testing helps uncover vulnerabilities that have not been detected through routine security assessments. Automated tools can only go so far in identifying weaknesses, but a skilled penetration tester can find hidden flaws that might be overlooked. These hidden vulnerabilities could be exploited by attackers, leading to significant breaches. Penetration testing provides a thorough evaluation, ensuring that even the most obscure vulnerabilities are identified and addressed.

**Validating Security Controls:** Regular penetration testing validates the effectiveness of existing security controls. It assesses whether the security measures function as intended and can withstand an attack. This validation is crucial for ensuring that investments in security are effective and provide the necessary protection. It also helps identify areas where controls need to be strengthened or updated.

CHAPTER 18    PENETRATION TESTING

**Enhancing Incident Response:** Penetration testing prepares organizations for real-world attacks by improving their incident response capabilities. The organization's response to simulated attacks is evaluated during a penetration test. This evaluation helps identify gaps in incident response procedures and provides an opportunity to refine and enhance these processes. Effective incident response is critical for minimizing the impact of actual security incidents.

**Meeting Compliance Requirements:** Many regulatory frameworks and industry standards mandate regular penetration testing. Compliance with these requirements is essential for avoiding legal and financial penalties. Penetration testing demonstrates that an organization is proactive in identifying and mitigating risks, which are often critical to regulatory compliance. It also assures stakeholders that the organization is committed to maintaining high security.

**Improving Security Awareness:** Penetration testing often includes social engineering components, which test employees' awareness and adherence to security policies. These tests can reveal weaknesses in employee training and highlight the need for enhanced security education. By improving security awareness among staff, organizations can reduce the likelihood of successful social engineering attacks. A well-informed workforce is a key defense against many types of cyber threats.

**Protecting Reputation and Trust:** A successful cyber attack can significantly damage an organization's reputation and erode trust with customers and partners. Penetration testing helps prevent such incidents by identifying and mitigating vulnerabilities before they can be exploited. By proactively addressing security weaknesses, organizations can maintain their reputation and ensure they are seen as reliable and trustworthy. This protection of reputation is crucial in maintaining competitive advantage and customer loyalty.

**Reducing Financial Risk:** Cyber attacks can result in significant financial losses due to data breaches, downtime, and remediation costs. Penetration testing helps reduce these financial risks by identifying vulnerabilities that could lead to costly incidents. By addressing these vulnerabilities proactively, organizations can avoid the substantial expenses associated with cyber attacks. This proactive approach is a cost-effective way to manage and mitigate financial risks related to cybersecurity.

**Staying Ahead of Attackers:** The cyber threat landscape constantly evolves, with new vulnerabilities and attack techniques emerging regularly. Penetration testing helps organizations stay ahead of attackers by continuously assessing and improving their security posture. This proactive approach ensures that defenses are always up-to-date-and capable of countering the latest threats. Staying ahead of attackers is crucial for maintaining a robust security framework.

**Supporting Business Continuity:** Penetration testing contributes to business continuity by protecting critical systems and data. A successful cyber attack can disrupt business operations and result in significant downtime. By identifying and mitigating vulnerabilities, penetration testing helps ensure that business operations can continue without interruption. This support for business continuity is vital for maintaining productivity and minimizing operational risks.

**Enhancing Risk Management:** Penetration testing is a key component of a comprehensive risk management strategy. It provides detailed insights into potential threats and vulnerabilities, allowing organizations to prioritize and address the most significant risks. This informed approach to risk management helps organizations allocate resources effectively and ensure that the most critical issues are addressed promptly. Enhanced risk management leads to a more resilient security posture.

**Strengthening Customer Confidence:** Customers expect their data to be protected by the organizations they interact with. Penetration testing demonstrates a commitment to security and assures that customer data is safeguarded. This commitment to security strengthens customer confidence and can be a differentiating factor in a competitive market. Building and maintaining customer trust is essential for long-term business success.

**Facilitating Continuous Improvement:** Penetration testing is not a one-time activity but an ongoing process. Regular testing provides continuous feedback on the effectiveness of security measures and highlights areas for improvement. This continuous improvement process is essential for adapting to new threats and ensuring security measures remain effective. Organizations can build a dynamic and resilient security framework by embracing continuous improvement.

# Risks of Not Implementing the Control

Penetration testing is crucial for identifying and addressing vulnerabilities within an organization's IT infrastructure. Without regular and thorough penetration testing, organizations expose themselves to risks that could have severe implications for their security posture, financial stability, and overall operational effectiveness. The following points detail the key risks associated with not implementing penetration testing, underscoring the importance of this proactive security measure.

**Undetected Vulnerabilities:** Without penetration testing, vulnerabilities within the system may remain undiscovered. Attackers can exploit these vulnerabilities, leading to unauthorized access, data breaches, and system compromises. The presence of undetected vulnerabilities significantly increases the risk of a successful cyber attack, which can have devastating effects on the organization's operations and reputation.

**Ineffective Security Controls:** Security measures not regularly tested may not function as intended. Penetration testing validates the effectiveness of these controls by simulating real-world attacks. Without this validation, organizations cannot be certain that their security controls can thwart actual threats, leaving them vulnerable to breaches and other security incidents.

**Compliance Failures:** Many regulatory frameworks and industry standards require regular penetration testing. Failure to conduct these tests can result in non-compliance, leading to legal penalties, fines, and a loss of certifications. Non-compliance can also damage an organization's reputation and erode trust with customers and partners, further impacting business operations.

**Inadequate Incident Response:** Organizations not performing penetration testing may have gaps in their incident response procedures. These gaps can hinder the organization's ability to detect, respond to, and mitigate security incidents effectively. Effective incident response is critical for minimizing the impact of cyber attacks, and penetration testing helps identify and address weaknesses in these processes.

**Increased Financial Risk:** Cyber attacks can result in significant financial losses due to data breaches, operational disruptions, and remediation costs. Penetration testing helps identify and mitigate vulnerabilities that could lead to these costly incidents. By not implementing penetration testing, organizations expose themselves to a higher risk of financial losses associated with cyber attacks.

**Reputation Damage:** A successful cyber attack can severely damage an organization's reputation. Customers and partners expect robust security measures to protect their data and interests. Failure to implement penetration testing increases the likelihood of a breach, which can lead to loss of trust, customer attrition, and long-term reputational harm.

**Loss of Competitive Advantage:** Security is a key differentiator in today's digital economy. Organizations not prioritizing penetration testing may fall behind their competitors in terms of security maturity. This can lead to losing competitive advantage as customers and partners seek more secure alternatives.

**Operational Disruptions:** Cyber attacks can cause significant disruptions to business operations. Penetration testing helps identify vulnerabilities that could be exploited to cause such disruptions. Organizations risk operational downtime by not conducting these tests, which can affect productivity, revenue, and customer satisfaction.

**Intellectual Property Theft:** Organizations possess valuable intellectual property (IP) that cyber attackers can target. Without penetration testing, vulnerabilities that could lead to IP theft may go unnoticed. IP loss can have serious consequences, including loss of competitive edge and financial damage.

**Data Breaches:** Data breaches can expose sensitive information, leading to privacy violations and regulatory penalties. Penetration testing helps identify weaknesses that could be exploited to breach data. Without these tests, organizations are at a higher risk of experiencing data breaches, which can have long-term legal and financial implications.

**Insider Threats:** Penetration testing often includes scenarios that simulate insider threats. These tests help assess the organization's ability to detect and respond to malicious actions by employees or contractors. Insider threats may go undetected without penetration testing, posing a significant risk to the organization's security.

**Strategic Misalignment:** Organizations not conducting penetration testing may have a misaligned security strategy. Regular testing provides valuable insights that help refine and improve security measures. Without these insights, organizations may invest in ineffective or misaligned security initiatives, reducing overall security effectiveness.

# What Questions Should You Ask?

To effectively implement a robust penetration testing program, cybersecurity leaders must start by asking the right questions. These questions help define the testing process's scope, objectives, and methodologies, ensuring that it aligns with the organization's security goals and risk management strategies. By systematically addressing these critical inquiries, leaders can build a comprehensive framework that effectively identifies and mitigates potential vulnerabilities. The following questions are essential for forming the basis of this important work.

**What are the specific objectives of the penetration test?** Defining the objectives is crucial for setting clear goals and expectations for the penetration testing process. Objectives might include identifying vulnerabilities, testing the effectiveness of security controls, or assessing the organization's incident response capabilities. Clear objectives ensure the testing is focused and aligned with the organization's security priorities. This clarity helps measure the success of the penetration test and understand its impact on the overall security posture.

**Which systems and assets are in scope for the penetration test?** Identifying the systems and assets that will be tested is a fundamental step in planning a penetration test. This includes determining which network segments, applications, and devices should be included. A well-defined scope ensures that critical assets are thoroughly tested while avoiding unnecessary risks to less critical systems. This approach helps prioritize resources and focus on the most significant areas of potential vulnerability.

**What are the rules of engagement for the penetration test?** Establishing rules of engagement (RoE) is essential for conducting penetration tests safely and effectively. RoE outlines the parameters within which testers must operate, including acceptable hours for testing, notification protocols, and specific prohibited attack methods. Clear RoE helps prevent unintended disruptions to business operations and ensures the testing process is controlled and predictable. This helps protect both the organization and the testers from potential risks.

**Who will conduct the penetration test?** Deciding whether to use internal resources or external vendors for penetration testing. External vendors bring an objective perspective and specialized expertise, while internal teams may have a more profound knowledge of the organization's

CHAPTER 18  PENETRATION TESTING

systems. The choice depends on the specific needs and resources of the organization. Ensuring that the testers have the necessary skills and experience is crucial for the effectiveness of the test.

**How will sensitive data be protected during the test?** Protecting sensitive data during penetration testing is paramount to prevent accidental leaks or breaches. This includes ensuring that data access is controlled and sensitive information is handled securely. Clear protocols for data protection help mitigate the risks associated with penetration testing. This focus on data security is essential for maintaining trust and compliance with regulatory requirements.

**What is the remediation process for identified vulnerabilities?** Defining the remediation process is critical for addressing vulnerabilities discovered during the penetration test. This includes prioritizing vulnerabilities based on their severity and potential impact and assigning responsibilities for remediation. A clear and structured remediation process ensures that identified issues are addressed promptly and effectively. This approach helps continuously improve the organization's security posture.

**How will the findings be communicated, and to whom?** Effective communication of penetration test findings is essential for ensuring that the right stakeholders are informed and that appropriate actions are taken. This includes preparing detailed reports and presentations for executives, IT staff, and other relevant parties. Clear and concise communication helps in understanding the findings' implications and making informed decisions about remediation and future testing. This transparency is key to fostering a culture of security within the organization.

**What are the metrics for measuring the success of the penetration test?** Establishing metrics for success helps in evaluating the effectiveness of the penetration test. Metrics might include the number of vulnerabilities discovered, the time taken to remediate issues, and improvements in security controls. These metrics provide a benchmark for assessing the test's impact and planning future security initiatives. This data-driven approach ensures the penetration testing program is continuously refined and improved.

**How frequently will penetration tests be conducted?** Determining the frequency of penetration tests is essential for maintaining a proactive security posture. Regular testing helps identify new vulnerabilities and assess the effectiveness of remediation efforts. The frequency of tests should be based on factors such as changes in the IT environment, emerging threats, and regulatory requirements. Consistent and periodic testing is crucial for staying ahead of potential threats.

**What is the budget for the penetration testing program?** Allocating a budget for penetration testing ensures that sufficient resources are available for thorough and effective testing. This includes costs for tools, personnel, and external vendor services. A well-defined budget helps plan and execute the testing program without financial constraints. This financial planning is vital for sustaining a robust penetration testing initiative.

**How will the organization handle false positives and false negatives?** Addressing false positives and negatives is important for ensuring the accuracy and reliability of the penetration test results. False positives can lead to wasted resources, while false negatives can leave vulnerabilities undetected. Establishing procedures for validating findings helps distinguish between real threats and benign issues. This validation process is essential for maintaining the credibility of the penetration testing program.

**What legal and ethical considerations must be addressed?** Ensuring compliance with legal and ethical standards is critical for conducting penetration tests responsibly. This includes obtaining proper authorization, respecting privacy, and adhering to regulatory requirements. Legal and ethical considerations help protect the organization and the testers from potential liabilities. This adherence to standards is fundamental for maintaining the integrity and professionalism of the penetration testing process.

# Recommended Training

A robust training program is essential for equipping IT/cybersecurity staff and employees with the knowledge and skills to protect the organization against cyber threats. Training should be tailored to address the specific roles and responsibilities of different groups within the organization, ensuring everyone understands their part in maintaining a secure environment. Comprehensive training programs help reduce the risk of cyber incidents by enhancing awareness, improving technical skills, and fostering a security-conscious culture. The following training recommendations address the diverse needs of IT staff, administrators, and general employees, contributing to a more resilient security posture.

**Security Awareness Training:** All employees should attend security awareness training. This training should cover the basics of cybersecurity, including recognizing phishing emails, creating strong passwords, and understanding the importance of data protection. The outcome of this training is an increased awareness of common threats and how to avoid them. Educating employees on these topics significantly reduces the risk of successful social engineering attacks and other user-targeted threats.

**Phishing Simulation Training:** IT and cybersecurity staff and all other employees should participate in phishing simulation exercises. These exercises involve sending simulated phishing emails to employees to test their ability to recognize and appropriately respond to phishing attempts. The training includes reviewing the results and providing feedback on identifying and handling phishing emails. This practical approach helps employees develop a critical eye for suspicious communications, reducing the risk of credential theft and other phishing-related incidents.

**Incident Response Training:** This training is crucial for IT and cybersecurity staff. It should include the steps to take during a security incident, such as identifying the incident, containing the breach, eradicating the threat, and recovering affected systems. The outcome is a well-prepared team that can respond swiftly and effectively to security incidents. Proper incident response training reduces the impact of cyber attacks by ensuring that incidents are managed efficiently and effectively.

**Advanced Penetration Testing Training:** Cybersecurity professionals and IT staff responsible for security testing should undergo training. This training covers techniques and tools used by attackers to exploit vulnerabilities and methodologies for conducting thorough penetration tests. The outcome is a team capable of identifying and addressing security weaknesses before attackers can exploit them. Enhanced penetration testing skills strengthen security posture and proactive threat mitigation.

**Secure Coding Practices Training:** Developers and software engineers should participate in secure coding practices training. This training focuses on writing code resistant to common vulnerabilities, such as SQL injection, cross-site scripting (XSS), and buffer overflows. The outcome is a development team that can create more secure applications, reducing the risk of security flaws in software products. Secure coding practices help prevent many types of attacks and improve the overall security of the organization's software.

**Network Security Training:** Network administrators and IT staff should receive training on network security principles and best practices. This includes configuring firewalls, implementing intrusion detection and prevention systems, and managing network access controls. The outcome is a team that can protect the organization's network infrastructure from external and internal threats. Network security training helps reduce the risk of unauthorized access and network-based attacks.

**Data Protection and Privacy Training:** All employees, especially those handling sensitive data, should undergo data protection and privacy training. This training covers data handling best practices, regulatory requirements, and the importance of safeguarding personal and sensitive information. The outcome is a workforce that understands the significance of data protection and is equipped to handle data securely. Effective data protection practices help prevent data breaches and ensure compliance with privacy regulations.

**Social Engineering Defense Training:** All employees should receive this training to help them recognize and respond to social engineering attacks. The training includes identifying common tactics attackers use, such as pretexting, baiting, and tailgating. The outcome is an increased ability to detect and thwart social engineering attempts. By training employees to be vigilant against these attacks, the organization can reduce the risk of security breaches initiated through human manipulation.

**Mobile Device Security Training:** With the increasing use of mobile devices for work purposes, training employees on mobile device security is essential. This training covers best practices for securing mobile devices, such as using encryption, updating software regularly, and avoiding public Wi-Fi for sensitive transactions. The outcome is a workforce that can securely use mobile devices for business activities. Improved mobile device security helps protect sensitive information accessed or stored on these devices.

**Cloud Security Training:** IT and cybersecurity staff should receive training on cloud security principles and practices. This includes understanding cloud service models, securing cloud infrastructure, and managing access to cloud resources. The outcome is a team that can effectively secure cloud environments and ensure the safe use of cloud services. Cloud security training helps mitigate risks associated with cloud computing, such as data breaches and misconfigurations.

**Compliance and Regulatory Training:** Employees, especially those in roles related to governance, risk, and compliance, should undergo training on relevant cybersecurity regulations and standards. This training covers requirements such as GDPR, HIPAA, and PCI DSS, as well as the steps needed to achieve and maintain compliance. The outcome is an informed workforce that can ensure the organization meets its legal and regulatory obligations. Compliance training helps avoid legal penalties and enhances the organization's reputation for security and privacy.

**Physical Security Training:** Physical security training is essential for all employees to understand the importance of securing physical access to the organization's premises. This training includes best practices for access control, visitor management, and securing sensitive areas. The outcome is a workforce that is vigilant about physical security threats and knows how to prevent unauthorized access. Physical security training helps protect the organization's physical assets and complements its cybersecurity efforts.

# Actionable Recommendations

Implementing a robust penetration testing program requires a strategic approach, careful planning, and continuous improvement. Specific, actionable recommendations must be followed to ensure the program is effective and aligned with organizational goals. These recommendations encompass various aspects of penetration testing, from defining the scope and selecting the right personnel to ensuring data protection and maintaining compliance. The following points provide detailed guidance on implementing a comprehensive and effective penetration testing strategy.

**Define Clear Objectives:** Establishing clear objectives is essential for guiding the penetration testing process. Objectives should align with the organization's overall security goals, such as identifying vulnerabilities, assessing the effectiveness of security controls, and improving incident response capabilities. Clear objectives ensure the testing is focused and relevant, providing valuable insights that drive security improvements. This clarity helps set expectations and measure the success of the testing efforts.

**Determine Scope and Boundaries:** Clearly define the scope and boundaries of the penetration test to ensure that critical assets are thoroughly evaluated. The scope should include specific systems, applications, and networks to be tested and exclude areas that are out of scope to prevent unnecessary risks. Defining the scope helps prioritize resources and focus efforts on the most critical areas, ensuring comprehensive coverage of the organization's key assets.

**Establish Rules of Engagement:** Develop rules of engagement (RoE) to outline the parameters within which testers will operate. RoE should specify acceptable testing hours, communication protocols, and prohibited attack methods. Clear RoE helps prevent unintended disruptions to business operations and ensures that the testing is conducted safely and ethically. This structured approach protects the organization and the testers from potential risks and misunderstandings.

**Select Qualified Personnel:** Choose qualified personnel to conduct the penetration testing, whether internal staff or external vendors. Ensure testers have the necessary skills, experience, and certifications to perform thorough and effective tests. Using qualified personnel enhances the credibility and reliability of the test results, assuring that the identified vulnerabilities are accurate and relevant. This selection process is crucial for the success of the penetration testing program.

**Develop a Comprehensive Testing Plan:** Create a detailed testing plan that outlines the methodology, tools, and techniques to be used during the penetration test. The plan should include reconnaissance, vulnerability identification, exploitation, and reporting steps. A well-structured testing plan ensures that all aspects of the penetration test are covered systematically, providing a clear roadmap for testers to follow. This planning helps in achieving consistent and repeatable results.

**Protect Sensitive Data:** Implement measures to protect sensitive data during the penetration testing. This includes ensuring that data access is controlled and sensitive information is handled securely. Data protection protocols help mitigate the risks associated with penetration testing, such as accidental leaks or breaches. Ensuring data security is essential for maintaining trust and compliance with regulatory requirements.

**Prioritize Remediation Efforts:** Establish a process for prioritizing and addressing vulnerabilities identified during the penetration test. This process should be based on each vulnerability's severity and potential impact, with critical issues addressed first. Effective prioritization ensures that the most significant risks are mitigated promptly, improving the organization's security posture. This approach helps efficiently allocate resources to where they are needed most.

**Communicate Findings Effectively:** Prepare detailed reports and presentations to communicate the penetration test findings to relevant stakeholders. Ensure that the communication is clear, concise, and tailored to the audience, whether they are executives, IT staff, or other parties. Effective communication helps stakeholders understand the implications of the findings and supports informed decision-making. This transparency is critical to driving security improvements and fostering a culture of security awareness.

**Measure Success with Metrics:** Establish metrics to evaluate the success of the penetration testing program. Metrics might include the number of vulnerabilities discovered, the time taken to remediate issues, and improvements in security controls. These metrics provide a benchmark for assessing the impact of testing efforts and planning future security initiatives. A data-driven approach ensures continuous refinement and improvement of the penetration testing program.

**Schedule Regular Testing:** Conduct penetration tests regularly to maintain a proactive security posture. Regular testing helps identify new vulnerabilities and assesses the effectiveness of remediation efforts over time. The frequency of tests should be determined based on factors such as changes in the IT environment, emerging threats, and regulatory requirements. Consistent and periodic testing is crucial for staying ahead of potential threats.

**Allocate Adequate Budget:** Ensure a sufficient budget for the penetration testing program. This includes tools, personnel, training, and external vendor services costs. A well-defined budget helps plan and execute the testing program without financial constraints, ensuring it is comprehensive and effective. Financial planning is vital for sustaining a robust penetration testing initiative.

**Address Legal and Ethical Considerations:** Ensure compliance with legal and ethical standards during the penetration testing. Obtain proper authorization, respect privacy, and adhere to relevant regulations to avoid legal and ethical issues. Legal and ethical considerations help protect the organization and the testers from potential liabilities, maintaining the integrity and professionalism of the penetration testing program.

# Simplified Security Controls (SSC)

Security controls are essential for any organization seeking to protect its digital and physical assets from cyber threats. Tailoring these controls to fit the specific needs of your business environment is crucial, as it ensures that the protection mechanisms are relevant and effective against the specific risks your organization faces. There are numerous sources to draw these controls from, including the well-regarded CIS Top 18, which provides a robust framework for crafting defensive strategies. The recommendations presented in this book are based on the CIS controls, among others, offering a comprehensive guide that can be adapted to serve a wide range of security needs. Before implementing these controls, it is vital to thoroughly review their design to ensure they align with your strategic objectives and operational practices. Additionally, after deployment, it is imperative to regularly test the controls to verify their effectiveness and to make necessary adjustments. This ensures that the controls continue to function as intended, safeguarding your organization against emerging threats and changing conditions.

## CHAPTER 18  PENETRATION TESTING

## CONTROL 1: ESTABLISH AND MAINTAIN A PENETRATION TESTING PROGRAM

**Control Objective:** To develop and sustain a comprehensive penetration testing program appropriate for the enterprise's size, complexity, and maturity. This program should encompass various scopes, including network, web applications, APIs, hosted services, and physical premises controls. It should outline frequency, limitations, points of contact, remediation processes, and retrospective requirements.

**Implementation Steps:**

**1.1. Program Development:** Establish a detailed penetration testing program that defines the scope, including network, web applications, APIs, hosted services, and physical premises controls.

**1.2. Define Frequency:** Set a regular schedule for penetration testing that aligns with the organization's risk profile and compliance requirements, ensuring tests are conducted at least annually.

**1.3. Establish Limitations:** Clearly define acceptable testing hours, prohibited attack types, and other limitations to ensure testing does not disrupt business operations.

**1.4. Designate Points of Contact:** Identify and designate specific individuals or teams responsible for overseeing the penetration testing process and addressing any issues.

**1.5. Remediation Process:** Develop a structured process for routing findings internally, prioritizing remediation efforts based on severity and impact.

**1.6. Retrospective Analysis:** Conduct retrospective reviews of penetration tests to assess their effectiveness and identify areas for improvement.

**Expected Outcome:** A well-defined penetration testing program ensures systematic identification and mitigation of vulnerabilities, enhancing the organization's overall security posture.

CHAPTER 18   PENETRATION TESTING

## CONTROL 2: PERFORM PERIODIC EXTERNAL PENETRATION TESTS

**Control Objective:** Conduct regular external penetration tests assessing the organization's exposure to external threats and identifying exploitable vulnerabilities. These tests should include a comprehensive reconnaissance of the enterprise and its environment.

**Implementation Steps:**

**2.1. External Testing Schedule:** Schedule external penetration tests at least annually, ensuring alignment with organizational risk and compliance needs.

**2.2. Reconnaissance:** Perform thorough reconnaissance to gather information on the enterprise's external footprint and identify potential entry points.

**2.3. Select Qualified Parties:** Engage qualified external penetration testing professionals with the necessary skills and experience.

**2.4. Testing Methodology:** Utilize clear box (white box) and opaque box (black box) testing methodologies to evaluate comprehensively.

**2.5. Reporting:** Develop detailed reports outlining discovered vulnerabilities, potential impacts, and recommended remediation steps.

**Expected Outcome:** Periodic external penetration tests provide insights into external vulnerabilities, enabling proactive risk mitigation and enhanced security defenses.

CHAPTER 18   PENETRATION TESTING

## CONTROL 3: REMEDIATE PENETRATION TEST FINDINGS

**Control Objective:** To ensure that vulnerabilities identified during penetration tests are remediated per the organization's remediation policies and priorities.

**Implementation Steps:**

**3.1. Remediation Policy:** Establish and maintain a remediation policy that outlines the criteria for prioritizing and addressing vulnerabilities.

**3.2. Assign Responsibilities:** Designate teams or individuals responsible for remediating identified vulnerabilities.

**3.3. Remediation Timeline:** Set clear timelines for addressing vulnerabilities based on their severity and potential impact.

**3.4. Verification:** Conduct follow-up testing to verify that vulnerabilities have been effectively remediated.

**3.5. Documentation:** Maintain detailed records of remediation efforts, including actions taken and outcomes achieved.

**Expected Outcome:** Effective remediation of penetration test findings reduces the risk of exploitation, ensuring a stronger security posture.

## CONTROL 4: VALIDATE SECURITY MEASURES

**Control Objective:** To validate and enhance the effectiveness of security measures following each penetration test, ensuring that defenses can detect and mitigate similar future threats.

**Implementation Steps:**

**4.1. Review Findings:** Analyze the results of each penetration test to understand the effectiveness of existing security measures.

CHAPTER 18   PENETRATION TESTING

**4.2. Modify Rulesets:** Update security rulesets, configurations, and capabilities to detect and respond to the techniques used during the penetration test.

**4.3. Enhance Monitoring:** Implement or improve monitoring and detection mechanisms based on the test findings.

**4.4. Training and Awareness:** Provide additional training to relevant staff based on the new techniques and vulnerabilities identified.

**4.5. Revalidate:** Conduct validation tests to ensure the modifications effectively enhance security measures.

**Expected Outcome:** Validating and refining security measures ensures continuous improvement in the organization's ability to detect and mitigate threats.

## CONTROL 5: PERFORM PERIODIC INTERNAL PENETRATION TESTS

**Control Objective:** Conduct regular internal penetration tests to identify vulnerabilities from an insider perspective, ensuring that internal systems and processes are secure.

**Implementation Steps:**

**5.1. Internal Testing Schedule:** Internal penetration tests are conducted annually to identify internal network and system vulnerabilities.

**5.2. Testing Methodology:** Clear box (white box) and opaque box (black box) testing methodologies comprehensively evaluate internal security.

**5.3. Simulate Insider Threats:** Include scenarios that simulate insider threats to assess the organization's ability to detect and respond to internal attacks.

**5.4. Reporting:** Develop detailed reports highlighting internal vulnerabilities and their potential impacts and recommended remediation strategies.

**5.5. Remediation and Validation:** Ensure identified vulnerabilities are remediated and validated through follow-up testing.

**Expected Outcome:** Regular internal penetration tests enhance the security of internal systems and processes, reducing the risk of insider threats and improving overall security posture.

# Index

## A

Access control lists (ACLs), 340, 341, 344, 392
Access control management
  audit trails, 160
  authentication, 159
  authorization, 160
  centralized/streamline access control, 179
  cybersecurity, 161–163
  cybersecurity leaders, 168, 169, 171
  granting access, 177
  least privilege, 157, 158
  MFA, 155, 178
  PAM, 156, 159
  RBAC, 155, 180
  recommendations, 174, 175
  revoking access, 177
  risks, 164–166
  service accounts, 160
  SoD, 160
  SSC, 176
  training, 171–173, 389
Access controls and authentication mechanisms, 355
Account management
  account auditing, 131
  account logging, 132
  administrative accounts, 130
  centralize account management, 154
  credential stuffing, 132
  cybersecurity, 132–135
  disabling dormant accounts, 152
  dormant accounts, 131
  inventory, 150
  MFA, 131
  password policies, 128, 130
  recommendations, 146–149
  restricting administrator privileges, 152
  risks, 136–139
  service accounts, 130, 153
  social engineering, 132
  SSC, 149
  SSO, 128, 131
  training programs, 143–146
  unauthorized access, 127
  unauthorized access/cyber threats, 140–143
  unique passwords, 151
  user credentials, 130

# INDEX

ACLs, *see* Access control lists (ACLs)
Administrative devices, 346
Advanced Configuration and Management training, 358
Advanced configuration management tools, 363
Advanced penetration testing training, 544
Advanced persistent threats (APTs), 277, 383, 516, 529, 532
Advanced threat protection (ATP), 249, 268, 269
Anomaly detection, 217, 377, 514
Application architectures, 463, 483
Application penetration testing, 465
Application software security, 463, 464, 466
  bug bounty programs, 469
  dynamic analysis, 468
  essentials
    competitive advantage, 472
    maintain customer trust, 471
    mitigate attack vectors, 470
    prevent financial loss, 471
    protect sensitive data, 470
    regulations and standards, 471
    secure development practices, 472
    secure integration, 472
    support business continuity, 471
    technological advancements, 471
  penetration testing, 468
  questionnaires
    compliance with industry regulations and standards, 477
    effective monitoring and logging, 478
    effective vulnerability management, 477
    handling security incidents and breaches, 477
    insider threats, 478
    potential security threats, 478
    regular security assessments and penetration testing, 477
    SDLC, 476
    secure coding practices, 476
    security challenges, 478
    security requirements, 476
    third-party components and libraries, 477
  risks of not implement
    attack surface, 475
    data breaches, 473
    financial losses, 473
    intellectual property (IP) theft, 474
    legal liability, 475

## INDEX

loss of competitive edge, 475
malware infections, 474
operational inefficiency, 475
regulatory penalties, 474
reputational damage, 474
service disruption, 474, 475
SBOM, 469
secure application development process, 467
secure coding practices, 468
security champions, 469
severity rating system, 469
SSC (*see* Simplified security controls (SSC))
SSDF, 470
static analysis, 468
third-party components, 468
threat modeling, 467
vulnerability management, 467
APTs, *see* Advanced persistent threats (APTs)
Artificial intelligence (AI), 2, 280
ATP, *see* Advanced threat protection (ATP)
Audit log management
   access control logs, 217
   adequate storage, 238, 239
   anomaly detection, 217
   audit logs, 212, 214
   centralized logging, 212, 216, 242, 243
   collect command-line, 242
   collect logs, 238
   collect URL request, 241
   comprehensive logging strategies, 219, 221, 222
   conduct reviews, 244
   cyber threats, 225–228
   detailed audit logging, 240
   DNS query logs, 218, 240, 241
   forensic investigation, 216
   functions, 214
   log analysis, 216
   management process, 237
   recommendations, 232–235
   retain audit logs, 243
   retention policies, 217
   risks, 222–225
   service providers, 244
   SSC, 236
   standardize time synchronization, 239
   system logs, 211
   time synchronization, 213, 217
   training programs, 229–232
Automating network monitoring, 362

## B

BCP, *see* Business Continuity Plan (BCP)
BEC, *see* Business email compromise (BEC)
BEC attacks, 406, 410
Behavioral analysis, 249, 278, 281, 423

# INDEX

Bring Your Device (BYOD) policies, 5, 6
Bug bounty programs, 469–470, 484
Business Continuity Plan (BCP), 79, 315, 442–443, 451
Business email compromise (BEC), 247, 250, 251, 257, 406, 410
BYOD policies, *see* Bring Your Device (BYOD) policies

## C

California Consumer Privacy Act (CCPA), 2, 289, 298, 317, 382, 388
CCPA, *see* California Consumer Privacy Act (CCPA)
Center for Internet Security (CIS), 23, 52, 85, 109, 115, 116, 128, 129, 150, 176, 203, 204, 236, 270, 302, 332, 364, 394, 427, 455, 472, 485, 520, 549
Centralized asset management system, 49
CIA, *see* Confidentiality, integrity and availability (CIA)
CIS, *see* Center for Internet Security (CIS)
CIS Password Policy Guide, 128
Clear box testing, 532, 533
Cloud-based technologies, 9, 39, 68, 78, 104, 112, 341
Cloud security, 376

Cloud security training, 78–79, 297–298, 390, 481, 545
Command and control (C2), 218, 532
Command-line audit logs, 213, 218
Commercial tools, 340, 342
Common Vulnerabilities and Exposures (CVE), 183, 185, 186
Common Vulnerability Scoring System (CVSS), 183, 185, 186, 194, 201
Communication plan, 503, 518
Compliance and regulatory training, 359, 545
Compliance-related training, 407
Comprehensive documentation, 341, 363
Comprehensive incident response plan, 317, 393–394
Comprehensive network monitoring and defense strategy, 373
Comprehensive network security strategy, 339
Comprehensive service provider management policy, 436
Comprehensive training programs, 51, 196, 229, 325, 357, 421, 449, 483, 514, 543
Comprehensive visibility, 49, 349, 372

# INDEX

Confidentiality, integrity and availability (CIA), 30, 60, 65, 309
Configuration management, 34, 98, 116, 203, 346, 363
Continuous vulnerability management
    advanced tools/procedures, 183
    authenticated scans, 185
    automated patch management, 206, 207
    automated vulnerability scans, 208, 209
    CVE, 185
    CVSS, 185
    cyber attackers, 181
    cybersecurity, 187–189
    detected vulnerabilities, 210
    enterprises, 183
    implementation, 193, 195, 196
    IOCs, 186
    layered approach, 182
    patch management, 185
    recommendations, 200–203
    remediation process, 205
    risks, 190–192
    scaling remediation, 182
    SCAP, 186
    SSC, 203
    training, 196–199
    vendors, 182
    vulnerability, 184
    vulnerability management process, 204
    zero-day exploit, 184
Contractual security clauses, 439
Cryptographic hashes, 35–36
C2, *see* Command and control (C2)
CVE, *see* Common Vulnerabilities and Exposures (CVE)
CVSS, *see* Common Vulnerability Scoring System (CVSS)
Cyber espionage, 384
Cyber insurance, 259, 284, 440–441
Cybersecurity Awareness training, 327, 359, 452
Cybersecurity best practices training, 389

# D

Data breach, 41, 65, 69, 75, 106, 137, 165, 190–191, 256, 287–288, 352, 381, 415, 444, 473, 508, 539
Data Execution Prevention (DEP), 306
Data exfiltration, 314
Data handling and protection, 410
Data loss prevention (DLP), 58, 82, 95
Data protection
    access control lists, 87
    access control systems, 62
    access management, 74
    asset management, 60
    classification, 58, 73
    cloud security, 68

INDEX

Data protection (cont.)
    competitive markets, 68
    cost savings, 67
    customer trust, 66
    cyber threats, 60
    data breaches, 65
    data classification, 61, 90
    data disposal, 63
    data inventory/mapping, 64, 86
    data lifecycle, 57
    data management process, 85
    data retention/disposal
        practices, 58
    data retention policy, 63
    data sharing, 66
    dispose data, 89
    DLM, 61
    DLP, 63, 95
    document data flows, 91
    employee training, 58
    encryption, 62, 76
    end-user devices, 90
    enforce data retension, 88
    future-proofing, 68
    holistic approach, 57
    processing and storage
        systems, 94
    recommendations, 79–84
    regulatory compliance, 66
    remote work, 67
    removable media, 92
    reputation, 67
    risks, 69–72
    safe handling, 73
    SCM, 64
    security, 65
    sensitive data, 92, 93, 96
    software management, 59
    SSC, 85
    strategic planning/
        implementation, 73
    threats, 66
    training, 76–79
    unauthorized software, 59
Data protection and privacy
    training, 388, 544
Data recovery
    air-gapped backup, 315
    automated backups, 334
    backups, 311, 313
    backup verification, 315
    BCP, 315
    cloud-based backup
        solutions, 311
    cybersecurity, 316–318
    definition, 313
    enterprises, 309
    implement practices, 322–324
    isolated instance, 336
    malware infection, 310
    monitoring systems/
        networks, 312
    procedures, 310
    process, 332
    protect recovery data, 335
    ransomware, 310
    recommendations, 328–331
    risks, 319–321

SSC, 332
test data recovery, 337
training, 325–327
Decommissioning procedures, 440, 454
DEP, *see* Data Execution Prevention (DEP)
Digital signatures, 35
Disaster recovery plan (DRP), 315, 318, 326, 330
DMARC, *see* Domain-based Message Authentication, Reporting and Conformance (DMARC)
DNS, *see* Domain name system (DNS)
DNS filtering, 251, 262, 266, 268
DKIM, *see* DomainKeys Identified Mail (DKIM)
DLP, *see* Data loss prevention (DLP)
Domain-based Message Authentication, Reporting and Conformance (DMARC), 252, 260
DomainKeys Identified Mail (DKIM), 252, 260, 274
Domain name system (DNS), 213, 218, 248, 251
DRP, *see* Disaster recovery plan (DRP)
Due diligence, 439, 453
Dwell time, 503
Dynamic analysis, 468, 483

# E

EDR solutions, *see* Endpoint detection and response (EDR) solutions
Effective incident response plan, 83, 102, 362
Email and browser protections
  attackers, 247
  BEC, 250, 251
  block unnecessary file types, 275
  browser-based attacks, 248
  browser vulnerabilities, 253
  content filtering, 251
  customer trust, 258
  cybersecurity leaders, 261–263
  cybersecurity strategies, 253, 255, 256
  data breach, 256
  DMARC, 252
  encryption, 252
  filtering services, 271
  implement DMARC policies, 274
  insurance costs, 259
  intellectual property, 258
  losses, 258
  malware infection, 257
  network-based URL filters, 272
  non-compliance, 258
  operational disruption, 258
  phishing, 250, 260
  pop-up blockers, 251

## INDEX

Email and browser
protections (*cont.*)
  recommendations, 266–270
  regular audits, 249
  reputational damage, 257
  risks, 256
  robust anti-malware
    protections, 276
  spam filtering, 253
  SSC, 270
  technical defenses, 248
  training, 263–266
  unauthorized or unnecessary
    browser, 273
  web access technologies, 248
  web browsers, 248
End-of-life (EOL) components,
  340, 345, 354, 363
Endpoint detection and response
  (EDR) solutions, 301,
  392, 517
Enterprise assets/software
  additional controls, 120
  automatic device lockout, 124
  automatic session locking, 118
  configuration management
    tools, 98
  configuration process, 117
  default accounts, 122
  digital environments, 100–102
  documentation/policy
    development, 99
  enterise workspaces, 125
  firewall management, 119

network devices, 118
organization's operations/
  culture, 108–110
recommendations, 113–115
remotely wipe data, 124
risks, 105–107
secure configuration
  management, 121
secure configurations, 98, 105
service providers, 97
SSC, 116
stakeholder, 103
training, 111–113
trusted DNS servers, 123
uninstallation, 122, 123
EOL components, *see* End-of-
  life (EOL) components)

## F

False positives, 376, 379, 391
Federal Financial Institutions
  Examination Council
  (FFIEC) guidelines, 436,
  440, 441, 447
FFIEC guidelines, *see* Federal
  Financial Institutions
  Examination Council
  (FFIEC) guidelines

## G

GDPR, *see* General Data Protection
  Regulation (GDPR)

General Data Protection
    Regulation (GDPR), 2, 18,
    41, 62, 77, 103, 106, 112,
    133, 137, 165, 196, 219, 231,
    255, 258, 289, 296, 298, 317,
    359, 382, 388, 411, 412, 422,
    450, 471, 474, 477, 481, 545

# H

Hardware asset management
    active management, 4
    asset inventory, 4
    asset tracking, 6
    automation, 1
    BYOD policies, 6, 7
    compliance requirements, 2
    cybersecurity, 13, 14, 16
    dynamic asset management, 9
    dynamic discovery tools, 25
    end-user devices, 4
    hardware types, 3
    holistic approach, 2
    incident response, 8
    integrated security
        ecosystems, 2
    inventory, 23
    IoT devices, 5
    manual processes, 1
    monitoring and tracking, 26
    network devices, 5
    portable and mobile devices, 5
    privacy, 10
    proactive vulnerability
        management, 28
    recommendations, 20–22
    remote assets, 6
    resource optimization, 9
    risk management, 8
    risks, 11–13
    secure configuration and
        management, 27
    servers, 6
    SSC, 23
    strategic decision-making, 10
    training, 17–20
    unauthorized author, 24
Health Insurance Portability and
    Accountability Act (HIPAA),
    219, 435
HECVAT, *see* Higher Education
    Community Vendor
    Assessment Toolkit
    (HECVAT)
HIDS, *see* Host-based intrusion
    detection solutions (HIDS)
Higher Education Community
    Vendor Assessment Toolkit
    (HECVAT), 437
HIPAA, *see* Health Insurance
    Portability and
    Accountability Act (HIPAA)
HIPS, *see* Host-based intrusion
    prevention solutions (HIPS)
Host-based intrusion detection
    solutions (HIDS), 396

# INDEX

Host-based intrusion prevention solutions (HIPS), 400–402
Human expertise, 371–373

## I, J

IAM, *see* Identity and Access Management (IAM)
Identity and Access Management (IAM), 129, 297
Incident classification, 503–504
Incident containment, 501–502
Incident detection, 501
Incident eradication, 502
Incident recovery, 502
Incident reporting, 410
Incident response, 375, 376, 379, 380, 385, 505
Incident response and management training, 358
Incident response management
  communication, 498
  communication plan, 503
  cybersecurity strategy, 497
  dwell time, 503
  essentials
    accountability and transparency, 507
    collaboration and coordination, 507
    customer trust, 506
    ensure regulatory compliance, 505
    impact on business operations, 504
    organizational resilience, 505
    post-incident reviews and continuous improvement processes, 507
    protect sensitive data, 505
    reduce financial losses, 505
    support business continuity, 506
    threat detection and response, 506
  incident classification, 503
  incident containment, 501
  incident detection, 501
  incident eradication, 502
  incident recovery, 502
  IRP, 501
  IRT, 503
  post-incident review, 500, 502
  questionnaires
    communication plan, 512
    compliance with legal and regulatory requirements, 513
    containment strategies, 512
    criteria for classify incidents, 513
    detect and report incidents, 511
    document and review incidents, 512
    eradication, 512

# INDEX

incident response
  process, 511
recover and restore normal
  operations, 512
regular training and
  exercises, 513
threat intelligence into
  incident response, 513
recommended training
  programs, 514
  advanced threat
    hunting, 516
  cybersecurity policy
    awareness, 516
  data protection and privacy
    training, 515
  endpoint security
    training, 516
  incident reporting
    procedures, 515
  incident response planning
    workshop, 514
  incident simulation
    exercises, 516
  network security basics, 515
  phishing awareness and
    prevention, 514
  secure password
    management, 515
  social engineering
    defense, 515
  threat detection and
    monitoring training, 514

regular scenario-based training
  and exercises, 498
risks of not implement
  competitive advantage, 510
  data breaches, 508
  extended downtime, 508
  financial losses, 508
  intellectual property (IP)
    theft, 509
  legal liabilities, 509
  psychologically impact
    employees, 510
  recovery costs, 510
  regulatory non-
    compliance, 508
  reputational damage, 509
scenario-based training, 504
SSC (*see* Simplified security
  controls (SSC))
strategic approach
  compliance with
    regulations, 519
  conduct regular training and
    drills, 518
  develop comprehensive
    incident response plan, 517
  external expertise, 519
  implement robust detection
    mechanisms, 517
  incident classification
    criteria, 518
  incorporate threat
    intelligence, 518

565

INDEX

Incident response
    management (*cont.*)
        post-incident review
            process, 518
        roles and
            responsibilities, 517
        securing endpoints, 519
        security-aware culture, 519
        threat intelligence and hunting,
            499, 502
Incident response plan (IRP), 385,
    390, 394, 440, 501
Incident response program, 497
Incident response team (IRT), 503
Incident response
    training, 388
Incremental backups, 314
Indicators of compromise (IOCs),
    186, 373, 375, 380
Insider threats, 66, 71, 108, 133,
    137, 165, 222, 223, 383, 413,
    478, 481, 539
Intellectual property (IP) theft, 289,
    382, 445
Internal threat intelligence
    capability, 373, 380
Internet of Things (IoT), 3, 5, 107
Intrusion detection systems (IDS),
    282, 299, 393, 517
Intrusion prevention systems (IPS),
    299, 393
IOCs, *see* Indicators of
    compromise (IOCs)
IoT, *see* Internet of Things (IoT)

IP theft, *see* Intellectual property
    (IP) theft
IRP, *see* Incident response plan (IRP)
IRT, *see* Incident response team (IRT)
IT Assets training, 360

# K

Key Performance Indicators
    (KPIs), 202
KPIs, *see* Key Performance
    Indicators (KPIs)

# L

Living-off-the-land (LotL), 279, 281
Log management, 211, 376
LotL, *see* Living-off-the-land (LotL)

# M

Machine learning (ML), 2, 217, 249,
    268, 280
Malware, 166, 251, 257, 265, 280
Malware defenses
    anti-malware
        signature, 304
    anti-malware software, 303
    behavior-based anti-malware
        software, 308
    centralized management, 278,
        279, 307
    configuring anti-malware
        software, 305, 306

cyber environment, 283–287
disable autorun/autoplay, 305
end-users, 278
incident response, 282, 283
multifaceted approach, 277
recommendations, 299, 301
risks, 287–291
SSC, 302
training, 295–298
vulnerabilities, 291–294
Managed security service providers (MSSPs), 519
MDM, *see* Mobile device management (MDM)
MFA, *see* Multi-factor authentication (MFA)
ML, *see* Machine learning (ML)
Mobile device management (MDM), 125, 262
Mobile device security training, 390, 545
MSSPs, *see* Managed security service providers (MSSPs)
Multi-factor authentication (MFA), 115, 128, 130, 131, 141, 143, 155, 158, 161, 172, 175, 267, 298, 300, 340, 344, 360, 361, 393

# N

National Institute of Standards and Technology (NIST), 109, 115, 470, 472

Network anomalies, 355
Network architecture diagrams, 340, 354
Network configurations, 340–342
Network devices, 339
   and configurations, 354
   default settings, 339
   vendor support, 340
Network infrastructure management, 342
   ACLs, 344
   administrative devices, 346
   configuration management, 346
   cyber threats, 342, 346
   default configurations, 343
   effective management, 342, 346
   EOL components, 345
   essential
      attack surface, 352
      competitive edge, 353
      customer trust, 349
      data breaches, 352
      data interception, 351
      enhance incident response, 347
      ensure regulatory compliance, 347
      financial losses, 352
      ineffective incident response, 352
      minimize attack surfaces, 347
      network downtime, 351
      operational inefficiency, 353

INDEX

Network infrastructure
    management (*cont.*)
        protection against evolving
            threats, 347
        regulatory non-
            compliance, 351
        remote work, 348
        reputational damage, 353
        scalability and
            growth, 349
        sensitive data,
            safeguarding, 348
        technological
            advancements, 350
        unpatched vulnerabilities,
            350, 351
        visibility and control, 349
    MFA, 344
    network monitoring, 345
    network segmentation, 345
    patch management, 344
    secure protocols, 344
    vulnerability management, 343
Network intrusion detection
    systems (NIDS), 397
Network monitoring and defense,
    373, 374
    anomaly detection, 377
    cloud security, 376
    collaboration and information
        sharing, 380
    compliance and regulatory
        requirements, 379
    comprehensive network
        monitoring, 380
    detection and response, 378
    false positives, 376, 379
    human error and
        misconfigurations, 378
    incident response and forensic
        investigation, 375, 380
    IOCs, 375
    log management, 376
    maintain business
        continuity, 381
    proactive threat
        management, 379
    questionnaires
        effective incident
            response, 385
        incident response plan, 385
        insider threats, 386
        logging and reporting, 385
        network traffic, 385
        security measures, 387
        threat intelligence, 386
        threats and
            vulnerabilities, 386
        tools and technologies, 386
        training and awareness
            programs, 387
        user access, 386
    risks associated with not
        implement, 384
        APTs, 383
        cyber espionage, 384

INDEX

data breaches, 381
financial losses, 381
insider threats, 383
intellectual property (IP)
    theft, 382
legal and regulatory
    penalties, 382
lose of competitive
    advantage, 383
operational disruption, 382
ransomware attacks, 383
reputational damage, 382
SIEM systems, 375
situational awareness, 379
SOC, 377
SSC (*see* Simplified security
    controls (SSC))
strategic approach
    access control measures, 393
    access controls and least
        privilege, 484
    advanced threat detection
        technologies, 393
    bug bounty program, 484
    CI/CD security checks, 483
    comprehensive incident
        response plan, 393
    comprehensive network
        monitoring strategy, 391
    comprehensive training
        program, 483
    dedicated SOC, 392
    EDR solutions, 392
    hardened configuration
        templates, 484
    inventory, third-party
        components, 483
    network segmentation, 392
    regular code reviews and
        security audits, 482
    regular security assessments
        and penetration tests, 484
    regular vulnerability
        assessments and
        penetration tests, 391
    robust incident response
        plan, 484
    SDLC, 482
    security policies, 392
    SIEM system, 391
    static and dynamic analysis
        tools, 483
    threat modeling
        sessions, 483
    user training and awareness
        programs, 393
threat hunting, 377
threat intelligence, 376, 380
threat landscape, 378
training recommendations
    access control and identity
        management training, 451
    access control management
        training, 389
    advanced threat detection
        training, 423

INDEX

Network monitoring and
defense (*cont.*)
business continuity and
disaster recovery
training, 451
cloud security training,
390, 481
compliance and regulatory
training, 422, 481
compliance and regulatory
update training, 451
contract management and
legal compliance
training, 450
cybersecurity awareness and
culture training, 452
cybersecurity best practices
training, 389
data protection and privacy
training, 388, 421, 450
incident response and
reporting training, 450
incident response training,
388, 421, 480
insider threat detection
training, 481
mobile device security
training, 390, 423
network security
fundamentals training, 388
network security
training, 423
password management
training, 421

penetration testing
training, 480
phishing and social
engineering awareness
training, 450
phishing awareness training,
388, 421
regular security awareness
training, 480
regular security drills and
simulations, 390
remote work security
training, 422
secure coding practices
training, 389, 479
secure configuration
training, 422
secure software
development training,
423, 451
security auditing and
monitoring
training, 451
security education
programs, 482
security logging and
monitoring training, 481
security policy and
procedures training, 388
service provider risk
assessment training, 450
social engineering
awareness training,
389, 422

# INDEX

third-party component management training, 480
threat modeling workshops, 479
vendor management best practices training, 452
vulnerability management training, 479
TTPs, 375
Network security
effective account management, 340
regular training and awareness programs, 341
training and educating staff, 357
Network security fundamentals training 358, 388
Network security training, 544
Network segmentation, 51, 345, 362
Network Time Protocol (NTP), 217, 233
NIDS, *see* Network intrusion detection systems (NIDS)
NIST, *see* National Institute of Standards and Technology (NIST)

# O

Ongoing monitoring, 31, 75, 331, 439
Opaque box testing, 532, 533

# P, Q

PAM, *see* Privileged Access Management (PAM)
Password hygiene, 406, 410
Patch management, 28, 33, 100, 185, 194, 201, 293, 344
Penetration testing, 465, 468, 527
benefit, 528
clear box testing, 532
command and control (C2), 532
complexity and potential risks, 529
cyber threats, 528
essentials
compliance requirements, 535
continuous improvement process, 537
enhance incident response, 535
identify hidden vulnerabilities, 534
protect reputation and trust, 535
reduce financial risk, 535
risk management strategy, 536
stay ahead of attackers, 536
strengthen customer confidence, 536
support business continuity, 536
validate security controls, 534

571

# INDEX

Penetration testing (*cont.*)
  exploitation, 531
  legal and ethical
    considerations, 533
  opaque box testing, 533
  physical penetration testing, 533
  process-related
    vulnerabilities, 529
  questionnaires
    budget, 542
    communication, 541
    false positives and
      negatives, 542
    frequency, 542
    internal resources/external
      vendors, 540
    legal and ethical
      considerations, 542
    metrics for success, 541
    objectives, 540
    protect sensitive data, 541
    remediation process, 541
    rules of engagement
      (RoE), 540
    systems and assets, 540
  reconnaissance, 531
  red team exercises, 529
  red teaming, 532
  regular security
    assessments, 530
  remediation, 533
  risks of not implement
    compliance failures, 538
    data breaches, 539
    inadequate incident
      response, 538
    increased financial risk, 538
    ineffective security
      controls, 537
    insider threats, 539
    intellectual property (IP)
      theft, 539
    loss of competitive
      advantage, 538
    operational
      disruptions, 539
    reputation damage, 538
    strategic misalignment, 539
    undetected
      vulnerabilities, 537
  rules of engagement (RoE), 532
  scope, 528
  social engineering, 531
  SSC (*see* Simplified security
    controls (SSC))
  strategic approach, 546
    allocate adequate
      budget, 549
    clear objectives, 546
    communicate findings, 548
    comprehensive testing
      plan, 547
    metrics, 548
    prioritize remediation
      efforts, 548
    protect sensitive data, 547
    qualified personnel, 547
    regular testing, 548

rules of engagement (RoE), 547
scope and boundaries, 547
testing scope, 533
tool for modern cybersecurity, 530
training recommendations
  advanced penetration testing training, 544
  cloud security training, 545
  compliance and regulatory training, 545
  data protection and privacy training, 544
  incident response training, 543
  mobile device security training, 545
  network security training, 544
  phishing simulation training, 543
  physical security training, 546
  secure coding practices training, 544
  social engineering defense training, 545
validation process, 528
vulnerability scanning, 531
Personally identifiable information (PII), 66
Phishing, 231, 250, 260, 282, 409, 429, 450–451
Phishing attacks, 257, 388
Phishing awareness training, 263, 295, 326, 388, 421
Phishing Simulation and Training, 359
Phishing simulation exercises, 543
Phishing simulations, 407, 411
Physical penetration testing, 533
Physical security training, 546
PII, *see* Personally identifiable information (PII)
Post-incident review, 502
Privileged Access Management (PAM), 144, 148, 156, 159, 162, 169
Proactive management, 32, 38, 190, 340
Problem-ticketing systems, 183, 186–187

# R

Ransomware attacks, 282, 313, 383
RBAC, *see* Role-based access control (RBAC)
Reconnaissance, 531, 551
Recovery Point Objectives (RPOs), 311, 313, 322
Recovery Time Objectives (RTOs), 311, 314
Red teaming, 529, 532
Regression testing, 186
Regular network audits, 361

Regular vulnerability assessments, 356
Regulations and standards, 356
Regulatory compliance, 364, 440
Regulatory compliance training, 411
Remote work security, 408, 410
Risk assessment, 28, 35, 102, 424, 439, 450
Risk-based remediation strategy, 205
Robust access controls, 158, 166, 174, 331, 361, 393
Role-based access control (RBAC), 155, 158, 161, 174, 198, 331, 393
Role-specific training, 409
RPOs, *see* Recovery Point Objectives (RPOs)
RTOs, *see* Recovery Time Objectives (RTOs)

# S

SaaS, *see* Software as a Service (SaaS)
SAM, *see* Software asset management (SAM)
Sarbanes-Oxley Act (SOX), 41, 219, 231
SBOM, *see* Software bill of materials (SBOM)
SCAP, *see* Security Content Automation Protocol (SCAP)
Scenario-based training, 498, 504
SCM, *see* Security Configuration Management (SCM)
SDLC, *see* Software development lifecycle (SDLC)
Secure application development process, 467
Secure coding practices training, 359, 389, 544
Secure communication protocols, 362
Secure protocols, 344, 355
Secure Remote Work Practices training, 360
Secure software development framework (SSDF), 470
Security audits, 83, 113, 440, 451
Security awareness and skills training
    business email compromise (BEC), 410
    data handling and protection, 410
    essentials
        adaptation to evolve threats, 413
        compliance with regulations, 412
        cost-effective risk management, 414
        employee empowerment, 414
        enhanced incident response, 412

human error reduction, 412
improved vendor and
   partner security, 414
phishing attack
   mitigation, 412
reduction of insider
   threats, 413
strengthened security
   culture, 413
support for remote work, 413
incident reporting, 410
password hygiene, 410
phishing, 409
phishing simulation, 411
questionnaires, 418
   delivery methods, 419
   incorporate employee
      feedback, 420
   metrics and evaluation
      methods, 418
   ongoing engagement, 419
   participation, 420
   potential resistance, 420
   roles and
      responsibilities, 419
   security threats, 418
   security tools, 419
   stakeholder
      involvement, 418
   training sessions, 419
remote work security, 410
risks of not implement
   damage to business
      partnerships, 417

data breaches, 415
financial losses, 416
insider threats, 416
insufficient incident
   response, 415
intellectual property
   theft, 416
loss of customer rust, 416
operational disruptions, 416
organization's security
   posture, 417
phishing attacks, 415
regulatory non-
   compliance, 415
vulnerability to emerge
   threats, 417
roles-specific training, 409
security awareness
   program, 409
security culture, 410
security updates and
   patches, 411
social engineering, 409
SSC (*see* Simplified security
   controls (SSC))
strategic approach
   clear and measurable
      objectives, 424
   conduct thorough risk
      assessment, 424
   continuous updates and
      reminders, 425
   effectiveness, training
      program, 426

INDEX

Security awareness and skills training (*cont.*)
  encourage active participation, 426
  implement phishing simulations, 426
  incorporate feedback and continuous improvement, 426, 427
  multiple training formats, 425
  real-world scenarios, 425
  role-based training modules, 424
  schedule for regular training sessions, 425
Security awareness program, 171, 406–409
Security awareness training, 76, 143, 148, 171–172, 327, 408, 543
Security champions, 469
Security Configuration Management (SCM), 34–35, 50–51, 64
Security Content Automation Protocol (SCAP), 183, 186
Security culture, 39, 149, 287, 410, 413
Security incident thresholds, 500
Security information and event management (SIEM) systems, 104, 372, 375, 391, 517

Security Operations Center (SOC), 377, 379, 392
Security updates and patches, 411
Sender Policy Framework (SPF), 274
Service provider classification, 438
Service provider inventory, 438
Service provider logs, 218
Service provider management, 435, 436
  contractual security clauses, 439
  cyber insurance, 440
  decommissioning procedures, 440
  due diligence, 439
  essentials
    business continuity planning, 442
    collaboration with service providers, 443
    cybersecurity landscape, 443
    incident response procedures, 442
    legal and financial liabilities, 442
    operational disruptions, 442, 443
    proactive risk management, 443
    regulatory compliance, 441
    sensitive data, 441
    third-party breaches, 441

## INDEX

trust and transparency with service providers, 442
incident response plan, 440
ongoing monitoring, 439
questionnaires
    data security and privacy, 448
    incident response protocols, 448
    insurance coverage and liability considerations, 449
    regular tracking and reporting, 449
    regulatory requirements, 447, 448
    scope of services, 447
    security measures, 447
    service providers, 447
    service provider's security posture, 447
    structured onboarding process, 448
    terminating and decommissioning service providers, 449
regulatory compliance, 440
risk assessment, 439
risks of not implement, 444
    exposure to advanced threats, 446
    financial losses, 444
    inadequate incident response, 445
    IP theft, 445
    legal liabilities, 445
    operational disruptions, 444
    regulatory non-sompliance, 444
    reputational damage, 445
    supply chain vulnerabilities, 446
security audits, 440
service provider classification, 438
service provider inventory, 438
SSC (*see* Simplified security controls (SSC))
strategic approach
    collaborative security practices, 455
    comprehensive inventory, 452
    conduct thorough due diligence, 453
    develop incident response protocols, 453
    develop risk classification framework, 453
    enforce data handling standards, 454
    implement continuous monitoring, 453
    regularly review and update policies, 454
    secure decommissioning procedures, 454
    security clauses in contracts, 453

INDEX

Service provider
    management (*cont.*)
        training and awareness
            programs, 454
        utilize third-party risk
            management tools, 454
    third-party risk management
        platforms, 439
Severity rating system, 466, 469
Shared Assessments program, 437
SIEM systems, *see* Security
    information and event
    management (SIEM) systems
Signature-based detection,
    278, 281
Simplified security controls (SSC),
    23, 52, 85, 364
    application software security
        accept and address reports,
            software vulnerabilities, 486
        application
            vulnerabilities, 490
        causes, security
            vulnerabilities, 487
        comprehensive code-level
            security checks, 494
        inventory, third-party
            components, 488
        regular penetration
            testing, 494
        secure application
            development process, 485
        secure design principles, 492

standard hardening
    configurations, 490
third-party software
    components, 489
threat modeling, 495
train developers in secure
    coding and application
    security practices, 491
trusted and thoroughly
    vetted modules/
    services, 493
incident response management
    effective
        communication, 524
    incident handling, 520
    incident response
        process, 522
    key roles and
        responsibilities, 523
    post-incident reviews, 525
    reporting security
        incidents, 522
    routine incident response
        exercises, 524
    security incident
        thresholds, 526
    timely and accurate
        reporting, 521
network monitoring
    and defense
        access for remote assets, 399
        application layer
            filtering, 403

578

INDEX

centralize security event alerting, 395
collect network traffic flow logs, 400
deploy HIDS, 396
deploy HIPS, 400
deploy NIDS, 397
deploy NIPS, 401
deploy port-level access control mechanisms, 402
filtering traffic between network segments, 398
tune security event alerting thresholds, 404
penetration testing
comprehensive penetration testing program, 550
external penetration tests, 551
internal penetration tests, 553
remediate penetration test findings, 552
validate security measures, 552
security awareness and skills training
authentication practices, 429
comprehensive security awareness program, 428
conduct role-specific security awareness and skills training, 434
data handling and disposal practices, 430
recognize and thwart social engineering attacks, 428
reduce data breaches risk and unauthorized access, 433
reporting and response to security incidents, 431
timely identification and resolution, software update issues, 432
unintentional data exposure, 431
service provider management
classify service providers, 458
comprehensive service provider management policy, 457
ensure service provider contracts, 459
inventory of service providers, 456
monitor service providers, 461
regular assessments, service providers, 460
secure decommissioning, service providers, 462
Single sign-on (SSO), 128, 131, 156, 159
Situational awareness, 372, 373, 379

579

# INDEX

SOC, *see* Security Operations Center (SOC)
Social engineering, 132, 252, 409, 531
Social engineering awareness training, 146, 389, 422
Social engineering defense training, 265, 515–516, 545
Social engineering tactics, 127, 248, 282, 407
Software as a Service (SaaS), 232, 235, 466
Software asset management (SAM), 31, 32, 46, 48
Software assets
  active management, 31
  allowlisting, 33, 55, 56
  asset management, 32
  authorization, 53
  cryptographic hashes, 35
  cybersecurity, 29, 31
  cyber threats, 43–45
  digital signatures, 35
  inventory, 53
  inventory management, 30
  organization digital and physical resources, 36–39
  patch management, 33
  recommendations, 49–51
  risk assessment, 35
  risks, 40–42
  SCM, 34
  software compliance, 34
  software inventories, 32, 55

software libraries, 56
software lifecycle, 35
SSC, 52
technical controls, 30
training programs, 46–48
unauthorized software, 30, 34, 54
vulnerability management, 33
Software bill of materials (SBOM), 469, 480
Software development lifecycle (SDLC), 476, 482
SOX, *see* Sarbanes-Oxley Act (SOX)
Spam filtering, 253
SPF, *see* Sender Policy Framework (SPF)
SSC, *see* Simplified security controls (SSC)
SSDF, *see* Secure software development framework (SSDF)
SSO, *see* Single sign-on (SSO)
Static analysis, 468, 483
System logs, 211, 216

# T

Tactics, techniques and procedures (TTPs), 373, 375, 380, 499, 502, 518, 532
Testing scope, 528, 533
Third-party components, 464, 468, 469, 477, 480, 483

Third-party risk management platforms, 439–440, 448, 453
Threat hunting, 377, 499
Threat intelligence, 187, 283, 374, 376, 380, 386, 394, 502
Threat modeling, 464, 465, 467
Traditional signature-based detection methods, 278, 281
TTPs, *see* Tactics, techniques and procedures (TTPs)

## U

U.K. Cyber Essentials, 436, 440, 441

## V

Virtual private networks (VPNs), 115, 262, 266, 343, 369, 370, 408

VPNs, *see* Virtual private networks (VPNs)
Vulnerability assessments, 197, 293, 356, 358, 391
Vulnerability management, 33, 343, 465–467, 477
Vulnerability scanning, 28, 193–194, 200, 531

## W, X, Y

WDEG, *see* Windows Defender Exploit Guard (WDEG)
Web browser plugins, 252
Windows Defender Exploit Guard (WDEG), 306

## Z

Zero-day exploit, 182, 184, 282

GPSR Compliance

The European Union's (EU) General Product Safety Regulation (GPSR) is a set of rules that requires consumer products to be safe and our obligations to ensure this.

If you have any concerns about our products, you can contact us on

ProductSafety@springernature.com

In case Publisher is established outside the EU, the EU authorized representative is:

Springer Nature Customer Service Center GmbH
Europaplatz 3
69115 Heidelberg, Germany

www.ingramcontent.com/pod-product-compliance
Lightning Source LLC
LaVergne TN
LVHW010331260326
834688LV00036B/658